International law from MUP

The Melland Schill name has a long-established reputation for high standards of scholarship. Each volume in the series addresses major international-law issues and current developments. Many of the previous volumes, published under the name 'Melland Schill Monographs', have become standard works of reference in the field. Interdisciplinary and accessible, the series is vital reading for students, scholars and practitioners of international law, international relations, politics, economics and development.

The law of international organisations

N. D. White

Manchester University Press

Manchester and New York

distributed exclusively in the USA by St. Martin's Press

Published by Manchester University Press
Oxford Road, Manchester M13 9NR, UK
and Room 400, 175 Fifth Avenue, New York, NY 10010, USA

Distributed exclusively in the USA
by St. Martin's Press, Inc., 175 Fifth Avenue, New York, NY 10010, USA

British Library Cataloguing-in-Publication Data
A catalogue record for this book is available from the British Library

Library of Congress Cataloging-in-Publication Data
White, N. D., 1961–
    The law of international organisations / N. D. White.
        p.   cm.—(Melland Schill studies in international law)
    Includes index.
    ISBN 0–7190–4339–5 (hc.)—ISBN 0–7190–4340–9 (pbk.)
    1. International agencies   I. Title.   II. Series.
JX1995.W483   1996
    341.2—dc20   96–16159

ISBN 0 7190 4339 5 *hardback*
        0 7190 4340 9 *paperback*

First published 1996

00 99 98 97 96   10 9 8 7 6 5 4 3 2 1

Typeset in Great Britain
by Northern Phototypesetting Co Ltd, Bolton
Printed in Great Britain
by Bell & Bain Ltd, Glasgow

Contents

Contents

Series editor's preface

In the twentieth century much of international diplomacy, and in turn, international law, has been developed in the context of international organisations. Given the undisputed importance of international organisations there are suprisingly few contemporary monographs that deal with them on the basis that there is a general body of law applicable to them. This book is therefore a welcome addition to the Melland Schill series. It cleverly blends complex theories with an extensive account of practice. It manages to present the functioning and operation of international organisations in an interesting and accessible manner. Debates over competence and decision-making procedures often appear abstract and formalistic – 'lawyers' law'. However, they reveal much about the constitutional structure of international society and its direction.

Dominic McGoldrick,
International and European Law Unit,
University of Liverpool

Preface

Inter-governmental organisations appear to be a central component of modern international society. The sheer number, variety and complexity of these institutions create an impression of chaotic activity, sometimes of immense importance, sometimes of profound impotence. Organisations can act in a governmental capacity; on other occasions they resemble the simple diplomatic conferences of the nineteenth century, with the result that some organisations challenge the supremacy of the nation State, others simply facilitate the continued dominance of the established international actors.

One way of trying to make sense of the legal and political evolution of international organisations is to assess the various approaches to international order. Although such a theoretical analysis can be seen as abstract, it has immense practical implications in that these approaches each have a shaping effect on the development of the personality, powers and practice of international organisations; this is primarily because they reflect the various political philosophies of the States represented in these institutions. The current prevalence of one approach to the status and role of organisations is mainly explained by the ideology of the dominant group of States in the international order. However, it is unlikely that one single approach can explain the legal and political development of institutions due to the fact that historically each organisation will have been differently influenced due to the changing geopolitical shape of the world. In addition, there are often quite wide variations in approach within what are sometimes only temporary groupings or alliances of States, for instance between the revolutionary and Marxist approaches of the Non-Aligned and Socialist States united during the 1960s and 1970s; or between the functionalist, rationalist and realist approaches of Western States. Furthermore, account must be taken of approaches which challenge the established State-centred orthodoxies, for instance the critical approach. In some ways the critical arguments for a more just and equitable approach to world order accord with the agendas of non-governmental organisations, although a detailed account of the influence of these organisations is beyond the scope of this book.

These different approaches are used throughout this book in an attempt not only to explain the political shape of international organisations, but also to clarify often obscure doctrinal debates about the legal nature and attributes of institutions. In other words, the law of international organisations, concerning issues such as legal personality, voting, suspension, powers, and decision-making capacity, is not simply described in formal terms because that does not fully explain the development and content of the law. Furthermore, as these organisations expand their competences, there is an inevitable clash between organisations of different types, reflecting different approaches to world order, principally between universal, regional and functional organisations. The current institutional structure of the international legal and political order is discussed in order to provide an assessment of how problems of overlap and supremacy are dealt with in law and in practice.

The powers and practice of organisations in the areas of trade and economic matters are not the subject of separate treatment, but are dealt with throughout the book. However, three areas of substance are discussed, namely: collective security, human rights, and environmental matters, in order to assess the impact of international organisations in developing, supervising, and perhaps enforcing, laws in these areas. These chapters not only provide an analysis of organisational powers and practice in areas of fundamental importance, but help to clarify aspects of the legal and political attributes of institutions, and the division of competence between them.

N. D. White
Nottingham
August 1995

Abbreviations

ACC	Administrative Committee on Co-ordination
ADF	Arab Deterrent Force
A.J.I.L.	*American Journal of International Law*
ALADI	Latin-American Integration Association
A/PV	General Assembly Provisional Records
ASEAN	Association of South East Asian Nations
ATS	Antarctic Treaty System
BFSP	British and Foreign State Papers
Bull.EC	*Bulletin of the European Communities*
B.Y.B.I.L.	*British Year Book of International Law*
CFSP	Common Foreign and Security Policy
CIS	Commonwealth of Independent States
CITES	Convention on Trade in Endangered Species
CMF	Commonwealth Monitoring Force
CMLR	*Common Market Law Reports*
COG	Commonwealth Observer Group
COMECON	Council for Mutual Economic Assistance
COMSAT	Communications Satellite Corporation
CSCE	Conference on Security and Cooperation in Europe
CTS	Consolidated Treaty Series
EBRD	European Bank for Reconstruction and Development
EC	European Community
ECA	Economic Commission for Africa
ECB	European Central Bank
ECE	Economic Commission for Europe
ECHR	European Court of Human Rights
ECJ	European Court of Justice
ECOMOG	Economic Community of West African States Monitoring Group
ECOSOC	Economic and Social Council
ECOWAS	Economic Community of West African States
ECR	European Court Reports
ECSC	European Coal and Steel Community

EDC	European Defence Community
EEC	European Economic Community
EFTA	European Free Trade Association
EHRR	European Human Rights Reports
EPC	European Political Cooperation
ERTA	European Road Transport Assocition
EU	European Union
Euratom	European Atomic Energy Community
FAO	Food and Agriculture Organisation
G7	Group of Seven Industrialised Countries
GAOR	General Assembly Official Records
GATT	General Agreement on Tariffs and Trade
GEF	Global Environmental Facility
GSO	Geostationary Orbit
HRC	Human Rights Committee
IAEA	International Atomic Energy Agency
IATA	International Air Transport Association
IBRD	International Bank for Reconstruction and Development
ICAO	International Civil Aviation Organisation
I.C.J. *Rep.*	International Court of Justice Reports
I.C.L.Q.	*International and Comparative Law Quarterly*
I.J.I.L.	*Indian Journal of International Law*
ILC	International Law Commission
I.L.M.	*International Legal Materials*
ILO	International Labour Organisation
I.L.R	*International Law Reports*
IMF	International Monetary Fund
IMO	International Maritime Organisation
INMARSAT	International Maritime Satellite Organisation
INTELSAT	International Telecommunications Satellite Organisation
ITU	International Telecommunications Union
Keesing's	*Keesing's Record of World Events*
LAFTA	Latin-American Free Trade Association
LNTS	League of Nations Treaty Series
MEP	Member of European Parliament
NAFTA	North American Free Trade Association
NATO	North Atlantic Treaty Organisation
NGO	Non-governmental organisation
N.I.L.R	*Netherlands International Law Review*
NPFL	National Patriotic Forces of Liberia
OAPEC	Organisation of Arab Petroleum Exporting Countries
OAS	Organisation of American States
OAU	Organisation of African Unity
OECD	Organisation for Economic Cooperation and Development

OECS	Organisation of Eastern Caribbean States
OEEC	Organisation for European Economic Cooperation
OJ	*Official Journal* (of the European Communities)
ONUC	United Nations Operation in the Congo
ONUCA	United Nations Observer Group in Central America
ONUVEN	United Nations Observer Mission to Verify the Electoral Process in Nicaragua
OPEC	Organisation of Petroleum Exporting Countries
OSCE	Organisation on Security and Cooperation in Europe
PAUTS	Pan American Union Treaty Series
P.C.I.J.	Permanent Court of International Justice
PLO	Palestine Liberation Organisation
SCOR	Security Council Official Records
S/PV	Security Council Provisional Records
SWAPO	South West African People's Organisation
UKTS	United Kingdom Treaty Series
UDI	Unilateral Declaration of Independence
UNAVEM	United Nations Angola Verification Mission
UNCIO	United Nations Conference on International Organisations
UNCTAD	United Nations Conference on Trade and Development
UNDOF	United Nations Disengagement Observer Force
UNDP	United Nations Development Programme
UNEF	United Nations Emergency Force
UNEP	United Nations Environment Programme
UNESCO	United Nations Educational, Scientific and Cultural Organisation
UNHCR	United Nations High Commissioner for Refugees
UNICEF	United Nations Children's Fund
UNIDO	United Nations Industrial Development Organisation
UNIFIL	United Nations Interim Force in Lebanon
UNIIMOG	United Nations Iran–Iraq Military Observer Group
UNIPOM	United Nations India–Pakistan Observation Mission
UNITA	National Union for the Total Independence of Angola
UNITAF	Unified Task Force
UNMOGIP	United Nations Military Observer Group in India and Pakistan
UNOMIL	United Nations Observer Mission for Liberia
UNOSOM	United Nations Operation in Somalia
UNPROFOR	United Nations Protection Force
UNSF	United Nations Security Force
UNTAG	United Nations Transition Assistance Group
UNTEA	United Nations Temporary Executive Authority
UNTS	United Nations Treaty Series
UNTSO	United Nations Truce Supervision Organisation
UPU	Universal Postal Union

WEU	Western European Union
WHO	World Health Organisation
WMO	World Meteorological Organisation
WTO	World Trade Organisation
YB	Yearbook (of the European Convention on Human Rights)
ZANU	Zimbabwean African National Union

1

Theories of international organisation

International lawyers tend to define and describe international (here meaning inter-governmental) organisations in a narrow, formalist or 'black letter' fashion. Professor Virally, for instance, gives us the following working legal definition of an international organisation:

> ... an organization can be defined as an association of States, established by agreement among its members and possessing a permanent system or set of organs, whose task it is to pursue objectives of common interest by means of co-operation among its members.

Such an approach then leads to an analysis of the various aspects of the definition – the inter-State nature of international organisations, 'their voluntaristic basis, their possession of a permanent system of organs, their autonomy and their co-operative function',[1] followed by attempts to assess each international organisation in terms of its 'fit'.

Such descriptive analyses help to give an understanding of the legal nature and legal functions of an organisation, but they fail to provide either a systemic or contextual understanding of international organisations. International organisations have evolved in terms of their legal powers and functions because they are part of a wider economic and political system. Indeed, if one takes a traditional Marxist approach to law, the whole legal 'superstructure' of norms and institutions are simply a product of the changing economic and technological conditions in international society.[2] Marxism too can be accused of being far too narrow with its simple instrumentalist approach. It can be argued, for instance, that law does often have a determining effect and that it is simply not a reflection of the material base.[3] The point is that international organisations need to be examined, whether for legal, economic, or political reasons, in their wider context. In this, the system theories of the political scientist can be of value. This can take the form of either macro-analysis, helpfully defined by Professor Abi-Saab as consisting of

> efforts ... to explain alterations in the structures and functions of the international organization by changes in the international system. This can be viewed in two ways: either the international organization is considered a system and the international

1

system is looked on as its environment; or the organization is considered an element (actor or subsystem) of a broader set, the international system.

Or micro-analysis which views the international organisation itself as the system to be analysed.[4] The purpose, in this chapter, will not be to undertake a pure systems analysis of international organisations, but to take the approach into account, and analyse the various theories concerning the structure of the international system.

The idea behind this chapter will be to give the reader a conceptual and contextual framework which can be used to analyse the substantive workings of international organisations. This will entail an examination of the narrow functionalist approach taken by the World Court in its judgments (for example in the *Reparation* case – see below), to the wider functionalism of David Mitrany, as well as the other main evolutionary approach to world order – rationalism. The more overtly politicised revolutionary, realist and critical approaches will be considered. Pieces of evidence gleaned from the practice of international organisations will be given, but the emphasis will be on the theoretical rather than the practical, the aim being to assess the relative value of these approaches, particularly in providing an explanation for the recent, somewhat frenetic, activity of international organisations.

Functionalism

Functionalism, that is, an analysis of the international system, its actors and norms, in terms of the areas of co-operation needed to make the system work at various levels of efficiency or justice, takes on many forms from the relatively narrow legal approach to interpreting the constitutions of international organisations, to the much wider political theory which looks at how the system works and how it may develop.[5]

The International Court of Justice's advisory opinion in the *Reparation*[6] case embodies the narrow legal approach to functionalism. The Court, in opining whether the United Nations had the capacity to bring an international claim in the name of the Organisation for the death of one of its agents, stated that

> Throughout its history, the development of international law has been influenced by the requirements of international life, and the progressive increase in the collective action of States has already given rise to instances of action upon the international plane by certain entities which are not States. The development culminated in the establishment in June 1945 of an international organization whose purposes and principles are specified in the Charter of the United Nations.

As will be seen, this bears a resemblance to the functionalist approach of the political scientist, who sees increased State co-operation in the performance of certain functions as part of the development of the international order. However, the Court's approach is not truly that of the political scientist, at least the macro-ana-

2

lyst, who looks primarily at the functions needed to be performed in the international system, and then looks to see if international organisations have developed to achieve those purposes. Instead, the Court, following a legal micro-analytical approach, concentrates on the functions and purposes of the particular organisation as embodied in its legal instruments. The Court stated that 'the rights and duties of an entity such as the Organization must depend upon its purposes and functions as specified or implied in its constituent documents and developed in practice'.[7] Although eschewing a purely formalist or literalist approach to treaty interpretation in favour of a more teleological approach by looking at the goals and functions of the Organisation, the Court, as a narrow legal forum, did not attempt to interpret the legal documents by reference to the functions *needed* to be performed by the particular organisation given the current state of international relations. Instead, specific provisions of the legal documents were interpreted by reference to the functions as listed in the more general provisions of the same legal documents. The Court did not refer to the international order to help it decide on the rights and duties of the UN, instead it refers to the UN order as established in its constituent document.

The functionalist approach adopted by international lawyers is characterised by a rejection of the idea that international organisations are simply 'vehicles for conference between the member nations'. Instead, it is argued, they have a degree of autonomy.[8] In particular, this school of thought advances the idea that international organisations have law-making capacity sometimes beyond that provided in their constitutions. For example the UN Charter in Article 25 provides that decisions of the Security Council are binding on member nations, in a different context under the 1957 Treaty of Rome and subsequent treaties, legislation adopted by the Council of Ministers and the Commission is directly binding on members of the European Union. Whereas the formalist would argue that beyond this the United Nations or other organisations do not have any greater law-making capacity than that literally found in their treaty make-up, scholars like Professor Higgins argue that they do.

> With the development of international organizations, the votes and views of States have come to have legal significance as evidence of customary law. Moreover, the practice of States comprises their collective wills as well as the total of their individual acts; and the number of occasions on which States see fit to act collectively has been greatly increased by the activities of international organizations. Collective acts of States, repeated by and acquiesced in by sufficient numbers with sufficient frequency, eventually attain the status of law. The existence of the United Nations ... now provides a very clear, very concentrated focal point for State practice.[9]

This approach which recognises that international organisations have become a much more significant source of customary international law, must be contrasted with the narrow approach adopted by other Western writers, who argue that the traditional sources of international law do not include the debates and resolutions of international organisations, citing primarily Article 38 of the Statute of the

International Court of Justice.[10] The wider, functional, approach which sees States sometimes being bound by the rules formulated in international organisations when they have not consented to them, enabling those organisations to fulfil the functions assigned to them by those very same member States, is a relatively radical approach to organisations in the context of Western *legal* philosophy, but is quite narrow when the wider *political* view of functionalism is looked at.

A broader attitude to functionalism can be traced back to the founder of the functionalist approach – David Mitrany. Professor Mitrany's functionalist approach elaborated in 1943[11] starts from an analysis of the world's first attempt at creating a universal international organisation, the League of Nations. In his opinion, the League of Nations' failure was not simply that it lacked teeth, or that it failed to use its teeth, but that it had failed to supplant the activities and functions of nation States. States, as the supreme actors in the international system, did not allow the League to develop in any way which would undermine that supremacy. The only possible alternatives to the established State-dominated and divided international society would be either to create a world State or to 'overlay political divisions with a spreading web of international activities and agencies, in which and through which, the interests and life of all nations would be gradually integrated'.[12] Ironically, there was some limited evidence of a web of economic and political trans-State co-operation and activities during the First World War in the form of joint Allied Councils and Commissions[13] but these disappeared relatively quickly at the end of the conflict to be replaced by a return to national sovereignty and a *laissez-faire* philosophy – entrenched views which the League of Nations was incapable of changing. The Second World War also created the conditions for the merging of State activities in the fight against the Axis powers, and the question Professor Mitrany asked was whether the end of the conflict should be marked by the formal adoption of a general framework by which State activities would be merged, or should it be allowed to occur naturally?

The advantage of a functionalist approach to international organisation would be that it would occur incrementally. International bodies would take on more and more common functions but this would not cause a violent reaction from nation States. As Professor Mitrany explains:

> ... the most intractable and disruptive of international principles, the principle of state equality, may well be tamed by specific functional arrangements which would not steal the crown of sovereignty while they would promise something for the purse of necessity.[14]

He explains that many international problems such as the distribution of raw materials and migration could not be solved in any other way. In other words the functional approach reflects what will inevitably occur out of a need to deal with problems which are intractable given an international system based on the traditional concept of State sovereignty, which can simply be defined 'as the supreme power of the State over its populace and territory, independent from any external authority'.[15]

4

Indeed, Professor Mitrany sees the 'functional selection and organisation of' common interests in international relations as a continuation of the process started, albeit in a very weak fashion before the League of Nations, with the establishment, for example, of: the General Postal Union established in 1864, the International Telegraphic Union established in 1865, the International Meteorological Union established in 1878, as well as bodies established under the League system, for example the International Labour Organisation (ILO). He identifies the basic idea for the functional organisation of international activities:

> The essential principle is that activities would be selected specifically and organized separately, each according to its nature, to the conditions under which it has to operate, and to the needs of the moment. It would allow, therefore, all freedom for practical variation in the organization of the several functions, as well as the working of a particular function as needs and conditions alter.[16]

The nature of the function would determine the power and structure of the international organisation which would naturally evolve to regulate the task. This view seems to envisage that rather than having a universal organisation such as the UN with a fixed constitution, the system should consist of many organisations of specific or limited competence, dealing independently with economic, social and security issues, each with different make-ups. In other words, although the exercise of functions in areas of common interest would be centralised, there would be no complete centralisation of all the functions within one world body. It does not appear that the current structure of international organisations entirely fits this theory, formulated as it was in 1943. On the other hand, there has been a development of many organisations of limited competence such as the General Agreement on Tariffs and Trade/World Organisation (GATT/WTO), and the specialised agencies of the UN such as the International Civil Aviation Organisation (ICAO), the International Bank for Reconstruction and Development (IBRD), the International Monetary Fund (IMF), the World Health Organisation (WHO), the Food and Agriculture Organisation (FAO), and the Industrial Development Organisation (UNIDO), to name the most prominent, as well as those organisations which are the successors of the nineteenth-century bodies listed above – the Universal Postal Union (UPU), the International Telecommunications Union (ITU), and the World Meteorlogical Organisation (WMO). It can be seen from this list that these bodies cover areas of common interest between States, and as Professor Bowett reports these agencies have 'varying constitutional forms and techniques' for dealing with them.[17]

However, there is also the world body, the United Nations, which, in part, centralises some of the areas of common interest. Nevertheless, Mitrany does not rule out a central co-ordinating body but this would be driven by functional necessity. So co-operation may occur between two regional agencies dealing with a similar problem, and this process might lead to a truly international organisation dealing with a particular area, say rail transport. That organisation may then co-ordinate with another agency dealing with a related area, say road transport, and so the process continues naturally.

However, Mitrany states that the functional approach does not necessitate that 'international action must have some over-all *political authority* above it' because this would create, in effect, a world government. World government would stultify the natural development inherent in the functional approach because any change would require the agreement of the States within the world body leading inevitably to confrontation on purely political grounds, confrontation, fuelled by the dogma of State sovereignty and State equality, which is less likely in agencies developed to deal with a particular common problem. Mitrany's functional model of world order is not necessarily contradicted by the development of the UN. In looking at the relationship between the United Nations' Economic and Social Council (ECOSOC) and its specialised agencies, it can be seen that the system does not lead to the imposition of central political control on those agencies and how they tackle the various common areas of social and economic concern.[18]

It can be seen therefore, that in the area of humanitarian, social and economic co-operation, there is some evidence in the current system of the functional approach, although probably not as much as Professor Mitrany envisaged. However, in the area of security matters the current system does appear to diverge from Mitrany's approach. The UN Charter does provide for the centralisation of collective security, through its executive organ, the Security Council. Furthermore, Articles 53 and 103 of the Charter assert the supremacy of the world body over regional or other treaty-based security organisations, with the exception of collective defence pacts in Article 51. Mitrany is of the opinion that security is 'something indispensable but also … something incapable by itself of achieving the peaceful growth of an international society. It is in fact a separate function like the others, not something that stands in stern isolation, overriding all others'.[19] According to Mitrany, security should be allowed to develop along the functional lines outlined for economic and social co-operation, perhaps with limited organisations joining together in regions, and then regions co-operating together. The growth of collective security has not occurred quite in this fashion but there is increasing co-operation and co-ordination between the United Nations and regional bodies such as the Organisation of American States (OAS), the Organisation of African Unity (OAU), defence pacts such as the North Atlantic Treaty Organisation (NATO), as well as other looser forms of international agency such as the Conference (now Organisation) on Security and Co-operation in Europe (CSCE/OSCE), in the post-Cold War era. Nevertheless, security is seen at the UN as paramount, contrary to Professor Mitrany's belief that it is no more important than economic and social matters. Indeed, it could be argued that peaceful conditions cannot be established until a certain degree of economic and social development has occurred throughout the world.

According to Mitrany, the problem with the international system is that 'because of the legalistic structure of the state and of our political outlook, which treat national and international society as two different worlds, social nature …

6

has not had a chance so far to take its course'.[20] Social activities are only allowed to extend as far as the frontier and are not allowed to be linked with the same activities in other States. The gradual removal of these artificial boundaries by increased co-operation in areas of common concern would lead to an international system by way of 'natural selection and evolution, tested and accepted by experience', perhaps, but not necessarily, a federal order, with the possibility of a 'union of peoples, not of States'.[21] International organisations composed of rigid legal structures, imposed to complement rather than supplant the State-based structure of international society would not successfully fulfil the needs of that society.

This powerful argument must be borne in mind when examining the current structure of international organisations, in particular the United Nations, which despite the Preamble of the Charter – it commences with the words 'WE THE PEOPLES OF THE UNITED NATIONS DETERMINED' to promote 'the economic and social advancement of all peoples' as well as to maintain peace and security – appears firmly to be based on the principles of State equality and sovereignty embodied in Article 2 of the Charter.

Professor Mitrany summarises his approach in the following passage:

> Co-operation for the common good is the task, both for the sake of peace and of a better life, and for that it is essential that certain interests and activities should be taken out of the mood of competition and worked together. But it is not essential to make co-operation fast to a territorial authority, and indeed it would be senseless to do so when the number of those activities is limited, while their range is the world.[22]

This vision has been developed by the neo-functionalists whose aim is 'to formulate sophisticated functionalist techniques for identifying the extent to which international co-operation leads to inter-state integration and for measuring the significance of the roles both attributed and accruing to the central institutions rather than the participating states'.[23] Its value is self-evident, but one problem, at least, can be highlighted, that is the current apparent trend, at least in the West, away from centralisation, both within the State and in international relations, with the resurgence of the *laissez-faire* philosophy, free trade and competition, with the obvious exception of European economic integration

Rationalism and positivism

Following a natural law tradition derived from the Ancient Greeks, and applied to international law by Grotius in the seventeenth century, rationalism is the 'belief that everything is explicable, that is, that everything can in principle be brought under the single system'.[24] Before looking at one or two examples of rationalist thought *vis-à-vis* international organisations, the general thrust of this approach will be given. Professor Goodwin helpfully summarises the rationalist position. Rationalists view the international order as a crude system capable of limited order and regularity though the exercise of Lockean-type natural rights (such as the right of self-defence). Nation States are like the individuals in Locke's state of nature, without a government, but not in a Hobbesian state of anarchy. Professor Goodwin continues:

> From this premise the rationalist goes on to argue that a rational and moral political order analogous to that found at the domestic level needs to be and can be created in international society as it exists today, that is, in a society of sovereign states, so transforming that society into a true community or 'comity' of nations. World institutions provide the framework for the realisation of this order, for expressing and nurturing the intellectual and moral solidarity of mankind, and for the application of what are conceived to be universally valid moral and legal principles, perceptible through reason, which will lead to the general renunciation of the use of force 'save in the common interest' and to the inauguration of the rule of law.[25]

According to the rationalist viewpoint, as international society evolves with the passage of time, it will increasingly move in the direction of world government. The difference between the rationalist approach and the functionalist approach can be seen in that rationalism predicts the development of international organisations towards world government whereas the functionalists see this as being achieved only if it is the final building block in the functional development of international organisations. In addition, rationalists see the development of international society moving towards more legal formalities and the rule of law – the idea that everybody in the system, government as well as governed, are subject to immutable and neutral legal principles. The functionalists, on the other hand, are keen to reduce the role of rigid legal structures which they see as getting in the way of international or regional agencies dealing effectively with common problems. In this respect the functionalists are nearer to the realist tradition reviewed below.

Rationalism must not be confused with positivism which advocates the systematic and scientific analysis of, in this case, international relations, in order to describe them and explain their workings. Positivism, with its emphasis on a value-free, neutral approach to study, is not committed to the idea that international society is or ought to be developing towards world government. Positivism is an attempt to describe the workings of the system as it 'is' rather than what it 'ought' to be. However, rationalism is not simply concerned with what 'ought' to be, it is equally concerned with what 'will' be. Positivists though, tend to confine their analysis to the description of the facts as can be observed.

Looking at the legal positivist movement, for instance, we can see that each jurist, in attempting to describe the role of international law, comes to a different conclusion despite analysing the same facts. John Austin, for instance, writing in 1833, dismisses international law as 'law improperly so called', being no different conceptually from rules of honour between gentlemen, or the rules of fashion 'current in the fashionable world'. This narrow view of international law is in part dictated by Austin's pseudo-scientific categorisation of laws, with law 'properly so called' being defined as the command of a sovereign backed by a sanction.[26]

Professor Hart, on the other hand, writing in 1961, heavily criticised the idea that law is simply a command. Instead, he states, it is a form of social rule, consisting not only of convergent behaviour but also reflected in the fact that members of society use law as a yardstick against which behaviour is judged, reflected in the fact that they will criticise other members if they breach the rule. Such is the role of law in a primitive society. Once a society becomes more complex, these 'primary rules' of òbligation are supplemented with 'secondary' rules of recognition, change and adjudication, enabling the society to overcome the problems of being uncertain, static and inefficient. One can see from this that Professor Hart has an evolutionary view of a legal system, characterised by the increasing centralisation of coercion. This would seem to fit the rationalist ideas of international society becoming increasingly centralised as it develops. However, when Professor Hart briefly examines the international legal system, he see it as simply consisting 'of a set of separate primary rules of obligation which are not united' by any rule of recognition, or having any separate rules of adjudication or any great ability to change. For Hart, then, international law is a primitive system, though he implicitly leaves open the question of its further development.[27]

Apart from the different basic definition of 'law', one way of explaining the difference between Austin's and Hart's approach to international law is that the former was writing in a period of absolute sovereignty and therefore dismissed international law and any notion of anything superior to nation States (except God), whereas Hart was writing after the birth of the United Nations and the explosion in the importance of international rules and principles. This difference itself seems to support the rationalist contention that international society is developing. Austin saw international society as not being governed by law, Hart saw it being governed by law but only in a very primitive and generally sanction-free sense.

Hans Kelsen, writing in the same period as Hart, on the other hand, saw national law and international law as part of one system with international law being supreme. For Kelsen, municipal legal systems, consisting of a network of norms, can only exist if they are 'by and large, effective'. International law only recognises effective government within a State. International law also determines the existence or emergence of a State as well as its government. A government may change, but as long as the elements of a State are present, as determined by international law, such as territory, population, government and new requirements such as self-determination, then the State continues to exist, its validity determined by international law. International law is in fact a set of higher norms, with its own basic norm, which may delegate to each national order a wide degree of discretion as to the laws it adopts. When national law conflicts with international law, Kelsen is of the opinion that, like national law which conflicts with the constitution of a State, the law is not void *ab initio*, but is valid until annulled. The same applies in international law so that a national law adopted in contradiction to international law is the potential object of an international sanction to force compliance with international law. The more numerous conflicts found between international law and national law than within national legal systems is explained by the fact that there are weak institutions to enforce compliance in the international legal system. International law itself does not appear to be subject to the overriding principle of effectiveness, a fact not explained by Kelsen.

Kelsen's theory contains other weaknesses, not the least of which is his definition of the basic norm as the apparently empty proposition that 'states ought to behave as they have customarily behaved', although this enables him to assert that all principles of international law are applicable to the national legal order.[28] However, it does contain within it the basic idea that the international legal system, although weak, is supreme, and does have the potential to develop towards greater centralisation and some form of world government, where the weak basic norm he identifies would be replaced by some form of written constitution empowering a central body with the enforcement of community norms. To this extent, his approach can be seen as furthering the rationalist argument.

As indicated by Professor Goodwin, Secretary General Hammarskjöld adopted a rationalist posture during his term as Secretary General. This was embodied in the introduction to the sixteenth annual report of the Secretary General in 1961.[29] He contrasted the view of some members of the UN who saw the Organisation 'as a static conference machinery for resolving conflicts of interests', with the view of others, and his own, that the UN is 'a dynamic instrument of governments through which' States should seek reconciliation and 'try to develop forms of executive action, undertaken on behalf of all the Members, and aiming at forestalling conflicts and resolving them … in a spirit of objectivity and in implementation of the principles and purposes of the Charter'. The contrast is essentially between the traditional approach to international organisations commencing with the Concert of Europe in 1815, which views organisations as simply arenas or fora for resolving differences between sovereign and equal States, and the rationalist view that international organisations increasingly become autonomous actors with centralised executive power over member States as the international system develops.

Hammarskjöld supported his thesis by looking at the purposes and principles of the UN Charter. He saw these as embodying basic rules of international ethics derived from those fundamental principles accepted in national societies. Professor Zacher accurately summarises these basic principles as 'the prevention of armed conflict through negotiation, the prohibition of the use of force "save in the common interest", equal economic opportunity, political equality, and the rule of law or justice'.[30] The latter is of particular significance for it carries 'the world community … far in the direction of an organized international system', with roots 'in the history of the efforts of man to eliminate from international life the anarchy which he had already much earlier overcome on the national level'. The thesis is clearly that the international system will, and should be encouraged to, follow the national system, with not only the rule of law based on just principles but also the emergence of a central power to administer the system as well as create new law. A necessary part of this order is the outlawing of the use of force except if centrally authorised to achieve community purposes. States still have the right of self-defence, preserved in Article 51 of the Charter, but simply as a temporary measure until the central authorities take over. Again the parallel with municipal law is clear.

Although the organs of the United Nations 'have features in common with a standing international diplomatic conference' their activities go beyond such an arena 'and show aspects of a parliamentary or quasi-parliamentary character'. The fact that decisions are adopted by a majority as opposed to the traditional requirement of unanimity shows this parliamentary tendency. In addition, despite the fact that the Assembly powers, apart from internal organisational matters, are simply recommendatory, there is 'scope for a gradual development in practice of the weight of the decisions' particularly if they are based on the 'application of the binding principles of the Charter and of international law'.[31] The move towards government in the United Nations is made even more palpable by the presence of a power in the executive organ, the Security Council, to make binding decisions, embodied in Article 25 of the Charter. Even in that body the requirement of unanimity has been dropped in favour of majority decision making although each of the permanent members possesses a veto.

Although Hammarskjöld was well aware of the deficiencies in the working of the Organisation, his view of the potential of the body to be a first step towards world government has become even more relevant with the end of the Cold War and the resurgence of the UN. It is too early to assess how far the United Nations has gone towards this view, though the explosion in UN activity in the 1990s, in military and economic coercion, peacekeeping and peaceful settlement efforts, is clear for everybody to see, but it is pertinent to note the present Secretary General, Boutros Boutros-Ghali, has echoed some of his predecessors' sentiments. In his report to the Security Council on enhancing the effectiveness of the United Nations, entitled *An Agenda for Peace*, adopted pursuant to the first meeting held by the Security Council at the level of heads of State and government on 31 January 1992, the Secretary General states:

> In these past few months a conviction has grown, among nations large and small, that an opportunity has been regained to achieve the great the Charter – a United Nations capable of maintaining peace and security, of securing justice and human rights and of promoting, in the words of the Charter, 'social progress and better standards of life in larger freedom' … Globalism and nationalism need not be viewed as opposing trends, doomed to spur each other on to extremes of reaction. The healthy globalization of contemporary life requires in the first instance solid identities and fundamental freedoms … Respect for democratic principles at all levels of existence is crucial: in communities, within States and within the community of States.[32]

Further, he states that 'the challenge to the United Nations is comprehensive: to become at last an effective collective instrument of global peace and security, to foster responsible relations within the community of States, to ensure the respect of the rights of all peoples to self-determination, to achieve international co-oper-ation in the solution of economic, social, intellectual, ecological and humanitar-ian problems'.[33] Again the vision is one of a community of nations operating within one system of principles under the guidance, if not the governance, of the United Nations.

Realist and policy-oriented approach

In many ways the realists are like the positivists in that they are concerned with the world condition as it is rather than as it ought to be. Unlike the positivists, who in the main, concentrate on the legal situation, the realists are more concerned with what they see as the all-pervading struggle for power between States or blocs of States. World organisations are simply a reflection of this power struggle.

> World order is ... a function of a balance of power checking and restraining the over-weening ambitions of the powerful. The task of world institutions is to add stability to the balance and to facilitate the adjustment of shifting power relationships without resort to large-scale or unlimited war.[34]

This parallels the Marxist concept of peaceful coexistence and reflects a United States' based approach to world order. International organisations, from the real-ist perspective, are useful devices for diffusing great power struggles, for example during the Cuban Missile crisis,[35] but their effectiveness is dependent on the rela-tionship between the powerful States, particularly in the Security Council.

> In short, world institutions are seen as essentially diplomatic contrivances, standing diplomatic conferences, not organs of government. Consequently it is what states do and not the precise institutional pattern that matters most.[36]

In addition, the realists play down the value of universal legal principles as some-how being able to constrain the exercise of power, or at least they argue that for international law to be 'real' law, there is a need for effective enforcement of its provisions, an ability only possessed by the most powerful States. Professor D'Amato states:

> In the international system, at least, we have states which occasionally break the rules of international law and which seem not to be deterred by expressions of social dis-approval from the other states. This is a reality of international life. Therefore, unlike the tribal society where social disapproval may constitute an effective sanction, inter-national society needs a physical sanction to underscore its legal rules. Otherwise, the rules will occasionally be flouted. Perhaps they will be ignored most often when the 'chips are down,' which is exactly when they most need to be enforced.[37]

This is contrary to the Hartian view that the international legal system is a primi-tive legal system kept together by condemnation and disapproval, often to be found in resolutions of international organisations. For D'Amato, 'legal systems typically enforce their own rules by removing one or more entitlements of persons who violate the rules'.[38] In a municipal legal system this may take the form of a removal of an individual's right to liberty whereas in the international legal system enforcement involves a State reacting to a violation of one of its entitlements, such as territorial integrity or diplomatic immunity, by 'a counter-violation of the same or a different entitlement'.[39] So when the American Embassy in Teheran was occupied in 1979 with the approval of the new revolutionary regime in Iran, the United States was not only entitled to take tit-for-tat measures against Iranian diplomats, but also other measures such as the seizure of Iranian assets, and presumably, though this is not explicitly dealt with by D'Amato, the use of force to attempt the rescue of the diplomats. This is a vision of a self-help society which only benefits States who are powerful enough to assert their (perceived) entitlements under international law. Self-help is not restricted to simple retaliation in kind, for this is not effective enough as it often 'fails to deter the original entitlement violation but in fact reinforces it'.[40] The vision is of a totally decentralised international society, in which international organisations play a peripheral, if not non-existent, role, in formulating and upholding international law.

The policy-oriented approach to international law and organisations, shares with the realist tradition a critical attitude to universality of legal norms seeing them as meaningless, sometimes even dangerous, but this is combined with a more positive agenda. The policy-oriented school sees the world in terms of a great ideological power struggle but goes further to combat the Marxist vision of society with a vision of its own.

Professor McDougal, founder of the school, puts forward his vision of a minimum 'world public order', where community use of coercion is designed to serve the goals of human dignity.[41] In order to discover the goals and values of the international community, one must first reject the universal approach to international law adopted by the traditionalist.

> In this grave posture of world affairs it can only make sense to put aside the veil that is provided by false conceptions of the universality of international law ... The effective authority of any legal system depends in the long run upon the underlying common interests of the participants in the system and their recognition of such common interests ... The discrediting of claims to universality which are in fact false is thus a first necessary step toward clarifying the common goals, interpretations, and procedures essential to achieving an effective international order capable of drawing upon the continuous support essential to global security by consent.[42]

This will include the cessation of 'glorifying specific institutional practices instead of glorifying the goal values of human dignity'. An 'institutional device' which has been used to suppress underlying goal values is international law. The question remains, what are the goal values? McDougal provides the answer:

> A value is a preferred social event; and if we were to begin to list all the specific items of food and drink, of dress and of housing, and of other enjoyments, we should quickly recognize the unwieldiness of the task. Hence for the purpose of comparing

individuals and peoples with one another we find it expedient to employ a brief list
of categories where there is a place for health, safety, and comfort (well being), for
affection, respect, skill, enlightenment, rectitude, wealth, and power.[43]

Institutions, of whatever shape or composition, from regional government to
world organisations, should be concerned with protecting and enhancing these
goal values, although the implicit assumption is that the larger, and more global,
an organisation becomes, the less it will be able effectively to secure these values.
It is clear from the list of values and the tests that McDougal applies to them, that
they are basic Western economic and democratic ideals concerned with individual rights such as freedom of religion, speech, opinion; the freedom to accumu-
late wealth and property through the exercise of one's own abilities and skills; the
protection of the basic unit of Western society – the family.[44] These values should
be protected by the public and legal orders including international law and organisations. In other words the world order is driven by the goals of the community,
a sensible enough proposition, until the list of goals is analysed. The problem,
then, is lack of objectivity. The approach is motivated, to a large degree, by
antipathy to the Soviet Union – 'the most ruthless and comprehensive tyranny
man has ever known'.[45] It is an approach firmly entrenched in the 'bipolar
world'.[46] Above all the theory advocates the decimation of universal norms in
preference to those which advance the goal values as identified by the policy
school.

> Yet the spokesmen of totalitarian powers are the ones who ... pay most punctilious
> deference to the supposed universality of international law. And why? Strange as it
> may seem at first glance, the most convincing interpretation is that the existing imper-
> fections can be used by them to help prevent further advances toward a world order
> with genuine measures of security. For it is in the name of such universal doctrines
> of international law as sovereignty, domestic jurisdiction, nonintervention, indepen-
> dence, and equality – all of which appear to fortify claims to freedom from external
> obligation – that the case is made to resist the institutional reconstructions which are
> indispensable to security.[47]

For example, the policy school argues that the literal meaning of the UN Charter
should be ignored if it is necessary to secure goal values. Thus the US-led, UN-
authorised response to the North Korean attack in 1950, though not compatible
with Article 27 nor Chapter VII of the Charter, is approved of because it secured
South Korea from communism – the negation of goal values – as well as preventing aggression.[48] The policy approach has also been used to justify military
coercion entirely outside the UN Charter framework, which, remember, prohibits
the use of force except in strict self-defence or by the Security Council under
Chapter VII, if the use of force is intended to secure goal values. This type of
argument has been advanced on many occasions by American jurists, for
example, to justify the United States' invasion of Grenada in 1983.[49] Furthermore,
despite the ending of the Cold War, it can be argued that the policy approach
is beginning to dominate in international organisations, with an increasingly

flexible use of the UN and other organisations to achieve goal values such as democracy, as well as greater support for civil and political rights. The economic sanctions imposed by the United Nations in 1993 and the Organisation of American States (OAS) in 1991 against Haiti after the democratically elected government had been removed by a military junta is just one example.

Revolutionary approach

The revolutionary approach has at its heart the Marxist model for international law and society. Marxists adopt a 'materialist conception of history' whereby the economic situation is the 'ultimately decisive' factor in determining the shape and form of society.[50] Marxists identify 'five socio-economic formations: primitive communal, slave, feudal, capitalist, and communist',[51] the transition being explained in terms of a change in the economic foundations of society. When looking at the norms governing relations between societies or countries, Marxists logically identify four types of international law, namely 'international law of the slave-owning society, feudal international law, bourgeois international law, and contemporary international law',[52] as well as a superior type of inter-State law governing relations exclusively between socialist States. 'Contemporary international law', on the other hand, is a compromise between those States remaining at the capitalist stage of development and those having achieved the higher stage of socialism if not pure communism. Soviet Marxists like Tunkin reject the idea of law being based on a community ideal, instead seeing it as essentially superstructural and a reflection of the power, or more specifically, class struggles within society, national and international. The economic struggle between capitalist and socialist countries is, according to Marxists, a reflection of the struggle between classes, which are in turn a product of the economic base.

> Of course, states, not classes, enter into international relations; international relations are relations among states. But the foreign policy of states is determined by the predominant class in these states; this is class policy. Therefore the struggle of the two systems, socialist and capitalist, affects relations among socialists and capitalist states.[53]

This struggle is not directly carried out by force of arms, Marxists above all else recognised the futility of nuclear war, but by economic competition between the two systems. International law thus serves the purpose of allowing the two competing systems to coexist peacefully but only temporarily until world communism is achieved. International law is not formed from a general consensus on community norms but is arrived at by compromise, often with the result that there is no true agreement at all, simply an ambiguous norm which can equally be used to justify the socialist and Western positions. One can cite here the agreement in several General Assembly resolutions whereby peoples fighting for self-determination are stated to be entitled to receive 'support' from outside States.[54] The word 'support' was said by Western States simply to allow for political and diplomatic encouragement, whilst socialist States seemed to view it, at least in their practice, as allowing some form of military or, at least, financial support.

Kartashkin, another Soviet jurist, seems to suggest that this sort of ambiguous compromise is to be found in norms and principles of international law having a 'class character', which are ideologically contentious. He cites human rights norms as coming within this class. More genuine agreement is likely to be achieved in norms of international law having a 'technical character', relating to international trade, postal and telegraphic communication, for example.[55] To this extent there are parallels with the functional approach, but whereas the functionalists see such technical co-operation mushrooming thereby reducing the role of the State in international society, Marxists see co-operation in these technical areas as being expedient for socialist States. Once the economic competition between capitalist and socialist States is won and world communism is achieved, States, being essentially superstructural, will disappear to be replaced by a vague ordering.

For Marxists, therefore, international organisations are primarily seen as fora or arenas for peaceful coexistence with the capitalist States. This is made clear in the following socialist definition of an international organisation as 'a stable, clearly structured instrument of international co-operation, freely established by its members for the joint solution of common problems and the pooling of efforts within the limits laid down in its statutes'.[56] The emphasis is on a body with relatively limited autonomy acting within its agreed statutes, therefore allowing little scope for the doctrines of implied or inherent powers which would allow the organisation to develop a large degree of autonomy.[57] In addition, the organisation, although an arena for co-operation in technical matters, is characterised by bitter ideological confrontation in class matters. There is no room within this conception for world government. International organisations are firmly based on the concept of sovereign equality of States so belying any notion that an international organisation can have or develop any will independent of the will of the sovereign member States.[58] This is made clear in the following statement by Brezhnev:

> The United Nations is not some sort of self-sufficient power nor some kind of universal supergovernment. Its actions and the positions it takes up merely reflect the existing balance of forces between the States of the world, which is the prevailing trend in international life.[59]

This is not simply a mirror of the realist view examined above. The Marxist view is that the principles of the UN Charter reflect the socialist concept of peaceful coexistence, thus the Organisation reflects not only the balance of power but also is a vehicle for the socialist countries to put forward their aims and principles in the battle against capitalism. The Organisation is not simply an arena for maintaining the *status quo*, although it does reflect the balance of power at any given moment. The position maintained by the socialist countries up until the end of the Cold War was that the balance of power in international organisations was shifting slowly towards the socialist ideal. Once victory was achieved then the United Nations and other international organisations would be swept away to be replaced by an undefined system based on socialist principles.

Certainly there was a marked contrast in the United Nations between the first decade when the West was dominant, and the late 1950s up until the end of the 1980s when the socialist States and newly decolonised majority formed an alliance on issues which appeared contrary to Western interests. This led to some socialist commentators re-evaluating the stress laid by Soviet theorists on class struggle on the international stage to a more general conflictive approach to international relations. This led one Romanian commentator to state in 1982:

> In brief, no politics in the international arena is purely co-operative or exclusively conflictual. The very existence of highly conflicting purposes or interests between States implies, and indeed, requires, some degree of co-operation between the United States and the U.S.S.R. in drafting the two nuclear treaties on tests and proliferation. On the contrary, even in the closest forms of co-operation between nations there is always an element of conflict … It is the peculiar dialectical relationship between conflict and co-operation in international politics that explains better than anything else the vacillations occurring in East-West or North-South relations.[60]

This dialectic, or continuing process of conflict and resolution, has led to the United Nations changing from a *status quo* institution into an 'accelerating factor in decolonization'.[61] This conflictive approach has been taken up by the developing countries, sometimes known as the Group of 77 Non-Aligned States, extending it beyond decolonisation to cover a new international economic and legal order. According to the developing countries' revolutionary approach, the USSR had an impact on the domination of international law and institutions by the European and Western powers by helping to 'purge international relations and the law of nations of the phenomena of imperialism and colonialism which they contained'.[62] However, after an initial period of revolutionary ardour, the Socialist States simply accepted the *status quo* waiting for the world proletarian revolution hiding behind the doctrine of peaceful coexistence, a doctrine which enabled the superpowers to create two opposing blocs. The developing countries on the other hand, by mainly pursuing a policy of non-alignment, wished to use the majority they hold in the international institutions to further their own ideals of a new international economic order based on a redistribution of power and wealth from North to South.

The Third World wish to use their voting strength to create law, indeed, unlike Western lawyers, they see the adoption of resolutions within the General Assembly of the United Nations as creating new law. The West's reaction to this is 'to continue to act in international organisations like States unjustly stripped of some "right" to supremacy', and by using their superior economic power to undermine the growth in revolutionary ideals coming from the majority of Non-Aligned States. Furthermore, Western States started to put more emphasis on non-universal organisations and fora for protecting their interests, including the use of the veto power in the Security Council, the use of the weighted-voting mechanism in the IMF and the International Bank for Reconstruction and Development (IBRD), as well as greater reliance on more informal arenas such as the G7 or Group of Seven Industrialised Countries, whilst at the same time either reducing their financing of, or even withdrawing from, universal organisations. In addition, the West continued to advocate the traditional international norms, such as the protection of political sovereignty, and constantly undermined any attempt to elevate the concept of economic sovereignty to a similar position.[63] This has not dissuaded the developing countries from using their voting power to adopt resolutions strengthening the norms of economic sovereignty and non-intervention,[64] as well as putting forward a more radical agenda for a new international economic order.[65]

The revolutionary approach of the developing countries to the United Nations is to use it as a vehicle, not simply for reform of the international system, but for a radical change from a Western-dominated society to a more equitable and democratic system. The emphasis on sovereign equality found in Marxism is present, but the difference is a much wider approach to the interpretation of the power of the United Nations, in particular the General Assembly. Bedjaoui states:

> It has been claimed that certain of the General Assembly's resolutions apparently contradict the Charter itself. Today, however, it is fully recognised that the General Assembly is quite competent to interpret the Charter, not only in its letter but also in its spirit. Thus certain resolutions might indeed appear to be a 'development', of the Charter, but they follow the same lines and go in the same direction. In addition, it is acknowledged that the General Assembly has powers and competences which are inherent in its work. This is the framework within which it takes decisions, and these cannot be without legal force.[66]

Whilst it can be argued strongly that, as the revolutionary approach of the Marxists to international organisations has been severely curtailed with the West's 'victory' in the Cold War,[67] the conflictive approach of the developing countries to economic matters, though perhaps submerged by the Security Council's current focusing of the UN's activities on security matters, is still present in the General Assembly and other universal organisations. With the East-West divide gone, it is probable that North-South issues will become even more significant in the work of international organisations, although, as the following section shows, the critical lawyers maintain that the West has such an ideological hold on international society in the post-Cold War era that the revolutionary ardour of the developing countries has largely been subdued. In effect, the end of the Cold War has not only led to the demise of Marxism but also Non Alignment.

Critical approach

The critical approach to law emerged as a post-Marxist and post-realist stream of philosophy coming from the United States in the 1970s. It involves a straightforward attack on liberalism and the overriding liberal notion of the rule of law. The general aim of this post-modernist or post-structuralist perspective has been summarised thus:

> While traditional jurisprudence claims to be able to reveal through pure reason a picture of an unchanging and universal unity beneath the manifests variability of laws, legal institutions and practices, and thus to establish a foundation in reason for actual legal systems, critical legal theory not only denies the possibility of discovering a universal foundation for law through pure reason, but sees the whole enterprise of jurisprudence ... as operating to confer a spurious legitimacy on law and legal systems.[68]

On the international plane, the critical theorists see the Euro-centric 'international law of sovereign equality, based as it is on the same structure of ideas as that which governed liberal politics for the past two centuries' as being incapable of dealing with the problems of the modern world.[69]

Furthermore, a critical analysis of international law reveals that it is *indeterminate*, a similar idea to the Marxist understanding that many international laws can be interpreted to support the widely differing views of those countries agreeing to the compromise formula. Furthermore:

> Most fields of international law are covered by widely formulated directives such as 'self-determination', 'territorial integrity', 'non-use of force', 'self-defence' etc. which in legal argument can be opposed to each other and interpreted to support the most varied and often conflicting positions. International practice, including the pronouncements of the International Court of Justice, enables professional jurists to pick any number of precedents to support their particular rule and their preferred interpretation thereof.[70]

This sounds familiar to readers of realist jurisprudence, in particular Karl Llewellyn's multiplicity of precedents and precedent techniques,[71] but the point is more fundamental – there is no distinct mode of legal reasoning, law is simply politics in disguise. After establishing this, the critical lawyers prefer an open-ended debate about values instead of a narrow doctrinal debate about the relative weight of laws and precedents.[72]

Related to this claim that international law lacks *objectivity* is the critics' claim that the claim by international law to be *neutral* is 'even at best a half truth concealing the many ways political power is channelled through the system'.[73] The law's claim to neutrality legitimates the whole political and legal system, allowing it to be exploited by the rich and powerful countries to the detriment of the poor and developing countries.[74] This can be seen to a large extent in many international organisations such as the GATT/WTO, the World Bank, in a relative sense the European Union where the smaller and poorer nations of Europe have fewer votes in the Council of Ministers, and in the United Nations where, despite the large majority of developing countries in the General Assembly, in the executive body, the Security Council, domination is by the economically and politically powerful nations, particularly, with the end of the Cold War, the Western States, represented by the United States, the United Kingdom and France.

Domination of the system, including international organisations, by the rich and powerful States is not necessarily carried out in a conscious fashion by the representatives of those States – they simply assume that the imposition of Western values and the extension of the market philosophy to the international plane is a natural and perfectly legitimate exercise. Indeed, since the Western way claims to be the only true path to follow, all others are deemed to be wrong and hence illegitimate.[75] It is the aim of the critical lawyers to delegitimate this claim to the truth, to reveal it as an exercise of power and domination, and to reveal a fairer and more equitable system.

The critical lawyers believe that ideas are of fundamental importance to any society, international or national. Indeed, they argue that ideas constitute (form or make up) society. In international society, a dominant world view has taken hold, which projects the image of a new world order replacing the old balance of power, in which the rule of law accompanied by the protection of democracy and human rights dominates. This is a purportedly neutral and autonomous system of law, but in fact it is ridden through with Western values and ideas. The critical lawyers argue that the imposition of a free-market economy on every State under the guise of liberal democracy and the protection of civil and political, but not economic social and cultural rights, will simply continue the system of alienation and exploitation of individuals found in existing liberal systems. Indeed, with Western corporate dominance of this system, the exploitation of individuals within developing countries will be exacerbated. People, as individuals, or as representatives of developing States, will be persuaded to accept this view because of the powerful legitimating theories and ideas put forward by Western nations.[76] Indeed, one can see this domination developing at the United Nations and other international organisations, where Western conceptions of democracy and the rule of law are becoming agenda items and even the subject of resolutions adopted by Assemblies in which the majority of States are developing States.[77]

It is the critical lawyers' view that legal liberalism, in its functionalist, rationalist, positivist and realist forms, represents the *status quo* in society and that it seeks to mask the injustice of the system. They attempt to seek out the conflict-ridden substance that is hidden beneath that apparently smooth surface. Professor Kelman states:

> The descriptive portrait of mainstream liberal thought … is a picture of a system of thought that is simultaneously beset by internal *contradiction* (not by 'competing concerns' artfully balanced until a wise equilibrium is reached, but by irreducible, irremediable, irresolvable conflict) and by systematic repression of the presence of these contradictions.[78]

One of the contradictions in liberal legal thought identified by Kelman is 'the contradiction between a commitment to mechanically applicable rules as the appropriate form for resolving disputes (thought to be associated in complex ways with the political tradition of self-reliance and individualism) and a commitment to situation-sensitive, ad hoc standards (thought to be a commitment to sharing and altruism)'.[79] Duncan Kennedy, writing in the context of a municipal legal system, contrasts the individualism present in dominant liberal legal thinking, in the form of the application of rigid and precise rules, with the notion of altruism or collectivism:

> Altruism denies the judge the right to apply rules without looking over his shoulder at the results. Altruism also denies that the only alternative to the passive stance is the claim of total discretion as creator of the legal universe. It asserts that we can gain an understanding of the values peoples have woven into their particular relationships, and of the moral tendency of their acts. These sometimes permit the judge to reach a decision, after the fact, on the basis of all the circumstances, as a person-in-society rather than as an individual.[80]

The critical lawyers thus express a clear preference for the application of general flexible standards, to do justice in the individual case, rather than the application of rigid rules which, despite their neutral appearance, favour the dominant group in society, for that group is invariably the source of that law. Martti Koskenniemi puts this in an international context by pointing to the increasing use of 'equity' in international adjudications and practice as indicating a move away from the 'sense of fixity' dominant in international legal discourse, as well as 'a silent realization that legal concepts and categories might provide a context and a vocabulary for addressing social conflict – but that the substantive solution of conflict cannot be found from those concepts'.[81]

One of the fundamental contradictions identified by the critical lawyers of great relevance to international law, and in particular the law of international organisations, is the conflict between community values and sovereignty, as Koskenniemi points out.

> International law cannot take a stand on how states should live without losing its neutrality. The Rule of Law can seem legitimate only by being able to explain itself from the perspective of enhancing community (because it would otherwise support egoism) and safeguarding sovereignty (as its implications would otherwise remain collectivist). This is possible as long as legal concepts are formal, that is, stay at a sufficiently general and abstract level. But as soon as their interpretation or application seems to support some particular type of communal existence or some determined limit for sovereign authority, they become vulnerable from some opposing substantive perspective. From such perspective, formalism merely hides the law's preference for an objectionable substantive policy.[82]

In the context of international organisations, one can see the conflict between community interests and the doctrine of State sovereignty, still predominant in most bodies, particularly the UN, although it is under attack in the European Union, as that institution moves falteringly towards a federal structure. These two principles are poles apart and yet are used interchangeably by States. At one moment a State may claim the principle of non-intervention to protect its own, or another nation's, sovereignty, at the next be claiming that community concerns override that norm. Initially the United Kingdom blocked any UN Security Council involvement with the crisis in Southern Rhodesia relying on the principle of non-intervention as embodied in Article 2(7) of the UN Charter. It quickly changed its mind after UDI in 1965, when it became clear that the problem could not be resolved by the UK acting independently but needed the support of the international community in the form of sanctions to combat a denial of self-determination – designated a threat to the international community by the Security Council.[83] Similarly, Western and other States on the Security Council hid behind the façade of Article 2(7) in the days following Iraq's defeat in Kuwait in 1991, refusing to intervene in the internal affairs of Iraq to support the revolutions occurring in the north and south of that country. This fundamental principle of State sovereignty was set aside when public opinion changed the attitude of Western States to favour intervention to protect the lives of the Kurds and Shiahs, which was also seen as a threat to the international community by the Security Council.[84]

The point the critical lawyers make is that international law is riddled with such contradictions, not only between sovereignty and community, but between consensualism and non-consensualism, effectiveness and principle, *pacta sunt servanda* and *rebus sic stantibus*, and many others. To cite Koskenniemi again:

> ... the matter is not 'choosing' between facts or concepts but giving facts and concepts a defensible meaning. But because it is this act of projecting meaning which determines the sense of law (whether facts or rules), that act cannot be justified by further reference to law: it is a political choice.[85]

After revealing that law is neither objective nor neutral but a matter of politics, the critical approach is concerned to increase the level of flexibility in the international legal and political system, to avoid rigidity, and to promote plasticity of contexts,[86] which would enable countries and individuals to free themselves from the domination of the system by the powerful, and to assert genuine community concerns over outdated and misused concepts. To this end, international organisations and bodies should be more concerned with the development of equitable principles rather than the reinforcement of rigid, inflexible, but inherently indeterminate, rules. International lawyers, and international organisations, should be concerned with 'what is just in particular contexts and for particular participants'.[87]

Concluding remarks

Although each of the above theories claims in its own way to represent the 'truth' about international organisations and international law, each really represents a particular viewpoint, essentially of a political nature. Despite their appearance of objectivity and neutrality, functionalism, rationalism, positivism and realism are various justifications for the existing Euro-centric system, with each theory emphasising different 'liberal' structures and values as being essential to international and national society: the role and level of government, the rule of law, democracy (though not necessarily on the international plane) and individualism for example. Although there may be apparent disagreements between the decentralist philosophy of the functionalist and the strong government of the rationalist, or the importance of law for the latter and the lesser role given to rules by the realist, they are simply differences of emphasis, just as there are debates within Western States themselves as to the roles of government and law.

Ranged against these theories are the less dominant Marxist, revolutionary and critical approaches. The simple Marxian vision of international organisations as fora for class struggle, producing meaningless compromise laws, though mirroring to a certain extent the realist power-dominated approach, has fallen by the wayside with the end of the Cold War. The revolutionary attitude of the Non-Aligned States seems to have lost its impetus as the majority of developing States have become dependent on the West, in many cases adopting or, at least, mimicking, Western values. The remaining critical approach with its emphasis on equity, collectivity and redistribution, remains the most viable alternative vision of international society. It remains to be seen whether it will take hold in the practice of international organisations or whether it will, like Marxism, fail for want of a clear picture of the future of international organisations and international society, for without such a vision, the critical approach will not succeed in undermining the dominant Western ideology.

The influence of these approaches on the shaping of the law and practice of international organisations will be considered throughout the rest of this book.

Notes

[1] M. Virally, 'Definition and Classification of International Organizations: a Legal Approach', in G. Abi-Saab (ed.), *The Concept of International Organization*, 51 (1981).

[2] G. I. Tunkin, *Theory of International Law*, 36 (1974).

[3] See H. Collins, *Marxism and Law*, ch.2 (1982).

[4] Abi-Saab (ed.), *Concept*, 14–15.

[5] See P. H. F. Bekker, *The Legal Position of Intergovernmental Organisations*, 5–6, 43–4 (1994). Bekker takes a narrow functionalist view and applies it to the privileges and immunities of international organisations.

[6] I.C.J. *Rep.* (1949), 174.

[7] *Ibid.*, 178–9.

[8] R. Higgins, 'Western Interpretations of International Organizations as Reflected in Scholarly Writings', in Abi-Saab (ed.), *Concept*, 194.

[9] R. Higgins, *The Development of International Law through the Political Organs of the United Nations*, 2 (1963). The fact that Professor Higgins adopts a policy approach to international law illustrates the fine line between functionalism and the policy school, see R. Higgins, *Problems and Process: International Law and How We Use It*, ch.1 (1994).

[10] F. Vallat, 'Book Review', 13 *I.C.L.Q.* (1964), 1501.

[11] D. Mitrany, *A Working Peace System*, (1943).

[12] *Ibid.*, 6.

[13] See further P. Gerbert, 'Rise and Development of International Organizations: A Synthesis', in Abi-Saab (ed.), *Concept*, 38.

[14] Mitrany, *Working Peace*, 29.

[15] F. L. Grieves, *Supranationalism and International Adjudication*, 5 (1969).

[16] Mitrany, *Working Peace*, 33.

[17] D. W. Bowett, *The Law of International Institutions*, 108 4th edn (1982).

[18] *Ibid.*, 65–9.

[19] Mitrany, *Working Peace*, 38.

[20] *Ibid.*, 42.

[21] *Ibid.*, 43–4.

[22] *Ibid.*, 55.

[23] C. A. Cosgrove and K. J. Twitchett (eds), *The New International Actors: The United Nations and the European Economic Community*, 16 (1970). On functionalism, neo-functionalism and integration see C. F. Alger, 'Functionalism and Integration as Approaches to International Organization', in Abi-Saab (ed.), *Concept*, 123.

[24] *A Dictionary of Philosophy*, 298–9 London, Pan Books (1979). See also M. N. Shaw, *International Law*, 745, 3rd edn (1991).

[25] G. L. Goodwin, 'World Institutions and World Order', in Cosgrove and Twitchett (eds), *Actors*, 55–7.

[26] J. Austin, *The Province of Jurisprudence Determined*, 9–15, 138 (1833).

[27] H. L. A. Hart, *The Concept of Law*, 212–29 (1961).

[28] H. Kelsen, *Principles of International Law*, 553–88, 2nd edn (1967).

[29] UN doc. A/4800/Add.1 (1961) in A. W. Cordier and W. Foote (eds), *Public Papers of the Secretaries General of the United Nations. Volume 5. Dag Hammarskjöld 1960–1961*, 542–62 (1975)

[30] M. W. Zacher, *Dag Hammarskjöld's United Nations*, 22 (1970)

[31] Hammarskjöld, UN doc. A/4800/Add. 1 (1961).

[32] *Agenda for Peace*, 1–2 (1992).

[33] *Report of the Secretary General on the Work of the Organisation*, 47 UN GAOR (Supp. No. 1), 27 (1992).

[34] Goodwin, in Cosgrove and Twitchett (eds), *Actors*, 62.

[35] See N. D. White, *Keeping the Peace: The United Nations and the Maintenance of International Peace and Security*, 17–18 (1993).

[36] Goodwin, in Cosgrove and Twitchett (eds), *Actors*, 63.

[37] A. D'Amato, 'Is International Law Really "Law"?', 79 *Northwestern University Law Review*, (1985), 1293 at 1299.

[38] *Ibid.*, 1305.

[39] *Ibid.*, 1313.

[40] *Ibid.*, 1311.

[41] M. S. McDougal, *Studies in World Public Order*, 3–41 (1986).

[42] *Ibid.*, 8.

[43] *Ibid.*, 11.

[44] *Ibid.*, 17–19.

[45] *Ibid.*, 40.

[46] *Ibid.*, 13.

[47] *Ibid.*, 7.

[48] *Ibid.*, ch. 7. Criticising the 'absolutist' approach of Leo Gross, 'Voting in the Security Council: Abstention and Absence from Meetings', 60 *Yale Law Journal*, (1951), 209.

[49] See W. M. Reisman, 'Coercion and Self-Determination: Construing Charter Article 2(4)' and O. Schachter's response, 'The Legality of Pro-Democratic Invasion', in 78 *A.J.I.L.* (1984), 642.

[50] K. Marx and F. Engels, *Selected Works*, vol. 3, 487 (1970) cited in V. Karatashkin, 'The Marxist–Leninist Approach: The Theory of Class Struggle and Contemporary International Law', in R. J. MacDonald and D. M. Johnston (eds), *Structure and Processes of International Law*, 80 (1983).

[51] Kartashkin, in MacDonald and Johnston (eds), *Structure*, 81.

[52] *Ibid.*

[53] Tunkin, *Theory*, 36.

[54] See for example GA Res. 2625, 25 UN GAOR Supp. (No. 28) 121 (1970).

[55] Kartashkin, in MacDonald and Johnston (eds), *Structure*, 84.

[56] G. Morozov, 'The Socialist Conception of International Organization' in Abi-Saab (ed.), *Concept*, 175. See further, G. I. Tunkin, 'The Legal Nature of the United Nations', 119 *Hague Recueil*, (1966), 7.

[57] See further chapters 2 and 5.

[58] Morozov, in Abi-Saab (ed.), *Concept*, 178.

[59] Cited in Morozov, *Ibid.*, 179.

[60] S. Brucan, 'Power and Conflict in the Study of International Organization', in Abi-Saab (ed.), *Concept*, 163–4.

[61] *Ibid.*, 167. See GA Res. 1514, 15 UN GAOR Supp. (No. 16) 66 (1960).

[62] M. Bedjaoui, 'A Third World View of International Organizations. Action towards a New International Economic Order', in Abi-Saab (ed.), *Concept*, 209.

[63] *Ibid.*, 210, 217, 223–4.

[64] For example GA Res. 2131, 20 UN GAOR Supp. (No. 14) 10 (1965).

[65] For example GA Res. 3171, 28 UN GAOR Supp. (No. 30) 52 (1973).

[66] Bedjaoui, in Abi-Saab (ed.), *Concept*, 237.

[67] But see the Chinese view of international law and organisations, J. A. Cohen and H. Chiu, *People's China and International Law* (1974).

[68] A. Thomson, 'Critical Approaches to Law: Who Needs Legal Theory?', in I. Griggs-Spall, and P. Ireland (eds), *The Critical Lawyers' Handbook*, 2 (1992).

[69] M. Koskenniemi, *International Law*, xi (1992).

[70] *Ibid.*, xvii–xviii.

[71] K. N. Llewellyn, *The Common Law Tradition*, 75–92 (1960).

[72] R. M. Unger, 'The Critical Legal Studies Movement', 96 *Harvard Law Review*, (1983), 561 at 564–76.

[73] Koskenniemi, *International Law*, xii.

[74] D. Kairys 'Introduction', in D. Kairys (ed.), *The Politics of Law. A Progressive Critique*, 7 (1990).

[75] D. Trubek, 'Where the Action is: Critical Legal Studies and Empiricism', 36 *Stanford Law Review*, (1984), 575 at 592.

[76] D. Kennedy, 'Cost-reduction Theory as Legitimation', 90 *Yale Law Journal*, (1981), 1275 at 1283.

[77] See for example: the 1991 OAS Assembly Resolution on 'Democracy', OAS AG/Res. 1080, (XXI–0/91); 'Promotion of Democracy', OAS AG/Res. 1280 (XXIV–0/94); UN GA Res. 48/131, 'Enhancing the Effectiveness of the Principle of Periodic and Genuine

Elections', 48 UN A/PV (1993); UN GA Res. 48/132, 'Strengthening the Rule of Law', 48 UN A/PV (1993); UN GA Res. 49/190, 'Strengthening the Role of the United Nations in Enhancing the Effectiveness of Periodic and Genuine Elections and the Promotion of Democratization', 49 UN A/PV (1994).

[78] M. Kelman, *A Guide to Critical Legal Studies*, 3 (1987).

[79] *Ibid.*

[80] D. Kennedy, 'Form and Substance in Private Law Adjudication', 89 *Harvard Law Review*, (1976), 1685 at 1773.

[81] Koskenniemi, *International Law*, xvii.

[82] *Ibid.*, xxii.

[83] UN SC Res. 232, 21 UN SCOR Resolutions 7 (1966).

[84] SC Res. 688, 41 UN SCOR Resolutions 10 (1991).

[85] Koskenniemi, *International Law*, xxiii.

[86] R. M. Unger, *Passion: An Essay on Personality*, 7–27 (1984).

[87] Koskenniemi, *International Law*, xxvii.

2

The legal personality of international organisations

The importance of international organisations in the field of international relations is reflected in their international personality, in other words their ability to operate on the international plane in a manner distinct from their member States. The aim of this chapter will be to try to ascertain the true nature of international legal personality, and to attempt to ascertain whether international organisations, though recognised as subjects of international law, are still subservient to States as actors on the international plane. The approach to international organisations adopted by formalist, realist, Marxist,[1] and critical schools, views organisations simply as fora for attempting to resolve conflicts of national interest, and therefore lacking distinct personality. This will be contrasted with the functionalist, rationalist and conflictive (developing States') views, which put forward the idea that international organisations not only have a separate personality from the member States, but can and do have powers which States by themselves cannot have, although this is relatively rare. The most obvious example will be in the collective security field where organisations have wider rights than individual States which are restricted to self-defence.

The concept of personality

International personality appears to be a nebulous concept in international law. Vastly differing organisations can possess personality. For instance Article 210 of the 1957 Treaty of Rome establishing the European Economic Community[2] simply states that 'the Community shall have legal personality'. Similarly, the Statutes establishing the World Tourism Organisation adopted in 1970 and entering into force in 1975, state, in Article 31, that 'the Organization shall have legal personality'.[3] It is relatively rare for an inter-governmental organisation to state that it has personality, indeed, there appears no need for an express provision in the constituent treaty of an organisation for it to be deemed to possess personality. However, the existence of an express statement in the provisions of the treaty is useful because 'such provisions oblige the Members to accept the organization as a separate international person, competent to perform acts which under traditional international law could only be performed by States'. In addition, such constitutional provisions 'clarify the status of the organization for non-members. If a non-member were to doubt the organization's competence to perform international acts, a clear constitutional provision may be of some assistance'.[4]

It is quite often stated that the possession of personality by an actor on the international plane does not imply that it automatically has all the rights and is subject to all the duties inherent in the legal system.

> ... 'personality' as a term is only short-hand for the proposition that an entity is endowed by international law with legal capacity. But entity A may have the capacity to perform acts X and Y, but not act Z, entity B to perform acts Y and Z but not act X, and entity C to perform all three.[5]

This approach signifies that although the possession of personality by international organisations may produce certain common core features in the sense of rights, principally treaty-making capacity,[6] privileges and immunities,[7] limited *locus standi* before international tribunals and capacity to bring claims, and duties, in the sense of the 'responsibility of the organisation for its own illegal acts'[8], the extent of the personality of a particular organisation depends on its constituent document or to be more accurate:

> The acceptance of international organizations as international persons is important mainly for doctrinal purposes. It confirms that organizations and States belong to the same category of legal persons acting under international law. It confirms the *capacity* of international organizations to perform administrative acts in the international field. Whether a particular international organization also has *competence* to perform such acts depends on its own constitution.[9]

This view of the personality of international organisation exemplifies the 'objective approach', whereby 'the international legal order ... automatically ascribes personality to an entity fulfilling certain conditions'.[10] According to Professor Brownlie those criteria are:

1. a permanent association of states, with lawful objects, equipped with organs;
2. a distinction, in terms of legal powers and purposes, between the organization and its member states;
3. the existence of legal powers exercisable on the international plane and not solely within the national systems of one or more states.[11]

However, as Professor Rama-Montaldo points out, the 'objective approach' and the 'inductive approach', which starts 'from the basis of the existence of certain rights and duties expressly conferred upon the organization, and derives from these particular rights and duties a general international personality', are 'methods of determining whether or not an organization possesses international personality', whereas the 'formal' and 'material' approaches 'are concerned with the legal consequences attaching to the concept of personality'.[12]

The formal approach identified by Rama-Montaldo 'holds that no specific rights or duties emerge from the fact that an organization is endowed with international personality, but that it is necessary to have recourse to the provisions of the instrument setting up the organization'. Such an approach signifies that international personality is simply 'a descriptive notion' or a 'label' and lacks 'any practical usefulness'. It also means that each international organisation has to be examined on an individual basis, there being no real possibility of a unifying theory. This approach, which tends to restrict the impact of international organisations by advocating a very narrow interpretation of the constituent treaties as well as a very tight curb on the development of any autonomy by the institution, reflects the orthodox Marxist and realist positions, which simply see organisations as an ideological battleground to be used by States, in particular the superpowers and, to a lesser extent, the critical approach which sees organisations as furthering the imposition of power on the weak and disadvantaged States. All these wider theories, despite the fact that they are so different politically speaking, reinforce the formal approach to international personality.

However, in so far as the critical approach advocates the greater use of flexible concepts in international law and organisations, it can be seen as also advocating that international organisations 'should' attempt to develop an autonomous power and so act as a break on the monopoly of power by the powerful States. This view is certainly true of the revolutionary approach adopted by the developing States in trying to redress the North–South imbalance, and also to a lesser extent, the functionalists such as David Mitrany, who, while playing down the role of international legal factors in the development of a functional world order, would probably advocate as wide an approach to personality as possible since it would allow international organisations to respond to the needs of the world community and not be hidebound to the express words of their constituent treaties. The rationalists, with their ideal of world government, would argue that autonomy in international organisations is essential if the world is to move away from a system of sovereign equals to one where international organisations are in fact the supreme actors on the international plane.

It would seem therefore that the weight of theory not only supports an 'objective approach', but also a 'material approach' to personality, which, in contrast to the formal approach, identifies 'a certain category of rights and duties which' 'arise from the very personality of the organization, and thus to be enjoyed by every organization constituting an international person irrespective, in principle, of the particular provisions of the constitution'.[13] Some authors take a very wide view of personality when adopting this approach. One view is that 'the legal consequences arising from the personality of an organization are the right to employ all the means that the international legal order puts at the disposal of its subjects (a) for the fulfilment of their competences and (b) for asserting their rights'.[14] Professor Seyersted takes this argument to its logical conclusion by placing international organisations and States as legal equals.

Indeed, it is submitted that international organizations are basically *general* subjects of international law, having an inherent capacity, within ... constitutional limits ...

to perform all such acts as are performed by traditional subjects of international law, States; but that most Organizations are not in a factual position to perform all such acts, because they neither have the territory nor nationals, and because their purposes are limited in their constitutions.[15]

Personality in practice

Seyersted's approach is linked to his view of inherent powers, reviewed more fully in chapter 5. However, the basic thrust is clear, organisations have the same legal capacity as States, the only limitations being the presence of any provisions in the constituent treaty forbidding any legal acts, and the general purposes of the organisation in their widest sense, as well as the practical limitations inherent in any international organisation – such as lack of manpower, funding, weaponry etc. The legal personality of an organisation signifies that it possesses all those rights and duties inherent in being a subject of international law, these are then restricted in the light of the constituent treaties, in particular the purposes of the organisation in question. For example, the legal personality of the European Economic Community is limited to give effect to the purposes of the Organisation as stated in the original Article 2 of the Treaty of Rome 1957.

> The Community shall have as its task, by establishing a common market and progressively approximating the economic policies of Member States, to promote throughout the Community a harmonious development of economic activities, a continuous and balanced expansion, an increase in stability, an accelerated raising of the standard of living and closer relations between the States belonging to it.

More specific purposes are listed in Article 3 such as the elimination of customs duties; the establishment of a common commercial policy towards third countries; the abolition of obstacles to freedom of movement for persons, services and capital; the adoption of common agricultural and transport policies; and the 'approximation of the laws of Member States to the extent required for the proper functioning of the common market'. It can be seen that these are indeed wide purposes, even before the changes effected by the Single European Act of 1986, which obliged member States to complete the internal market by 1992,[16] and the 1992 Treaty on European Union (Maastricht Treaty),[17] which extends the purposes of European Community, as well as creating a new entity – the European Union. The additional purposes of the EC/EU include the development of: social, industrial, and technology policies; consumer protection, health and education initiatives; cooperation in immigration, asylum, drug trafficking and combatting organised crime; a common foreign and security policy; and a plan for monetary union.

Looking at these purposes, it can only be concluded that the European regional Organisation, as a whole, has an immensely wide international personality, superseding, in some respects, that possessed by its member States. Other organisations, on the other hand, which make the same claim to possess international personality, have much more modest purposes. The aforementioned World

Tourism Organisation, for instance, has as its aims 'the promotion and development of tourism with a view to contributing to economic development, international understanding, peace, prosperity, universal respect for, and observance of human rights and fundamental freedoms for all without distinction as to race, sex, language and religion'. Furthermore, according to Article 3 of its constituent document, 'the Organization shall take all appropriate action to achieve this objective', thereby allowing it to act independently on the international plane but only to achieve its purposes.

The approach whereby an international organisation, possessing the criteria identified by Brownlie, is assumed to possess all the rights and duties of an actor on the international plane subject to constitutional and practical limitations, has the advantage of greater conceptual clarity than the other approaches identified. It is also more fully in accord with the growth in competence and autonomy of international organisations since the Second World War. International personality is limited by the purposes (and sometimes functions if they are listed separately) of the organisation as defined in its treaties and, as shall be seen in later chapters, in the organisation's interpretation of its treaties.

The Constitution of the Food and Agriculture Organisation, a specialised agency of the UN established in 1945,[18] reflects this approach to international personality, when it states in Article 16 that 'the organization shall have the capacity of a legal person to perform any legal act appropriate to its purpose which is not beyond the powers granted to it by this Constitution'. This recognises that a general claim to international personality is not required for international personality is inherent in such an organisation: its rights and duties on the international plane simply being limited by the purposes of the organisation. Turning to the purposes of the FAO as defined in the Preamble, these are 'raising levels of nutrition and standards of living' of individuals; 'securing improvements in the efficiency of the production and distribution of food and agricultural products'; 'bettering the conditions of rural populations'; and 'contributing toward an expanding world economy and ensuring humanity's freedom from hunger'. Article 1 of the Constitution then lists the functions of the FAO to include the collection, analysis and dissemination of information, and the recommendation of national and international action on issues relating to nutrition, food and agriculture. However, even if it were possible to read these functions as somehow limiting the purposes of the FAO, such an approach would be nullified by Article 1(3)(c) which states that one of the general functions of the FAO is 'to take all necessary and appropriate action to implement the purposes of the Organization as set forth in the Preamble'.

Judicial consideration

The World Court in the *Expenses* case seemed to adopt this principle of 'functional limitation'[19] when considering whether expenditures authorised by the UN General Assembly relating to the UN Operation in the Congo (ONUC) and the

31

UN Emergency Force (UNEF) in the Middle East constituted 'expenses of the Organization' within the meaning of Article 17(2) of the UN Charter. The World Court stated:

> In determining whether the actual expenditures authorized constitute 'expenses of the Organization within the meaning of Article 17, paragraph 2, of the Charter', the Court agrees that such expenditures must be tested by their relationship to the purposes of the United Nations in the sense that if an expenditure were made for a purpose which is not one of the purposes of the United Nations, it could not be considered an 'expense of the Organization'.
>
> The purposes of the United Nations are set forth in Article 1 of the Charter. The first two purposes as stated in paragraphs 1 and 2, may be summarily described as pointing to the goal of international peace and security and friendly relations. The third purpose is the achievement of economic, social, cultural and humanitarian goals and respect for human rights. The fourth and last purpose is: 'To be a center for harmonizing the actions of nations in the attainment of these common ends.'
>
> The primary place ascribed to international peace and security is natural, since the fulfilment of the other purposes will be dependent upon the attainment of that basic condition. The purposes are broad indeed, but neither they nor the powers conferred to effectuate them are unlimited.[20]

These rather conservative sounding words from the World Court hide a flexible functionalist approach to the questions of personality and powers of the United Nations. The Court identifies the goals of the Organisation as being very wide, indeed, one can see that they could not be much wider, covering every aspect of humanity's existence and impinging on the areas commonly recognised as within the sovereignty of States – particularly economic, social and cultural areas. However, when looking at the functions of the various organs entrusted with the achievement of these goals then there are limitations, in particular the fact that in most areas, including the economic, social and cultural provinces, the powers of the organs are simply recommendatory. However, in the field of collective security, the powers of the UN are potentially very wide, particularly when considering the Security Council's mandatory powers as recognised in Article 25. If this is seen alongside the functions of the Security Council as defined in Article 24(1), namely the possession of 'primary responsibility for the maintenance of international peace and security', then in this field, at least, the personality of the Organisation is immense if not unlimited. Furthermore, in considering the question of the ability to create a peacekeeping force by the *General Assembly*, the Court was happy to assume that such an action was within the powers of the Organisation and within the functions of that organ (as well as the Security Council), in that the General Assembly possesses wide subsidiary powers in the field of peace and security in Articles 10 and 14 of the Charter.[21] Thus the Court had little problem in finding that the Organisation had the capacity to create a peacekeeping force, even though there is no express provision in the Charter granting that power. The approach of the Court which relies heavily on the goals and functions of the Organisation can be confused with the policy-oriented approach identified in chapter 1. However, it must be remembered that the policy approach replaces the goals of the organisation with the goals identified as necessary for a world order, and it may well be that the two sets of goals are incompatible.

The concept of international personality of the United Nations was discussed more thoroughly by the World Court in the earlier *Reparation* case.[22] The UN General Assembly sought the advice of the International Court on the issue of whether the United Nations could bring an international claim, with a view to obtaining reparation, against the State responsible for injuries to an agent of the United Nations suffered in the course of performing his duties. The Court saw this as directly raising the issue of personality. The functionalist – in this case almost policy-oriented – approach of the Court was made clear from the outset of the judgment when it stated that 'the subjects of law in any legal system are not necessarily identical in their nature or in the extent of their rights, *and their nature depends on the needs of the Community*' (author's italic). The needs of the international community have led, according to the Court, to an increasing amount of collective action and the creation of 'certain entities which are not states', culminating in the creation of the UN in 1945, 'whose purposes and functions are specified in the Charter'. The Court then emphasised that for the UN 'to achieve these ends the attribution of international personality is indispensable'.[23]

The Court noted that the Charter 'has not been content to make the Organization ... merely a centre "for harmonising the actions of nations in the attainment of those common ends"', as stated in Article 1(4) of the UN Charter. In other words the Organisation is not simply a forum, or a meeting place for States to air their differences, but an autonomous actor, 'which occupies a position in certain respects in detachment from its Members', identifiable by the presence of separate organs; also 'by giving the Organization legal capacity and privileges and immunities in the territory of each of its Members', and 'by providing for the conclusion of agreements between the Organization and its Members'.[24] These features are common to most international organisations.

After having identified the tasks of the UN in a similar manner to the *Expenses* case, the Court then made a general pronouncement on the personality of the UN.

> In the opinion of the Court, the Organization was intended to exercise and enjoy, and is in fact exercising and enjoying, functions and rights which can only be explained on the basis of a large measure of international personality and the capacity to operate upon an international plane. It is at present the supreme type of international organization, and it could not carry out the intentions of its founders if it was devoid of international personality. It must be acknowledged that its Members, by entrusting certain functions to it, with the attendant duties and responsibilities, have clothed it with the competence required to enable those functions to be effectively discharged.

Nevertheless, the Court emphasised that this was not to say that the UN was the same thing as a State, nor that it possessed the same rights and duties as a State 'but what it does mean is that it is a subject of international law and capable of possessing international rights and duties, and that it has the capacity to maintain its rights by bringing international claims'.[25] Furthermore, the Court then suggests that in terms of the hierarchy of international actors, nation-State supremacy remains unchallenged.

> Whereas a State possesses the totality of international rights and duties recognised by international law, the rights and duties of an entity such as the Organization must depend upon its purposes and functions as specified or implied in its constituent documents and developed in practice.[26]

Whilst a recognition of the functional limitation on the personality of the UN, this statement regarding the relationship between States and organisations seems a little too traditionalist, particularly in the light of developments in the UN and other organisations such as the European Union since the judgment was given in 1949. At that time, the UN blocked by the superpowers from fully developing its potential, did not seem to impinge on the supremacy of the nation State, but since that time the UN has developed immensely and has taken to asserting its rights and enforcing the duties of its members in a variety of ways not envisaged by the Court nor sometimes readily reconcilable with the Charter – for instance by demanding compensation from Iraq for its invasion of Kuwait, and by imposing severe disarmament conditions on that country after its defeat by a UN authorised military action.[27] The end of the Cold War has freed the UN to develop and expand its powers in a much wider functionalist way than envisaged by the World Court.

However, having said that, the International Court in 1949 was not averse to recognising a right which cannot readily be implied from any of the express provisions of the Charter, and in so doing recognising that the UN had rights overlapping with those customarily belonging to States. Indeed, there appears to be no reason for not extending the capacity to bring an international claim against a member or outside State which has caused injury to the Organisation by a breach of its international obligations towards it,[28] to all inter-governmental organisations of an autonomous nature, subject to the controlling, but very leniently applied principle of functional limitation. In recognising this capacity the Court saw international organisations as having a right similar to the traditional right of States to exercise diplomatic protection when injury or loss has been caused by another State to their nationals. The Court stated that the bases of these rights were different, in that it labelled the Organisation's right as consisting of 'functional protection in respect of its agents', whilst a State's right is 'diplomatic protection of its nationals', but the Court recognised that the two overlapped with the 'risk of competition between the Organization and the national state'.[29]

The Court applied the principle of functional limitation in a fashion which appears to allow for a wide interpretation of the functions and powers of an organisation thereby permitting the possession of a vast array of rights by the Organisation.

> The Charter does not expressly confer upon the Organization the capacity to include, in its claim for reparation, damage caused to the victim or to persons entitled through him. The Court must therefore begin by enquiring whether the provisions of the

Charter concerning the functions of the Organization, and the part played by its agents in the performance of those functions, imply for the Organization power to afford its agents the limited protection that would consist in the bringing of a claim on their behalf ... Under international law, the Organization must be deemed to have those powers which, though not expressly provided in the Charter, are conferred upon it by necessary implication as being essential to the performance of its duties ...

Having regard to the purposes and functions already referred to, the Organization may find it necessary, and has in fact found it necessary, to entrust its agents with important missions to be performed in disturbed parts of the world. Many missions, from their very nature, involve the agents in unusual dangers to which ordinary persons are not exposed ... Both to ensure the efficient and independent performance of these missions and to afford effective support to its agents, the Organization must provide them with adequate protection.[30]

This extract shows that the Court has adopted a very wide approach to the interpretation of the rights and powers of international organisations by not only looking at the express powers of the Organisation but allowing a wide measure of implied powers. In many ways it could be argued that this interpretation is in fact inconsistent with the doctrine of implied powers and is more readily suitable to the concept of inherent powers as identified by Professor Seyersted and reviewed more thoroughly in chapter 5.

It is clear, however, that the Court's lenient approach to the functional limitation of an organisation's personality allows for the argument that an organisation does possess a wide range of rights and duties on the international plane, a range which will not necessarily be static, but will develop with time, in accordance with the needs of the international community, perhaps to the extent of rivalling, or indeed overthrowing the supremacy of the nation State. For instance, the UN could claim not only the right to afford 'functional protection' to its agents in the form of bringing a claim but also the right to use force to protect its agents, as States have claimed the right to protect their nationals abroad by the use of military force. Furthermore, since a State's right to use force to protect nationals abroad is not without dispute in that it is only used by Western States with the ability to project their military might overseas, it may be, given time, that the only legitimate way for endangered nationals, UN agents, or indeed the human rights of any population, to be protected by the use of force is under UN authority. This scenario which envisages the centralisation of the use of force, under UN authority as States gradually give up their more dubious claims to be able to use force, fits the rationalist model of increasing development towards world government. The question of whether the world community has actually moved in this direction to any great extent will be discussed in chapters 7 and 8.

From this analysis it is submitted that it is only possible in very general terms to delimit the criteria and rights ensuing from an organisation possessing international personality. The criteria identified by Professor Brownlie have been identified above, the core rights and duties ensuing from personality have also been identified and are summarised by Professor Rama-Montaldo.

As in the case of States, international personality is not a mere formal concept but entails precise legal consequences which may be summed up as enabling the person to operate on an international plane, manifesting itself as a distinct entity and entering into relationships with other international persons.

Having said this, Professor Rama-Montaldo is at pains to point out that 'special care must be taken not to confuse the field of rights arising from international personality common to all international organizations, and the field of implied powers or functions particular to each organization'.[31] He gives the following illustration:

... there may be considered 'inherent' in the personality of an international organization a capacity to manifest its will *vis-à-vis* other subjects of international law by means of a treaty, or a recognition, or a claim: but the application of that will, for example to the creation of armed forces, or the administration of territory, or the acquisition of territory by occupation, or the use of the high seas by a fleet, or the participation in activities of other international organizations, is not 'inherent' in its personality but pertains to the scope of its expressed or implied functions or powers.[32]

Another way of looking at the issue of personality is to accept the common core of rights inherent in international personality as recognised by Rama-Montaldo, but to state as Professor Seyersted does above, that these are only an aspect of the personality of international organisations, and that if organisations are treated as equal to States then they have those inherent rights and duties belonging to States, and are only limited by the functions and purposes as identified in their constitutions. Such an approach is perhaps more in accordance with the principle of functional limitation which is not a rigid doctrine but will operate to allow certain institutions such as the UN to assert a capacity far beyond the common core of rights, whilst others, such as the World Tourism Organisation will operate only at the core.

A similar relaxed approach to functional limitation has been shown by the European Court in the *Commission* v *Council* case of 1971[33] in considering the powers of the European Community to conclude agreements with third countries in pursuit of its transport policy. In considering the impact of Article 210 of the Treaty of Rome 1957, which, remember, states that 'the Community shall have legal personality', the Court interpreted it to mean 'that in its external relations the Community enjoys the capacity to establish contractual links with third countries over the whole field of objectives defined in Part One of the Treaty', including the development of a common transport policy. As well as recognising that the capacity to enter into treaties is an important consequence of international personality, the Court took a wide view of the limitations on this aspect of personality by looking at the goals of the Community, in particular Article 3(e) of the Treaty of Rome which mentions the adoption of a common policy in the sphere of transport as one of the objectives of the Community. The wide approach to functional limitation is made clear when the Court stated:

To determine in a particular case the Community's authority to enter into international agreements, regard must be had to the whole scheme of the Treaty no less than to its substantive provisions. Such authority arises not only from an express conferment by the Treaty – as is the case with Article 113 and 114 for tariff and trade agreements and with Article 238 for association agreements – but may equally flow from other provisions of the Treaty and from measures adopted, within the framework of those provisions, by the Community institutions.

The autonomy and power of the Community which arise from its considerable personality is emphasised by the Court when it makes it clear that every time the Community lays down common rules in whatever form, with a view to implementing a common policy as established in the objectives of the Treaty of Rome (or subsequent amending treaties), then 'the Member States no longer have the right, acting individually or even collectively, to undertake obligations with third countries which affect those rules'. When such common rules are created by the Community institutions 'the Community alone is in a position to assume and carry out contractual obligations towards third countries affecting the whole sphere of application of the Community legal system'. Indeed, the Court not only emphasises the high degree of autonomy of the Community from its member States but also the supremacy of the Community within the pursuit of those objectives:

These Community powers exclude the possibility of concurrent powers on the part of Member States, since any steps taken outside the framework of the Community institutions would be incompatible with the unity of the Common Market and the uniform application of Community law.[34]

It is to this issue of autonomy (and supremacy) that the analysis now turns in that it appears that the main distinguishing feature of personality is that organisations possessing it have autonomy from the member States and indeed, in highly developed organisations, the centralisation of power is so great that the relationship between the organisation and member States can become hierarchical. Before looking at organisations with autonomy and supremacy it would be useful to mention bodies which lack autonomy and are simply fora for States to meet.

International organisations as arenas

Theorists belonging to the politically opposed schools of realism and Marxism both agree that inter-governmental organisations are simply meeting places which both reflect the balance of power in the world and are useful for the powerful States to meet to discuss and possibly resolve their differences. This view of organisations in general is incorrect, in fact there are relatively few organisations which seem to fit this description. Indeed, most of those that do fit this description are not generally recognised as international organisations in the full sense since they lack at least one of the criteria of personality such as organs, and, most

importantly, autonomy. They are in many ways simply fora for the world's politicians to meet and air their differences.

A good example of this type of organisation is the Commonwealth, formerly
the British Commonwealth of Nations which emerged out of the decolonisation
of the British Empire. The Commonwealth describes itself as 'a voluntary association of independent sovereign States, each responsible for its own policies,
consulting and co-operating in the common interests of their peoples and in the
promotion of international understanding and world peace'.[35] There is no formal
constitution and most business in the field of international relations is carried out
at biennial heads-of-government meetings,[36] adopting a series of declarations
such as the 1977 Gleneagles Agreement to prevent sporting contacts with South
Africa so long as that country continued with its apartheid policies. The Commonwealth's dealings with South Africa and its attempts to end the apartheid
system where a good example of one of the Commonwealth's activities in international relations. It first agreed a package of sanctions in August 1986, but without that agreement forming a treaty or resting on a mandatory treaty power, the
sanctions, as with all Commonwealth 'measures', were not binding. They were
'lifted' at the 28th biennial Commonwealth heads-of-government meeting in
October 1991 when the process of reform in South Africa seemed to be irrevoca-
bly under way.[37]

Another informal international body which, unlike the Commonwealth, has an
increasing amount of *de facto* power and influence in international relations, is the
Group of Seven Industrialised Countries (known as the Group of Seven or G7).
This involves the regular meeting of the finance ministers or heads of government
of France, Germany, Italy, Japan, Canada, the United States and the United Kingdom. The President of the Commission of the EU has been invited as an observer
since 1978, and since the summit in June 1994 the Russian government seems to
be a member making it effectively the Group of Eight. The body arose out of the
informal meetings of the finance ministers of France and West Germany in the
early 1970s which grew from 1975 to 1976 into the G7.[38] The aims of the body
are to discuss international problems but also increasingly to attempt to set, or
influence, the international agenda, mainly in the area of economic concerns but
also extending to diplomatic and political problems. The G7 heads-of-government meeting in Naples in July 1994 contained statements on combatting unemployment within G7 countries and also encouragement for the peace process in
Bosnia. As a meeting place for the major Western powers, the wider purposes of
the G7 is to maintain the *status quo* within the West but also, implicitly, to advocate Western political and economic policies throughout the world.

There are other examples of loose associations of States whose aim is to enable
countries to attempt to resolve common problems. A recent example is the Commonwealth of Independent States (CIS) established by the Minsk Agreement of 8
December 1991,[39] consisting of the countries emerging from the former Soviet
Union. Although still at a very early stage of development, this arena has been
used at various levels to attempt to solve diverse problems arising from the break-

up, such as the division of armaments possessed by the former Soviet Union, and the continuation of civil aviation amongst the new States. The CIS is developing an institutional structure, and in 1993 a Charter was signed which may result in an organisation having international personality covering economic, social, defence and human rights areas. The Alma-Ata Declaration signed at the same time as the Minsk Agreement makes it clear that the CIS is 'neither a state, nor a super-state structure'.[40]

Other bodies, while sharing the characteristics of the above in that they serve mainly as fora for the resolution of specific problems have developed institutional and more formal mechanisms for this purpose. In this respect they occupy a hybrid position, somewhere between the category of bodies normally accepted as possessing international personality and those, such as the Commonwealth and the G7, which do not. The main examples of these bodies are the Conference on Security and Co-operation in Europe (CSCE) and the General Agreement on Tariffs and Trade (GATT).

The CSCE is essentially a process, in the form of a continuing series of meetings, dealing with security and human rights issues. It was started during the period of *détente* between the superpowers with the adoption of the Helsinki Final Act of 1975,[41] by Eastern and Western European States as well as Canada, the Soviet Union and the United States. This conference or process has rapidly expanded since the end of the Cold War and currently has over fifty members including the newly independent republics of the former Soviet Union, the newly independent Baltic States, States from the former Yugoslavia, and has created institutions and structures so that in many ways it appears to be an international organisation. However, the 1975 Final Act, not being a treaty, has given rise to question marks as to the constitutional development of many of the powers now apparently possessed by the CSCE, and it is perhaps true to say that the obligations created by the CSCE process are 'political rather than legal'.[42] In 1990 in the Paris meeting, the States involved in the CSCE process, acting as the CSCE Council, invested the Consultative Committee and the Committee of Senior Officials of the CSCE with the authority to execute fact-finding and monitoring missions. This was further enhanced in 1992, whereby the Council adopted a document which developed the CSCE's fact-finding capacity as well as its good offices, conciliation and dispute settlement powers. A further meeting laid down concrete peacekeeping (but not enforcement) provisions.[43]

One way of explaining the legal basis of these powers is by arguing that as individual States possess these consensual pacific settlement powers under customary international law, then so does the CSCE process, it simply enhances them by making them collective.[44] The uncertainty over the legal basis of the CSCE and the question marks over its personality may lead to the further enhancement of the Organisation and its formal foundation in a treaty. Indeed, another step towards this was made in December 1994, when the CSCE renamed itself the Organisation on Security and co-operation in Europe (OSCE).[45]

However, the presence of a treaty is just one element in the establishment of an autonomous international organisation possessing international personality. The CIS is treaty based but is only slowly moving in the direction of developing the institutional framework and powers of an autonomous international organisation possessing legal personality. The GATT, originally established in 1947, is in many ways simply a treaty, not a constitution of an international organisation. Professor Bowett succinctly describes GATT in the following manner:

> This is not a specialised agency and is more an international treaty than an international organisation. As a treaty, it establishes a common code of conduct in international trade, it provides machinery for reducing and stabilising tariffs and a forum for regular consultation on international trade. The annual sessions of the Contracting Parties ... afford an opportunity for multilateral tariff negotiations which produce tariff schedules: these become binding contractual commitments when adopted by the meeting of the Contracting Parties and, by virtue of the Most Favoured Nation Clause, tariff concessions registered with one Party become available to all Parties. Quantitative restrictions on imports are in principle forbidden, but exceptions exist for agriculture and for Parties experiencing balance-of-payments difficulties or desiring to protect infant industries in a developing country ...
>
> The institutional forms of GATT are extraordinarily elementary. When GATT was drafted it was assumed that the ITO, the International Trade Organisation, would be created and would therefore provide the appropriate institutional machinery. Mainly due to U.S. opposition, this did not occur, so that it has been left for the conferences or "sessions" of members to devise a *de facto* machinery of a Council, Committees, sub-committees and working groups.[46]

Unlike the CSCE, the GATT is treaty based, but that treaty does not provide for formal decision-making processes by specific organs acting independently from the State parties to the Treaty. Although operating in the economic sphere as opposed to the area of security, in many ways the GATT is like the CSCE, developing organs and mechanisms for resolving disputes, but because of the lack of treaty provisions for these bodies,[47] doubts have to be cast over whether the GATT or the CSCE have international legal personality.

The absence of an executive decision-making organ has meant that the GATT has struggled to achieve agreement between the parties (numbering over one hundred) at the various sessions. The latest round of multilateral trade negotiations, the 'Uruguay Round', started in 1986 and ended on 15 December 1993. This calls into question the functionalist vision of Professor Mitrany who saw the gradual development of *effective* bodies, for dealing with economic issues, in particular, as fundamental to world order. The purposes of the GATT, as stated in the Preamble, are wide, namely that the parties' 'relations in the field of trade and economic endeavour should be conducted with a view to raising standards of living, ensuring full employment and a large and steadily growing volume of real income and effective demand, developing the full use of the resources of the world and expanding the production and exchange of goods', but the lack of mechanisms and personality have meant that the GATT lacks the necessary autonomy and power to do little more than maintain the *status quo* and thereby prolong Northern dominance of world trade.

However, with the successful completion of the Uruguay round of negotiations in December 1993, the participants decided to establish a World Trade Organisation (WTO) by 1995 to replace the cumbersome GATT machinery and to 'develop an integrated, more viable multilateral trading system'.[48] The WTO shall, by Article 2 of the Agreement Establishing the World Trade Organisation, 'provide the common institutional framework for the conduct of relations among its members' and to this end it creates a biannual Ministerial Conference to carry out the functions of the WTO, and a General Council to carry out the functions of the Ministerial Conference between its meetings, both bodies being composed of representatives of all members. The other committees established by the Agreement to oversee the implementation of the various trade agreements are generally open to all member States.[49] The lack of a small, executive committee limits the autonomy of the proposed new Organisation, although Article 9 does put limits on the consensus decision-making procedures of GATT by providing for majority and qualified majority voting in instances where decision making by consensus cannot be achieved. This development in voting, as well as the robust institutional reforms including the institutionalisation of dispute settlement under the authority of the Dispute Settlement Body (DSB)[50] outlined in Annex 2 which allows for the adoption of decisions of panels of three experts unless the DSB decides otherwise by consensus, make the new Organisation an autonomous international actor in the area of world trade as opposed to simply being an arena for States.

International organisations as autonomous actors

To identify the criteria of autonomy of an international organisation it is necessary to repeat the features of international personality as identified by Professor Brownlie: 'a permanent association of states, with lawful objects, equipped with organs'; 'a distinction, in terms of legal powers and purposes, between the organization and its member states'; and 'the existence of legal powers exercisable on the international plane and not solely within the national systems of one or more states'.[51] Of course the power invested in those organs, the degree of independence from member States, and the extent and type of powers exercisable on the international plane, determine the extent of an organisation's personality. Given the generality of these three features of autonomy it is possible to place most international organisations within this category. The purpose here is to give a few examples of different types of autonomous organisations. However, if the organs, independence and powers of an organisations are so well developed as to place the organisation, in some respects, in a position of superiority to its members then it is possible to argue that these organisations belong, at least in part, to a separate category, one dealt with under the next heading.

To start with, two examples of organisations of limited competence will be looked at to ascertain their degree of autonomy. These organisations have been set up by members to perform specific functions. The Organisation for Economic Co-operation and Development (OECD), an exclusively Western organisation,[52] is the successor to the Organisation for European Economic Co-operation (OEEC) established in 1948 to administer aid to Western Europe under the Marshall plan and to promote economic co-operation between the countries of that region. Its success in achieving this, its effective replacement by the EEC and the European Free Trade Association (EFTA), and the desire for an organisation to deal more with the problems caused by the inter-dependence of Western economies, led the United States, France, Britain and West Germany to lay the foundations for the OECD. The Convention on the Organisation for Economic co-operation and Development entered into force in 1961.

The OECD has distinct organs, namely a Council, an Executive Committee, a Secretary General and various subsidiary bodies. Of these organs, the Executive Committee, the Secretary General, and the other committees, are the subsidiary bodies, servicing the Council.[53] The Council is 'composed of all the Members' and is 'the body from which all acts of the Organisation derive'.[54] In terms of decision-making powers, Article 5 provides that the Organisation can 'make recommendations to Members', 'enter into agreements with members, non members States and international organisations', and most significantly 'to take decisions which, except as otherwise provided, shall be binding on all the Members'. Article 6 requires unanimity for decisions or recommendations to be adopted, with the caveat that abstentions do not invalidate any resolution, the only effect being that the abstaining member is not bound.

Although the Council is invested with a mandatory power to bind members, the requirements of unanimity and representation of all the members in the Council means that the sovereignty of member States is not undermined. Member States cannot be subjected to a decision which they object to. In this sense the OECD, although autonomous, is not superior to its members. The presence of mandatory powers, although an important factor in establishing autonomy, is not necessarily an indication of a supranational organisation.

The aims of the OECD are established in Article 1, namely 'to achieve the highest sustainable economic growth and employment and a rising standard of living in Member countries, while maintaining financial stability, and thus to contribute to the development of the world economy'; 'to contribute to sound economic expansion in Member as well as non-Member countries in the process of economic development'; and 'to contribute to the expansion of world trade on a multilateral, non-discriminatory basis in accordance with international obligations'.[55] To this end Article 3 declares that the members provide the Organisation with information, consult on policies and most importantly 'co-operate closely and where appropriate take co-ordinated action'.

These powers and purposes are not merely aimed at members but are also designed to facilitate economic development in non-member countries, a particular task of the Development Assistance Committee established by the Council. As regards the members' achievements in the economic field the Council has established an Economic Policy Committee which reviews economic developments in member countries, while the Economic and Development Review Committee carries out economic surveys of member countries by the so-called 'confrontation method, each country's economic situation and policies being examined by a panel of representatives of other members'.[56] The setting up of these supervisory organs by the Council has enhanced the autonomy of the Organisation by making the membership submit to regular review of their economic performance, as well as being subjected to potentially harmful criticism. The OECD's reports are seen as influential in Western circles, and members cannot avoid them as they are not subject to veto in the Council. In many ways the OECD is more *effective* than the GATT in the economic sphere, although in general the OECD's functions are supervisory, rather than being concerned with the actual multilateral negotiation of trade.

For organisations to fulfil the requirements of functionalism, their *raison d'être* should be to combat common problems, eventually leading to the diminution of the nation State as individuals realise that there needs are being met more and more by international bodies rather than governments. Organisations of limited competence, above of all types of organisation, should meet these requirements. However, as the OECD illustrates, the aim of these organisations is more often the maintenance of an ideology. The Western domination of the OECD simply means that as an organisation it is concerned with the improvement, and, if possible, exportation, of Western economic philosophy, namely free-market capitalism, under the guise of universal economic development. In this respect the OECD and other Western organisations, seem to lend support to the critical approach to international organisations, in that its superficial aims of promoting economic development in an neutral and objective way simply disguise the true power structure and ideology of the West. The critical lawyers would see the organisation's relative autonomy – its independence – from member States as simply furthering the illusion of neutrality and further hiding the true political nature of the organisation.

However, not all autonomous organisations have emerged to further the Western liberal dominance of international society. Some organisations could be said to be truly functional such as the International Civil Aviation Organisation (ICAO), whilst others follow the revolutionary conflictive approach and attempt to set up rival organisations and structures to combat the Western type. With the collapse of the Soviet Union and the Eastern bloc, organisations such as the Warsaw Pact, and the Council for Mutual Economic Assistance (COMECON), Marxist international organisations have all but disappeared, but this has not meant the end of the revolutionary approach to international organisations. An early example of developing countries attempting to combat the Western influence, in this case in the form of multinational oil companies, was the establishment of the Organisation of Petroleum Exporting Countries (OPEC) in 1960, and the Organisation of Arab Petroleum Exporting Countries (OAPEC) in 1968, the latter being responsible for the oil embargo that crippled Western economies in 1973.

To use OPEC as an example, it can be seen from its constitution not only that it is a 'permanent intergovernmental organisation', but that its main purpose 'shall be the co-ordination and unification of the petroleum policies of Member countries and the determination of the best means for safeguarding their interests, individually or collectively'.[57] Article 4 in particular reflects the conflictive origins of the Organisation in that it obliges member countries to act 'in a sprit of solidarity by rejecting offers of beneficial treatment by any oil company that is employing sanctions against one or more of the member countries'.[58] In addition, membership is restricted not simply to countries with a substantial net export of crude petroleum, but to those which have 'fundamentally similar interests to those of member countries'.[59] Members are exclusively developing countries.

As an organisation, OPEC meets the criteria for autonomy, having permanence, separate organs (the Conference, the Board of Governors, and the Secretariat), independent aims and purposes and the power to influence world oil prices. Indeed, in terms of *factual* personality, the power to influence world affairs, OPEC is well endowed. However, in terms of *legal* personality, although clearly autonomous there is no provision which can be construed as giving OPEC any supranational competence. The Conference consisting of all member countries is the 'supreme authority of the Organization'. 'All decisions of the Conference, other than on procedural matters shall require the unanimous agreement' of all members.[60] Furthermore, Article 5 asserts that the 'Organization shall be guided by the principle of ... sovereign equality'.

Other autonomous organisations clearly have a functional base in that their purposes and activities are aimed at dealing effectively with areas of common concern amongst States. The ICAO, a specialised agency of the UN, is just one example of such an institution. The rapid development in international air transport during the Second World War led to States replacing the Paris Convention of 1919 with the more complex Chicago Convention of 1944,[61] and accompanying International Air Services Transit Agreement (the 'Two Freedoms' Agreement),[62] and the International Air Transport Agreement (the 'Five Freedoms' Agreement).[63] These agreements established a new legal regime for civilian air transportation, although the Five Freedoms Agreement has had little impact, States preferring to regulate the commercial freedoms of the air by bilateral agreements.

Despite the fact that States have preferred bilateralism to multilateralism in the granting of commercial freedoms, and in this way have not developed the legal regime as far from the Paris Convention as may have been intended, the role of the ICAO is still of great importance since its activities are mainly concerned with standard setting and regulation. The purposes of the ICAO are to be found in Article 44 of the Chicago Convention, namely 'to develop the principles and techniques of international air navigation and to foster the planning and development of international air transport', more specifically: to ensure safety, regularity, efficiency; to encourage the arts of aircraft design, and the development of airways, aircraft and airports. Although Article 44 also mentions the promotion of economical air transport and the prevention of economic waste caused by unreasonable competition, the preponderance of bilateral agreements has meant that rate and tariff setting has largely been left to the International Air Transport Association (IATA) a non-governmental organisation consisting of representatives of the world's airlines. In this way, the ICAO has not been able to function fully as intended.

In terms of institutional structure, the ICAO has an Assembly consisting of all members who adopt decisions by majority,[64] a Council composed of thirty-three members, elected by the Assembly, an Air Navigation Commission and several sub-committees appointed by the Council. The Council is the permanent governing body of the ICAO, again adopting decisions by a majority.[65] It has several tasks including a legislative function under Article 54(l), namely to adopt 'international standards and recommended practices' as Annexes to the Chicago Convention. According to Article 37 these standards cover such areas as communication systems, navigation aids, rules of the air, air traffic control procedures, airworthiness of aircraft, logbooks, aeronautical charts, aircraft in distress, and the investigation of accidents. Each member State undertakes to 'collaborate in securing the highest practicable degree of uniformity in regulations, standards [and] procedure'. As well as certain administrative functions such as the administration of the Organisation's finances, the Council has a judicial function according to Article 84 which provides that 'if any disagreement between two or more contracting States relating to the interpretation and application of this Convention or its Annexes cannot be settled by negotiation, it shall, on the application of any State concerned in the disagreement, be decided by the Council'.[66] The fact that only one of the parties to the dispute needs to complain distinguishes the Council as a judicial organ from the World Court of the UN which requires both parties to consent to the case being heard.

The ICAO has been successful in developing standards and practices in air transport and navigation – its standards are the international standards. It clearly has a large degree of autonomy on the international plane enhanced by the fact that both the Assembly and the Council have the power to enter into agreements with other international organisations by Articles 64 and 65, as well as carrying out functions under the Transport and Transit Agreements. Furthermore, the Council's judicial and legislative competences, the fact that, as a body representing only a fifth of the total membership, it can act independently of that membership, suggest not only that the ICAO as an organisation has a large degree of international personality in the field of air transport, but also that it has within it that hierarchical element, with the Council as the supreme organ, that can not only act independently of member States, but can also set standards and decide disputes against the wishes of one or more members. In other words it has that element of supremacy in its particular functional field. However, it is not clear whether the standards set by the Council in the form of annexes are considered to be fully binding, at least not in the sense of a treaty commitment.[67] The fact that the Annexes, although extremely important, are not viewed as having the same legal force as treaty obligations themselves, is shown by the fact that on extremely important issues, such as the changes suggested after the shooting down of the Korean airliner by the Soviet Union in 1983, the ICAO amended the Chicago Convention in accordance with Article 94, rather than simply adopting revised rules of the air within one of the Annexes to the Convention.[68] Indeed, even if the standards are seen as mandatory there are mechanisms in the Treaty which allow a member State, with some exceptions, to decide not to comply with a particular international standard.[69]

Supranational organisations

According to the rationalist, international relations is moving towards world government in which the sovereign nation States' supremacy will be replaced by international organisations and the rule of law. It is true to say that this vision remains to a large degree unfulfilled in that most organisations fall within the category of simple arenas for negotiation and dispute resolution, or more significantly in the category of autonomous actors having a large degree of personality within their own particular spheres, but not replacing the nation State as supreme actors in the international field. The post-1945 proliferation of autonomous international organisations as opposed to simple fora, supports the rationalist proposition that the world order is moving towards more centralisation, but it does not by itself signify the final step of world government. For the rationalist vision of a world community to be realised there must be at least signs of a movement towards regional or world government.

Professor Schermers in concluding that supranational organisations in the true sense do not exist as yet on the international plane, identifies five elements required for supranationality, namely 'that decisions of the organization must be binding on Member governments', 'organs taking the decisions should not be entirely dependent on the co-operation of all participating governments' (for instance by allowing for majority voting or allowing decision making by a body of independent individuals), organisations 'should be empowered to make rules which directly bind the inhabitants of Member States', organisations 'must have the power to enforce' their decisions, and finally that organisations 'should have some financial autonomy'. It may be that it is only possible to speak at the moment of 'relative' supranationality but the following discussion illustrates that there are elements of it in some organisations.[70]

As has already been discussed in chapter 1 under the heading of rationalism, the United Nations has some elements of world government within its organs and in its practice. It has a very weak 'legislative' organ, the General Assembly, which although only generally empowered to adopt recommendations, can build up a body of law through consistent adoption of resolutions on a particular subject. The fact that by Article 18 of the UN Charter resolutions on important questions can simply be adopted by a two-thirds majority means that it can create law, albeit much more slowly, in the face of negative votes and abstentions.

The UN has a much more powerful 'executive' organ, the Security Council, consisting of fifteen member States, requiring a vote of nine with the concurrence, in the form of a positive vote or abstention, of the five permanent members – France, Britain, the United States, Russia and China.[71] This clearly means that the Security Council can adopt resolutions which may operate against the interests of a significant number of member States. However, the Security Council's main concern is in the field of international peace and security, where it can adopt binding decisions as well as recommendations. It can impose sanctions and take military action against a member State under Chapter VII of the UN Charter and thereby enforce its decisions. In this respect it appears to fulfil the rationalist ideal of a fully centralised decision-making institution in the field of international peace. Its practice in this area will be considered more fully in chapter 7.

The UN also has a judicial organ, the International Court of Justice, which can be used on the basis of consent by States for solving their disputes according to international legal norms, as well as giving advisory opinions, *inter alia*, on the legality of action by the other organs of the United Nations, but only if so requested by those organs.[72] The limited powers of the World Court seem to be a weakness if the UN is to fulfil, at least in the field of peace and security, the role of world government, since there appears to be no mechanism by which the Court can automatically judge the behaviour of States or the behaviour of the other organs of the United Nations. This signifies an absence of the rule of law so critical for the development of a world government. It is important according to the rationalists that all actors on the international plane be governed by law, otherwise there is nothing to prevent the misuse of power in the General Assembly by a majority of States, or in the Security Council by a minority of States, nor is there anything to prevent a State from breaching international law then refusing to submit its dispute to the International Court. This important issue will be returned to in chapter 5.

Despite deficiencies which will be identified and analysed throughout the course of this book there is no doubt that the United Nations is currently the supreme type of international organisation having a legal personality that is in certain aspects superior to nation States. It will be seen for instance in the course of chapter 7 that the Security Council can take coercive action including the use of military measures against a State if it deems the situation to be a 'threat to the peace' according to Article 39 of the UN Charter, whereas States are only permitted by Article 51 to use military force in self-defence in response to an 'armed attack' – a much narrower legal concept. It follows that the Security Council has, at least in theory, superior powers to nation States in this area. In this respect the United Nations not only has the personality equal to the State as suggested by Professor Seyersted, but has arguably a greater personality in terms of the powers it can exercise on the international plane.

Turning now to the leading example of nascent government on the regional level, it is necessary to briefly trace the development of the European Union (EU) to ascertain whether there is a movement towards supranationalism or federalism, which can be categorised as a form of government of States.

The dream of a 'United States of Europe' was not simply a post-Second World War phenomenon. After the First World War Giovanni Agnelli, founder of the Italian Fiat company, and Attilio Cabiati, an economist, wrote,

> Without hesitation we believe that, if we really want to make war in Europe a pheno-
> menon which cannot be repeated, there is only one way to do so and we must be out-
> spoken enough to consider it: a federation of European states under a central power
> which governs them. Any other milder version is an illusion.[73]

The essential element in this federal ideal is the centralisation of governmental power. They point to the two constitutions of the United States to illustrate their point that nothing short of a federal State in Europe will be sufficient. The first constitution of the United States of 1781 essentially created a league of sovereign independent States, an unworkable system according to Agnelli and Cabiati, since the 'essence of sovereignty is legal omnipotence ... it cannot acknowledge a higher sovereignty without destroying itself'.[74] The 1788 Constitution recognised this problem and replaced the old constitutional system with a central government with legislative and executive power. Of course if the European Union eventually emerges as a federal State along the lines of the United States then it will have the equivalent international legal personality, and not that of an organisation, which in theory may be the same as a State but in practice is functionally limited.

One group having such a vision for Europe was the European Union of Feder-alists established in Paris in 1946. At its first conference in 1947 the Union pro-vided a little more detail as to what elements were needed for a federal system:

> Federalists must declare firmly and without compromise that it is absolute national
> sovereignty that must be abated, that a part of that sovereignty must be entrusted to a
> federal authority assisted by all the functional bodies necessary to the accomplish-
> ment, on the federal plane, of its economic and cultural tasks, whether in whole or in
> part. In particular the authority must possess:
> (a) a government responsible to the peoples and groups and not to the federated states;
> (b) a Supreme Court capable of resolving possible disputes between state members of
>   the Federation;
> (c) an armed police force under its own control ...[75]

A federal system entails not simply autonomy for the central body in certain areas, but entails full government, representing the people of Europe and not simply a Council of State members, as well as an independent police force to impose its will. The Supreme Court must not only adjudicate disputes between State members as stated but also must control the activities of the centre if the rationalist vision of a rule of law is to be achieved.

The ideal of a European federal union was tempered by the politicians of Europe who wanted greater co-operation in order to compete with the superpowers but were not ready for wholesale European integration. The result was a gradual move towards greater centralisation of powers, the first steps being the creation by 'the Six' of France, West Germany, Italy, Belgium, Netherlands, and Luxembourg, of the European Coal and Steel Community in 1952,[76] with a consultative Assembly, High Authority, Council and a Court. It must be remembered as well that this was part of a wider process of institutionalisation in Europe with the creation of the Organisation for European Economic Co-operation (OEEC) in 1948, the North Atlantic Treaty Organisation (NATO), and the Council of Europe in 1949, all institutions separate from the Community.

The success of the common market in coal and steel led to the expansion along functionalist lines of the idea of economic integration in the creation of the European Economic Community (EEC) and the European Atomic Energy Community (Euratom)[77] (governing the peaceful uses of nuclear power) in 1957. The EEC was based on the idea of free trade within a large market, and although it created a 'new legal order'[78] independent of member States with centralised decision-making power (by majority vote in certain cases),[79] having direct effect in national legal systems without the need for national parliamentary approval, its concern was with economic integration rather than a political union. Decision making in the Community was a mixture of inter-governmental, in the Council of Ministers, and supranational in the independent but unelected, Commission.[80] The Assembly, to which MEPs were elected for the first time in 1979, had limited advisory and supervisory powers under the 1957 Treaty,[81] not permitting it to represent the people of Europe in more than a token fashion. It can be seen therefore that under the 1957 Treaties the EEC had limited international personality, with its concentration on the creation of a common market, and its restriction at the decision-making level primarily to control by member governments.

Nevertheless, there was sufficient centralisation in the Treaty of Rome as enhanced by the 1965 Treaty establishing a Single Council and a Single Commission of the European Communities (the Merger Treaty)[82] to encourage those States fearing a loss of sovereignty – the United Kingdom, Norway, Sweden, Denmark, Austria, Portugal, Iceland, and Switzerland, to form the separate European Free Trade Association (EFTA) in 1959, which was explicitly based on the premise of no surrender by member States of their sovereignty.[83] However, the success of the EEC/EC/EU led to the UK, Denmark and Ireland joining in 1972, Greece in 1981, Spain and Portugal in 1986, and Austria, Sweden and Finland in 1995 bringing the membership to fifteen.

In terms of international legal personality, the EEC, by adopting a common external tariff, was able to negotiate as a single entity in the GATT trade rounds.[84] 'The Community was set to become a very important force in the global economy, an economic giant. But this did not, at this stage, extend to foreign or defence policy. She was not a political giant'.[85] The Community in effect served liberal functionalist purposes namely the 'removal of impediments to voluntary and hence mutually beneficial transactions between individuals who happen to live on different sides of a border'.[86] It did not as yet serve the rationalist aim of political integration towards a central European government. The Single European Act of 1986 and more particularly the Treaty on European Union of 1992 can be said to have made tentative steps towards this aim with an increase in interventionist supranational activities (in the form of greater majority voting in the Council and a greater co-operative role for the Assembly, now called the European Parliament) in the field of economic, social and industrial policy, to be dealt with by the original EC itself (the so-called first pillar of the Maastricht Treaty). However, the Common Foreign and Security Policy (CFSP), and the areas of justice and home affairs (the second and third pillars), are to be left to inter-governmental co-operation, although the mechanisms for action in these areas are to be brought within the Treaty framework for the first time.[87]

If we turn to look at the CFSP as introduced by the Maastricht Treaty, it can be seen that this is building on the process of European Political Co-operation (EPC) started in the 1970s, whereby member States' agreements on a common position became Community Law only when adopted by the Council of Ministers of the EC. This process was formalised first by the 1986 Treaty and then by the Maastricht Treaty, but is still clearly separate from 'the supra-national aspects of the European Community (such as majority voting, the role of the European Parliament and the European Court of Justice)'.[88] With the defence policy of the European Union being in the hands of the already established inter-governmental Western European Union, established in 1954,[89] the separation of defence and foreign policy from the supranational activities of the EC appears complete. The absence of legal control over the CFSP by the European Court of Justice is another defect in the rationalist ideal of the rule of law governing the activities of the Organisation. In the area of economic integration, the European Court of Justice has adopted a strong, policy-based role to the extent that it can be compared with the US Supreme Court even though the EC is not fully a federal system.[90] Its absence in the area of foreign policy, signifies that member States are not yet prepared wholeheartedly to follow a federal road.

This has led one commentator to suggest that the European Union has no legal personality on the international plane, unlike the EC. He points to the absence of a provision similar to Article 210 of the Treaty of Rome, the absence of treaty-making power by the Union, unlike the European Community, and clear statements in the *travaux préparatoires* to the effect that no personality was intended.[91] However, neither the lack of an explicit treaty reference to personality, nor explicit treaty-making powers, is fatal to the implication of personality. The fact that the Maastricht Treaty envisages joint action by the Council of Ministers on the international plane,[92] binding on members, sometimes directed at situations in other countries not members of the EU, such as Iraq and the former Yugoslavia,[93] then there can be no doubt that the European Union has objective international personality irrespective of the views of some of the member States. Indeed, it could be argued that inherent personality, which carries with it duties as well as rights, would theoretically survive an explicit statement by all the member States that the organisation had no personality. The personality may only be that of an autonomous actor in the field of foreign and security policy in contrast to its personality in the economic area. In addition, the provisions in the Maastricht Treaty for qualified majority voting in the Council are extended to the CFSP although the norm in these situations is still one of unanimity.[94] This signifies a greater centralisation of power than perhaps envisaged by some member States and may be an area for future development.

Designating the EC as a supranational organisation in some fields does not signify that it is in effect a federal system,[95] this lies in future development, nor does it signify that the member States have transferred all their sovereignty to Brussels. It means that in certain areas, primarily in economic issues, the EC, through the Commission and the Council of Ministers and increasingly the European Parliament, the activities of which, as well as those of the member States, are controlled by the European Court, is supreme. One or two examples may be given to illustrate the point.

Article 155 of the Treaty of Rome empowers the Commission, *inter alia*, to 'ensure the proper functioning and development of the common market' in particular the application of the Treaty and 'the measures taken by the institutions pursuant thereto'. One aspect of this policing role is explained by Freestone and Davidson:

> ... the basic competition regulation, Regulation 17/62, empowers the Commission to collect relevant data and to require individuals and businesses to supply data to it. Violations of the Treaty's competition provisions (Articles 85 and 86) may be punished by substantial fines not in excess of one million units of account or 10% of annual turnover. All decisions taken by the Commission are subject to review by the ECJ. *The centralised policing of a common policy is not only unique within the EEC it is also unique in the world.*[96]

The supremacy of the European Community in implementing the common commercial policy is made clear in the following statement by Marise Cremona.

> In addition to expressly granted external powers, for example in the implementation of the common commercial policy ... or the power to conclude Association Agreements ... the Community has been held to possess whatever external powers are necessary in order to implement an internal policy effectively (... expounded by the Court of Justice in *Commission* v *Council (ERTA)* [1971]). In addition, external powers even under the common commercial policy may extend beyond the fields expressly mentioned in Article 113 to cover new aspects of commercial policy reflecting changing conditions in world trade, such as trade in services for example.
>
> The dynamic character of the Community's external policies is important in this context because it indicates that the boundary between the powers of the Community, the Union and Member States will need continual redefinition ... [An example] can be made in relation to the protection of human rights ... which also appears in Article F [of the Treaty on European Union], raising questions as to participation in relevant treaties such as the European Convention on Human Rights and Fundamental Freedoms.

> *The dynamic nature of the Community's powers has another implication: insofar as those powers are exclusive, their extension into new areas or new aspects of existing fields will exclude Member States. It has been clear since 1975 that the Community's powers in implementing the common commercial policy are exclusive in the sense that the Member States do not possess concurrent powers.*[97]

The growing omni-competence of the European Community is, somewhat paradoxically, recognised in the much-vaunted 'subsidiarity' principle, 'Maastricht's supposed safeguard against an over ambitious Community',[98] introduced into the EC Treaty by the Treaty on European Union. Article 3(b) provides:

> In areas which do not fall within its exclusive competence, the Community shall take action, in accordance with the principle of subsidiarity, only if and in so far as the objectives of the proposed action cannot be sufficiently achieved by the Member States and can therefore, by reason of the scale or effects of the proposed action, be better achieved by the Community.

This provision can in many respects be seen to justify the Community's development towards a federal goal rather than being a means of preventing it. It seems to imply a political hierarchy with the Community being at the highest level, or more accurately 'subsidiarity establishes a presumption that the primary responsibility and decision making competence should rest with the *lowest possible* level of authority of the political hierarchy',[99] in other words the member States. This view of federalism and the subsidiarity principle would

> serve as a means of maintaining a high degree of administrative decentralization: EC Member States surrendered their pretensions to pure and undiluted sovereignty, but each retains its own governmental apparatus to administer national legislation and those services which remain in its competence and to implement EC legislation. Yet, distribution of power of this kind is not simply a mechanical device or an exercise ir the division of labour in the Community organization. It places restrictions on the discretion and freedom of manoeuvre of the central authority and inevitably encourages substantial decentralization of political power.[100]

The encouragement to decentralise in the subsidiarity principle assumes the centralisation of power in the Community. The hierarchical nature of the European Community can be contrasted with the inter-governmental nature of the CFSP aspect of the European Union which simply 'comprises an aggregation or pooling of existing Member State powers'.[101] Therefore it can be said that whilst the Community has extensive international legal personality of a supranational and sometimes federal nature, the Union is, as yet, simply an autonomous actor.

Concluding remarks

Conceptually, the international legal personality of international organisations is equivalent to that of States. In other words, organisations have, in theory, the same rights and duties as States. However, constitutional and practical limitations

– the 'functional limitation' – on the capacity of international organisations signifies that it is only possible to identify a common core of rights such as treaty-
making capacity and privileges and immunities. In this way, States appear to
maintain their supremacy over most international organisations. In many ways it
makes little practical difference to state that international organisations may have
personality beyond the common core if their constitutions and practical circumstances allow. The end result appears to be the same. However, the latter approach
which starts from the common core, as opposed to the totality of rights and duties
possessed by a full actor on the international stage, fails to take account of the fact
that organisations do appear to have the potential to evolve, along a combination
of rationalist and functionalist lines, towards federal Statehood. The expansion of
organisations' powers, and the apparent evolution from fora, to autonomous
bodies, to supranational organisations, and finally to federal States, indicates that
organisations do potentially have the legal personality of States. Indeed, it has
been argued that in some cases international organisations have a greater personality than States in certain limited areas, an inevitable consequence of the centralisation, and therefore, the enhancement of powers. This is not to say that all
international organisations will evolve into supranational entities, many will
remain as powerful autonomous actors, or as simple arenas, depending on the
functions and purposes of the organisation and the practical limitations upon
them.

Notes

[1] But see C. Osakwe, 'Contemporary Soviet Doctrine on the Juridical Nature of Universal International Organizations', 65 *A.J.I.L.* (1971), 502–21.

[2] 298 UNTS 11.

[3] 985 UNTS 339.

[4] H. G. Schermers, *International Institutional Law*, 774, 2nd edn (1980).

[5] D. P. O'Connell, *International Law*, vol. 1, 82, 2nd edn (1970).

[6] D. W. Bowett, *The Law of International Institutions*, 341–5, 4th edn (1982). But see I.
Brownlie, *Principles of Public International Law*, 683–4, 4th edn (1990).

[7] P. H. F. Bekker, *The Legal Position of Intergovernmental Organizations*, 96 (1994).

[8] Bowett, *Institutions*, 362–3.

[9] Schermers, *Institutional Law*, 776–7.

[10] M. Rama-Montaldo, 'International Legal Personality and Implied Powers of International Organizations', 44 *B.Y.B.I.L.* (1970), 111 at 112.

[11] Brownlie, *Principles*, 681–2.

[12] Rama-Montaldo, 44 *B.Y.B.I.L.* (1970), 113.

[13] *Ibid.*, 116.

[14] *Ibid.*, 117.

[15] F. Seyersted, *United Nations Forces*, 155 (1966). See further F. Seyersted, 'International Personality of International Organizations: Do their capacities really depend upon
their constitutions?', 4 *I.J.I.L.* (1964), 1.

[16] UKTS 31 (1988), Cmnd 372.

[17] 31 *I.L.M.* (1992), 247.

[18] UKTS 47 (1946), Cmnd 6955.

[19] Rama-Montaldo, 44 *B.Y.B.I.L.* (1970), 122.

[20] *Certain Expenses of the United Nations*, I.C.J. *Rep.* 1962, 151 at 167–8.

[21] *Ibid.*, 163.

[22] *Reparation for Injuries Suffered in the Service of the United Nations*, I.C.J. *Rep.* 1949, 174.

[23] *Ibid.*, 178.

[24] *Ibid.*, 178–9.

[25] *Ibid.*, 179.

[26] *Ibid.*, 180.

[27] SC Res. 687, 46 UN SCOR Resolutions (1991).

[28] I.C.J. *Rep.* 1949, 180–1.

[29] *Ibid.*, 182–6.

[30] *Ibid.*, 182–3.

[31] Rama-Montaldo, 44 *B.Y.B.I.L.* (1970), 155.

[32] *Ibid.*, 143.

[33] Case 22/70, [1971] ECR 263.

[34] *Ibid.*, 274–6.

[35] Declaration adopted on 22 January 1971 by the Commonwealth Heads of Government Conference at Singapore, cited in I. A. Shearer, *Starke's International Law*, 106, 11th edn (1994).

[36] The Commonwealth does have an active and well-developed Secretariat.

[37] *Keesing's* (1991), 38552.

[38] 29 *Yearbook of International Organizations*, vol. 1, 632 (1992–3).

[39] 2 *Europa World Year Book*, 33rd edn (1992), 2270.

[40] 2 *Europa World Year Book*, 33rd edn (1992), 2271. For further discussion see A. G. Khodakov, 'The Commonwealth of Independent States as a Legal Phenomenon', 7 *Emory International Law Review* (1993), 13.

[41] 14 *I.L.M.* (1975), 1292.

[42] D. McGoldrick, 'The Development of the Conference on Security and Co-operation in Europe – From Process to Institution', in B. S. Jackson and D. McGoldrick (eds), *Legal Visions of the New Europe*, 176 (1993).

[43] 31 *I.L.M.* (1992), 976; 31 *I.L.M.* (1992), 1390; 32 *I.L.M.* (1993), 551.

[44] But see chapter 9 on the CSCE and fact finding in the area of human rights.

[45] Budapest document, 15 *Human Rights Law Journal* (1994), 459–52. Under this declaration the CSCE Council becomes the Ministerial Council, the Committee of Senior Officials becomes the Senior Council, and the Permanent Committee becomes the Permanent Council.

[46] Bowett, *Institutions*, 117–18.

[47] But see Article 38(2)(f) of the 1947 GATT, 55 UNTS 194.

[48] Preamble, *Agreement Establishing the World Trade Organization*, 33 *I.L.M.* (1994), 15.

[49] *Ibid.*, Article 4.

[50] *Ibid.*, Article 4(3).

[51] Brownlie, *Principles*, 681–2.

[52] 888 UNTS 179.

[53] *Ibid.*, Articles 9 and 10.

[54] *Ibid.*, Article 7.

[55] See also Article 2, *Ibid.*

[56] P. J. G. Kapteyn *et al.*, *International Organization and Integration* vol. 2.B – 2.J, Dir.2.B.7, 4–5 (1983).

[57] 443 UNTS 247, Articles 1 and 2.

[58] Kapteyn *et al.*, *International Organization*, vol. 2.K., Dir. 2.K.3.2.

[59] 443 UNTS 247, Article 7c.

[60] *Ibid.*, Articles 9–10.

[61] 15 UNTS 295.

[62] 84 UNTS 389.

[63] 171 UNTS 387.

[64] 15 UNTS 389, Article 48(c).

[65] *Ibid.*, Article 52.

[66] See *Appeal Relating to the Jurisdiction of the ICAO Council (India v Pakistan)*, I.C.J. *Rep.* 1972, 46.

[67] 15 UNTS 389, Articles, 37 and 90. J. Naveau, *International Air Transport in a Changing World*, 54 (1989).

[68] Article 3 bis, 23 *I.L.M.* (1984), 705.

[69] 15 UNTS 389, Article 38. N. M. Matte, *Treatise on Air-Aeronautical Law*, 212 (1981).

[70] Schermers, *Institutional Law*, 29–30.

[71] Article 27 of the UN Charter.

[72] Articles 36 and 65 of the Statute of the International Court of Justice.

[73] Extracted in D. Weigall and P. Stirk (eds), *The Origins and Development of the European Community*, 6–7 (1992).

[74] *Ibid.*, 7.

[75] Extracted in Weigall and Stirk (eds), *Origins and Development*, 42. In 1995 preliminary discussions as to the establishment of EUROPOL, a European police force took place.

[76] 261 UNTS 140.

[77] 298 UNTS 167.

[78] Case 26/62, *Van Gend en Loos v Netherlandse Administratie der Belastingen*, [1963] ECR 1 at 12. The ECJ held that community legislation was not only directly applicable to member States, as provided for in Article 189 of the Treaty of Rome, but also that it could be directly effective, creating rights before national courts for individuals. The case provides an excellent example of judicial creativity by the European Court.

[79] See chapter 3.

[80] Weigall and Stirk (eds), *Origins and Development*, 93.

[81] See D. Freestone and J. S. Davidson, *The Institutional Framework of the European Community*, 76–84 (1988).

[82] UKTS 15 (1979), Cmnd 7460.

[83] Weigall and Stirk (eds), *Origins and Development*, 94.

[84] See further Op. 1/94, *Re the Uruguay Round Treaties*, [1995] CMLR 205.

[85] Weigall and Stirk (eds), *Origins and Development*, 115.

[86] H. Schmieding, *Europe after Maastricht*, 12 (1993).

[87] *Ibid.*, 21–2.

[88] M. Cremona, 'The Common Foreign and Security Policy of the European Union and the External Relations Powers of the European Community', in D. O'Keefe and P. M. Twomey (eds), *Legal Issues of the Maastricht Treaty*, 248 (1994).

[89] Article J.4.2. of the Treaty on European Union 1992.

[90] Freestone and Davidson, *The Institutional Framework*, 27.

[91] M. R. Eaton, 'Common Foreign and Security Policy', in O'Keefe and Twomey (eds), *Maastricht Treaty*, 224.

[92] Article J.3.1 of the Treaty on European Union 1992.

[93] See chapter 7.

[94] Articles J.3.2 and J.8.2 of the Treaty on European Union 1992.

[95] Although there are significant federal elements in it, T. C. Hartley, *Foundations of European Community Law*, 10–11, 3rd edn (1994).

[96] Freestone and Davidson, *Institutional Framework*, 63. Author's italic.

[97] Cremona, in O'Keefe and Twomey (eds), *Maastricht Treaty*, 249. Author's italic. See also Op. 1/94, *Re the Uruguay Round Treaties*, [1995] *CMLR* 205.

[98] Schmieding, *Europe after Maastricht*, 20.

[99] N. Emiliou, 'Subsidiarity: Panacea or Fig Leaf?', in O'Keefe and Twomey (eds), *Maastricht Treaty* 66. Author's italic.

[100] *Ibid.*, 82–3.

[101] Cremona, in O'Keefe and Twomey (eds), *Maastricht Treaty*, 250.

3

Composition and structure of international organisations

The aim of this chapter is not simply to give the reader a basic run through of the common institutional legal problems such as membership, composition, representation, voting, withdrawal, suspension and expulsion,[1] but to continue to look at the wider issues of international organisations raised in the first two chapters, in particular the impact of institutions on the doctrine of sovereign equality, so long the cornerstone of international relations. The inspiration for this chapter comes from Professor Bowett, who writes:

> The sovereign State not only tended, in the nineteenth century, to be thought of as the only real subject of international law, but, in the context of the nineteenth-century conferences, which, represented the beginnings of international organisation, equality meant 'the right of every interested State to participate on an equal footing, (and) conceding to the delegations of every State an equality of voting strength whenever votes are taken and requiring unanimity for all important decisions and ... limiting the assembly to decisions *ad referendum* ...'. The assumptions that only States ought to be represented in the international sphere, that States should enjoy complete equality of vote, and that decisions required unanimity could, if carried to their logical conclusions, well-nigh stultify the promotion of common interests through the medium of international organisations. Our present purpose, therefore, is to show how far, by a constant process of development and experiment, these supposed consequences of the doctrine of sovereign equality have been evaded by the different techniques of membership, representation, voting and the like.[2]

The point could be taken further in that, as we have seen in chapter 2, some organisations are not merely autonomous from their membership and therefore compete in the provision of services with States, but others have powers not possessed by States, making them in some ways superior to nation States. These autonomous and supreme international organisations could be said to have limited the doctrines of sovereignty and sovereign equality themselves, not merely limited the consequences of them.

Membership

Some international organisations can be labelled as having universal membership, some limited, either regionally, functionally or politically. Membership of so-called universal organisations is not necessarily open to all States nor are all eligible States members. The League of Nations formed in 1919 was the first real attempt at a universal organisation, Article 1(1) of the Covenant[3] provided that 'the original members of the League of Nations shall be those of the Signatories which are named in the Annex as shall accede without reservation to this Covenant'. Furthermore, Article 1(2) made membership open to 'any fully self-governing State, Dominion or Colony not named in the Annex ... if its admission is agreed to by two-thirds of the Assembly, provided that it shall give effective guarantees of its sincere intention to observe its international obligations ...'. One of the original signatories, and one of the driving forces behind the formation of the League, was the United States, but President Wilson failed to persuade the United States' Congress to ratify the Covenant and the United States did not become a member. Thus at the outset the League was not a universal organisation, and despite the fact that its membership rose to 59, it was dogged by impotence and withdrawal so that by its formal dissolution in April 1946 it only had 40 members.

The world's second attempt at establishing a *global* international organisation, the United Nations, was more successful. Article 3 of the UN Charter states that the 'original Members of the United Nations shall be the States which, having participated in [the San Francisco conference], or having previously signed the Declaration by United Nations of 1 January 1942, sign the present Charter and ratify it in accordance with Article 110'.[4] Article 4 outlines the procedure for the admission of new States to the United Nations.

1. Membership in the United Nations is open to all other peace-loving states which accept the obligations contained in the present Charter and, in the judgment of the Organization, are able and willing to carry out these obligations.
2. The admission of any such state to membership in the United Nations will be effected by a decision of the General Assembly upon the recommendation of the Security Council.

In 1945 the membership of the United Nations numbered 51 (little more than its predecessor) and was, with the exception of the Soviet Union and its allies, Western dominated, but by the end of the Cold War in 1989 the membership had increased to 159, the bulk of the increase consisting of newly independent States (loosely known as the Non-Aligned group or the Group of 77), dramatically altering the balance of voting power in the General Assembly. The end of the Cold War saw a further dramatic increase in membership so that on 15 December 1994 when Palau was admitted, the number of member States stood at 185. The major part of this increase was caused by the 'fall-out' occurring at the end of the Cold War. Clear examples are the former Soviet republics of Armenia, Azerbaijan,

Georgia, Kazakhstan, Kyrgyzstan, Republic of Moldova, Tajikistan, Turk-menistan and Uzbekistan,[5] as well as the more recent acquisitions to the former Soviet empire, the Baltic States of Latvia, Lithuania, and Estonia. The same can be said about those new States emerging from the collapse of the Communist regime in Yugoslavia, namely, Bosnia and Herzegovina, Croatia, Slovenia, and the Yugoslav Republic of Macedonia, in addition to the new member States of Namibia, the Democratic People's Republic of Korea, the Republic of Korea, Eritrea, the Czech Republic and Slovakia. The remainder of the post-Cold War membership increase consists of so-called micro-States of Micronesia, Liechten-stein, the Marshall Islands, San Marino, Monaco, Andorra and Palau.

On the question of admission of new members Article 4(1) lays down the cri-teria to be applied. However, it has become obvious, particularly during the Cold War, that member States, particularly the superpowers in the Security Council, exercised their judgment as to new applicants according to wider geopolitical cri-teria. This is in contradiction to the legal requirements of Article 4(1), a position made clear by the General Assembly of the UN, which requested an advisory opinion of the International Court of Justice in 1948. The Court agreed with the General Assembly.

> A Member of the United Nations which is called upon, in virtue of Article 4 of the Charter, to pronounce itself by its vote, either in the Security Council or in the Gen-eral Assembly, on the admission of a State to membership in the United Nations, is not juridically entitled to make its consent to the admission dependent on conditions not expressly provided for by paragraph 1 of the said Article; and that in particular, a Member of the Organization cannot, while it recognizes the conditions set forth in that provision by the State concerned, subject its affirmative vote to the additional condition that other States be admitted to membership in the United Nations together with that State.[6]

As Professor Schermers relates:

> the major powers in the Security Council did not accept this view, however. The Soviet Union ha[d] rejected it from the beginning; the United States implicitly rejected it in 1975 when it blocked the admission of the Democratic Republic of Viet-nam and the Republic of Vietnam for reasons other than those mentioned in Article 4 of the UN Charter.[7]

The specialised agencies of the UN also aspire to universal membership subject to any functional limitations inherent in the purposes of the organisations. For instance the World Meteorological Organisation (WMO) established as an inter-governmental organisation in 1947, currently with over 170 members, has the purposes of facilitating 'world-wide co-operation in the establishment of net-works of stations for the making of meteorological observations' as well as infor-mation exchange, standardisation, and research in meteorology. With these functions in mind, its constitution provides that membership is only open to those States possessing a meteorological service, as well as the founding States.[8] Other UN specialised agencies, on the other hand, although set up to fulfil certain goals, do not delimit their membership by reference to functions. The International Maritime Organisation (IMO), established in 1948, presently with over 140 member States, has the function of providing co-operation among members on matters affecting international merchant shipping as well as the encouragement of the highest practicable standards of maritime safety and efficiency of navigation, the prevention and control of marine pollution and the removal of governmental discriminatory action affecting shipping. Membership is not restricted to States with merchant shipping fleets, but is open to all States.[9] Other organisations' membership restrictions reflect their wartime origins. For instance Article 92(a) of the Convention on International Civil Aviation of 1944, which, *inter alia*, established the ICAO, states 'this Convention shall be open for adherence by members of the United Nations and States associated with them, and States which remained neutral during the present world conflict', referring not to the UN Organisation but to those parties adhering to the Declaration by United Nations of 1942. As regards new members, Article 93 provides that admittance of States which were enemies of the Second World War allies is subject to a four-fifths majority vote 'provided that in each case the assent of any State invaded or attacked during the present war by the State seeking admission shall be necessary'. Despite these potentially divisive origins, the ICAO, as with the UN itself, has developed into a universal organisation of currently over 175 members.

Regional organisations by their very nature limit their membership on geographical grounds. As we have seen in chapter 2, membership of the European Union has expanded from the original six to fifteen with the prospect of further expansion into eastern Europe. The conditions of membership are contained in Article O of the Maastricht Treaty of 1992, replacing a similar provision, Article 237, in the Treaty of Rome of 1957.

> Any European State may apply to become a Member of the Union. It shall address its application to the Council, which shall act unanimously after consulting the Commission and after receiving the assent of the European Parliament, which shall act by an absolute majority of its component members. The Conditions of admission and the adjustments to the Treaties on which the Union is founded which such admission entails shall be the subject of an agreement between the Member States and the applicant State. This agreement shall be submitted for ratification by all the contracting States in accordance with their respective constitutional requirements.

The admission of new member States to an organisation such as the EU may create the need for many amendments to the constituent treaties, not the least the negotiation of voting rights in the Council and the European Parliament. Furthermore, unlike the UN, the only substantive condition contained in Article O and its predecessor is that the applicant has to be a 'European State', any other criteria will presumably be at the complete discretion of each member State. However, when France blocked the application of the United Kingdom in 1961 and 1967, it could be argued that the European Court of Justice could have declared France to be in breach of the EC treaties since it was acting for political purposes foreign to the spirit and aims of the Community.[10] Despite this argument, it appears that as with the UN Security Council, a veto of an application for membership may be exercised by a member State of the EU in the Council, for whatever reason.

Other regional organisations place limits on membership in addition to those that are geographical. The Association of South East Asian Nations (ASEAN), established by the Bangkok Declaration of 1967,[11] is 'open for participation to all States in the South-East Asian Region subscribing to the aforementioned aims, principles and purposes', namely accelerated economic growth, the promotion of regional peace and security and the rule of law, and general collaboration and mutual assistance in the economic, social, cultural, technical, scientific, industrial and agricultural fields. The process by which applications are vetted to ensure compliance is not clear, though presumably consent must be given by either the Ministerial Meeting or the Standing Committee, organs created by the Bangkok Declaration.

The League of Arab States, established in 1945, simply states that it 'shall be composed of the independent Arab States that have signed this pact' and allows other independent Arab States 'the right' to adhere by application to the Council.[12] The fact that the Pact states that every Arab State has the 'right' to become a member, presumably removes any political discretion on the part of the members of the Council to veto an application, unlike the discretionary process envisaged by the EU and ASEAN. A similar non-discretionary approach appears in the Charter of the Organisation of African Unity (OAU), signed in 1963, which lays down in Article 4 that 'each independent sovereign African State shall be entitled to become a member of the Organization'.[13] This entitlement may have been tested if South Africa has applied for membership during the years of the apartheid regime, given the emphasis in the Charter on the struggle against neo-colonialism in all its forms. Article 28 simply declares that admission shall be decided by a simple majority in the Assembly (consisting of all members). Such a majority was obtained for the admission of the Saharan Arab Democratic Republic (Western Sahara) in 1984 despite objections, particularly from Morocco, as to the sovereignty and independence of Western Sahara.[14]

The Arab League also has provision in its 'Annex on Palestine' for the Council to 'designate an Arab delegate from Palestine to participate in its work until this country enjoys actual independence'. The Palestine Liberation Organisation (PLO) has been so designated, and Palestine was confirmed as a full member of the League in 1976. The presence of what would traditionally be described as non-State actors in international organisations is not a rarity, though in the case of the PLO, the normal procedure has been to grant it observer status, allowing it to speak at meetings and to submit documents, but not the right to vote. For instance the PLO was invited by the General Assembly of the UN in 1974 to participate as an observer.[15] However, following the Palestine National Council's Declaration of Independence in 1988,[16] the PLO applied for full membership of the World Health Organisation (WHO) in May 1989. The WHO's constitution provided that 'membership in the Organization is open to all States'.[17] The United States successfully objected to this on the grounds that the PLO was neither a State nor the government of one and that it should remain as an observer at the UN and within the specialised agencies.[18]

Other countries have been permitted to become members of an organisation before they have achieved independence. Burma, Indonesia and Tunisia became members of the FAO before the date of their independence,[19] and in 1977 the UN General Assembly requested all specialised agencies to grant full membership to the UN Council for Namibia,[20] when Namibia did not finally achieve independence until March 1990. Furthermore, the UN's membership in 1945 included parts of the Soviet Union, namely Byelorussia and the Ukraine, to attempt to redress the imbalance in voting power at the UN between West and East. These members have since become States with the collapse of the Soviet Union.

Finally, one international organisation may be able to take part in the proceedings of another organisation. The EC's role in GATT has been mentioned in chapter 2. Furthermore, the EC was admitted to full membership of the FAO in 1991 following an amendment of the FAO constitution to extend membership to 'regional economic integration organizations' as well as 'nations'. As Professor Kirgis relates, under this amendment to the FAO Treaty 'a regional economic integration organization shares its membership, in effect, with its member States. Depending on what competence its member States have delegated to it and what they have retained, it may participate and cast the number of votes of its members or they may participate and cast their own votes'.[21] This confusing state of affairs is perhaps explained by the fact that, in the FAO at least, the EC is treated as being at least equal in competence to its member states. However, the basic principle of international organisations is that non-State entities may be represented either as observers or as full members only if the constitution of the organisation so permits. Some treaties only allow for State members,[22] and indeed, membership of all inter-governmental organisations is self-evidently dominated by States, which by itself suggests that organisations have not made great inroads into the supremacy of States in international relations. However, when we turn to look at the issues of representation and voting, it will be seen that organisations have undermined the principle of sovereign equality and in certain instances have actually eroded the concept of sovereignty itself.

Withdrawal

The constituent treaties of international organisations may contain a right of withdrawal for member States. Most specialised agencies' constitutions contain the right of withdrawal but not the United Nations itself, in contrast to its predecessor. Article 1(3) of the League of Nations Covenant provided that 'any member of the League may, after two years notice of its intention to do so, withdraw from the League, provided that all its international obligations under this Covenant shall have been fulfilled at the time of its withdrawal'. Between 1924 and 1940, sixteen States withdrew from the League, including Germany, Italy and Japan, weakening the universality of the Organisation as well as its effectiveness, and helping the slide towards war with no international forum for States to air their differences or attempt to resolve their disputes. It may be because of this that the United Nations Charter contains no provisions for withdrawal.

Nevertheless, this did not stop Indonesia from notifying the Secretary General of the United Nations of its withdrawal from the Organisation on 20 January 1965, the reason given being the election of Malaysia to the Security Council.[23] In practice, Indonesia did appear to fully withdraw in this period, a fact evidenced not only by its physical absence from the UN, but also by the removal of the Indonesian flag and nameplate, and its absence from formal membership lists. However, on 19 September 1966, Indonesia informed the Secretary General that it had decided 'to resume full co-operation with the UN and to resume participation in its activities starting with the twenty-first session of the General Assembly'.[24] In response, the President of the General Assembly stated 'it would appear that the Government of Indonesia considers that its recent absence from the Organization was based not upon a withdrawal from the UN but upon a cessation of co-operation. The action taken so far by the UN on this matter would not appear to preclude this view'.[25] Since no State objected to this approach it appears that Indonesia's membership had continued during its period of non-participation.[26]

Despite the fact that there are several more instances of States withdrawing or attempting to withdraw from international organisations in the absence of a constitutional withdrawal clause,[27] there are strong arguments to suggest that such actions are unlawful. Professor Schermers provides two of the most compelling. First, 'the way in which the organizations have reacted to the withdrawals and in which the States in questions have later returned to the organizations raise doubts about the validity' of the withdrawals.[28] Second, the argument that State sovereignty necessarily dictates that each State has complete freedom to decide if it wants to continue its membership is readily countered by Professor Schermers:

> Each establishment of an international organization means a transfer of some powers from the national government to another administrative body. The acceptance of independent administrative tribunal therefore invalidates the argument that State sovereignty should necessitate the right of States to unilaterally withdraw from international organizations ... By binding itself to an organization a State voluntarily sacrifices a part of its freedom of action. There can be no special reason to assume that the powers thus transferred can be withdrawn unilaterally.[29]

Thus, in the absence of a clause permitting withdrawal, a sovereign State has no right to withdraw from an organisation.[30] Its sovereign freedom of action is curtailed by its membership and by its transfer of powers, no matter how limited or how great, to the organisation. Sovereignty is therefore circumscribed by membership.

Suspension and expulsion

Clauses permitting an organisation to expel or suspend a member are again to be found only in constituent treaties of some organisations. Expulsion, even where permitted, seems an extreme remedy and one that is perhaps not readily reconcilable with any of the various approaches to international organisations. If an organisation is set up to perform a function, or as a rudimentary form of world or regional government, or simply as a forum for States to discuss and attempt to resolve their differences, expulsion of a State member for whatever reason appears to undermine all of these aims. As Professor Schermers states, 'expulsion is a token of impotence, and the more primitive a legal system, the more evident this lack of power will be. The Member that cannot be controlled is expelled from the community'.[31]

It may be because of this that there is little practice in the field of expulsion from international organisations, even when the constitution supplies the power. The League of Nations expelled the Soviet Union in 1939 for aggression against Finland, and the World Bank expelled Czechoslovakia for non-payment of its shares of the capital in 1954.[32] Attempts have been made, in the absence of an expulsion clause, to expel South Africa from various specialised agencies of the UN, the reason being that country's system of apartheid. However, the effects of these efforts are not clear, as South Africa withdrew from the ILO in 1964 before the Organisation could formally amend its constitution to allow for expulsion, and terminated co-operation with the WHO in 1964. In 1979, the Universal Postal Union (UPU) formally expelled South Africa, although many members refused to accept the legality of this and continued to treat South Africa as a member of the Organisation.[33]

There appears to be very few examples of completely effective expulsions in the absence of an empowering provision, perhaps the OAS's expulsion of Cuba in 1962 being the clearest. The resolution of the Organ of Consultation of the OAS declared that as a consequences of 'its repeated acts', namely the establishment of a political system based on Marxist–Leninist ideology and the acceptance of extra-continental support from Communist powers, 'the present government of Cuba has voluntarily placed itself outside the inter-American system' and should therefore be excluded from the Organisation.[34] Two factors tend to undermine the legitimacy of this apparent expulsion. The fact that six members abstained on the resolution casts doubt on the legality of such an act. Second, the resolution only debars the government of Cuba from participation, Cuba is still formally a member and will be permitted to participate again either on a change of government or a change of policy on the part of the OAS.

In the absence of an expulsion clause, the limited practice examined above would suggest that expulsion is not permitted.[35] However, it would be difficult to deny the legality of expulsion if organisations developed a consistent practice on the matter in the future, particularly if it is accepted that an autonomous international organisation, being separate from the State members, has the inherent right to control its membership, although there may be strong pragmatic reasons, outlined above, to argue against such a development.

The United Nations Charter does permit expulsion in Article 6 which provides that 'a Member of the United Nations which has persistently violated the principles contained in the present Charter may be expelled from the Organization by the General Assembly upon the recommendation of the Security Council'. This power has not been used although there were attempts in the early 1970s to expel South Africa from the Organisation. In 1974 the General Assembly called upon the Security Council to 'review the relationship between the United Nations and South Africa in the light of the latter's constant violation of the principles of the Charter and the Universal Declaration of Human Rights'.[36] In the same year, a draft resolution was put before the Security Council which recommended to the General Assembly the immediate expulsion of South Africa from the Assembly within the terms of Article 6 of the Charter.[37] The United Kingdom, France and the United States vetoed the resolution. The Assembly then proceeded to reject the credentials of the representatives of the South African government,[38] the legality, and the effects, of which seem to be unclear.[39] For the most part since 1974 until the end of apartheid and universal elections in 1994, the South African government did not take its seat in the Assembly.

The UN's dealing with South Africa in 1974 could equally be seen as an attempted suspension of South Africa.[40] The UN Charter provides for the right of suspension in Article 5, which provides:

> A Member of the United Nations against which preventive or enforcement action has been taken by the Security Council may be suspended from the exercise of the rights and privileges of membership by the General Assembly upon the recommendation of the Security Council. The exercise of the rights and privileges may be restored by the Security Council.[41]

There has been little practice by the UN in this area, although the case of the membership of Yugoslavia appears to be best discussed under the heading of suspension. In May 1992, with the break-up of the former Yugoslavia under way and the UN admitting Slovenia, Bosnia and Croatia as new members, a question mark was raised over the continuing occupation of the Yugoslav seat by the rump Yugoslav authorities in Belgrade, despite their continuing claim to the seat.[42] This element of doubt developed further in September 1992 when the Security Council adopted Resolution 777 which considered 'that the State formerly known as the Socialist Federal Republic of Yugoslavia has ceased to exist' and therefore that:

> the Federal Republic of Yugoslavia (Serbia and Montenegro) cannot continue automatically the membership of the former Socialist Republic of Yugoslavia in the United Nations; and therefore recommends to the General Assembly that it decide that the Federal Republic of Yugoslavia (Serbia and Montenegro) should apply for membership in the United Nations and that it shall not participate in the work of the General Assembly.

The General Assembly duly endorsed the Security Council's recommendation.[43] The Security Council had taken mandatory enforcement action against Serbia and Montenegro in the form of a trade embargo in May 1992,[44] and therefore seemed to have the power to suspend Yugoslavia under Article 5. Indeed, the effects of the UN action appear to be those of suspension in that while Yugoslavia's delegation can still attend meetings it cannot vote or participate, it continues to have its seat and its flag still flies. The curious feature appears to be that it is required to apply for membership in the face of precedents, most recently the succession of Russia to the Soviet Union's seat without the need for membership application, although the UN may have been driven by the requirement in Article 4(1) that members, or more correctly applicants for membership should be 'peace-loving' States, given Serbian support for the Bosnian–Serb war effort.[45] The UN, legally speaking, seems to have combined Articles 4 and 6, when perhaps it should simply have suspended Yugoslavia from enjoying the rights and privileges of membership under Article 6. There are, of course, strong arguments for stating that the exclusion of Serbia and Montenegro simply increases its international isolation thereby preventing useful contact between it and the international community and perhaps increasing its stubbornness. Nevertheless, the UN's lead was taken up by the International Atomic Energy Agency (IAEA) which decided to make the Federal Republic of Yugoslavia apply for membership, and was foreshadowed by the CSCE which suspended Yugoslavia in July 1992.[46]

Representation of States

To be entitled to be representatives of a member State of an international organisation, delegates will generally have to prove that they are entitled to represent their State. Proof is given in the form of credentials, normally a letter issued by the Head of State or Government (sometimes the Foreign Minister) listing the names of the members of the delegation. These credentials are then verified by a committee created by the main organ of the organisation (the credentials committee), and normally such a process does not present a problem. However, it has already been seen that the Credentials Committee and the General Assembly of the UN used this device to deny the South African government full representation at the UN in the 1970s.

From an objective standpoint, if a State is to be properly represented in an international organisation, and be subject to the obligations and pressures that the organisation can bring to bear on that State, the credentials to be recognised should be those of the government in effective control of the State, irrespective of whether the State is an international pariah. This was the view taken in 1950 by Secretary General Lie,

> It is submitted that the proper principle can be derived by analogy from Article 4 of the Charter. This Article requires that an applicant for membership must be able and

willing to carry out the obligations of membership. The obligations of membership can be carried out only by governments which in fact possess the power to do so. Where a revolutionary government presents itself as representing a State, in rivalry to an existing government, the question at issue should be which of the two governments in fact is in a position to employ the resources and direct the people of the State in fulfilment of the obligations of membership. In essence, this means an inquiry as to whether the new government exercises effective authority within the territory of the State and is habitually obeyed by the bulk of the population.[47]

Although perhaps adopting an unduly Austinian definition of sovereign power, the point is that it is better to have the representatives of the despotic but effective government in an international organisation than the alternative but ineffective 'government', for membership of an international organisation not only confers rights upon States, it imposes duties, and these duties can include the requirement of self-determination or the observance of human rights.

The Secretary General was putting forward an opinion as regards the question of Chinese representation at the UN. The Nationalist representative present since the formation of the UN was not removed from seat at the UN, including the permanent seat on the Security Council, until 1971 under the rules of procedure governing credentials. Simply put, the West dominated the UN to the extent that it could oppose any attempt to reject the credentials of the Nationalist government, which had taken refuge in Taiwan, in favour of the Communist government which occupied the whole of mainland China. Eventually, the growth in the membership of the UN enabled the General Assembly to adopt a resolution[48] which resolved to 'restore all its rights to the People's Republic of China ... and to expel forthwith the representatives of Chiang Kai-shek from the place which they unlawfully occupy'.[49] The Secretary General reported to the Council that he was satisfied under rule 15 of the Rules of Procedure,[50] and the Council welcomed the Communist Chinese on 21 November 1971, following a change of tack by the United States from a policy of confrontation with China to one of *rapprochement*. The Republic of China (Taiwan) is no longer a member of the UN even though Article 23, which sets out the composition of the Security Council, still refers to the 'Republic of China' and not the 'People's Republic of China'. Attempts to admit Taiwan as a separate member of the UN were thwarted by Taiwan and the People's Republic insisting that there was only one China and therefore only one Chinese representative.

Another infamous case of credentials being denied to the effective government of a State occurred following the December 1978 Vietnamese invasion of Cambodia (Kampuchea). The atrocious Pol Pot government of 'Democratic Kampuchea' was driven into a small area near the border with Thailand. The Vietnamese installed a new government of the 'People's Republic of Kampuchea'. At the 34th session of the General Assembly in 1979, both the governments of 'Democratic Kampuchea' and the 'People's Republic of Kampuchea' claimed the right to represent Cambodia. The Assembly's Credentials Committee recommended by a vote of 6 to 3 that the Assembly accept the credentials of the

'Democratic' delegation.[51] The General Assembly followed this recommendation and seated the representatives of the Pol Pot regime,[52] a situation that was to remain unchanged until the Cambodian peace process was under way in 1990.

The denial of the credentials to the governments of South Africa, the People's Republic of China and Cambodia reflect one of the various ways the international community, according to the dominant political groupings at the time, react to so-called international pariahs, States ostracised by the rest of the international community for their actions, in the case of South Africa for its system of apartheid, China and Vietnam for their ideology and their aggressive acts. Although theo-retically sovereign and equal, some States can be denied the rights (and the duties) of membership and in some ways of Statehood itself, by an organisation's refusal to accept their representatives. In contrast, the international community can act with alacrity when it wishes to accept a friendly State and its representatives into an organisation.

The break-up of the Soviet Union led to the creation of fifteen newly indepen-dent States. The Russian Federation was by far the largest in terms of military and economic power as well as geographically. On 21 December 1991, eleven repre-sentatives of the loose association of independent States constituted as the CIS decided that 'the States of the Commonwealth support Russia's continuance of the membership of the [USSR] in the United Nations, including permanent mem-bership of the Security Council, and other international organizations'.[53] In a letter sent a few days later, Boris Yeltsin, the President of the Russian Federation, informed the UN Secretary General, that membership of the Soviet Union in the Security Council and all other UN organs was being continued by the Russian Federation. In addition, the letter stated that Russia remained responsible in full for the rights and obligations of the former Soviet Union under the UN Charter.[54]

Russia's claim to the permanent seat in the Security Council led to speculation that this would spark off a reassessment of those States entitled to hold a perma-nent seat. However, the three Western permanent members, France, the United States and Britain, with the acquiescence of China, skilfully managed a special Security Council summit, attended by Heads of State and government. The summit was held on 31 January 1992, ostensibly to adopt a general declaration on the effectiveness of the UN, but in reality to endorse Russia's claim to the per-manent seat. President Yeltsin took part in the meeting and no mention was made of his right to do so.[55] Russia was therefore treated as a successor to the perma-nent seat rather than as a new member, in accordance with past practice of the United Nations, for instance in the case of India, an original member of the Organisation, which broke into two States in 1947 on independence. India was treated as continuing its membership without interruption, whereas Pakistan, was treated as a new State having to apply for UN membership.[56] The Security Coun-cil's approach to the issue of Russian membership has two drawbacks. First of all it confirms and enhances the perception of the Security Council as an exclusive and in many ways old-fashioned club, consisting of the most important actors, the permanent members, above the non-permanent members and the ordinary membership of the UN, in effect a three-tiered structure contrary to the formal sovereign equality of States. Second, and less significantly, the process leaves Article 23 of the UN Charter unchanged, stating that the permanent membership includes the USSR as opposed to Russia. Any change in Article 23 will necessitate the amendment procedure embodied in Article 108 which requires a two-thirds vote in the General Assembly and ratification by two-thirds of the members of the UN including all the permanent members.

Representation of the community

The composition of the Security Council is the prime example of how, in some international organisations, the executive body, that is the smaller body with the greater power to take action, is controlled by a small number of States, in contrast to the plenary organ, where all members are represented, usually at an annual session, normally under the principle of one State, one vote. The voting mechanism in the Security Council, reviewed below, ensures that the permanent members of France, Britain, the United States, Russia and China, have a veto over any issue which they perceive to affect their interests. The other ten members of the Council, the non-permanent members, are elected for terms of two years 'due regard being specially paid, in the first instance to the contribution of Members of the United Nations to the maintenance of international peace and security and to the other purposes of the Organization, and also to equitable geographical representation'.[57]

The membership of the Security Council was increased from 11 to 15 in 1965, but this still fails to make the Council representative of the whole membership of the United Nations. In 1945 the ratio of members of the Organisation to members of the Council was 11:51, a proportion of total membership amounting to nearly 22 per cent; now it is 15:185, just over 8 per cent of the membership being represented in the Council. It would take a Security Council of 40 members to return to the original ratio, and a member of the UN cannot be expected to be elected to the 'club' for many years. The General Assembly, in recommending an increase of Security Council membership in 1963, also laid down the guidelines for the equitable composition of the non-permanent membership, namely, five from Afro-Asian States, one from Eastern Europe, two from Latin America, two from Western European and other States.[58] The increasing gap between the Security Council and the General Assembly of the UN led to an increasing divorce in terms of the aims and objectives of the Organisation, particularly in the area of peace and security, reviewed in chapter 7. The potential hierarchical relationship between the Council (as the superior organ) and the Assembly (as the subsidiary organ) was not unduly felt during the Cold War due to the extensive use of the veto by the permanent members, but with the end of the Cold War the Security Council has started to use its formidable range of powers, with little consultation with the whole membership. The Security Council, with its mandatory powers, can oblige members of the UN to comply with its decisions, embodying, in effect, a crude form of government of all States by a few States.

Non-plenary organs of other international organisations have a similar bias towards the most powerful members though this can sometimes be justified on the basis of the functions of the institution. The Council of the ICAO for instance consists of thirty-three contracting States elected by the plenary body, the Assembly, giving adequate representation to 'the States of chief importance in air transport'; States 'which make the largest contribution to the provision of facilities for international civil air navigation'; and other States 'whose designation will ensure that all the major geographic areas of the world are represented on the Council'.[59] The Council of the ICAO thus contains the major aviation powers for obvious reasons but does not explicitly name any States unlike the UN Security Council where an argument could be mounted for stating that membership should be given to those States with the greatest military power, those who are major contributors to peacekeeping operations, as well as equitable geographical representation. Such a composition could be justified along functional lines, in that the objectives of the Security Council are to maintain international peace and security, not to secure lifelong permanent membership for a handful of States whose military and peacekeeping capacities may be quite limited.

In the case of the United Nations, despite the wording of Article 24 which suggests that the Security Council is simply 'acting on behalf' of the membership, there is no method for the plenary body to control the activities of the Security Council. Similarly, the Assembly of the ICAO, the plenary organ, delegates 'to the Council the powers and authority necessary or desirable for the discharge of the duties of the Organization' by Article 49 of the Chicago Convention. Nevertheless, as has been seen in chapter 2, the Council of the ICAO has many independent powers and as the permanent organ it 'runs' the ICAO.

A more equitable composition of an international organisation can be found in the constitution of one of the oldest, the International Labour Organisation (ILO), formed in 1919, and brought into relationship with the UN in 1945 as a specialised agency.[60] Its purposes are outlined in the Preamble to the Constitution of the ILO, principally the improvement of working conditions. As Professor Bowett states: 'the fact that the Organisation is designed to promote the interests of part of the Community *within the State*, as opposed to the interests of the State as such, has led to a form of representation of interests other than the State interest which was unique at its inception'.[61] This uniqueness of representation is found in the fact that all decisions within the Organisation's organs are taken on a tripartite basis. In the annual General Conference each member is represented by a delegation consisting of two government delegates, one employer's delegate and one worker's delegate, each delegate having one vote, requiring either a simple majority or qualified majority for a decision to be adopted. The Governing Body, according to Article 7, shall consist of 56 persons, 28 representing governments, 14 representing employers and 14 representing workers. Of the 28 persons representing governments, 10 shall be of chief industrial importance, again reflecting the functional nature of the Organisation.

The ILO is a good example of where individual's interests are properly represented in an international organisation, where normally such bodies are mainly if not solely concerned with representing State interests. The only other organisation which seeks to allow individuals some sort of representation is the European Union, where 'the European Parliament is elected by individuals within each member State, with each member State having a different number of seats in the Parliament allocated to it, ranging from 99 for Germany to 6 for Luxembourg. However, the European Parliament has limited powers compared to the Council (representing States) and Commission (individuals appointed by States). The ILO remains a unique organisation allowing for individuals and States to be represented at the same level. The structure of the ILO, with its smaller Governing Body, shares a feature with the UN and the ICAO in allowing membership to be affected by decisions adopted in a small organ by a majority vote. However, unlike the UN Security Council, the Governing body of the ILO is limited to control of the International Labour Office (the Secretariat of the Organisation) and preparing for meetings of the General Conference.

In the case of the ILO the non-plenary organ is clearly subordinate to the plenary body, which will necessarily mean that sovereignty is not so easily impinged, though if the voting structure of the General Conference is looked at, it can be seen that majority decision making allows for decisions to be adopted against the interests of a minority of States.[62] The difference between the ILO and the UN is that while both allow for the plenary body to adopt decisions by a majority or qualified majority, thereby affecting the interests of a minority of States voting against, the UN, through the non-plenary Security Council, can adopt decisions which impinge on the sovereignty of the majority of members without their consent, though it could be argued that by becoming members of the UN each State has consented, by Article 25 of the UN Charter, to be bound by the decisions of the Security Council. Such an argument tends to forget that membership of the UN, although technically optional, is in fact essential for most States in the world, and there must be doubts about the nature of the 'consent' given to the Security Council to take executive action.

An organisation with a small executive organ with the power to adopt mandatory decisions by a majority vote is the one which most infringes on the sovereignty of nations, in that a small number of States can curtail the freedom of the remainder even though a majority of the membership of the organisation may be opposed to it. Of the organisations looked at so far, the United Nations appears to be the only one to fit this model, although the European Union with its increase in qualified majority voting in the Council could be argued to fit this model (the argument against being that the Council is composed of the whole membership and unanimity or consensus is often sought). Others approach the UN model, but given the aims and objectives of the UN, no organisation can approach it in terms of the power and capabilities it possesses and in particular those that it entrusts to the Security Council. Other organisations may have non-plenary organs which can adopt mandatory decisions on the basis of unanimity, others adopting recommendations by majority or by unanimity. In these cases too, substantial inroads can be made into a member State's sovereignty, although the absence of mandatory powers means that a member State's sovereign freedom cannot be immediately affected.[63]

Other organisations' principal organs consist of the whole of the membership (as in the case of the Arab League or the new WTO). If those organs are required to adopt decisions by consensus or unanimity then that particular organisation is closer to being simply an arena or forum as opposed to an autonomous international actor capable of affecting the sovereignty and sovereign equality of member States. Whereas the GATT is simply such an arena, the proposed new WTO, although its full membership organs are expected to achieve consensus where possible, can adopt decisions by a majority.[64] Thus the WTO is a relatively tentative institutional development in the area of world trade. In the case of the Arab League, Article 7 of the Pact provides that 'the decisions of the Council taken by a unanimous vote shall be binding on all the member States; those that are reached by a majority vote shall only bind those which accept them'. Such a provision does not encroach upon the sovereignty of States in that it mean that each member of the League can only bind *itself* by voting for a resolution in the Council. In other organisations such as the UN, the Security Council can bind *other* States by resolution. Each organisation's institutional structure and powers has to be examined individually to ascertain the capacity of the organisation for making inroads into a member's sovereignty.

Voting

The post-1945 institutional order has witnessed a move away from unanimity as a basis of decision making in favour of majority voting. This move, as much as any other development, has led to the factual decline of sovereign equality, in that decisions can be adopted against the votes of a minority of States, and also the doctrine of sovereignty, in that decisions can be made by a majority which affect the sovereign interests of a minority (or sometimes even a majority) of States, particularly if the organisation in question has the power to make binding decisions as opposed to recommendations. The vast majority of organisations simply have a recommendatory power, but a few have mandatory powers. This aspect of decision making will be reviewed in the next chapter.

In the League of Nations system, the normal rule was one of unanimity for both Council and Assembly, a requirement embodied in Article 5 of the Covenant. The contrast between this and the UN Organisation makes clear the move away from unanimity and sovereign equality. In the UN Security Council, Article 27 provides that 'decisions of the Security Council on procedural matters shall be made by an affirmative vote of nine members' whilst decisions on all other matters 'shall be made by an affirmative vote of nine members including the concurring votes of the permanent members'. This embodies the concept of the veto for the five permanent members which will be examined below; suffice it to say that Article 27 contains elements of both qualified majority for the whole Council, and unanimity by the permanent members on substantive issues. As regards the General Assembly, Article 18 provides that each member of the Assembly shall have one vote and that 'decisions on important questions shall be made by a two-thirds vote of those present and voting', while 'decisions on other questions, including the determination of additional categories of questions to be decided by a two-thirds majority, shall be made by a majority of the members present and voting'. This is an example of qualified majority voting on certain issues, an issue returned to below.

Although most organisations, including the specialised agencies of the UN, can take decisions by a majority of some form or other, there are still a number of organisations where unanimity is still required. The Council of Europe, for instance, established in 1949, whose aim is to achieve greater unity in areas of common concern and take common action in economic, social, cultural, scientific and human rights matters among its members from both Western and Eastern Europe, requires unanimity in most cases. The Committee of Ministers, the executive organ of the Council, on which all States are represented, adopts its resolutions on 'important matters', according to Article 20, with 'the unanimous vote of the representatives casting a vote, and of a majority of representatives entitled to sit on the Committee'.[65] This rather peculiar formula means that a State can block a resolution if it wants to simply by casting a negative vote. A State can thus protect itself from a resolution which may affect its interests. Although, on this issue, the powers of the Committee are recommendatory, it can formulate its conclusions in the form of a treaty. This process has led to the adoption of the Convention for the Protection of Human Rights and Fundamental Freedoms 1950, and the European Social Charter 1961, reviewed in chapter 9. Although the treaties emerging from the Council of Europe can only be binding if member States ratify them, those outside the treaties will have question marks raised against their commitment to human rights, one of the main aims of the Council of Europe.

Unanimity must not be confused with consensus which 'is usually defined as the making of decisions without a vote and without formal objection by any member state'.[66] Very few international organisations provide for consensus decision making in their constitutions, although it is embodied in the proposed new WTO as the normal method. The WTO can perhaps be seen as the culmination of a development in institutions towards consensus decision making wherever possible despite the formal provisions of the Treaty. This development is explained by Professor Schermers:

> Consensus is strongly influenced by the legal rules on voting. When unanimity is required, decisions can only be made by consensus. All Members have the right of veto, and no concession need to be made. When majority voting is possible, Mem-

bers may prefer to co-operate in reaching consensus on a proposal which they dislike, in order to avoid a majority decision on a proposal which they find still more objectionable. The risk of being out-voted may encourage stubborn Members to compromise. Furthermore, concessions made in order to reach consensus can be more easily defended at home when the alternative is being out-voted. Consensus, therefore, can be more easily obtained in organizations which do not require unanimity.[67]

Article 18 of the UN Charter does not expressly recognise consensus decision making. Indeed, during the Cold War, the majority of members of the General Assembly regularly adopted resolutions on issues concerning security, economic order and self-determination against the votes of a substantial minority of often quite powerful States. The climate in the late 1980s and 1990s has changed to the extent that the majority of General Assembly resolutions are now adopted without a vote. The main disadvantages of consensus decision making are that it is time-consuming and, more significantly, the content of the resolutions may be watered down and become, in Marxist terms, meaningless compromises used to justify opposing viewpoints. Consensus decision making cannot be seen as protecting the sovereignty of States, for if a State wishes to protect its interests by blocking a resolution, it cannot do so, since the resolution will still be adopted by a majority. Consensus decision making is not a return to unanimity. Indeed, the constitution of the new WTO only sees consensus as desirable; if it cannot be achieved majority voting is permissable.[68]

Despite the political desirability of consensus decision making, most international organisations' constitutions legally allow for resolutions to be adopted by a simple majority, sometimes a qualified majority (normally two-thirds of members).[69] As has already been stated Article 18 of the UN Charter permits the General Assembly to adopt resolutions on 'important questions' by a two-thirds majority of those members present and voting, whilst other resolutions are adopted by a mere majority. Although the main examples of 'important questions' are given: recommendations with respect to the maintenance of international peace and security; the election of non-permanent members to the Security Council; the election of members of the Economic and Social Council; the election of members of the Trusteeship Council; the admission of new Members to the UN; the suspension of rights and privileges of membership; the expulsion of Members; questions relating to the operation of the trusteeship system; and budgetary questions, it can be argued that an incomplete list creates confusion. Other organisations do not leave this gap and simply list the questions which require a two-thirds majority. The UN Educational, Scientific and Cultural Organisation (UNESCO), a specialised agency of the UN, established in 1946 with the purpose of 'promoting collaboration among the nations through education, science and culture,' requires a simple majority except in cases provided for in other provisions of the UNESCO Convention.[70]

Nevertheless, despite this slight differences in approach it is clear that organisations established under the principle of majority voting can adopt resolutions which severely affect the interests of a minority of States. Both the UN General

Assembly and UNESCO can only operate, in the main, by recommendation, but in the case of the Assembly at least, the constant repetition of principles in resolutions can either add to or reinforce the corpus of international law and thereby bind States which originally voted against the resolution. Some immensely influential General Assembly resolutions have been adopted not by unanimity or by consensus but by majority decisions. For instance in 1960 the General Assembly adopted the famous Declaration on the Granting of Independence to Colonial Territories and Peoples, the content of which condemns as illegal the 'subjection of peoples to alien subjugation, domination and exploitation' and States that 'all peoples have the right to self-determination'.[71] No States voted against the resolution but nine (mainly Western States) did abstain. The 1960 resolution has since formed the bedrock of the development of the legal principles of decolonisation and self-determination. In 1962 the General Assembly adopted the Resolution on Permanent Sovereignty over Natural Resources which recognises the right of States to expropriate foreign property.[72] Fourteen States were unable to vote for this resolution, including France who voted against. Subsequently, in one of the most pro-Western interpretations of the international legal principles governing expropriation, Professor Dupuy, a French international lawyer, in the 1977 arbitral award in *Texaco* v *Libya*, stated that the resolution reflected customary international law.[73] It is also interesting to note that in discerning the principles governing the indirect use of military force by one State against another the World Court in the *Nicaragua* case relied principally on General Assembly resolutions, namely the 1965 Declaration on Non Intervention, the 1970 Declaration on Friendly Relations and the 1974 Definition of Aggression.[74] Although the latter two were adopted by consensus and only Britain abstained on the first, the importance of General Assembly resolutions as sources of custom can be seen. In addition, the Court adopted a Hartian view of custom by defining it not only as general conformity of behaviour by States but also reaction by the community when the customary rule has been broken, not simply the views of the law breaker and the victim, but the *general* critical reaction of the community.[75] In many ways the principle governing the non-use of force in international relations embodied in Article 2(4) of the UN Charter was upheld during the Cold War not by the Security Council enforcing compliance with the norm but by the consistent condemnation of States breaching the principle by the General Assembly, almost always by a majority vote. For instance, it repeatedly condemned the Soviet Union's armed intervention in Afghanistan until the Soviet withdrawal in 1989, resolutions voted for by the vast majority of States,[76] and adopted a similar resolution condemning the United States' invasion of Panama in 1989 although by a smaller majority.[77]

Though the UN Organisation provides for majority voting in its organs, the basic principle is one nation, one vote – the smallest nations in the United Nations – the so-called micro-States – have an equal say in the General Assembly as the most powerful, despite the fact that in terms of contributions to the budget the larger States contribute the most. The United States contributes 25 per cent of the regular budget (and around 30 per cent of the peacekeeping budget), whilst the smaller ones pay 0.01 per cent.[78] Japan and Germany are the second and fourth largest contributors to the regular budget although neither is 'rewarded' with a permanent seat on the Security Council and the right of veto. Under such a system resolutions may be adopted by a majority of States possibly resulting in greater expenditure for the Organisation even though they are opposed by those States which contribute the most financially. It could be argued that while the UN has moved away from formal sovereign equality by allowing for majority decision making, it has not fully or fairly done this to reflect the real interests and power of States. A further step away from formal sovereign equality which would allow organisations greater formal and factual power to adopt decisions affecting the sovereign interests of States would be the principle of weighted voting.

Weighted voting

The problem with weighted voting, whereby certain States are given more votes or voting power than others, is 'the criterion on which extra weight should be given. Should it be population, national income, power, or some other criterion' such as contributions to the budget of the organisation?[79] Weighted voting may be credible and acceptable in functional organisations whose purposes and powers are confined to achieving limited goals, but seems inapplicable to organisations such as the United Nations which have such a vast array of goals that it would be impossible to agree on a set of criteria.[80]

The main organisations which use weighted voting are the two UN specialised agencies which serve as world financial institutions, the International Monetary Fund (IMF) and the International Bank for Reconstruction and Development (IBRD). Professor Schermers outlines the reasons for the use of weighted-voting procedures in these organisations both of which were established at the end of the Second World War.[81] First, 'their task is confined so precisely to one field that criteria for weighting can be found there', second, and perhaps more significantly 'insufficient money would have been made available had the donating States not obtained a preponderant influence in decision-making'. Schermers then summarises the voting system agreed upon:

(1) Every member has 250 votes (the nationality element).
(2) In the FUND: Every Member has one additional vote for each part of its quota, equivalent to one hundred thousand Special Drawing Rights [SDRs]. In the BANK: Every Member has one additional vote for each share of stock held (the interest element).[82]

The purposes of the IMF are to promote international monetary co-operation by means of exchange rate stability and orderly exchange arrangements and assistance to members in financial difficulties by making financial resources available to them. On joining the fund, each member is assigned a quota reviewed every five years, based largely on the State's economic strength. The member pays its subscription which is equal to its quota, into a common pool of currencies, from which all members may draw during balance-of-payment difficulties. The withdrawal must be approved by majority vote in the Executive Board of the IMF which consists of twenty-four directors, five of whom are appointed by the five members having the largest quota in the Fund (USA, Japan, Germany, France and the UK).[83] The size of the quota is also significant in three respects. First of all, the amount of quota determines the cumulative amount of outstanding loan a State can have from the IMF. Second, as we have seen, the quota determines the State's voting power over IMF policies in the Board of Governors, in which each member is represented, with its shares of votes. Third, the quota determines how many SDRs the member receives when SDRs are distributed.

The dominance of the financial institutions by the economically powerful States is continued in the structure and voting of the IBRD (sometimes known, together with the International Development Association and the International Finance Corporation, as the World Bank). However, while the Bank lends to poor countries, the IMF may lend to any member country lacking sufficient foreign currency to cover short-term obligations to creditors in other countries. As from 1 April 1989, the World Bank requires IMF approval for some of its loans to developing countries due to its poor track record of lending in the 1970s and early 1980s. The purposes of the IBRD are to promote the economic development of member countries by making loans to governments below conventional interest rates in instances where capital is not available at reasonable rates from other sources; to provide member countries with technical assistance on matters relating to their economic development; and to try to increase the effectiveness of international economic development by fostering co-operation among the donors of financial and technical assistance. The powers of the Bank are vested in the Board of Governors, consisting of one representative from each member. The Board delegates most of its functions to the Executive Directors, consisting of twenty-four directors, five again being appointed by the States having the largest capital subscription (USA, Japan, Germany, France and the UK). With the voting power of each director being proportionate to their capital subscriptions, decisions can be adopted by a majority of the votes cast,[84] although consensus is normally sought, a position also adopted by the Executive Board of the IMF.

From this brief description of the structure, purposes and voting system of the IMF and the IBRD, it can be seen that it is dominated by the Western industrial powers. In 1994, on the Executive Board of the IMF, the US director held 17.84 per cent of the vote, Germany and Japan 5.55 per cent each, and Britain and France 5 per cent each, which along with other Western votes, ensures the continued dominance of the Organisation by the West, although its share has decreased since 1947 when the US held 31.5 per cent of the votes.[85] Although it may be argued that the World Bank in particular helps the economic development of developing countries especially by investing in projects, this does not disguise the fact that such projects must invariably be approved by Western States and will in many ways reflect their ideology of a free-market economy.

Weighted-voting mechanisms found in other organisations can also be justified on functional grounds, a good example being the commercial satellite organisations. The Agreement Relating to the International Telecommunications Satellite Organisation (INTELSAT), established in 1971, provides in the Preamble that the parties have the aim of 'achieving a *single* global telecommunications satellite system',[86] and currently has over 120 State members. The ultimate authority within the INTELSAT institutional structure – the Board of Governors – which adopts, amongst other things, major policy decisions on the functioning of the satellite network, is composed of twenty-eight governors. Of these governors some have a seat on the basis of their investment shares, which in turn are based on the degree of usage by the member of the space segment for communication purposes. In addition, any five or more members from the same ITU (International Telecommunications Union) region, which are not otherwise represented on the Board, may together select one governor, regardless of their total investment. Article 9 of the Agreement provides that each governor shall have a vote proportionate to that part of the investment share of the member or group of members he represents with the proviso that no governor may cast more than 40 per cent of the total number of votes. The latter proviso is intended to prevent domination of the Organisation by the United States which, via its designated telecommunications entity, the Communications Satellite Corporation (COMSAT), dominated the interim INTELSAT body established by Western States in 1964. Western States' domination of the Organisation inevitably continues with their technological superiority in the telecommunications industry, though Board decisions are normally made unanimously. However, when unanimity is not achieved, decisions are made on the basis of a weighted vote based either upon two-thirds of the voters' investment shares, or upon the support of all but three of the governors.[87]

A similar structure of voting is to be found in the International Maritime Satellite Organisation (INMARSAT) created in 1976,[88] with the purpose of providing a space segment to improve maritime communications and thereby improving safety at sea. The Council of INMARSAT is composed of twenty-two representatives of members or groups of members with the largest investment shares and four representatives of elected members. On the Council no representative may cast a vote in excess of 25 per cent and although normally the Council will endeavour to achieve unanimity in its decisions, substantive decisions may be taken by a two-thirds majority of the investment shares represented on the Council. Again the developed Western States, having the largest investment shares to reflect their contribution to the maritime satellite technology used, dominate the Organisation. However, although the Soviet Union and its allies formed their own satellite organisation, INTERSPUTNIK, in 1971, the USSR joined INMARSAT in 1979 and INTELSAT in 1991 thereby changing the balance in these organisations and also ensuring the development of global telecommunications networks along functionalist lines.

Although most weighted-voting mechanisms are to found in functional organisations, there is an example of such a mechanism in a regional organisation – the
European Union, although there 'is considerable discrepancy between the treaty
provisions relating to the voting [in the Council] and actual practice'.[89] The 1957
Treaty of Rome's provisions on voting have been untouched by the Maastricht
Treaty except to provide for greater use of majority voting. In formal terms, the
normal method of voting in the Council, according to Article 148(1) is by simple
majority. However, simple majority voting is displaced when the Treaty so provides, which it does to such an extent as to make simple majority voting the
exception rather than the norm. Where the treaties provide for qualified majority
voting, Article 148(2) provides that the votes of the members shall be weighted
with Germany, France, Italy and the United Kingdom having 10 votes each; Spain
8; Belgium, Greece, the Netherlands and Portugal 5 each; Austria and Sweden 4
each; Denmark, Ireland and Finland 3 each; and Luxembourg 2. Decisions
required to be adopted by a qualified majority must be adopted by at least 62 out
of 87 votes, although under the Ioánnina Compromise agreed in March 1994, 23-
5 opposing votes would be sufficient to continue debate for a reasonable period in
order to attempt to achieve consensus.[90] On occasions the treaties specify a unanimous vote, for instance in the case of admission of new members.[91]

Despite these elaborate voting provisions, which only recognise unanimity in a
specified number of cases, the practice of the Council has been to introduce a *de
facto* veto. The situation was analysed in 1988 by Freestone and Davidson:

> The Treaty provides for a large number of decisions to be taken by a majority vote
> but it is used in less than 5 per cent of Council decisions, largely because of the Lux-
> embourg Compromise … After a major constitutional crisis in 1965, between the
> French and other Community states, a statement was issued in January 1966 that
> 'where in the case of decisions which may be taken by a majority vote on a proposal
> of the Commission, very important interests of one or more partners are at stake, the
> Members of the Council will endeavour within a reasonable time, to reach a solution
> which can be adopted by all the members of the Council'. The French insisted fur-
> ther, however, that such discussion shall be continued until 'unanimous agreement is
> reached'. In practice the French view has prevailed and hence a *de facto* 'veto' has
> been introduced into Council procedure.[92]

Nevertheless, although the 'political veto' has continued to operate after the
Maastricht Treaty 1992, since it is a 'mere matter of convention its scope will
always depend upon the consensus among the Member States at any given time:
if a majority of Member States oppose a vote (or refuse to vote) because they respect the right of one Member State to claim that its vital interests are at stake, the
measure will be blocked; if they do not a vote will be taken'.[93]

The other main decision-making organ of the European Union, the Commission, consisting of twenty independent, Council-appointed members, with at least
one from each member State, is empowered to make decisions by a simple majority,[94] although consensus is normally sought. The general powers of the Commission are outlined in Article 155 of the Treaty of Rome, namely: the policing and

enforcement of the treaties and Community legislation, the formulation of recommendations and proposals sometimes as a prerequisite to Council action, and the adoption of primary legislation in certain instances as well as secondary legislation delegated by the Council.

The inability of the Council of the principal European regional organisation to move away from the traditional approach to voting reflects a continued dominance of sovereignty even within one of the most advanced (in terms of integration and regional government) organisations in the world, although the expanding roles of the Commission and Parliament counteract this to some extent. Other organisations formally embed the concept of the veto within their constitutions, so that while the Council of the European Union allows a *de facto* veto for each member State of the organisation, the Security Council of the UN has a *de jure* veto but only for the five permanent members of the Security Council on substantive matters with the proviso in Article 27(3) that 'in decisions under Chapter VI, and under paragraph 3 of Article 52, a party to a dispute shall abstain from voting'. Procedural matters require an affirmative vote of nine out of the fifteen members and in practice include: inclusion of items on the agenda, removal of an item from the list of matters of which the Council is seized, rulings of the President, suspension and adjournment of meetings, invitation to non-members to participate in meetings, and convocation of an emergency special session of the General Assembly.[95]

The right of veto was further strengthened in the Yalta formula, presented to the San Francisco Conference in explanation of the right of veto. The Yalta formula introduced the prospect of the 'double-veto' signifying that 'any decision regarding the preliminary question as to whether or not such a matter is procedural must be taken by vote of [nine] members of the Security Council, including the concurring votes of the permanent members'.[96] The big powers ensured that the veto was not only to apply to proposed enforcement action by the Council under Chapter VII of the Charter, but also by the 'chain of events' theory contained in the Yalta formula, to proposals for the pacific settlement of disputes under Chapter VI. The major powers justified this power by stating that any pacific measures 'may initiate a chain of events which might in the end require the Council under its responsibilities to invoke measures of enforcement'.[97]

Debates over the applicability of the chain-of-events theory and the double veto can be found in the early meetings of the Council,[98] but these diminished during the Cold War by the permanent members developing the practice of using the veto to defeat any type of proposal either under Chapter VI or Chapter VII unless it was clearly procedural. The only development in this period which limited the extent of the veto was the practice that developed which meant that abstention by a permanent member on a vote on a substantive matter did not constitute a veto. The only other limitation to be found in the wording of Article 27 and the Yalta formula was that parties to a dispute should abstain from voting on a proposed resolution coming within Chapter VI, thereby preventing a veto by a permanent member involved in such a situation. This formal limitation has been virtually ignored by all members of the Security Council. For instance the French and British were clearly 'parties' to the Suez Crisis of 1956 but their vetoes were still accepted as valid even though proposed resolutions in the Security Council were clearly drafted under Chapter VI.[99] More recently the United States used its veto twice following its military intervention in Panama in December 1989 to block proposals which did not foresee Chapter VII action.[100] This practice seems to be a breach of the Charter in particular when one looks at the Permanent Court's advisory opinion on whether the League's Council's otherwise unanimous vote was affected by the negative vote of a party to the dispute in question. The Court held that the negative vote could not affect the decision of the Council stating that:

> according to the Covenant itself, in certain cases and more particularly in the case of settlement of a dispute, the rule of unanimity is applicable, subject to the limitation that the votes cast by representatives of the interested party do not affect the required unanimity ... The well-known rule that no one can be a judge in his own suit holds good.[101]

The veto was used indiscriminately during the Cold War. In the period 1946-86 the number of vetoes for the permanent members was China 22, the Soviet Union 121, UK 26, France 16, and the USA 57. The USSR cast 77 of its vetoes in the first ten years when the UN was Western dominated, whereas the United States cast 45 of its vetoes in the period 1976-86, when the Non-Aligned and Socialist bloc tended to combine and dominate the UN.[102] With the end of the Cold War in the late 1980s, the number of vetoes has decreased dramatically. This indicates a greater degree of co-operation between the permanent members with the demise of the Soviet Union and the traditional refusal of China to use its veto unless its interests are greatly affected. Although the demise of the veto for the present has led to greater unanimity on the Council, at least between the permanent members, it has also led to the adoption of a greater number of enforcement resolutions adopted under Chapter VII, imposing sanctions or taking military measures against States, thereby affecting the sovereignty not only of these target States, but also of the rest of the membership of the UN which are obliged to carry out the will of the Security Council. The implications of this will be examined more fully in chapter 7.

Concluding remarks

Although States dominate the membership of international organisations, and usually join under the principles of untainted sovereignty and sovereign equality, it appears that once a State has joined there is a presumption against lawful withdrawal, unless the constitution provides otherwise, and further that a State can be expelled or suspended by an organisation against its will, if the organisation is constitutionally so empowered. These suggest an undermining of sovereignty, although it is possible to argue that a State knows the rules when it joins, and

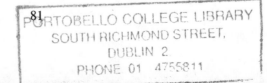

consent is an expression of sovereign will. However, this argument misses the point that membership of some organisations is becoming imperative for States, and the fact that if the constituent treaty is silent on the issues, it can certainly be maintained that a State has still lost its 'sovereign' right of withdrawal, and perhaps further, that the organisation has the 'inherent' right to control its membership by expulsion or suspension though there are strong pragmatic reasons against allowing this. Nevertheless, if a constituent treaty is silent on the matter and the organisation decides to expel a member State, it is difficult to argue that this is unconstitutional particularly if the practice is repeated. The cases of South Africa and Yugoslavia before the UN reveal the flexibility with which an organisation interprets its constituent document, and the difficulty of clearly demonstrating the illegality of such actions. As shall be seen in chapter 5, there is a general presumption against institutional actions being declared *ultra vires*.

The undermining of sovereignty by the growth of organisational competence is made much clearer by the concentration of power in the hands of a few States in small executive organs or by weighted-voting techniques, or in the hands of a larger number of States by majority voting in plenary organs. This allows for decisions to be adopted against the will of a large number of member States. Apart from the occasional functional justification for this development, it appears to be either a development towards world government with an increased centralised legislative capacity, or more simply a reflection of the fact that powerful States (at the moment the West) are shaping international organisations in their image while offering the panacea of sovereign equality. The latter may be the more acceptable explanation because while there has been an increase in governmental activity by international organisations, it has not been accompanied by a solidification of constitutional laws and procedures, instead there have simply been numerous politically expedient actions, for example in the issue of representation of governments before the UN. In other words, without the development of the rule of law, the rationalist vision is defective, and instead the realist or critical positions appear to have been reached. This can be reinforced by recognising the fact that although many organisations follow Western goals, for instance the promotion of democracy, these organisations themselves are not subject to democratisation, either to ensure more equitable representation of States, or more fundamentally, of peoples, with the limited exceptions of the ILO and the European Parliament in the case of peoples.

Notes

[1] Other issues such as amendment and financing will not be dealt with here, see H. G. Schermers, *International Institutional Law* 1012–51, 804–992, 2nd edn (1980).

[2] D. W. Bowett, *The Law of International Institutions*, 383, 4th edn (1982).

[3] 225 CTS 195.

[4] Article 110(1) of the UN Charter provides that 'the present Charter shall be ratified by signatory states in accordance with their respective constitutional processes'.

[5] Belarus, formerly Byelorussia, and the Ukraine have been members since 1945 originally at the insistence of the Soviet Union of which they were a part, in order to provide some balance in the UN between the two power blocs.

[6] *Admission of a State to the United Nations, (Charter, Art.4)*, I.C.J. *Rep.* 1948, 65.

[7] Schermers, *International Institutional Law*, 51, 2nd edn (1980).

[8] 77 UNTS 143. Articles 2 and 3.

[9] 298 UNTS 48. Articles 1 and 5.

[10] Schermers, *Institutional Law*, 51.

[11] P. J. G. Kapteyn *et al.*, *International Organization and Integration*, vol.2.B-2.J, 2.F.2.a (1983).

[12] 70 UNTS 248, Article 1.

[13] 479 UNTS 39.

[14] G. J. Naldi, *The Organization of African Unity*, 30–2 (1989).

[15] GA Res. 3237, 29 UN GAOR Supp. (No. 31) 4 (1974). See Y. Z. Blum, *Eroding the United Nations Charter*, ch. 4 (1993).

[16] UN doc. S/20278 (1988). See also GA Res. 43/177, 43 UN GAOR Supp. (No. 49) 62 (1988), which decided that 'Palestine' should be used in UN records instead of 'Palestine Liberation Organization', without considering the question of membership.

[17] 14 UNTS 186, Article 3.

[18] F. L. Kirgis, *International Organizations in their Legal Setting*, 158–64, 2nd edn (1993).

[19] *Yearbook of the International Law Commission*, 1969 2, 35.

[20] GA Res. 32/9E, 32 UN GAOR Supp. (No. 34) (1977).

[21] Kirgis, *International Organizations*, 165.

[22] On associate membership see Schermers, *Institutional Law*, 142–4.

[23] *Yearbook of the United Nations*, (1964), 189–92.

[24] UN doc. A/6419 (1966).

[25] GA 1420 plen. mtg, 21 UN GAOR (1966).

[26] Schermers, *Institutional Law*, 102. See further Blum, *Eroding the Charter*, ch. 2. A similar situation appears to have arisen in the Council of Europe when Turkey walked out in April 1995 following criticism of its invasion of northern Iraq, *The Times*, 28 April 1995.

[27] Schermers, *Institutional Law*, 65.

[28] *Ibid.*, 69.

[29] *Ibid.*

[30] See also Article 56 of the Vienna Convention on the Law of Treaties, 1969.

[32] *Ibid.*, 117. The withdrawal by Greece from the Council of Europe in 1969 pre-empted a suspension under Article 8 of the Statute of the Council of Europe, 9 *I.L.M.* (1970), 396–416.

[33] Schermers, *Institutional Law*, 79–81.

[34] OAS Doc. OEA/Ser.F/11.8 (1962).

[35] Bowett, *International Institutions*, 393.

[36] GA Res. 3207, 29 UN GAOR Supp. (No. 31) 2 (1974).

[37] UN doc. S/11543 (1974).

[38] GA Res. 3206, 29 UN GAOR Supp. (No. 31) 2 (1974).

[39] Kirgis, *International Organizations*, 585–600. See also Blum, *Eroding the Charter* 43–55.

[40] L. Gross, *Selected Essays on International Law and Organization*, 328–9 (1993).

[41] See also Article 19 of the UN Charter.

[42] UN doc. A/46/PV.86, 22 (1992), US.

[43] GA Res. 47/1, 47 UN GAOR (1992).

[44] SC Res. 757, 47 UN SCOR Resolutions (1992).

[45] See Y. H. Blum, 'UN Membership of the "New" Yugoslavia: Continuity or Break?', 86 A.J.I.L. (1992), 830.

[46] Kirgis, *International Organizations*, 603, 619.

[47] UN doc. S/1466 (1950).

[48] The resolution was adopted by a two-thirds majority instead of a simple majority normally required for issues of representation, see Schermers *Institutional Law*, 207.

[49] GA Res. 2758, 26 UN GAOR Supp. (No. 29) (1971).

[50] Rule 15 provides that 'the credentials of the representatives on the Security Council ... shall be examined by the Secretary General who shall submit a report to the Security Council for approval'.

[51] UN doc. A/34/500 (1979).

[52] GA Res. 34/2, 34 UN GAOR Supp. (No. 46) 12 (1979).

[53] UN doc. A/47/60 Annex 5 (1991).

[54] UN doc. S/23319 (1991).

[55] SC 3046 mtg, 47 UN SCOR (1992).

[56] Memorandum from the UN Secretariat, UN doc. A/CN.4/SER.A/Add 1 (1962). But see recent practice as regards the former Yugoslavia examined above.

[57] Article 23 of the UN Charter.

[58] GA Res. 1991, 18 UN GAOR Supp. (No. 15) (1963).

[59] Article 50 of the Convention on International Civil Aviation. On a similar point, Article 28 of the IMO Convention provided that the Maritime Safety Committee shall be composed of sixteen members elected by the Assembly being 'states having an important interest in maritime safety' eight of whom 'shall be elected from the ten largest shipowning States'. A dispute arose at the first session of the Assembly when neither Liberia (on paper the third largest shipowning State) nor Panama (eighth largest) were elected. An advisory opinion of the ICJ was sought. The Court determined that the Maritime Safety Committee was not properly constituted as the criterion of the largest ship-owning States 'depends solely upon the tonnage registered in the countries in question' and not the tonnage as actually owned by nationals of the State. The IMO amended its constitution in 1974 to provide that the Safety Committee 'shall consist of all members'. *Constitution of the Maritime Safety Committee of the Inter-Governmental Maritime Organisation*, ICJ *Rep*. 1960, 150 at 171.

[60] 15 UNTS 35.

[61] Bowett, *International Institutions*, 109.

[62] For a thorough review of the balance of power in the organs of the UN specialised agencies, see Bowett, *International Institutions*, 121–9.

[63] See chapter 4.

[64] See chapter 2.

[65] 87 UNTS 103.

[66] Kirgis, *International Organizations*, 215.

[67] Schermers, *Institutional Law*, 393.

[68] Agreement Establishing the World Trade Organisation, Article 9, 33 *I.L.M.* (1993), 1 at 19.

[69] For the different types of majority decision making procedures and their definitions

see Schermers, *Institutional Law*, 406–16.

[70] 4 UNTS 275, Articles 1(1), 4(8)(a).

[71] GA Res. 1514, 15 UN GAOR Supp. (No. 16) 66 (1960).

[72] GA Res. 1803, 17 UN GAOR Supp. (No. 17) 15 (1962).

[73] 53 *I.L.R.* (1977), 389, para. 87.

[74] *Case Concerning Military and Paramilitary Activities in and Against Nicaragua*, I.C.J. *Rep.* 1986, 99, 101, 103–4, 106–7. GA Res. 2131, 20 UN GAOR Supp. (No. 14) 10 (1965); GA Res. 2625, 25 UN GAOR Supp. (No. 28) 121 (1970); GA Res. 3314, 29 UN GAOR Supp. (No. 31) 142 (1974).

[75] ICJ *Rep.* 1986, 98.

[76] Starting with GA Res. ES–6/2, 6 UN GAOR ESS Supp. (No. 1) 2 (1980).

[77] GA Res. 44/240, 44 UN GAOR (1989).

[78] See P. R. Baehr and L. Gordenker, *The United Nations in the 1990s*, 59–62 (1992).

[79] Schermers, *Institutional Law*, 397.

[80] C. W. Jenks, 'Some Constitutional Problems of International Organisations', 22 *B.Y.B.I.L.* (1945), 41.

[81] 2 UNTS 10.

[82] Schermers, *Institutional Law*, 398–400. The SDR is an interest-bearing international reserve asset created by the IMF in 1969. All IMF accounts are denominated in terms of the SDR. On 31 December 1994 the SDR was worth $1.46.

[83] Article of Agreement of the International Monetary Fund, Article 12.

[84] Articles of Agreement of the International Bank for Reconstruction and Development, Article 5(3).

[85] Of the Executive Directors of the IBRD, the US holds 17.42 per cent, Japan 6.58 per cent, Germany 5.08 per cent, and France and the UK 4.87 per cent each. 1 *Europa World Yearbook*, 36th edn (1995), 70, 82.

[86] 1220 UNTS 21.

[87] See further F. Lyall, *Law and Space Telecommunications*, 103 (1989).

[88] 1143 UNTS 105.

[89] D. Freestone and J. S. Davidson, *The Institutional Framework of the European Communities*, 67 (1988).

[90] 1 *Europa World Yearbook*, 36th edn (1995), 151.

[91] Article 237 of the Treaty of Rome, Article O of the Treaty on European Union.

[92] Freestone and Davidson, *Institutional Framework*, 103.

[93] T. C. Hartley, *The Foundations of European Community Law*, 22–3, 3rd edn (1994).

[94] Articles 157 and 163 of the Treaty of Rome.

[95] S. D. Bailey, *The Procedure of the UN Security Council*, 199, 2nd edn (1988).

[96] UNCIO, vol. 11, 713.

[97] *Ibid.*, 714.

[98] S. D. Bailey, *Voting in the Security Council*, 69–73 (1969).

[99] SC 749 mtg, 11 UN SCOR (1956). UN docs S/3710, S/3713/Rev. 1 (1956).

[100] 27(1) *UN Chronicle* (1990), 67.

[101] *Interpretation of Article 3, Paragraph 2, of the Treaty of Lausanne (Frontier between Iraq and Turkey)*, P.C.I.J. Ser. B No. 12, 21 November 1925, 31–2.

[102] Bailey, *Procedure*, 209.

4

The decision-making capacity of international organisations

This chapter will consider the nature of powers exercised by international organisations. World or regional government requires mandatory or binding decision-making capacity.[1] This chapter will be concerned with discerning any elements of this in established international organisations. The impact of the more usual type of decision, the recommendation, will be considered, as will other types of decisions, for example declaratory resolutions and determinations. The impact of treaties drafted within organisations will be looked at. One of the purposes will be to ascertain whether there is any element of organisational legislative competence to rival the traditional forms of creating international law, namely customary law and treaties, both of which are created by States. By this method it will be possible to discover whether organisations, have altered, or have the capacity to alter, the dominance of international society by the nation State. The greater the impact of organisations' decisions on the international plane, the easier it is to accept the rationalist contention that international society is moving towards greater centralisation and government. The potential impact of the rule-making powers of international organisations has been expressed by Professor Kirgis:

> Since the decline in the 18th Century of natural law as the acknowledged basis for international order, the orthodox view has been that the only legitimate source for an international right or obligation is the express or tacit consent of each state to which it applies. This positivist doctrine finds expression in the sources of international law enumerated in *article 38(1)* of the Statute of the International Court of Justice, particularly the first two sources – international conventions (treaties) and custom. But treaty formulation and custom-building can be slow and cumbersome processes; moreover, once a rule is embodied in a treaty or in custom, it may be difficult to adapt it to keep pace with changing circumstances. As the face of the world changes at an accelerating rate, international law has to try to find ways to keep up. One way is to nudge away from strict positivism; that is away from the notion that any new or amended rule of international law can be applied to a given state only if that state has expressly consented to it. Norms of general application can then come into existence as norms do in domestic law for individuals and corporate entities through legislation and administrative rule-making.[2]

Effective institutional rule making is not necessarily limited to the making and

possible enforcement of binding decisions, but can be effected by recommendations, declarations, determinations, and obviously by organisations themselves
drafting and putting forward treaties for ratification by members and possibly
non-members as well.

Binding decisions

As a general rule of modern international institutional law, it has been accepted that
international organizations cannot take binding external decisions unless their constitutions expressly so provide.

Few constitutions allow international organizations to take binding external decisions. In their mutual relations, and often in relation to their subjects, Members are
obliged to comply with these decisions. The absence of sanctions may diminish the
actual effect of such binding decisions, but it does not deprive them of their legal
force. In practice, it may mean that the effect of binding international decisions is less
than that of similar decisions under national law. The gap between binding and non-
binding decisions may also have been narrowed from the other side, as some non-
binding decisions have a considerable practical influence.[3]

The establishment of supranational organisations would seem to require the ability of the organisation in question to promulgate binding rules, for without that
power the ability of the institution to control its State members would be lacking.
However, as has been seen in chapter 2, there are only partial examples of supranational organisations, principally the UN and the EU. The power of these bodies
to adopt mandatory resolutions will be analysed in this section, but it must be
made clear that organisations which do not display sufficient elements of centralisation to be labelled supranational can have mandatory powers.

The main examples of autonomous, as opposed to supranational, organisations
having the express constitutional power to make binding decisions are the Western European Union (WEU) and the Organisation of American States (OAS). In
both cases the binding powers relate to the question of peace and security, which
along with the mandatory powers of the UN Security Council, perhaps indicate
that when States establish organisations they are prepared to vest them with binding powers in the area of peace and security, more so than in other areas. This
tends to support the rationalist contention that for world government to develop
there must be a minimum level of world security. Professor Mitrany, the leading
functionalist, argued, on the other hand, that peace and security was not necessarily a precondition to world order, instead he suggested that basic economic
conditions ensuring freedom from want and hunger were more desirable and more
likely to be dealt with effectively by the development of functional organisations.
There is little evidence of this, at least in terms of organisations having the ability to decide on economic policy and assistance to States or peoples. Mandatory
decision-making powers in the economic sphere seemed to be confined to the
European Union, which is perhaps more an example of countries which having

already attained an acceptable standard of wealth have, by integration and some centralisation, improved their material well-being even further by the creation of a common market.

Nevertheless, there are certain indications in the process of European integration, that the functionalist agenda is being followed. The Preamble of the Treaty Establishing the European Coal and Steel Community of 1951, the first 'Community' treaty creating 'a common market, common objectives and common institutions',[4] makes it clear that the vision of Robert Schuman and Jean Monnet behind[5] the creation of a common coal and steel market, was to bond the member States together economically so that they were unable to fall out militarily. One preambular paragraph reads as follows:

> Resolved to substitute for age-old rivalries the merging of their essential interests; to create by establishing an economic community, the basis for a broader and deeper community among peoples long divided by bloody conflicts; and to lay the foundations for institutions which will give direction to a destiny henceforward shared.

Whereas there was sufficient consensus to create the basis for a European common market, the attempt in 1954 to create a treaty aimed at establishing a European Defence Community (EDC), with a unified European Army under a single European political and military authority, failed.[6] In its place emerged the Western European Union, which in security terms, was based firmly on the notion of a collective defence pact along the lines of the North Atlantic Treaty Organisation (NATO).[7] However, vestiges of the centralised mandatory decision-making power intended for the EDC can be found in Protocol 3 on the Control of Armaments:

> When the development of atomic, biological and chemical weapons in the territory on the mainland of Europe of the High Contracting Parties who have not given up the right to produce them has passed the experimental stage and effective production of them has started there, the level of stocks that the High Contracting Parties concerned will be allowed to hold on the mainland of Europe shall be decided by a majority vote of the Council of Western European Union.

The WEU was overshadowed during the Cold War by NATO, which allied a greater number of Western States under a defence umbrella, and consequently its mandatory powers were not exercised. Nevertheless, the generally more unstable post-Cold War era has led to a revitalisation of the WEU, in particular in the Maastricht Treaty of 1992, which provides in Article J.4. for the establishment 'in time' of a 'common defence' and requests that the WEU, 'which is an integral part of the [European] Union, to elaborate and implement decisions and actions of the [European] Union which have defence implications'. It appears from the European experiment that the development of defence and security powers by an international organisation are the culmination of a process starting with economic integration. It may be that under the Maastricht provisions the WEU will become integrated within the EU, an integration which will be accompanied by the enhancement of the mandatory powers of the WEU.

The functionalist argument, however, is refuted in other instances of organisations possessing the power to make binding decisions. In the case of the OAS, the Organisation, which is concerned with economic, social, defensive and security matters, only possesses mandatory powers in the area of security. The Charter of the OAS of 1948 (the Bogotá Charter) contains within it the concept of a defensive pact,[8] but its founders also intended it to have wider powers in the field of security. Article 28 provides that:

> If the inviolability or the integrity of the territory or the sovereignty or political independence of any American State should be affected by an armed attack or by an act of aggression that is not an armed attack, or by an extracontinental conflict, or by a conflict between two or more American States, or by any other fact or situation that might endanger the peace in America, the American States, in furtherance of the principles of continental solidarity or collective self-defence, shall apply the measures and procedures established in the special treaties on the subject.

For the type of action envisaged, attention must be paid to the special treaties on the subject that also form part of the inter-American collective security network. The main treaty is the Inter-American Treaty of Reciprocal Assistance (Rio Treaty) of 1947,[9] Article 6 of which adds to Article 5 of the Bogotá Charter that the Organ of Consultation of Foreign Ministers of the OAS 'shall meet immediately in order to agree on the measures which must be taken in the case of aggression to assist the victim of the aggression or, in any case, the measures which should be taken for the common defense and for the maintenance of peace and security of the Continent'. Article 8 was revised in 1975 to explicitly enumerate the types of measures that can be taken by the OAS:

> For the purposes of this Treaty, the measures on which the Organ of Consultation may agree will comprise one or more of the following: recall of chiefs of diplomatic missions; breaking of diplomatic relations; breaking of consular relations; partial or complete interruption of economic relations or of rail, sea, air, postal, telegraphic, telephonic ... communications; and the use of armed force.

Article 17 provides that the Meeting of Consultation shall take its decisions by a vote of two-thirds of the States which have ratified the Treaty, and Article 20 provides that 'decisions which require the application of measures specified in article 8 shall be binding upon all the' State parties 'with the sole exception that no state shall be required to use armed force without its consent'. The practice of the OAS in this area will be reviewed in chapter 7.

Binding decision-making capacity is not a power solely limited to some security organisations, but can be found in functional organisations, although its occurrence is rarer. The current Constitution of the Universal Postal Union (UPU) of 1964,[10] provides in Article 1 that the UPU is 'a single postal territory for the reciprocal exchange of letter post items' with guaranteed freedom of transit throughout the Union. The Organisation's ability to facilitate the global postal service is enhanced by the provisions of Article 22 which provides that the UPU's

General and Detailed Regulations as well as the Universal Postal Convention, all of which are regularly updated[11] and contain more detailed rules on the workings of the UPU as well as rules applicable to the international postal service, are binding on member States.[12]

Those organisations with elements of supranationalism identified in chapter 2, by their very nature possess decision-making powers. It is true that the United Nations' organs operate in the main by the adoption of non-binding recommendations, particularly the General Assembly, although even that body has certain decision-making powers, as recognised by the International Court in the *Expenses* case:

> ... the functions and powers conferred by the Charter on the General Assembly are not confined to discussion, consideration, the initiation of studies and the making of recommendations; they are not merely hortatory. Article 18 of the UN Charter deals with 'decisions' of the General Assembly 'on important questions'. These 'decisions' do indeed include certain recommendations, but others have dispositive force and effect. Among these latter decisions, Article 18 includes the suspension of rights and privileges of membership, expulsion of Members, and 'budgetary questions'.[13]

As Professor Schermers states 'the examples mentioned by the Court could be classified as internal rules with important external effects',[14] and it may be doubted whether the Assembly has the power to make binding 'external rules', namely 'rules extending beyond the functioning of the organization itself'.[15] However, as shall be seen in chapter 5, the World Court opined in the *Namibia* case that the Assembly had the power to 'decide' to terminate South Africa's mandate over South West Africa. Although apparently of a different order to budgetary and membership matters, the termination of a UN mandate could be viewed as an internal decision,[16] or alternatively the General Assembly's 'decision' could be viewed simply as a declaration or, more accurately, a determination (see below), which required the mandatory powers of the Security Council to make it a formally binding decision.[17]

Furthermore, the World Court's decision in the *Namibia* case indicates that the Security Council's mandatory powers can be exercised beyond the limits of Chapter VII of the UN Charter. The Court referred to Article 25 of the Charter which provides that 'the Members of the Security Council agree to accept and carry out the decisions of the Security Council in accordance with the present Charter'. The Court then analysed the applicability of Article 25 to resolutions, such as the one confronting it, adopted outside the confines of Chapter VII.

> It has been contended that Article 25 of the Charter applies only to enforcement measures adopted under Chapter VII of the Charter. It is not possible to find in the Charter any support for this view. Article 25 is not confined to decisions with regard to enforcement action but applies to 'decisions of the Security Council' adopted in accordance with the Charter. Moreover, that Article is placed, not in Chapter VII, but immediately after Article 24 in that part of the Charter which deals with the functions and powers of the Security Council. If Article 25 has reference solely to decisions of

the Security Council concerning enforcement action under Articles 41 and 42 of the Charter, that is to say, if it were only such decisions which had binding effect, then Article 25 would be superfluous, since this effect is secured by Articles 48 and 49 of the Charter.

The Court then stated that 'the language of a resolution of the Security Council should be carefully analysed before a conclusion can be made as to its binding effect'.[18] Nevertheless, the Court's approach means that the Security Council can adopt binding decisions on a wider variety of matters than previously thought, though of course these matters are still within the general field of the maintenance of international peace and security (reviewed in chapter 7).

The European Union on the other hand has the power to adopt mandatory decisions in a much wider field. The principal decision-making powers of the Organisation under the Treaty of Rome are in the economic field though, in adopting a common economic position *vis-à-vis* third States, this power has been used infrequently to deal with situations which are really security matters. In the past, the adoption of a common European position on the issue of economic sanctions against outside States has been taken through a procedure which was a curious combination of use of the institutional machinery along with an informal meeting of the Foreign Ministers of member States known as the EPC (European Political Co-operation). Decisions reached in this forum did not give rise to enforceable obligations under Community law. In the case of economic sanctions, the EPC unanimously agreed on a common European position, on other occasions the matter was taken on board by the Council of Ministers in the form of a binding regulation or decision. Only in the latter instance was the decision binding. For example, a regulation was adopted following the Argentinian invasion of the Falklands in 1982 suspending the import of all products originating from Argentina.[19] The treaty base for this power is Article 113 of the Treaty of Rome which provides for a 'common commercial policy' covering, *inter alia*, external trade.

The move towards a common foreign policy entirely within a defined, treaty-based, institutional framework was partially achieved by Article 30 of the Single European Act of 1986. It provided, *inter alia*, that '[t]he Ministers for Foreign Affairs [of the EC] ... shall meet at least four times a year within the framework of the European Political Co-operation' to 'ensure the swift adoption of common positions and the implementation of joint action'. The move towards a common foreign and security policy was completed by Article J of the Treaty of European Union (Maastricht Treaty) of 1992. By Article J.8.1 the EPC is replaced by the European Council which shall 'define the principles of and general guidelines for the common foreign and security policy'. Further, Article J.8.2 states that the Council (of Ministers) 'shall take the decisions necessary for defining and implementing the common foreign and security policy on the basis of the guidelines adopted by the European Council. It shall ensure the unity, consistency and effectiveness of action by the Union'.[20]

The activities of the European Community and Union in the field of peace and security will be reviewed in chapter 7. The Organisation's ability to adopt binding decisions, whether in the field of economic affairs (where the vast majority of decisions are made),[21] or in the fields of peace and security, social policy,[22] and justice and home affairs,[23] is derived from Article 189 of the amended Treaty of Rome which provides:

> In order to carry out their task and in accordance with the provisions of this Treaty, the European Parliament acting jointly with the Council, the Council and the Commission shall make regulations and issue directives, take decisions, make recommendations or deliver opinions.
>
> A regulation shall have general application. It shall be binding in its entirety and directly applicable in all Member States.
>
> A directive shall be binding, as to the result to be achieved, upon each Member State to which it is addressed, but shall leave to the national authorities the choice of form and methods.
>
> A decision shall be binding in its entirety upon those to whom it is addressed.
>
> Recommendations and opinions shall have no binding force.

Although using a variety of words, it is clear that the Community can, where empowered by the other provisions of the Treaty, take mandatory 'decisions'. Article 189 uses the term 'decision' for binding decisions applicable either to Member States, or individuals and companies. 'Regulations' are directly binding on member States, whilst 'directives' allow the member government scope as to the exact form of their implementation. The ability to bind natural and legal persons within member States as well as the member States themselves, is indicative of a higher level of supranationalism in the European Organisation than in the United Nations which can only bind members, which in turn must adopt the relevant legislation, if necessary, for the implementation of the Security Council's decisions. Early on in the life of the Coal and Steel Community, the European Court recognised the law-making effect of Community decisions when it described them as 'quasi-legislative measures adopted by a public authority with legislative effect erga omnes'.[24]

Recommendations

Recommendations are simply resolutions adopted by international organisations that do not bind the member States.[25] As Professor Schermers states:

> All international organizations are empowered to issue recommendations. The frequency with which they use this power depends mainly on the extent of their authority to issue further binding decisions. The recommendation is little used in organizations (like the EEC) which have such authority, and frequently used in organizations (like the UN and the specialized agencies) which do not.[26]

Without analysing the actual effect of recommendations on the membership of international organisations, it is possible simply to point at the lack of direct legal effect of such resolutions in order to reinforce a picture of most international organisations as simple fora for States to meet, air their differences, and adopt some sort of compromise communiqué of limited legal, though potentially of great political, value.[27] This may be the position with the informal meeting of certain groups of States such as the G7, but is not so in the case of properly constituted organisations formally adopting resolutions of a recommendatory nature. Such resolutions can have a significant independent legal effect, and enhance, rather than detract from, the autonomy of the particular organisation. Such an approach is favoured by Professor Higgins who states:

> With the development of international organizations, the votes and views of states have come to have legal significance as evidence of customary international law ... Collective acts by states, repeated by and acquiesced in by sufficient numbers with sufficient frequency, eventually attain the status of law.[28]

A different, but no less significant, analysis is given by Professor Schreuer:

> The limited and qualified authority of recommendations also requires a view of their legal consequences which is different from those of mandatory rules. By virtue of their non-binding character, they do not absolutely require a decision in conformity with their provisions. On the other hand, this does not mean that it is open to decision makers to ignore them arbitrarily. There is at least a duty to consider them in good faith.
>
> A recommendation can, moreover, usually serve as a presumption of legality in favour of conduct which is in accordance with its tenets. A State acting in accordance with the recommendations of [an international organization] will enjoy the benefit of the doubt should the legality of its conduct be called into question. On the other hand, action contrary to the provisions of a recommendation can result in the shifting of the burden of proof against the person violating it.[29]

The immense significance of General Assembly recommendations has already been deal with in chapter 3. The purpose here will be to review, albeit relatively briefly, the recommendatory powers of some of the specialised agencies and other functional organisations in order to assess the legal impact of this type of resolution.

The International Atomic Energy Agency (IAEA) is not a specialised agency of the UN, though it has an agreement with the UN by which it comes 'under the aegis of the UN' in that the Agency 'will function under its Statute as an autonomous international organization in the working relationship with the UN'.[30] Article 2 of the Statute of the IAEA of 1956 states the objectives of the Organisation in the following terms:

> The agency shall seek to accelerate and enlarge the contribution of atomic energy to peace, health and prosperity throughout the world. It shall ensure, so far as it is able, that assistance provided by it or at its request or under its supervision or control is not used in such a way as to further any military purpose.[31]

The agency has various functions outlined in Article 3, including the establishment and administration of safeguards to ensure that fissionable materials are not used 'to further any military purpose' when requested by the parties to any bilateral or multilateral treaties, or at the request of any State. For example the IAEA has verification duties under the 1968 Treaty on the Non-Proliferation of Nuclear Weapons.[32] As well as the creation and supervision of safeguards, the IAEA has the power 'to establish or adopt … standards of safety for protection of health and minimization of danger to life and property … and to provide for the application of these standards, at the request of the parties, to operations under' treaties or at the request of individual States. In fact the IAEA's standards, though only recommendatory, are often taken on board by Members without the formalities of Article 3 being complied with.[33] Given the dangerous nature of fissionable material, the IAEA's standards are viewed as having a legal effect independently of their incorporation into domestic legislation.

In addition, the IAEA can be requested to assist in the enforcement of a mandatory resolution of an international organisation as was the case with UN Security Council resolution 687 of 3 April 1991, which decided on the partial disarmament of Iraq under the supervision of a UN Special Commission and the IAEA, following Iraq's defeat and expulsion from Kuwait. Normally, however, the IAEA can only work with the consent of the State in question, as illustrated by North Korea's refusal to allow an IAEA team into the country to inspect nuclear facilities in June 1994.[34] Even in the case of Iraq, resolution 687, though a mandatory resolution of the Council under Chapter VII, was still agreed to by the Iraqis. The work of the IAEA and the Special Commission in Iraq is dependent on Iraqi co-operation, though Iraq is being coerced into compliance by the continuation of sanctions and the occasional unilateral airstrikes by Western States.[35]

Many functional organisations use the power of recommendation to great effect. Some like the World Health Organisation (WHO) and the International Labour Organisation (ILO) often use the recommendation in place of a convention or quasi-binding regulation, even though both organisations are expressly empowered to adopt conventions. The less formal, and technically non-binding recommendation, seems to be equally respected by members as a more formal and binding treaty commitment.

The Constitution of the World Health Organisation, originally adopted in 1946, puts forward the objective of the WHO in simple terms in Article 1, namely 'the attainment of all peoples of the highest possible level of health'.[36] The functions of the WHO, listed in Article 2 include: acting as the central authority on international health work; assisting governments when requested to improve health services; the provision of technical and emergency aid upon request by States; promoting research into diseases; promoting the prevention of accidental injuries; improving nutrition, housing, sanitation and working conditions; promoting co-operation among scientific groups; and providing information on health matters. In addition to the WHO developing 'international standards with respect to food, biological, pharmaceutical and other products', its standard-setting function is stated more widely, namely 'to propose conventions, agreements, regulations, and make recommendations with respect to international health matters'. The Health Assembly, consisting of all members, has the authority to adopt conventions by a two-thirds majority and regulations by a simple majority.[37] Conventions are binding on those members when accepted by their relevant constitutional procedures, and regulations are binding on all members except for those expressly contracting out. In this sense WHO regulations are not inherently binding, although in many ways they appear to be a hybrid between binding decisions and recommendations. Important regulations adopted by the WHO include the International Sanitary Regulations adopted initially in 1951, revised and renamed the International Health Regulations in 1969,[38] dealing with a wide variety of matters with many designed to prevent and control the spread of diseases such as cholera, the bubonic plague and yellow fever.[39]

The fact that States are bound by regulations unless they expressly contract out was meant to promote uniformity amongst the membership. In contrast to the adoption of conventions when members have to contract in by adopting the convention, regulations are *prima facie* binding on members. Nevertheless, Article 22 still permits members to opt out of regulations. It can be argued that the power to opt out is important for States, otherwise they could be bound by a decision adopted by a slender majority. However, the Health Assembly has adopted the approach that a reservation (as opposed to an opt-out) to regulations is not valid unless it is accepted by the Health Assembly – in effect the Assembly decides by majority on regulations and can by the same majority reject reservations to those regulations – an illustration of the legislative decision-making capacity of an organisation.[40] A State is still able to opt out entirely but is not entitled to accept the regulations subject to a reservation. It may be because of the political problems caused by its approach to the adoption of binding regulations, that the WHO:

usually acts by adopting nonbinding recommendations, rather than binding regulations. For example, in 1981 it adopted the International Code of Marketing of Breast-Milk Substitutes, a non binding code designed to contribute to the safe nutrition of infants, after considering whether to adopt it as a set of binding regulations. More than 130 states have given effect to its principles.[41]

Whereas it might be argued that the WHO's capacity to adopt regulations is in many ways a power of decision making (though the opt-out and the right to reservation are meant to prevent this), its capacity to adopt conventions, though little used, is not an example of mandatory legislation but is subject to acceptance by each individual member. The ILO has power to adopt and supervise conventions as well as having the ability to adopt recommendations, but no power to adopt regulations. The ILO has used both its power to promulgate conventions and its power to adopt recommendations extensively.[42] Valticos explains the basis on which the different powers are used:

International labour standards are contained in two different kinds of instruments: Conventions, which, following ratification, become binding on ratifying States, and

Recommendations which are not designed for the creation of obligations but are essentially guides for national action ...

The relative appropriateness of Conventions and Recommendations respectively to deal with a given question depends in each case on the subject-matter and the degree of maturity of the question. Recommendations may be adopted, in particular, when the complexity of the subject and the wide differences in the circumstances of the different countries make it impossible to provide for a universal and uniform mode of application of international standards, or where this is an exploratory measure, with a view to the subsequent embodiment of the standards in a Convention, or where a more detailed Recommendation aims at supplementing a Convention drafted in more general terms.[43]

The close relationship and compatibility of the two forms of law making are made clear from this statement. Formally, recommendations have less legal force than the binding treaty commitments undertaken by State parties, but practically the two methods are so interwoven that in many cases it would be very difficult for a State to claim to have accepted a convention without the clarifying or explanatory recommendations that surround it. For instance the ILO Convention Concerning Equal Remuneration for Men and Women Workers for Work of Equal Value of 1951[44] lays down a general principle of equal pay, while the Recommendation Concerning Equal Remuneration for Men and Women Workers for Work of Equal Value adopted by the General Conference[45] indicates methods in which members could implement the general principle.

Furthermore, to protect the integrity of the Conventions from which many recommendations arise, the Secretariat of the ILO, the International Labour Office, has, and this practice has been accepted by member States, not permitted reservations to the ILO Conventions. In 1951 the International Labour Office justified this approach on the grounds of the unique tripartite nature of the Conference consisting as it does of workers, employers and State representatives, and the fact that the Constitution of the ILO contemplates in Article 19(5)(b) and (d) the adoption or rejection of the convention as a whole by the legislatures of the members. In addition, to allow reservations might deny workers some of the rights granted to them in the convention if their national government so wished. Furthermore, the ILO Constitution is sufficiently flexible, with its provisions for modification and development, to enable members to propose changes.[46]

The rejection by the ILO and the WHO of reservations to conventions and regulations exemplifies the independence of these organisations from the practice normally associated with the adoption of treaties outside this organisational framework, when reservation to multilateral treaties are the norm unless the treaty prohibits them. If the treaty is silent then reservations are allowed unless they are incompatible with the object and purpose of the treaty.[47] Furthermore, the adoption of recommendations by both organisations, and this is indicative of many functional organisations, as a form of quasi-legislation, indicates that the 'recommendation', though formally non-binding, practically can be seen as binding.

When looking at the more political organisations such as the UN General Assembly, the recommendations must be treated with greater care so as to discern any element of legislation, though as has been stated above and in chapter 3, it is possible to see consistent resolutions, or resolutions adopted by consensus, as having a quasi-legislative effect.

Declarations

The ILO and the WHO's recommendations can be said in many ways to be declarations in that they declare general principles to be applicable to certain actions. Whether these have the status of law or are intended to become law needs to be discerned from the terms of the resolution, the background – to see if the resolution is a culmination of practice, and the statements, if any, accompanying or following the vote when States may make it clear that they do not consider themselves legally bound. In effect, particularly in consensus resolutions of a declaratory nature, it is arguable that there is a presumption of *opinio juris* on the part of States voting for the resolution unless they expressly opt out by stating that their vote is simply a political, not a legal, act.

It appears to be correct to state that no constitution of an autonomous international organisation contains the express power to adopt declarations.[48] However, it has become established and accepted practice for organisations to adopt declarations as a special type of recommendation, in other words as a power implied from the express recommendatory power. A declaration is a resolution which not only creates a presumption that action in conformity with it is lawful, but goes further and expects compliance by member States with the declaration. This is not to say that declarations are binding *per se*, it is simply to state that since declarations are meant to reflect or crystallise customary law, States, whether members of the Organisation or not, are bound to comply in accordance with their obligations under general international law. Declarations serve to focus members' concentration on consolidating and codifying customary international law. On certain occasions the UN General Assembly may attempt to reform the law or put forward new principles of law in the form of declarations. In these cases care must be taken to analyse the voting patterns and explanations of why a State is voting for or against the resolution, and, more particularly, to see if in subsequent practice the declaration is used and recognised by members and other States as an instrument of customary international law.

Examples of General Assembly declarations have been given in chapter 3. Certain declarations are declaratory of international legal norms or further help to crystallise such norms – for example the Declaration on the Granting of Independence to Colonial Territories and Peoples 1960 and the Resolution on Permanent Sovereignty over Natural Resources 1962. Furthermore, where there is a need for legal regulation, say in a newly developing area of State practice as in the case of outer space, General Assembly resolutions may fill the legal vacuum.[49] Other resolutions, on the other hand, such as the 1974 Definition of Aggression, have a dual purpose: first, to define and clarify aspects of customary law or the Charter; and second, to improve the effectiveness of the United Nations collective security machinery. In the case of the 1974 Definition of Aggression, the purpose was to provide a normative definition of aggression, but also to enable the Security Council to determine more readily that acts of aggression have occurred within the meaning of Article 39 and so possibly take measures to combat the aggression under Chapter 7 of the Charter.

The General Assembly continues to adopt resolutions which both codify (and, in some instances, legislate), and purport to enhance the effectiveness of the UN. Indeed, this type of resolution seems predominant at present as a result of the need to modernise a more dynamic UN in the post-Cold War era. However, it is arguable that in some instances the two goals of codification and improved efficiency are incompatible, by, for example, codifying a set of principles that prevent UN action. It is questionable whether the effectiveness of fact finding will be improved as a result of a recent General Assembly resolution, supported by all member States, entitled the Declaration on Fact Finding by the United Nations in the Field of the Maintenance of Peace and Security, adopted without a vote on 17 January 1992, following a report of the Sixth Committee which in turn was based on work by the Special Committee on the Charter.[50] Although the resolution recognised 'that the ability of the United Nations to maintain international peace and security depends to a large extent on its acquiring detailed knowledge about the factual circumstances of any dispute or situation', and that the competent organs of the UN should endeavour to undertake fact-finding activities that should be 'comprehensive, objective, impartial and timely', it still recognised, the legal principle embodied in Article 2(7) of the Charter, that 'the sending of a United Nations fact finding mission to the territory of any State requires the prior consent of that State'. Although the Assembly encouraged States to adopt 'a policy of admitting ... fact finding missions to their territory', the UN's respect for the sovereignty of its members undermines the proper institutionalisation and greater efficacy of fact finding, whether it be by the Security Council, the General Assembly, or the Secretary General. The fact is that even when States consent to such missions, they are often too late to contribute to prevent a conflict breaking out, and if a conflict is already under way, they do little towards its peaceful settlement.

Perhaps it would have been better for the Assembly to 'legislate' in this area, for example when there is Security Council authorisation, to permit fact-finding without consent. Indeed, it could be argued that the Security Council can adopt a 'decision' to send a fact finding team which is binding within the terms of Article 25. However, a 'clarification' of the law along these lines would not have been acceptable to a significant number of States desiring to prevent further encroachments on their sovereignty: this would have resulted in a resolution being adopted by a majority and less likely to be seen as a contribution to international law. The end result is a resolution which reflects current practice on non-intervention to the detriment of the efficiency of the United Nations and illustrates the problems that can emerge from the adoption of declarations by political bodies.[51]

In other organisations too there has developed the power, usually, but not exclusively, in the plenary body, to adopt declaratory resolutions. As with the United Nations General Assembly, this declaratory power is sometimes 'legislative' in that it develops nascent principles of international or regional law, or it is sometimes simply 'codificatory' in that it simply collects together the established rules of international or regional law on the subject. The latter resolution tends to support the realist and Marxist viewpoints that organisations are simply fora for the drafting and agreement of compromises which maintain the balance of power in international society by not purporting to disturb the *status quo*. Even within regional organisations containing developing States, the desire to preserve the current unstable structure of States by the governments of those States outweighs the revolutionary attitude of those States in other areas of international law and in other international organisations. The OAU, in 1967, adopted a Declaration Reaffirming the Principle of Respect for Sovereignty and Territorial Integrity of Member States,[52] which failed to address the pressing and still present tribal problems in Africa except in so far as to reaffirm the artificial colonial boundaries as the international ones. The solidification of the legal principle *uti possidetis juris*[53] by this declaration, combined with the assumption that self-determination was inapplicable, cemented the *status quo* in Africa but failed to address the problems such a principle creates, evidenced by the bloody civil war in Biafra in 1967,[54] and the many conflicts and other disasters before and since.

Other organisations have adopted a more radical agenda reflected in their declaratory resolutions. The OAS for instance, whilst not undermining the principle of *uti possidetis*, has curtailed the freedom of American governments to take whatever form they like. At its twenty-first regular session in June 1991 the OAS General Assembly adopted the Santiago Commitment to Democracy and the Renewal of the Inter-American System, under which the members declared their 'inescapable commitment to the defense and promotion of representative democracy and human rights in the region, within the framework of respect for the principles of self-determination and non-intervention'. At the same meeting, the Assembly approved a resolution on representative democracy,[55] by which it instructed the OAS Secretary General to call for an immediate convocation of a meeting of the Permanent Council in the event of a disruption in the democratic process within any member State. The Permanent Council is empowered to convene an *ad hoc* meeting of the Ministers of Foreign Affairs. This process was instituted for the first time in October 1991 when the democratically elected President Aristide of Haiti was deposed by a military coup. This eventually led to the imposition of sanctions against Haiti by the OAS illustrating a development whereby the organisation not simply legislates, in the form of a declaration, to promote a certain type of behaviour by its members – in this case democracy – but is also prepared to enforce that declaration. The OAS development of the principle of democracy is also perhaps illustrative of a move away from the maintenance of the *status quo* towards more equitable standards of behaviour or, perhaps more accurately, towards the adoption of Western ideology.

Determinations

Whereas declarations are in essence general principles of law set down in a non-binding resolution, determinations consist of the application of these general principles, or the principles of the constituent document, to a particular set of facts or a dispute. In some cases these determinative resolutions may be non-binding, but in other cases a more elaborate mechanism for dispute resolution within a particular organisation may include provision for an authoritative binding decision.[56]

General statements about the value and effect of resolutions must be made with a great deal of caution. Some determinations are overtly political and can be seen as lacking in significant legal content or effect. This can be seen in certain determinations adopted by the UN General Assembly, in particular its infamous resolution 3379 adopted on 10 November 1975, which simply 'determined that Zionism is a form of racism and racial discrimination'. The political impact of this resolution was great but its value as a determination of international law was undermined: by the fact that it was only adopted by a majority of 72 to 35 with 32 abstentions, by its alleged but largely unexplained legal inaccuracy,[57] and by the fact that it was 'repealed' in 1991 by a majority of 111 votes to 13 with 25 abstentions.[58]

The fact that there are examples of misdirected and probably inaccurate General Assembly determinations should not undermine the general value of its determinative capacity. Indeed, it appears inevitable that in a highly charged political atmosphere in which groups of States are competing for dominance that there are going to be resolutions which offend or even outrage a significant minority. The revolutionary approach to world order advocated by many developing States dictates that the political organs which they dominate in terms of voting power should be used in an antagonistic way. However, other determinations of the General Assembly may be adopted by a very large majority or by a consensus and so be acceptable as authoritative, as opposed to opinionated, legal determinations.

During the Cold War when the Security Council was deadlocked by the veto there were numerous examples of authoritative General Assembly resolutions adopted on issues and disputes. Indeed, during this period the focus of attention was on the General Assembly in order to discern the reaction of the world community to breaches of accepted international norms. In many ways it was the Assembly which maintained the critical attitude to miscreant States' behaviour, a reaction essential for the maintenance of a system based on customary law.[59] Many of these resolutions which applied principles of international and Charter law to situations, disputes and conflicts were not adopted by consensus, but because they were clearly based, unlike the Zionism resolution, on principles of international law, there was no doubt about their legal effect. For instance after the Soviet Union had intervened in Hungary and the Security Council was inevitably deadlocked by the Soviet veto, the Assembly declared 'that by using armed force against the Hungarian people' the Soviet Union was 'violating the political independence of Hungary' and violating the UN Charter.[60] The resolution was expressed as 'objective', containing no 'political intentions', and representing a 'historical judgment' by members voting for it.[61]

There are many other instances of General Assembly determinations which, although not binding in an institutional sense, are binding in the sense that they reflected customary international law. On the issue of apartheid in South Africa, the Assembly consistently determined that this was a breach of customary law[62] and a threat to the peace within the terms of the UN Charter. It is arguable that the latter determination is one which ought to have been left to the Security Council under Article 39 of the Charter, although in many ways the Assembly's determination that the 'situation in South Africa constitutes a threat to international peace and security' in 1965[63] was a more objective application of the concept that the Council's more limited determination in 1977 'that the acquisition of arms and related material constitutes a threat to the maintenance of international peace and security,' 'having regard to the policies and practices of the South African Government'.[64] The Security Council's more limited determination was accompanied by the imposition of a mandatory arms embargo, whilst the Assembly wished for the imposition by the Council of a more comprehensive set of sanctions under Chapter VII. In the post-Cold War period, with an active Security Council, there has been a reduction in the number of Assembly determinations, although they are still to be found. For instance the Assembly has determined that 'as the Republic of Bosnia and Herzegovina is a sovereign independent State and a member of the United Nations, it is entitled to all rights provided for in the Charter of the United Nations, including the right to self-defence under Article 51' to support its call that the Security Council arms embargo imposed against the whole of the former Yugoslavia in resolution 713 of 1991 be lifted as regards Bosnia.[65]

Article 39 of the UN Charter is most significant in that it expressly empowers the Security Council to make determinations which may have a tremendous legal and political impact. Article 39 states, in part, that 'the Security Council shall determine the existence of any threat to the peace, breach of the peace, or act of aggression'. The Council must make such a determination before utilising the coercive powers granted to it in Articles 41 and 42. In this way the concepts of 'threat to the peace', 'breach of the peace' and 'act of aggression' have great institutional legal significance. In addition, a finding of 'aggression' by the Security Council may have a wider legal impact in that under customary international law 'aggression' is a crime, entailing individual as well as State responsibility, though it is sometimes argued that this only applies to 'wars' of aggression not 'acts' of aggression in the sense of Article 39.[66]

There are a few examples of the Security Council making determinations of a 'threat to the peace', 'breach of the peace' or 'act of aggression' within the meaning of Article 39 during the Cold War, for instance it found that the situation in

Southern Rhodesia constituted a threat to the peace in 1966,[67]; that there was a breach of the peace in the region of the Falkland Islands in 1982,[68]; and that the Israeli attack on the PLO base in Tunis in 1985 was an act of aggression.[69] The end of the Cold War has seen a dramatic increase in the number of determinations under Article 39, in particular the concept of a 'threat to the peace' has been greatly extended to cover not only civil conflicts with international repercussions as in the former Yugoslavia[70] and Iraq[71] for example, but also to cover support for terrorism and the denial of democracy, in the cases of Libya[72] and Haiti[73] respectively. The concept of a breach of the peace has again been applied to inter-State conflicts, with the Iraqi invasion of Kuwait, while findings of aggression have again been sparse because of the wider implications. In all these cases the Council employed the coercive mechanisms of Chapter VII, normally in the form of binding economic sanctions, and occasionally with the use of military measures,[74] thereby enforcing its determinations under Article 39.

Although its express powers of determination are limited to Article 39, the Security Council, like the General Assembly has also developed a quasi-judicial capacity, making determinations based on international law as opposed to the institutional law of its constituent document. It appears odd that whereas Security Council determinations under Article 39 are not binding *per se* although they *may* be accompanied by binding decisions within the meaning of Article 25 of the UN Charter, the Council's resolutions based on its implied judicial powers of determination on questions of international law may or may not be binding in the institutional sense depending on the criteria laid down by the World Court in the *Namibia* case.[75] As well as having the potential to be binding Security Council 'decisions' within the meaning of Article 25, Security Council determinations are binding in a wider sense in that they are based on customary international law. For instance in 1965 the Security Council, in an early application of the principle of self-determination, stated that it regarded 'the declaration of independence by' the 'racist settler minority in Southern Rhodesia' 'as having no legal authority' and thereafter referred to the 'illegal racist minority regime in Southern Rhodesia'.[76] Another example of the use of this power can be found in the Security Council's determination that the declaration by the Turkish Cypriot authorities of the establishment of the Turkish Republic of Northern Cyprus was 'legally invalid',[77] because the 'State' in the northern part of the island was the result of an invasion by Turkey in 1974. In the same vein the Security Council decided in August 1990 'that the annexation of Kuwait by Iraq ... has no legal validity, and is considered null and void'.[78]

Despite misgivings about the lack of judicial procedure in the Security Council,[79] it is clear that such a power is invaluable in a legal system which is dependent for its continuance on clear and unequivocal condemnations of breaches of international law. The Security Council, like the General Assembly, is helping to uphold and bolster basic principles of international law using express and implied powers of determination. In other international organisations, the power to make determinations is more part of a dispute settlement mechanism between member

States. Mention has already been made in chapter 2 of the ICAO Council's dispute settlement powers under Article 84 of the Chicago Convention. A further example of this power to make authoritative determinations or rather in this case 'interpretations' of the constituent documents of an organisation can be found in Article 29 of the Article of Agreement of the International Monetary Fund (IMF) of 1947. This provides that 'any question of interpretation of this Agreement arising between any member and the Fund or between any Members of the Fund shall be submitted to the Executive Board for its decision'. A member can appeal from this decision to the Board of Governors 'whose decision shall be final' and who refer the matter to the Committee on Interpretation. The provision states that 'a decision of the Committee shall be the decision of the Board of Governors unless the Board of Governors, by an eighty-five percent majority of the total voting power, decides otherwise.' Although the Executive Board's and the Board of Governors' decisions are made under the weighted-voting system, described in chapter 3, decisions of the Committee on Interpretation are made on the basis of each Committee member having one vote. Despite some debate it appears that 'interpretations' under Article 29 are binding on member States.[80] The need for authoritative interpretations in this case is explained by Professor Kirgis:

> The Fund Agreement ... contains a number of significant provisions directly regulating the conduct of member states. Some of the provisions impose rather technical obligations regarding such matters as the convertibility of currencies and recognition by member states of some controls imposed by other member states on the availability or use of foreign exchange. Consequently it was thought important at the Bretton Woods Conference of 1944, when the Fund and World Bank Agreement were drafted, to include a provision for authoritative interpretation of each Agreement by in house organs able to bring expertise and expeditious decision making to the task.[81]

Conventions

Looking at the practice of organisations it appears that they have the power to conclude treaties with other organisations and States in the absence of a constitutional provision preventing it.[82] The UN Charter for instance expressly provides for the conclusion of trusteeship agreement between the UN and States, and agreements between the UN and specialised agencies,[83] but in its practice the UN has concluded headquarters agreements with States, agreements on co-operation with other organisations, and many status-of-forces agreements with States in which a peacekeeping force has been sent, all of which are not expressly authorised by the Charter. As Professor Seyersted points out 'only a small fraction of the treaties concluded by the United Nations fall within the categories authorized by the Charter. The same applies to a number of other Organizations'.[84]

As well as possessing the inherent power to become parties to treaties, many international organisations have in their practice developed the power to formulate conventions for ratification by members and sometimes non-members. In many instances this has taken place in the absence of an express constitutional provision, but the accepted view seems to be that the plenary bodies of organisations have that power in the absence of an express prohibition in the constituent document. The power to promulgate conventions is likened to the plenary body's power to adopt recommendations, in that until the convention is ratified by sufficient members it is simply a recommendation to be ratified.[85] Unlike the inherent power to conclude treaties with States and other organisations which places organisations on a par with States in terms of legal powers, the capacity to negotiate and propose conventions does not undermine the sovereign supremacy of States in that before a State can be bound by any such convention, it needs to have ratified it. The State still possesses the ultimate authority over whether to bind itself by a formal treaty commitment.

Although on a formal level, the sovereign capacity of a State to conclude treaties has not been limited by the development of convention-making powers within international organisations,[86] in one or two instances, the practical effect of treaty formation has been to reduce the freedom of States. Although under traditional treaty law, once a State has become a party to a treaty it is legally bound by the provisions of that treaty, the principle of *pacta sunt servanda*,[87] in many cases treaty commitments within multilateral treaties are ignored. A State will become a party to a treaty knowing that without supervision of that treaty by an international organisation or an institution set up under the treaty, its non-compliance is unlikely to be the subject of any collective action or criticism by the other members. Conventions adopted by international organisations are quite often supervised by those organisations or bodies set up under the treaties. When this happens, a State which has ratified the treaty simply for political effect will be collectively criticised by the supervising organisation or organ for non-compliance. This procedure is particularly apparent within the treaties and protocols of human rights adopted by organisations such as the Council of Europe, the United Nations and the Organisation of American States, reviewed more thoroughly in chapter 9.

The treaty-creating powers of the ILO have already been described above. Article 19 of the Constitution of the International Labour Organisation expressly empowers the Conference of the Organisation to adopt conventions by a two-thirds majority of the votes cast by the delegates present. Bearing in mind the fact that the Conference is composed of governmental and non-governmental delegates, it can be seen that the treaties promulgated by the ILO are not the product solely of inter-governmental negotiation. The control of the sovereign State over the negotiation process is undermined in the ILO. Indeed, this caused some States to object to the ILO's first conventions in the early years of that Organisation's existence.[88] However, the express power of the ILO has not been questioned since. Furthermore, Article 19(5) provides that members must not only have to bring the convention before the competent municipal authorities for the enactment of legislation and to have to report on the result, but also according to paragraph (e) if the member does not ratify the convention '... it shall report to the Director General of the International Labour Office, at appropriate intervals as requested by the Governing Body, the position of its law and practice in regard to the matters dealt with in the Convention, showing the extent to which effect has been given ... to any of the provisions of the Convention ... and stating the difficulties which prevent or delay the ratification of such Convention'. In other words a member State which has not ratified a convention, not only has to justify its position, but report on the discrepancies between its practice and the convention, despite the fact that it is not a party. The recalcitrant member State can thus be pushed into ratification. A similar though less onerous clause can be found in the Constitution of the World Health Organisation.[89]

Nevertheless, the capacity of a State to choose whether to ratify a treaty is still intact and in the absence of provisions similar to those found in the ILO Convention, the pressure on States to ratify is likely to be diffuse. This is essentially the defect with the convention-making powers of organisations in that its legislative potential is dashed on the rock of sovereignty. In many ways the organisation is better off formulating recommendations and declarations rather than conventions which often take a long while to enter into force. The 1982 United Nations Law of the Sea Convention[90] which took many years to negotiate and was signed by 159 States only entered into force, in accordance with its provisions, a year after the sixtieth ratification which occurred on 16 November 1993. Professor Schermers points to another problem with the requirement of ratification for treaties in assessing the Council of Europe in 1979:

> Participation in the ... conventions [adopted by the Council of Europe] is so varied that no two States are bound by the same conventions and very few conventions bind the same States. This has made it impossible for the organization to create a consistent body of law. A new rule cannot be based on a former one if they do not concern the same States. There is no "Council of Europe law" in the way that there is a "law of the European Communities". The Council of Europe cannot do more than create separate legal systems for individual conventions, such as the European Convention on Human Rights.[91]

Although the number of ratifications of the various Council of Europe conventions has increased since 1979 so has the number of members and so the problem remains. This situation is exacerbated when the organisation allows non-members to ratify conventions. This may increase the impact of the convention but it results in a series of 'stand alone' conventions, no different from treaties negotiated outside an organisational framework. In many ways, recommendations and declarations, although not binding, either in an institutional sense or under the principle *pacta sunt servanda*, do allow the organisation to build on previous resolutions. Once a coherent and consistent set of recommendations have been built up by an organisation over many years then it is very difficult for individual States to act contrary to their content. Furthermore, if the resolutions are indeed consistent and adopted by large majorities, their contents can pass into customary law very quickly, perhaps more quickly than a treaty might formally enter into force. Certainly many parts of the Law of the Sea Convention were accepted by many States as customary law almost from the outset.[92] In many ways the Law of the Sea Convention, and other widely unratified treaties, can be seen as a recommendation, or more accurately as a set of recommendations, some of which will pass into customary international law, others not.

Concluding remarks

In many ways treaty making by international organisations does not enhance their legislative role in that the organisation is simply facilitating one of the traditional forms of making international law. It could be argued that in the absence of wider binding decision-making powers, international organisations do not in general have the ability to act in a legislative manner. This view undervalues the archetypical resolutions produced by international organisations – recommendations and declarations. A widely supported recommendation or declaration can be seen to be a form of law – 'soft law' perhaps – which act as guides to states' behaviour. They are not binding in a customary sense, although they may eventually pass into customary international law, but they do create a presumption that behaviour contrary to them is *prima facie* unlawful.

To look at it another way, a State which is trying to justify its behaviour on the international stage will point to: treaty provisions, principles of customary international law, and recommendations or declarations of international organisations. The recommendations of certain international organisations such as the ILO, the IAEA, and the WHO as well as the UN General Assembly, are often treated by States as important as traditional sources of international law. Indeed, in certain areas such as health and employment, where there is little customary law, recommendations are seen as important as treaties. It is therefore inappropriate to dismiss the resolutions of organisations as simply a source of State practice when examining customary international law: they can be an independent source of law and to that extent, despite their relatively weak nature, illustrate the law-making capacity of international organisations. In this limited sense, there is a move towards greater governmental activity by organisations along rationalist lines, although, as we shall see in chapter 5, this does not completely fulfil the ideal of the rule of law which not only requires the creation and application of rules, but also legal control of the rule makers as well.

Codification of international norms is one of the important legislative functions of international organisations. However, it is arguable that this process, which does not always question the value of these norms, simply perpetuates the *status quo*. This stagnation of the international legal system can be overcome if organisations adopt resolutions aimed at reforming the more inequitable aspects of international law. This was certainly the revolutionary approach adopted by the Non-Aligned States in the plenary organs of international organisations in the 1960s and 1970s. However, the post-Cold War evidence is that such majorities are conforming more to the accepted norms. Nevertheless, there is also evidence to suggest that this simply does not consolidate the existing system by reinforcing Western dominance, it also has led to the adoption by the Non-Aligned States of certain reforming aspects of Western ideology, such as the 'right' to democracy, which, themselves, appear to deal with injustice. In this way, the agendas of international institutions – the Council of Europe, the OAS and the UN for example – seem to be converging to cover certain common areas beyond the traditional consensus norm governing the non-use of force.

Notes

[1] In this chapter the term 'decisions' is used in two senses: first in a generic sense as the formal output of international organisations, whether in the form of binding resolutions, recommendations, declarations, determinations or conventions; and second in a narrow sense of legally-binding decisions. When using decision in the latter sense, the phrase 'binding decisions' will be used. See H. G. Schermers, *International Institutional Law*, 363, 2nd edn (1980).

[2] F. L. Kirgis, *International Organizations in their Legal Setting*, 274, 2nd edn (1993).

[3] Schermers, *Institutional Law*, 648.

[4] 261 UNTS 140, Article 1.

[5] D. Weigall and P. Stirk (eds), *The Origins and Development of the European Community*, ch. 4 (1992).

[6] *Ibid.*, ch. 5.

[7] 19 UNTS 51, Articles 5 and 6.

[8] Article 27, 119 UNTS 4.

[9] 21 UNTS 77.

[10] 611 UNTS 7.

[11] See Universal Postal Convention and General Regulations of the UPU of 1984, Cmnd 9629.

[12] See also Article 25 of the UPU Constitution.

[13] *Certain Expenses of the United Nations*, ICJ *Rep*. 1962, 151 at 163.

[14] Schermers, *Institutional Law*, 596.

[15] *Ibid.*, 597–8.

[16] Indeed, Article 18(2) mentions 'trusteeship' questions alongside budgetary and membership issues as 'important decisions'. See further *Legal Consequences for States of the Continued Presence of South Africa in Namibia (South West Africa) Notwithstanding Security Council Resolution 276 (1970)*, ICJ *Rep*. 1971, 16 at 49–50.

[17] *Ibid.*, 51.

[18] *Ibid.*, 52–3. See R. Higgins, 'The Advisory Opinion on Namibia: Which UN Resolutions are Binding under Article 25 of the Charter?', 21 *I.C.L.Q.* (1972), 270.

[19] EC Regulation 877/82, *OJ* 1982 L102/1.

[20] Article J.8.2 also states that the 'Council [of Ministers] shall act unanimously, except for procedural questions and in the case referred to in Article J.3(2)'. Article J.3.2 provides that the 'Council shall, when adopting the joint action and at any stage during its development, define those matters on which decisions are to be taken by a qualified majority'.

[21] See Articles 8–130 of the Treaty of Rome, dealing with: the free movement of goods, persons, services and capital; the elimination of customs duties; agriculture; transport; tax-

ation; monetary and economic policy.

[22] See Articles 117–127 of the Treaty of Rome.

[23] See Article K of the Treaty on European Union.

[24] Case 8/55, *Fédération Charbonnière de Belgique* v *High Authority of the European Coal and Steel Community*, [1956] ECR 245 at 258.

[25] The only Organisation which appears to use the term 'recommendation' as a form of binding decision is the European Economic Coal and Steel Community, by Article 14 of its Treaty.

[26] Schermers, *Institutional Law*, 598–9.

[27] For views as to the limited nature of General Assembly recommendations see F. Vallat, 'The General Assembly and the Security Council of the United Nations', 29 *B.Y.B.I.L.* (1952), 96; D.H.N. Johnson, 'The Effect of Resolutions of the General Assembly of the UN', 32 *B.Y.B.I.L.* (1955–6), 97.

[28] R. Higgins, *The Development of International Law Through the Political Organs of the United Nations*, 3 (1963).

[29] C. H. Schreuer, 'Recommendations and the Traditional Sources of International Law', 20 *German Yearbook of International Law* (1977), 103 at 118.

[30] 281 UNTS 369.

[31] 276 UNTS 3.

[32] 729 UNTS 161.

[33] Schermers, *Institutional Law*, 606.

[34] IAEA Press Releases 94/27, 94/45.

[35] 9(2) IAEA Newsbriefs, (1994).

[36] 'Health is a state of complete physical, mental and social well-being and not merely the absence of disease or infirmity'. Preamble, WHO Constitution.

[37] Articles 21 and 22, 14 UNTS 186.

[38] WHO doc. WHA22.46 (1969). 764 UNTS 3.

[39] Recently invoked by the WHO in relation to an outbreak of the bubonic plague in India. See Press Release WHO/71, 28 September 1994.

[40] Kirgis, *International Organizations*, 315.

[41] *Ibid.*, 316. WHO Res. WHA 34.22 (1981).

[42] Kirgis, *International Organizations*, 276.

[43] N. Valticos, 'The International Labour Organization', in S. Schwebel (edn), *The Effectiveness of International Decisions*, 134–5 (1971).

[44] 165 UNTS 303.

[45] ILO Recommendation 90 (1951); 1 *ILO Conventions and Recommendations 1919–1991*, 531.

[46] 34 *ILO Official Bull.* (1951), 274 at 287–8.

[47] Article 19 of the Vienna Convention on the Law of Treaties 1969, 1155 UNTS 331. P. Reuter, *Introduction to the Law of Treaties*, 60–5 (1989).

[48] Schermers, *Institutional Law*, 611.

[49] GA Res. 1721, 16 UN GAOR (1961); GA Res. 1962, 17 UN GAOR (1963). See B. Cheng, 'United Nations Resolutions on Outer Space: Instant Customary International Law?', 5 *I.J.I.L.* (1965), 23.

[50] GA Res. 46/59, 46 UN GAOR (1991).

[51] See also GA 46/182, 46 UN GAOR (1991) on the Strengthening of the Coordination of Humanitarian Emergency Assistance of the United Nations.

[52] OAU doc. AHG/St 2 (4) (1967).

[53] See I. Brownlie, *Principles of Public International Law*, 134–5, 4th edn (1990).

[54] The OAU Assembly discussed the problem of Biafra and condemned secession in any member State and reaffirmed its support for the principle of territorial integrity. It declared the principle of self-determination to be inapplicable. OAU doc. AHG/Res. 51 (4) (1967).

[55] OAS doc. AG/Res. 1080, (21–0/91).

[56] See further J. Casteneda, 'Valeur Juridique des Résolutions des Nations Unies', 129 *Hague Recueil* (1970 I), 207 at 287–301.

[57] See T. M. Franck, *Nation against Nation: What Happened to the U.N. Dream and what the US can do about it*, 205–10 (1985). D. P. Moynihan, *On the Law of Nations*, 162–4 (1990).

[58] GA Res. 46/86, 46 UN GAOR (1991).

[59] H. L. A. Hart, *The Concept of Law*, 56, 91–2, ch.10, 2nd edn (1993).

[60] GA Res. 1131, 11 UN GAOR Supp. (No. 17) 64 (1956). Adopted by 55 votes to 8 with 13 abstentions.

[61] GA 618 mtg, 11 GAOR (1956), para.10, Peru.

[62] For example, GA Res. 3324, 29 UN GAOR Supp. (No. 31) 14 (1974).

[63] GA Res. 2054, 20 UN GAOR Supp. (No. 14) 13 (1965).

[64] SC Res. 418, 32 UN SCOR Resolutions 5 (1977).

[65] GA Res. 48/88, 48 UN GAOR (1993). See also GA Res. 49/10, 49 UN A/PV (1994).

[66] Y. Dinstein, *War, Aggression and Self-Defence*, 125, 2nd edn (1994).

[67] SC Res. 232, 21 UN SCOR Resolutions 7 (1966).

[68] SC Res. 502, 37 UN SCOR Resolutions 15 (1982).

[69] SC Res. 573, 40 UN SCOR Resolutions 23 (1985).

[70] SC Res. 713, 46 UN SCOR Resolutions (1991).

[71] SC Res. 688, 46 UN SCOR Resolutions (1991).

[72] SC Res. 748, 47 UN SCOR Resolutions (1992).

[73] SC Res. 841, 48 UN SCOR Resolutions (1993).

[74] See further chapter 7.

[75] ICJ *Rep*. 1971, 16 at 51–3. See further chapter 5.

[76] SC Res. 217, 216, 20 UN SCOR Resolutions 8 (1965).

[77] SC Res. 541, 38 UN SCOR Resolutions 15 (1983).

[78] SC Res. 662, 45 UN SCOR Resolutions 20 (1990). See also SC Res. 674, 45 UN SCOR Resolutions 25 (1990), which was expressly stated to be adopted under Chapter VII and which, *inter alia*, reminded 'Iraq that under international law it is liable for any loss, damage or injury arising in regard to Kuwait and third States, and their nationals and corporations, as a result of the invasion and illegal occupation of Kuwait by Iraq'.

[79] E. Lauterpacht, *Aspects of the Administration of International Justice*, 37–48 (1991).

[80] Kirgis, *International Organizations*, 436.

[81] *Ibid.*, 431–2. See also Article 11 of the Articles of Agreement of the International Bank for Reconstruction and Development, 1947.

[82] F. Seyersted, *United Nations Forces: In the Law of Peace and War*, 145–7 (1966). But see I. Brownlie, *Principles of Public International Law*, 683–4, 4th edn (1990).

[83] Chapter 12 of the UN Charter and Articles 57 and 63.

[84] Seyersted, *United Nations Forces*, 146.

[85] Schermers, *Institutional Law*, 625.

[86] The same principles of treaty law apply to conventions negotiated within an institutional framework to those negotiated outside it – Article 5 of the Vienna Convention on the Law of Treaties, 1969.

[87] Article 26 of the Vienna Convention on the Law of Treaties, 1969.
[88] Schermers, *Institutional Law*, 624.
[89] Article 20.
[90] 21 *I.L.M.* (1982), 1261.
[91] Schermers, *Institutional Law*, 622–3.
[92] R. V. Churchill and A. V. Lowe, *The Law of the Sea*, 15, 2nd edn (1988).

5

Powers and the legal regulation of international organisations

Many of the theoretical approaches to international organisations identified in chapter 1 concentrate on describing the institutional world order in terms of the power structures prevailing at the time. The positivists in general (with the obvious exception of Kelsen), Marxists and realists all tend to agree on the limited role of law in controlling the activities of organisations given that these bodies are formed on the back of political compromise, although the Soviet Union, in particular was always willing to claim that actions of the UN were beyond the powers of that organisation or *ultra vires*, when the actions in question went against the Soviet interest.[1] The functionalist approach tends to put effectiveness in fulfilling the aim of combatting common problems as the overriding principle whilst seeing excessive legal regulation and the rule of law as inhibiting this. The revolutionary and critical approaches advocate a more flexible, equitable approach to international organisations, which would necessarily remove the certainty required for a rule of law to develop, although the critical approach clearly states that a rule of law does exist in international relations, the trouble being that it is not an objective and neutral rule but one dominated by the ideology of the Western capitalist States. The only approach that posits a rule of law as a positive contribution to world order is that of the rationalist which foresees the development of international organisation towards world government, in which both governed and governors are subject to overriding legal principles; in essence a liberal vision of world society. This chapter is concerned mainly with assessing whether a rule of law exists enabling judicial institutions to control the activities of international organisations.

Or to put it another way, in a world order in which the rule of law is purportedly paramount, there must be a *legal* method of controlling the excesses of institutions. They too must be subject to international law. This chapter will contain an attempt to ascertain the existence of any developed doctrine of *ultra vires* in international law. This will entail looking at the judgments of the World Court in the *Expenses* and the *Lockerbie* cases amongst others, and other judicial institutions such as the European Court of Justice, as well as the writings of jurists, and the practice of international organisations. The hypothesis to be tested is whether there is the rule of law in international relations. An important element of this chapter will be an analysis of the extent of an organisation's powers including the doctrines of implied and inherent powers, the point being that the further an organisation can stretch its powers beyond those expressly granted to it in its constituent treaty, the more difficult it appears to be for international courts to develop a substantive doctrine of *ultra vires*. However, before looking in detail at the doctrines of *ultra vires*, implied and inherent powers, it is necessary to undertake an overview of the role of judicial institutions in the world order.

The role of judicial institutions

A number of organisations have, as one of their organs, a judicial body. For instance the International Court of Justice is listed as one of the 'principal organs of the United Nations' in Article 7(1) of the UN Charter, whilst the European Court of Justice is included in Part Five of the amended Treaty of Rome as one of the primary Community institutions. Others have added judicial bodies to their organisational make-up, but in these cases the judicial body is limited to hearing complaints in certain areas, usually the violation of human rights. For instance the Statute of the Inter-American Court on Human Rights was not adopted by the General Assembly of the Organisation of American States (OAS) until 1979.[2] Its nature and competence was defined in Article 1.

> The Inter-American Court of Human Rights is an autonomous judicial institution whose purpose is the application and interpretation of the American Convention on Human Rights. The Court exercises its functions in accordance with the provisions of the aforementioned Convention and the present Statute.[3]

The purposes of the Court are clearly limited and certainly do not include the possibility of judicial review of OAS actions, only review of the human rights obligations of OAS members. Indeed, only the European Court of Justice is expressly provided with the power of judicial review. The International Court of Justice may have the chance of reviewing the actions of the other organs of the UN in its advisory opinions or if a case is brought before it by a State which raises the issue of UN action. It can be seen from the outset that the possibility of developing international legal principles concerning *ultra vires* remains slight, although the jurisprudence of the European Court of Justice may serve as a model.

Most international judicial bodies are concerned with adjudicating disputes between States, some allow individuals the right of complaint, whilst others have the much more limited function, in international terms, of acting as staff administrative tribunals. Furthermore, some organisations have established quasi-judicial bodies, not empowered to perform full judicial functions of deciding cases according to the principles of international law, but limited to act as mediatory or fact-finding bodies. These different roles of international judicial institutions will be reviewed here before looking at the judicial-review function and the development, if any, of a doctrine of *ultra vires*.

The principal example of an international judicial body empowered to hear disputes between *States* is the International Court of Justice. In many ways the World Court is a very traditional judicial institution being based firmly on the Statute of the Permanent Court of International Justice of the League of Nations.[4] Whereas the founders of the UN greatly enhanced the powers of the 'executive' and 'legislative' organs of the UN (the Security Council and the General Assembly), they failed to give the 'judicial' body, the World Court, any new teeth. Unlike the other organs of the UN, the World Court is simply seen as an unbroken continuation of the League's judicial body.

The State-based nature of the International Court of Justice (ICJ) is emphasised in Article 93 which states that all members of the UN are *ipso facto* parties to the Statute of the ICJ, in addition to non-member States which 'may become ... part[ies] to the Statute ... on conditions to be determined in each case by the General Assembly upon the recommendation of the Security Council'. Switzerland, for instance, although not a member of the UN is a party to the ICJ Statute. The competence of the Court as defined in the Statute of the ICJ makes it clear that 'only States may be parties in cases before the Court'. The lack of any mandatory power to hear cases is emphasised by Article 36 of the Statute which delimits the jurisdiction of the Court. Normally the World Court depends upon the consent of all the State parties to a dispute before it has competence to hear it. This is made clear in Article 36(1) which provides:

> The jurisdiction of the Court comprises all cases which the parties refer to it and all matters specially provided for in the Charter of the United Nations or in treaties and conventions in force.

Consent to jurisdiction must be given by States in advance. The reference to 'all matters specially provided for in' the UN Charter seems to have no effect, certainly none towards creating some sort of compulsory jurisdiction. The Security Council has the power to *recommend* to members that they refer legal disputes to the ICJ.[5] The fact that this recommendatory power cannot compel a State to submit to the jurisdiction of the ICJ was made clear by the ICJ itself in the *Corfu Channel* case, when it rejected by a majority the British argument to the contrary, albeit in an *obiter dictum*.[6] However, there are a number of 'treaties or conventions in force' which contain provisions in them providing for disputes to be referred to the International Court. States which are party to these treaties, therefore, may be brought before the ICJ on the basis of their treaty commitment by another State party, even though they would not wish the case in question to be decided by the ICJ. For instance Article 14(1) of the 1971 Montreal Convention for the Suppression of Unlawful Acts Against the Safety of Civil Aviation[7] provides:

> Any dispute between two or more Contracting States concerning the interpretation or application of this Convention which cannot be settled through negotiation, shall, at the request of one of them, be submitted to arbitration. If within six months of the date of the request for arbitration the Parties are unable to agree on the organization

of the arbitration, any one of those Parties may refer the dispute to the International Court of Justice by request in conformity with the Statute of the Court.

Article 14(1) of the Montreal Convention and Article 36(1) of the Statute of the International Court of Justice formed the basis of Libya's request in 1992 for interim measures in its dispute with the United States and the United Kingdom over attempts to extradite the two Libyan terrorists accused of the Lockerbie bombing of December 1988 (the *Lockerbie* cases). Both the United States and the UK argued, *inter alia*, that the provisional measures requested by Libya should not be granted because the six-month period prescribed by Article 14(1) had not expired and also that Libya had not established that the defendant States had refused to arbitrate.[8] Clearly the United States and the UK, when becoming parties to the Montreal Convention, did not foresee it as being used against them in this way. Their blushes were saved by the Court considering that whatever the situation was before the adoption by the Security Council (on a proposal by Western States) of mandatory resolution 748 of 31 March 1992 (three days after the close of the hearings on the case) which imposed sanctions against Libya unless it handed over the Lockerbie suspects and renounced terrorism, 'the rights claimed by Libya under the Montreal Convention cannot now be regarded as appropriate for protection by the indication of provisional measures'.[9] The Western use of the Security Council, in effect, to block Libya's case before the ICJ, raises question marks about the abuse of power by the Security Council and the inability of the ICJ to control this. This issue will be returned to below.

Article 36 also provides for another source of jurisdiction for the ICJ, the so-called 'optional clause'. Paragraph 2 provides that 'the State parties to the present Statute may at any time declare that they recognise as compulsory *ipso facto* and without special agreement, in relation to any other State accepting the same obligation, the jurisdiction of the Court' in legal disputes. Although over fifty declarations recognising the compulsory jurisdiction of the Court have been made, many are hedged about with conditions and reservations in order to prevent disputes being taken to the ICJ involving the vital interests of a State. In this respect States have reinterpreted Article 36(3), which provides that the declarations under Article 36(2) 'shall be made unconditionally or on condition of reciprocity on the part of several or certain States, or for a certain time'. Although allowing for certain conditions to be attached to the optional clause, Article 36(3) does not expressly allow for reservations to be attached to the clause. The World Court has so far managed to avoid determining the legality of reservations which can, for instance, state that matters within the domestic jurisdiction of the State party as determined by that party are excluded from the jurisdiction of the Court. The optional clause remains of doubtful value.[10]

The World Court is the primary judicial forum for States to resolve their international disputes. International organisations have no *locus standi* before the Court and although, as shall be seen, it may give advisory opinions on questions put to it by UN organs or other authorised international organisations, the opportunities for the Court to review the activities of international organisations are few and far between. As regards its effectiveness as a judicial organ in helping to establish the rule of law amongst States, the World Court's consensual base prevents it from being little more than a standing arbitral body called into action when States feel they can afford that a dispute, often of a minor nature such as a frontier dispute or a maritime delimitation, be settled by judicial means. There is some evidence[11] that the Court is being used more now than during the Cold War but this may be because of the greater number of disputes that have come to a head in the unsettled post-Cold War era. Even its most significant decisions such as the *Nicaragua* case concerning the rules on the indirect use of force[12] have been undermined by non-compliance or even, in that particular case, refusal by the United States to appear despite the fact that the Court found it had jurisdiction.[13] Such actions by one of the most powerful States hardly indicates adherence to the principle of the rule of law.

Other organisations have a judicial organ to which member States can bring complaints, the main example is the European Court of Justice. However, whilst the World Court is a universal judicial body entitled to hear cases not only concerning alleged breaches of the UN Charter, the European Court of Justice is restricted to alleged breaches of the Treaties establishing the European Community or action taken by Community institutions thereunder. Article 164 states that the 'Court of Justice shall ensure that in the interpretation and application of this Treaty the law is observed'. Article 170 of the Treaty of Rome provides that 'a Member State which considers that another Member State has failed to fulfil an obligation under this Treaty ... may bring the matter before the Court of Justice', after consideration by the Commission. Furthermore, by Article 169, the Commission itself can bring a member State before the Court if the member has refused to comply with a Commission opinion that it has failed to fulfil its Treaty obligations. Like the World Court, the European Court of Justice's decisions are binding. However, whereas Article 59 of the Statute of the ICJ provides that 'the decision of the Court has no binding force except between the parties and in respect of that particular case', thereby simply imposing a treaty obligation on States to comply, the European Court of Justice's decisions are binding and enforceable according to Article 171 of the Treaty of Rome as amended by the Maastricht Treaty:

1. If the Court of Justice finds that a Member State has failed to fulfil an obligation under this Treaty, the State shall be required to take the necessary measures to comply with the judgment of the Court of Justice.
2. If the Commission considers that the Member State concerned has not taken such measures it shall, after giving that State the opportunity to submit its observations, issue a reasoned opinion specifying the points on which the Member State concerned has not complied with the judgment of the Court of Justice.

If the Member State concerned fails to take the necessary measures to comply with the Court's judgment within the time-limit laid down by the Commission, the latter may bring the case before the Court of Justice. In so doing it shall specify the amount of lump sum or penalty payment to be paid by the Member State concerned which it considers appropriate in the circumstances.

If the Court of Justice finds that the Member State concerned has not complied with its judgment it may impose a lump sum or penalty payment on it.

The second paragraph of this Article, added by the Maastricht Treaty of 1992, means that not only does the European Court have compulsory jurisdiction over member States, it has the power to enforce its decisions, making it an extremely powerful judicial body unlike the ICJ. Indeed, with the creation of the Court of First Instance by the Single European Act of 1986 to take some of the more mundane workload of the Court of Justice, there emerges:

the conceptual base of a hierarchic Community judicial system at the apex of which sits the Court of Justice. In the future, this base may be enlarged, either by expanding the jurisdiction of the Court of First Instance or by creating other tribunals of specialized jurisdiction.[14]

Equally significantly, the Maastricht Treaty, by enabling the Court to enforce compliance with the European Treaties, is ensuring that the rule of law, in the sense of European regional law, is complied with by member States.

As well as being the judicial adjudicator between State members of the European Community, the European Court of Justice's competence extends to judicial review of Community decisions. Natural or legal persons (*individuals* or companies) have *locus standi*, as well as member States, the Council and Commission, to bring actions for a review of Community Acts according to Article 173 of the Treaty of Rome. This power will be examined in the next section. Individuals can claim damages against the Community in an action before the Court of Justice in two cases. First, according to Article 181, where the Community is in breach of contract, the case may be heard by the European Court if the parties so designate. Second, in the case of non-contractual liability, Article 215 of the Treaty of Rome provides that the Community 'shall ... make good any damage caused by its institutions or by its servants in the performance of their duties'. Article 43 of the Statute of the Court of Justice makes it clear that proceedings for non-contractual liability must be brought within five years 'from the occurrence of the event giving rise thereto'.[15]

Whereas the European Court of Justice allows individuals some limited rights to enforce the *economic* laws of the regional organisations, other organisations allow individuals *locus standi* to enforce *human rights laws*. The Human Rights Committee (HRC) established by the 1966 International Covenant on Civil and Political Rights[16] can hear complaints of alleged violations of individual's human rights committed by the parties to the Convention as long as they are also parties to the First Optional Protocol which allows for individual petitions.[17] Whereas there are over 110 State parties to the Covenant itself there are only just under 70 State parties to the Optional Protocol. The limited *locus standi* given to individuals as compared to States is continued in the protection of human rights in Europe by the 1950 European Convention for the Protection of Human Rights and Fundamental Freedoms.[18] However, declarations under Article 25 of the Convention, which allows for the right of individual petition provided that the State party against which the complaint has been lodged has declared that it recognises the competence of the Court to hear such complaints, have been made by nearly all the State parties to the Convention. The work of the European Court of Human Rights will be reviewed in chapter 9 along with other organisations whose purpose is to secure the protection of human rights.

In addition, certain organisations have created staff administrative tribunals to deal with disputes between the employees of organisations and the organisations themselves. The reasons for this are outlined by Professor Bowett:

> The creation of international civil services, or secretariats, whose members are bound to the organisation by a contractual relationship, made desirable the establishment of special tribunals competent to determine disputes arising from that relationship, once the view was accepted that the members acquired legal rights which ought to be protected by a system of administrative justice, on the continental pattern, and not left to the unfettered discretion of the executive as is largely the practice in the Anglo-American systems.[19]

This final example of the *locus standi* given to *individuals* in certain areas will not be reviewed here. It is sufficient to point to the success of the ILO Administrative Tribunal in this respect; its Statute was amended in 1949 to allow several other organisations, particularly UN specialised agencies, to use it as their administrative tribunal. In addition, one of the reasons for the creation of the Court of First Instance by the Single European Act of 1986 was to take the burden of actions brought by Community employees against Community institutions off the European Court of Justice.[20]

Finally before moving on to look at the central purpose of this chapter, namely that of judicial review of actions of organisations, mention must be made of the fact that many organisations do not have a judicial organ either of general or specific competence, preferring instead to depend on the powers of their political organs. Although the scope for judicial input into organisations has increased over the years with the development in particular of human rights courts, it is true to say that there has not been a dramatic swing towards creating judicial institutions or submitting disputes to legal settlement by existing courts or arbitration procedures. The machinery of the Permanent Court of Arbitration established in 1899[21] has only been used to a limited extent.

One example of an organisation which has failed to make use of judicial techniques is the Organisation of African Unity (OAU). Article 3(3) of the Charter of the OAU provides that the member States agree to the 'peaceful settlement of disputes by negotiation, mediation, conciliation or arbitration'. Unlike the UN, the OAU is a much more loose-knit organisation relying primarily on informal diplomacy and the good offices of the OAU's Secretary General, despite the fact that the OAU Charter deliberately restricts the Secretary General to the role of an administrator.[22] On paper the OAU has, as one of its principal institutions, a Commission of Mediation, Conciliation and Arbitration established by Article 19 of the OAU Charter and in an Additional Protocol of 1964.[23] However, this organ has not become operational, reflecting the unwillingness of African States to submit to formal dispute resolution mechanisms and also the limited budget of the African Organisation. However, in June 1981 the OAU Assembly of Heads of State and Government adopted the African Charter on Human and Peoples' Rights (known as the Banjul Charter),[24] which provides for the creation of the African Commission on Human and Peoples' Rights. Although this quasi-judicial body can receive complaints from both individuals and States (without the need for a separate declaration for individual petitions on the part of State members), 'its powers of implementation and investigation are … weaker' in comparison to the European and inter-American systems.[25] These will receive fuller review in chapter 9.

Judicial review and the doctrine of *ultra vires*

From the brief analysis of the role of judicial institutions above, it can be seen that there is little opportunity for the development of a rule of law amongst member States in many organisations due to the simple fact that very few have developed judicial bodies, and in those organisations that have there may be few opportunities for judicial review of the competence of the organisation itself, bearing in mind that for a rule of law to be established, not only the members of the organisation, but the organisation itself, should be subject to legal principles and norms laid out in the constituent document. As has already been stated, only the UN and the EC have any developed jurisprudence on judicial review, and it will be the purpose here to review the activities and decisions of the International Court of Justice and the European Court of Justice in this respect.

There is no established procedure in the UN Charter or in the Statute of the ICJ for decisions of the organs of the UN to be reviewed by the Court, in contrast to the Community treaties examined below. The International Court may be given an opportunity to comment on the legality of UN resolutions either if so requested, directly or indirectly, in a non-binding, and therefore non-enforceable, advisory opinion in accordance with Article 65 of the ICJ's Statute, or if the matter arises in contentious proceedings between States under Article 36 of the Statute. Article 65 provides that 'the Court may give an advisory opinion on any legal question at the request of whatever body may be authorised by or in accordance with the Charter of the United Nations to make such a request'. All the principal organs of the UN, excluding the Secretariat, have been authorised 'by or in accordance with the Charter' to request advisory opinions as have most of the specialised agencies and a handful of other functional organisations. For instance, the WHO, requested an advisory opinion of great significance from the World Court in May 1993, namely whether the use of nuclear weapons would be a breach of a

State's obligations under international law including the WHO Constitution.[26] However, this mechanism is not used on a regular enough basis, and in particular is not so used to enable the ICJ to review the legality of decisions taken by the UN or other authorised organisations.[27] Furthermore, in the rare instances when the ICJ has the chance to act as a constitutional court, it has usually steered clear of declaring institutional acts as *ultra vires* and therefore illegal. Here, the main instances of this approach will be examined.

In the *Certain Expenses* case, more fully reviewed in the context of implied and inherent powers below, a financial crisis over payment for the UN's peacekeeping operations in the Middle East (UNEF I) and in the Congo (ONUC), led the UN General Assembly to request an advisory opinion from the Court on the question whether these expenditures constituted 'expenses of the Organization' within the meaning of Article 17(2) of the UN Charter. Given that the Assembly had created UNEF I and had taken over the mandating of ONUC when the Security Council was deadlocked, this question raised, in particular, the question of whether the General Assembly was entitled to authorise peacekeeping operations, or whether exclusive competence in the field of peace and security lay with the Security Council. As shall be seen in the remainder of this chapter, the Court did examine the UN Charter in terms of the division of competence between the Security Council and the General Assembly in the field of security, and in many ways the Court provides some clarification as to the powers of those two organs in the field of peacekeeping.

After analysing the structure and powers of the two principal UN organs and finding that the General Assembly was indeed empowered to create and mandate peacekeeping forces, the Court then tested whether the expenditures were compatible with the purposes of the UN. The Court then summarised the broad purposes set out in Article 1 of the Charter and stated:

> These purposes are wide indeed, but neither they nor the powers conferred to effectuate them are unlimited. Save as they have entrusted the Organization with the attainment of these common ends, the Member States retain their freedom of action. But when the Organization takes action which warrants the assertion that it was appropriate for the fulfilment of one of the stated purposes of the United Nations, the presumption is that such action is not *ultra vires* the Organization.

It must be stressed that the Court is prepared only to *presume* that the action is *intra vires* and that it leaves itself the option of being able to declare future actions *ultra vires*, if given the opportunity. The difficulty is that it rarely has the opportunity, hence the presumption. It would make for a totally inefficient security system if every resolution of the Security Council or General Assembly had question marks as to its legality hanging over it. States wanting to deny their obligations to the UN would simply maintain opposition to the resolutions on the basis of their alleged illegality, as France and the Soviet Union had done over the expenses crisis, and very little could be done to prevent this. However, if the decisions are presumed to be lawful until declared otherwise, States are under an undeniable obligation to comply.

The Court's desire to maintain a credible UN collective security system, enabling it to act when faced with international crises, and above all for its actions to be respected, is further heightened by the Court suggesting that even if the action was taken by the wrong organ but was still within the purposes of the UN, then there would still be a presumption that it was a valid action. In effect, each organ of the UN determines its own jurisdiction, and subject to the remote possibility of this being reviewed by the ICJ at a later stage, action taken under that assumed jurisdiction is valid to all intents and purposes. The Court points out that there is no established procedure for judicial review in the structure of the United Nations unlike 'in the legal systems of States' where 'there is often some procedure for determining the legality of ... a legislative or governmental act'. The fact that there is an absence of judicial review procedure in some municipal legal systems with their much more efficient centralised powers, strengthens the contention that it is unnecessarily legalistic and perhaps detrimental to expect such a procedure in an underdeveloped, quasi-centralised, international system. Such a procedure may be put in place once an efficient supranational structure is established as in the European Communities. On occasions, though, in advisory opinions, the Court may have the opportunity to comment on the constitutionality of UN actions.[28] Judge Sir Percy Spender makes this clear in a separate opinion:

> The question of constitutionality of action taken by the General Assembly or the Security Council will rarely call for consideration except within the United Nations itself, where a majority rule prevails. In practice this may enable action to be taken which is beyond power. When, however, the Court is called upon to, pronounce upon a question whether certain authority exercised by an organ of the Organization is within the power of that organ, only legal considerations may be invoked and *de facto* extension of the Charter must be disregarded.[29]

The further organisations move away from unanimity as the voting norm, the greater the chance of the majority pushing the powers of the organisation to the limits of the constitution and beyond.[30] Nevertheless, there has not been a parallel development of a procedure of judicial review, which would enable decisions to be quickly challenged and annulled if necessary, with the exception of the European Court of Justice. The lack of judicial-review mechanisms severely undermines the claim by the rationalists that world society is moving towards greater world government and the rule of law.

It must be stressed, however, that in the *Expenses* case, the World Court was prepared to examine the legality of the General Assembly's action in terms of its competence under the UN Charter; it did not abdicate its responsibility as the judicial organ of the UN in deference to the political power of the Assembly. However, what it did do, as shall be seen below, was to adopt a very liberal attitude to Charter interpretation. In effect the approach was to assert its ability to examine the actions of the Assembly but to do so in a very lenient way with the end result being the General Assembly was found competent. Perhaps this lenient approach is an inevitable consequence of the presumption against *ultra vires*.

A similar attitude can be found in the World Court's judgment in the *Namibia* case, following the Security Council's request for an advisory opinion on the question of the legal consequences for States of the continued presence of South Africa in Namibia notwithstanding the adoption by the Security Council of resolution 276 of 1970. Resolution 276 affirmed the General Assembly's 'decision' to terminate South Africa's mandate over Namibia,[31] and declared that the continued presence of South Africa was illegal and therefore all actions taken by the South African authorities in Namibia were illegal and invalid. It then called on all States to refrain from dealings with the South African government which would be inconsistent with its illegal presence in Namibia. This clearly raised vital constitutional issues, namely the power of the General Assembly to make decisions terminating mandates and the power of the Security Council to adopt a decision on illegality which is binding on member States in the absence of a determination of a threat to the peace or breach of the peace under Chapter VII of the Charter.

The World Court adopted a similar, somewhat contradictory, approach evidenced in the *Expenses* case, in that it stated first that 'a resolution of a properly constituted organ of the United Nations which is passed in accordance with that organ's rules of procedure, and is declared by the President to have been so passed, must be presumed to have been validly adopted'; and further that the Court 'does not possess powers of judicial review or appeal in respect of the decisions taken by the United Nations organs concerned';[32] but at the same time it did review the actions of the two organs and in so doing again adopted a very generous approach to the powers of the UN. As in the *Expenses* case, the opinion seemed to assume that the actions are lawful but proceeded to examine them with a view to justifying that assumption. The Court upheld the power of the General Assembly to terminate South Africa's mandate despite the fact that the Charter does not explicitly grant the Assembly powers to make binding decisions beyond budgetary and membership matters. In addition, the Court found that the Security Council's declaration of illegality and call to States not to have dealing with South Africa was a binding decision under Article 25 notwithstanding the previous understanding that mandatory decisions could only be made under Chapter VII.[33] Again these opinions constitute very liberal interpretations of the Charter, and can be used to support the doctrines of implied, and even inherent, powers examined below.

Judges Gros and Fitzmaurice dissented in the *Namibia* case basically on the grounds that the organs of the UN lacked competence to act in the fashion that they did. Judge Fitzmaurice was at pains to state that the Court could and should have reviewed the actions of, inter alia, the Security Council and declared them *ultra vires* when he stated that:

> limitations on the powers of the Security Council are necessary because of the all too great ease with which any acutely controversial international situation can be repre-

sented as involving a latent threat to peace and security, even where it is really too remote genuinely to constitute one. Without these limitations, the functions of the Security Council could be used for purposes never originally intended ...

Furthermore, he made it clear that he would be prepared to examine Security Council determinations of a 'threat to the peace' or 'breach of the peace' under Article 39 (although none were made in the case) to see if they were genuine for there was a very great danger of the Council 'artificially creat[ing a threat] as a pretext for the realisation of ulterior purposes'.[34] He was prepared to look behind the wordings of UN resolutions at the motives of those voting for them whilst the majority appeared to accept the resolutions at their face value.[35] Only the two dissenting judges would have been prepared to determine whether there really existed a 'threat to the peace', and if none existed, they would have been prepared to declare the resolution *ultra vires*.

The very issue of the Court being prepared to exercise true review powers to see if there really was an abuse of power by the Security Council in determining that there existed a 'threat to the peace' arose in the *Lockerbie* cases of 1992. The cases arose out of the bomb explosion on board Pan Am flight 103 which caused the death of all those on board over Lockerbie in Scotland on 21 December 1988. Two Libyan nationals and State employees were indicted in the United States and charged in Scotland for planting the bomb. In a joint declaration on 27 November 1991, the United States and Britain requested that Libya surrender the suspects for trial.[36] Lack of a satisfactory response to this led to the two Western countries proposing what was to become resolution 731 of 21 January 1992, which urged Libya 'immediately to provide a full and effective response to those requests so as to contribute to the elimination of international terrorism'. This resolution did not appear to be mandatory, it certainly was not adopted under Chapter VII, but during the debates leading to its adoption, both Western States mentioned the adoption of further resolutions imposing sanctions if Libya failed to comply.[37]

It was this threat which led to Libya instituting proceedings before the ICJ on the basis of Article 14(1) of the 1971 Montreal Convention, alleging that the United States and Britain had breached the 1971 Convention relying, *inter alia*, on Article 5(2) which obliges State parties to either try an alleged terrorist in their jurisdiction or extradite them to a State willing to exercise such jurisdiction. Libya asserted that it had submitted the case to the relevant Libyan authorities for the purpose of prosecution. Libya requested that the Court grant provisional measures enjoining the United States and the United Kingdom from taking action to compel or coerce Libya into surrendering the accused and to ensure that no steps be taken that would prejudice Libya's rights pending the outcome of the case.[38]

The Court heard the request for provisional[39] measures between 26 to 28 March. On 31 March 1992 the Security Council determined that 'the failure by the Libyan Government to demonstrate by concrete actions its renunciation of terrorism and in particular its continued failure to respond fully and effectively to the requests in resolution 731 (1992) constitute a threat to international peace and security', and acting under Chapter VII of the Charter, decided that Libya must comply with the extradition requests and renounce all forms of terrorism by 15 April 1992 or suffer sanctions. The Court delivered its opinion denying interim measures on 14 April and sanctions were imposed the next day.

The decision of the Court denying Libya's request for provisional measures was extremely short and lacked any real explanation.

> Whereas both Libya and the United States, as Members of the United Nations, are obliged to accept and carry out the decisions of the Security Council in accordance with Article 25 of the Charter; whereas the Court, which is at the stage of proceedings on provisional measures, considers that prima facie this obligation extends to the decision contained in resolution 748 (1992); and whereas, in accordance with Article 103 of the Charter, the obligations of the parties in that respect prevail over their obligations under any other international agreement, including the Montreal Convention.[40]

Decisions of the Security Council under Chapter VII appear to be in general beyond the purview of any review by the Court, at least at the provisional measures stage, because they are binding obligations which prevail over any other treaty commitment. The Court is certainly not willing to look behind the motives of the sponsors of resolution 748 in order to determine whether there really existed a threat to the peace from an incident that has occurred over three years previously.[41] This still leaves open three possibilities for review. First, that review is possible at the merits stage. Second, review is possible in the case of resolutions under Chapter VI. Third, review is possible in the case of binding Chapter VII resolutions which conflict with customary international law, particularly peremptory norms of international law from which there is no derogation – *jus cogens*.

The latter was raised in the 1993 application by the Bosnian government for provisional measures in order to halt the acts of genocide allegedly being committed by Serbia and Montenegro. The Bosnian government argued that the Security Council's mandatory arms embargo against the whole of Yugoslavia imposed in resolution 713 of 1991, after the Council had determined that the situation in the former Yugoslavia constituted a threat to the peace, prevented it from defending itself from the commission of these acts of genocide.[42] Only *ad hoc* Judge Lauterpacht thought that, although the Court had no power to review Council determinations of threats to the peace, since there was a conflict between members obligations under Article 25 of the Charter and a norm of *jus cogens* (that prohibiting genocide), the latter obligations prevailed and that resolution 713, being contrary to an established rule of *jus cogens*, might be legally null and void.[43]

The Court, in the *Lockerbie* cases, seemed to rule out review of Security Council resolutions, either under Chapter VI or VII, at the merits stage.

> Whereas the Court, while thus not at this stage called upon to determine definitely the legal effects of Security Council resolution 748 (1992), considers that, whatever the situation previous to the adoption of that resolution, the rights claimed by Libya under the Montreal Convention cannot now be regarded as appropriate for protection by the indication of provisional measures.[44]

123

It appears that the Court would not be prepared to examine the legality of Security Council resolutions, in terms of their constitutionality, only to determine the 'legal effects' of the resolution. Presumably this would mean a further consideration of whether a mandatory Council resolution prevails over Libya's rights under the Montreal Convention. Presumably the answer again would be based on Articles 25 and 103, although the Court may support its decision at the merits stage (if the case goes that far) by more elaborate reasoning. It would not entail an examination of the crucial determination by the Security Council that there was a threat to the peace, or the motives of those sponsoring or voting for the resolution. It may be argued that this still leaves room for judicial review,[45] but it appears to be a very restricted and unlikely option.

The separate and dissenting judgments in the *Lockerbie* cases again provide more fertile ground for those seeking some sign of judicial willingness to question the activities of the Security Council. Judge Lachs refers to the Court as 'the guardian of legality for the international community as a whole, both within and without the United Nations',[46] though this is certainly not precise enough to be interpreted as promising judicial review in the future. Judge Shahabuddeen simply asks a series of questions on this issue:

> ... whether a decision of the Security Council may override the legal rights of States, and if so, whether there are any limitations on the power of the Council to characterize a situation as one justifying the making of a decision entailing such consequences? Are there any limits to the Council's powers of appreciation? In the equilibrium of forces underpinning the structure of the United Nations within the evolving international order, is there any conceivable point beyond which a legal issue may properly arise as to the competence of the Security Council to produce such overriding results? If there are any limits, what are those limits and what body, if other than the Security Council, is competent to say what those limits are?[47]

Although seeing these as important issues to be discussed the judge is unsure as to how far the Court can enter into the debate. Judge Bedjaoui, on the other hand, appears adamant that the Court should be able to review the acts of the Security Council, not simply to determine their legal effects, but to assess their very legal core, namely their compatibility with the UN Charter. Referring to Article 24 of the Charter, which by reference to Article 1(1), provides that the Security Council must take measures 'in conformity with principles of justice and international law', he cites Judge Fitzmaurice in the *Namibia* case to the effect that the Security Council is as much a subject of international law as any member State, although he also seemed to recognise that generally the Court should not be used as a Court of Appeal from Security Council decisions, unless the Security Council was attempting to subvert the integrity of the Court. Further he seemed to accept the presumption that Security Council resolutions were valid unless the resolution was an attempt to deprive the Court of its jurisdiction.[48] Judge Weeramantry agreed that the Court was not vested with 'review or appellate jurisdiction', but when issues involving the interpretation of the Charter come before the

Court it 'acts as guardian of the Charter and international law for, in the international arena, there is no higher body charged with judicial functions and the determination of questions of interpretation and application of international law'. However, this guardianship does not go to questioning the discretion of the Security Council under Article 39 of the Charter to determine that a 'threat to the peace' exists.[49]

As with its previous decisions there appears to be an undercurrent in the Court in favour of seizing the rare opportunities for enhancing review of the legality of UN actions, but on balance this is a minority view, and in many respects those judges advocating it do not present very coherent or logical arguments in trying to balance assertions of the Court's 'guardianship' of the Charter against respect for the Security Council's freedom to act in the field of peace and security. Very few judges are prepared to question the competence of the Security Council in the area which has most impact on States, namely determinations under Article 39 which may lead to enforcement action under Chapter VII. Without that power, the ICJ cannot be seen as a constitutional court.

The timidity of the World Court judges to develop a power of judicial review, albeit from the scraps provided by the UN system, is to be contrasted with the judicial creativity of the European Court of Justice in the area of judicial review, albeit from a greater treaty base. While the Treaty of Rome empowers the European Court to exercise judicial review in several articles, the Court has seized on these provisions to develop impressive credentials as a constitutional court. The purpose here is not to fully review the activities of the European Court in this area for its jurisprudence is vast and the subject of many separate studies,[50] it is simply to give a flavour of its powers to enable the reader to contrast them with those of the World Court.

The main provisions giving the European Court of Justice powers of judicial review are Articles 173 and 175 of the amended Treaty of Rome.[51] Article 173 provides:

> The Court of Justice shall review the legality of acts adopted jointly by the European Parliament and the Council, of acts of the Council, of the Commission, and the ECB [European Central Bank] other than recommendations and opinions, and of acts of the European Parliament intended to produce legal effects vis-à-vis third parties.
>
> It shall for this purpose have jurisdiction in actions brought by a Member State, the Council or the Commission on grounds of lack of competence, infringement of an essential procedural requirement, infringement of this Treaty or of any rule of law relating to its application, or misuse of powers.
>
> The Court shall have jurisdiction under the same conditions in actions brought by the European Parliament and by the ECB for the purpose of protecting their prerogatives.
>
> Any natural or legal person may, under the same conditions, institute proceedings against a decision addressed to that person or against a decision which, although in the form of a regulation or a decision addressed to another person, is of direct and individual concern to the former.

The proceedings provided for in this Article shall be instituted within two months of the publication of the measure, or of its notification to the plaintiff, or, in the absence thereof, of the day on which it came to the knowledge of the latter, as the case may be.

The last paragraph is to ensure that Community legislation does not remain for a long period of time with question marks over it as to its constitutionality. Article 174 provides that if the Court finds that the action under Article 173 is well founded, it 'shall declare the act concerned to be void'. Article 175 deals with the case where the institutions of the Community have failed to act and thereby have breached of the Treaty, allowing member State and other institutions to bring an action after first calling on the institution concerned to carry out its obligations. Individuals and companies have *locus standi* on the same basis as Article 173. If the Court of Justice finds that the institution, by its inaction, has failed to comply with a treaty obligation, the 'institutions shall be required to take necessary measures to comply with the judgment of the Court of Justice'.

In a brief review such as this, it is only possible to give some examples of how the European Court of Justice has interpreted and developed these provisions. Indeed, before the Maastricht Treaty of 1992 amended the Treaty of Rome, Article 173(1) simply stated that 'the Court of Justice shall, review the legality of acts of the Council and the Commission other than recommendations or opinions', there being no explicit provisions for review of acts of the European Parliament. The Court remedied this defect in 1986 in the case, *Partie Écologiste 'Les Verts'* v *European Parliament*. In this case the European Parliament had allocated funds to the political parties for an information campaign leading to the direct elections to the Parliament in 1984. The French Green Party complained that by only allocating a small portion of the budget to new parties putting up candidates for the first time, the Parliament was discriminating in favour of established parties. The Court held that the Greens could bring proceedings against the Parliament under Article 173 as it then was. The Court made a statement which illustrates clearly its role as a constitutional court prepared to review actions of all the Community institutions:

... the European Economic Community is a Community based on the rule of law, inasmuch as neither its Member States not its institutions can avoid a review of the question whether the measures adopted by them are in conformity with the basic constitutional charter, the Treaty.[52]

The spirit of the Treaty, as embodied in particular in Article 164, was used by the Court to assert its right of judicial review of measures adopted by any Community institution which were intended to have legal effects. Parliament was not mentioned in the original text because it initially only had powers of consultation rather than substantive powers to adopt binding measures. The fact was that Parliament's powers had been extended so that it was possible for Parliament to exceed them. To remedy this an action of annulment must be available under Article 173. Indeed, in the case the Court did annul the measures adopted by the European Parliament. The Court's approach has, as can be seen in the up-to-date version of the Treaty, been taken into account.

Another example of the Court's liberal approach[53] to its review brief is its approach to what acts it is entitled to review. Article 189 lists the acts of the Council and Commission as regulations, directives, decisions, recommendations or opinions. The European Court has been willing to look at measures which have not carried the labels of the first three.[54]

The four grounds for annulment laid out in Article 173(2) have also been liberally interpreted by the European Court. The first two, lack of competence and infringement of an essential procedural requirement, roughly correspond to the English-law concepts of substantive and procedural *ultra vires*, although the approach of the European Court has been more 'interventionist' than the English courts in applying them.[55] On the third ground of annulment, treaty infringements or infringements of any rule of law relating to the application of the relevant treaty, the Court has interpreted the concept of any 'rule of law' very widely to include all legislation made by Community institutions pursuant to the Treaty, and general principles as are recognised in international law, and, borrowing from Article 215 on the non-contractual liability of the Community, 'general principles common to the laws of the Member States'.[56] This approach brings the European Community within the wider ambit of international law, so that the rule of law in the Organisation is not simply based on European law, but international law and the general principles of law found in the Members' legal systems. On the fourth ground for annulment, misuse of powers, the Court has found that 'the term includes not only the use of power for an unlawful purpose but also its use for a purpose, itself lawful, but not the one contemplated in conferring the power in question'.[57]

Although it is impossible here to give a full picture of the powers of judicial review of the European Court, it is sufficient to quote the following statement by President Ole Due,

> It is possible to conclude ... that the Court of Justice has found ways and means for filling the gaps in the judicial system of the Treaty text so as to provide full judicial protection of Member States, Community institutions and individuals against encroachment upon their rights and to offer opportunities for the Court to decide on practically any issue of a constitutional character which may arise in a Community context. Without any doubt, the Court exercises the functions of a Constitutional Court for the Communities.[58]

Although the European Court does not have any jurisdiction over the second and third pillars of the Maastricht Treaty (CFSP, justice and home affairs), its extensive competence over the EC, ECSC and Euratom (the Communities), demonstrates the vast gap in the development of the power of judicial review and the establishment of the rule of law between the European Court and the International Court of Justice. Rationalists may point to the European system as an indicator of how international organisations may progress towards government and the rule of law amongst States, but unless the International Court and other international judicial institutions follow its lead and seize opportunities to assert the supremacy of law over the actions of organisations, then the rationalists proposition will remain just an ideal. Furthermore, State members of international organisations must create more opportunities for judicial review, either by creating courts where none exist, or by enhancing the powers of those already established. However, this must be done in such a way as not to inhibit the effectiveness of the organisation in attempting to achieve the purposes for which it was established. In many ways, it appears that before a developed system of judicial review can be established within the UN and other organisations, those organisations must first develop governmental powers – become supranational organisations – so that they are able to achieve their aims more effectively. As we have seen, most organisations have not developed to this extent. It may be argued that to insist on a layer of judicial control over such bodies may have the effect of severely hindering their development, although the following sections show that the adoption of an inherent powers approach to organisations offsets this. In the case of the UN, the Security Council is showing elements of supranationalism in its use of binding powers under Chapter VII – the time may come when this is exercised so extensively that the UN members decide that a system of judicial review is necessary. Such a system cannot be developed out of the Statute of the ICJ but must be clearly established, taking account of the need for speedy and clear review, as an amendment to the Charter and Statute.

Implied powers

An international organisation has to respond to events to be able to fulfil its functions effectively. Even the most prescient founders of an organisation established in 1945 or 1985 cannot have foreseen the developments that have occurred since the establishment of the institution. To restrict organisations to the express provisions of their constituent treaties would therefore consign many organisations to playing a peripheral role in world affairs, although, exceptionally, Article 1 of the OAS Charter does explicitly limit the powers of the Organisation to those expressly conferred. Most organisations have a degree of autonomy as seen in chapter 2, and this means that they have a certain flexibility in interpreting their powers as contained in their constituent documents. However, the greater that flexibility is deemed to be, the more difficult it becomes to determine whether an action of an international organisation is *ultra vires* or not. In the World Court decisions looked at above and reassessed below, it will be seen that the presumption against *ultra vires*, and the wide doctrine of implied powers, are two sides of the same coin. Indeed, it can be argued that the concept of objective international personality necessarily results in a wide view of implied powers, or rather inherent powers, and a presumption against *ultra vires*.

The problem facing international lawyers is how far have organisations progressed in divorcing their activities from the institution's treaty base, and more importantly, whether this has been accepted in the law of international organisations. It appears to be accepted in the practice of international organisations, the decisions of judicial institutions, and the comments of international jurists, that there is an accepted doctrine of implied powers in international law. Early in the life of the United Nations, the World Court accepted such a doctrine in the *Reparation* case when it stated:

> The Court must therefore begin by inquiring whether the provisions of the Charter concerning the functions of the Organization, and the part played by its agents in the performance of those functions, imply for the Organization power to afford its agents the limited protection that would consist in the bringing of a claim on their behalf for reparation for damage suffered in such circumstances. Under international law, the Organization must be deemed to have those powers which, though not expressly provided in the Charter, are conferred upon it by necessary implication as being essential to the performance of its duties.[59]

The Court deemed that it was necessary for the UN to be able to bring a claim on behalf of its employees, though it did not state from which express (sometimes called 'delegated') power this implied power derived. It appeared to be derived more from the general nature and purposes of the UN as a body aimed at securing international peace and security, an aim requiring the extensive use of personnel in dangerous situations.[60] Judge Hackworth, in his dissenting opinion, pointed to the problem with the Court's approach:

> There can be no gainsaying the fact that the Organization is one of delegated and enumerated powers. It is to be presumed that such powers as the Member States desired to confer upon it are stated either in the Charter or in complementary agreements concluded by them. Powers not expressed cannot freely be implied. Implied powers flow from a grant of expressed powers, and are limited to those that are 'necessary' to the exercise of powers expressly granted. No necessity for the exercise of power here in question has been shown to exist. There is no impelling reason, if any at all, why the Organization should become the sponsor of claims on behalf of its employees.[61]

The difference in the approach of the majority and Judge Hackworth embodies the doctrinal confusion of what exactly is meant by implied powers. While accepting the Court's opinion in the *Reparation* case, Professor Schermers, on the one hand, seemingly ties implied powers to express powers by stating that 'many powers can only be exercised on the basis that other powers exist', while on the other hand he states that implied powers can be derived from the general principles and purposes of the Organisation as found in the opening Article of an organisation's constitution.[62] Formally speaking, the general purposes of the organisation are not realistically the powers of the organisation – these are to be found in the detailed body of the treaty defining the composition and powers of the various organs. However, Professor Schermers's dilemma seems to encapsulate the debate as to the extent of the doctrine of implied powers.

Professor Bowett, on the other hand, clearly opts for the wider approach while advising caution so that

> great care is taken to restrict implied powers to those which may reasonably be deduced from the purposes and functions of the organisation in question. Therefore the test is a functional one; reference [should be made] to the functions and powers of the organisation exercised on the international plane ... [63]

This seems to be the approach inevitably adopted by organisations in interpreting their treaties, but the wider the purposes of the organisation are, the greater the competence of the organisation to rely on implied powers. One exception to this appears to be the European Community, due mainly to the fact that the Treaty envisages the need for extra powers not expressly provided for. Article 235 provides:

> If action by the Community should prove necessary to attain, in the course of the operation of the common market, one of the objectives of the Community and this Treaty has not provided the necessary powers, the Council shall, acting unanimously on a proposal from the Commission and after consulting the European Parliament, take the appropriate measures.

This 'residual legislative power', combined with the greater use (as compared to other organisations) made by the European Community of its power to amend its treaties,[64] has 'possibly limited the development in Community law of the doctrine of *implied powers* ... Despite the generally expansive interpretation of the Treaty by the ECJ it is only in one field – that of external relations – that the doctrine of implied powers per se has been employed extensively'.[65]

The International Court of Justice has adopted a very generous view of the doctrine of implied powers, not only in the *Reparation* case but in the *Expenses* and *Namibia* cases mentioned above. In the latter case, the International Court found that the General Assembly's termination of South Africa's mandate was within its competence. It pointed to no specific Charter provisions but made the more general proposition that 'the United Nations as a successor to the League, acting through its competent organs, must be seen above all as the supervisory institution, competent to pronounce, in that capacity, on the conduct of the mandatory with respect to its international obligation, and competent to act accordingly'. The action of the Assembly in terminating the mandate was viewed by the Court 'as the exercise of the right to terminate a relationship in the case of a deliberate and persistent violation of obligations which destroys the very object and purpose of that relationship', in accordance with the general principles of international law governing termination of a treaty relationship for breach.[66]

As to the legal basis of Security Council resolution 276, the Court stated that:

> Article 24 of the Charter vests in the Security Council the necessary authority to take action such as that taken in the present case. The reference in paragraph 2 of this Article to specific powers of the Security Council under certain chapters of the Charter does not exclude the existence of general powers to discharge the responsibilities

conferred in paragraph 1. Reference may be made in this respect to the Secretary General's Statement, presented to the Security Council on 10 January 1947, to the effect that 'the powers of the Council under Article 24 are not restricted to the specific grants of authority contained in Chapters VI, VII, VIII and XII ... [T]he Members of the United Nations have conferred upon the Security Council powers commensurate with its responsibility for the maintenance of peace and security. The only limitations are the fundamental principles and purposes found in Chapter I of the Charter'.[67]

The Court's approach is liberal and functionalist 'so that powers *relating* to the purposes and functions specified in the constitution can be implied', rather than narrow and formalist whereby 'one can imply only such powers as arise by necessary intendment from the constitutional provisions'.[68]

Such a liberal approach is exemplified in the *Expenses* case when the Court did not stop to consider whether the development of a power to create and mandate peacekeeping forces by the General Assembly was *necessary* for the fulfilment of the express provisions of the Charter.[69] On the issue of the General Assembly's power, the Court stated that 'the provisions of the Charter which distribute functions and powers to the Security Council and to the General Assembly give no support to the view that such distribution excludes from the powers of the General Assembly the power' to adopt measures designed to maintain peace and security. The emphasis is not on the implication of powers necessary to make an express provision effective as in the *Reparation* case, but on the absence of any provision in the Charter prohibiting the exercise of such a power. The only limitation on the powers of the General Assembly in the field of peace and security is that, according to the Court, only the Security Council can 'order coercive action'.[70] In effect, the General Assembly's powers are only limited by provisions in the Charter which clearly prohibit such acts, in the case the restriction was that only the Security Council could order enforcement action under Chapter VII. Furthermore, in discussing the creation of the Congo force (ONUC) by the Security Council, the Court did not feel it necessary to identify the provisions of the Charter from which peacekeeping could be derived, it simply stated that 'the Charter does not forbid the Security Council to act through instruments of its own choice', and that ONUC was not a 'preventive or enforcement' action under Chapter VII and therefore did not come within the sole ambit of the Security Council but could be mandated by the General Assembly.[71]

Inherent powers

The Court certainly seemed to accept the British view on the creation of UNEF, contained in a Minister's response in the House of Commons to the question of which article of the Charter had the Force been created under, in terms of it not being created under any express provisions, but under a resolution of the General Assembly which was not prohibited by the Charter. The narrow view of the

Soviet Union that the only express mention made of the creation of any type of armed forces in the Charter was in Chapter VII, where only the Security Council was authorised to act, was rejected.[72] With the emphasis on UN organs having the power to undertake any action within the UN's purposes as long as the Charter does not expressly prohibit it, the Court, in many ways, seemed to have moved away from the doctrine of implied powers to that of inherent powers as argued for by Professor Seyersted.

> Indeed, it appears that while intergovernmental organizations, unlike States, are restricted by specific provisions in their constitutions as to the aims for which they shall work, such Organizations are, like States, in principle free to perform any sovereign act, or any act under international law, which they are in a factual position to perform to attain these aims, provided that their constitutions do not preclude such acts. While a minority of the members will always have the right to challenge the legality, from an internal point of view, of acts performed to attain aims other than those defined in the constitution, the minority cannot challenge acts performed in order to attain aims covered in the constitution merely on the basis that such acts were not 'essential' or 'necessary' to attain these aims. Thus it is not necessary to look for specific provisions in the constitution, or to resort to strained interpretations of texts and intentions, or to look for precedents or constructions to justify legally the performance by an intergovernmental organization of a sovereign or international act not specifically authorized in its constitution. As an intergovernmental organization it has an *inherent power* to perform such acts.[73]

Seyersted's view is very powerful and seems to be supported by the ICJ's approach, particularly in the *Expenses* case, where the Court seemingly accepted his view, as we have seen above, that action taken by the wrong organ within an organisation would not necessarily invalidate the act in relation to third parties. Seyersted's view of personality and powers is that international organisations, whatever their capacities or aims, whether large and powerful or small and weak, are like States in that they are full subjects of international law. It follows from this that 'they have an inherent capacity (not implied in any particular articles of their constitution) to perform any sovereign or international act which they are in a practical position to perform and which is not precluded by any provisions of their constitution. Their position thus differs from states in fact rather than in law'.[74]

Seyersted's view is certainly to be preferred to that of Professor Rama-Montaldo who draws an unworkable distinction between those non-expressed powers inherent in international personality of an organisation such as treaty-making powers, and those non-expressed powers which must be implied by necessary implication from the provisions of the constitution of an organisation, such as peacekeeping. Member States cannot object to inherent rights, which are not subject to the criterion of necessity, but can to alleged implied rights if the latter cannot be deemed to be necessary for the fulfilment of the provisions of the treaty.[75] Although he argues that the World Court in the *Reparation* and *Expenses* cases adopted this approach, he admits that powers can be implied not only to effect express provisions but also the wider functions of the organisation.[76] Although there may be technical merit in this approach, the end result is little different from Professor Seyersted's who argues that the objective international personality of organisations, which includes the inherent right to enter into treaties, also includes in law all the inherent rights of an international actor, the only limitation being the purposes and functions[77] of the organisation and the express limitations in the treaty. The difference is essentially as to the scope of personality. Rama-Montaldo starts from the proposition that the personality of organisations is much less than that of States but their rights can be added to by a wide approach to implied powers, whilst Seyersted starts from the position that the personality of organisations is the same as that of States, but that its inherent rights are limited by the provisions of the constitution. Both approaches in the end fall back on the purposes and functions of the organisation to ascertain the practical extent of the organisation's rights. It is submitted that Seyersted' approach is the one adopted by the World Court and international organisations as well as being the most workable.[78]

Seyersted's approach certainly seems to have been the norm in the practice of organisations as we shall see in chapters 7 to 10. Furthermore it has two clear advantages over the doctrine of implied powers. First, it satisfies the functionalist agenda by allowing an organisation to fulfil its aims and not be hidebound by the legal niceties of its individual, and often obscurely drafted compromise provisions; and second, it enables courts and commentators to review the actions of the organisations quickly and accurately since there are only two real legal controls on the actions of the organisation – that the action in question aims to achieve one of the purposes of the organisation, and that it is not expressly prohibited by any of the provisions of the constitution. Only if either of these legal thresholds is crossed can an international court, jurist or member State, claim that the action is *ultra vires*.

Concluding remarks

Although there has been a significant growth in human rights tribunals, it is true to say that the exponential growth in international organisations, both in terms of numbers and competence, has not been matched by a corresponding growth in judicial institutions. From the rationalist perspective, a lack of judicial input undermines a legal system, though a functionalist would applaud it on the grounds that excessive legalism stultifies an effective organisational order. However, the functionalist argument is rebutted by the European Court which plays a central role in a dynamic regional organisation, though it does not have jurisdiction over all aspects of EU activity.

It may be that a legal and political system only acquires developed judicial organs when government institutions have emerged. Judicial tribunals, upholding the rule of law by the application of neutral rules and by the development of the power of judicial review, appear to be in the distant future for international society, which still relies on political organs with quasi-judicial competence as well as community reaction as evidenced in international organisations. As yet, this 'inefficiency', in a Hartian sense, has not been remedied except in the case of the European Court. The inability and unwillingness of the World Court to develop a power of judicial review can partly be explained by a realistic lack of desire to limit the growth of the UN at the promising stage of development. A critical approach, however, would point to the naturally conservative approach of a court, relying on past practice and decisions, which simply reinforces the *status quo*, by, in this case, repeating the presumption against *ultra vires* and the lack of review powers.

In fact there is little difficulty in identifying a doctrine of *ultra vires* which still allows organisations to treat their constitutions as living documents capable of growth and expansion. The practice of organisations examined in chapters 7 to 10, as well as the decisions of the World Court reviewed here, indicate that although the justificatory terminology employed is usually one of 'implied powers', the reality is one of 'inherent powers'; so that the tests for whether an organisation's action is lawful are: whether it fulfils the purposes of the constituent treaty; and whether it is not prohibited by the treaty. It may be that because the powers of the UN are so wide and the provisions of the Charter so ambiguous that the World Court has developed the presumption against *ultra vires*. However, a clearly unconstitutional act under either of the two tests would have to be declared unlawful.

The doctrine of inherent powers allows for significant institutional growth without the need to go through cumbersome amendment machinery. It does not mean, however, that the rule of law, in terms of legal control of the organisation, has to be abandoned in that there is still an identifiable content to the doctrine of *ultra vires*. Nevertheless, without significant judicial practice, the doctrine remains theoretical rather than a practical limitation upon the activities of organisations, with the exception of the European Communities.

Notes

[1] See USSR's objection to the UN General Assembly's Uniting for Peace resolution of 1950, GA 301 mtg, 5 UN GAOR para. 138 (1950).

[2] 19 *I.L.M.* (1980), 1458.

[3] The American Convention on Human Rights (pact of San José) was adopted in 1969, 1144 UNTS 123. It is only open to OAS members.

[4] Article 92 of the UN Charter.

[5] Article 36(3) of the UN Charter.

[6] *Corfu Channel Case*, I.C.J. *Rep.* 1947–8, 15 at 31–2.

[7] 10 UKTS (1974), Cmnd 5524.

[8] *Case Concerning Questions of Interpretation and Application of the 1971 Montreal Convention Arising from the Aerial Incident at Lockerbie* (referred to as the *Lockerbie* case), *Libya* v *US*, I.C.J. *Rep.* 1992, 114 at 122.

[9] *Ibid.*, 126–7.

[10] J. G. Merrills, *International Dispute Settlement*, 111, 2nd edn (1991).

[11] K. Highet, 'The Peace Palace Heats Up: The World Court in Business Again?', 18 *Commonwealth Law Bulletin* (1992), 755.

[12] *Case Concerning Military and Paramilitary Activities in and Against Nicaragua (Nicaragua* v *US)*, I.C.J. *Rep.* 1986, 14.

[13] *Case Concerning Military and Paramilitary Activities in and Against Nicaragua (Nicaragua* v *US). Jurisdiction of the Court and Admissibility of the Application*, I.C.J. *Rep.* 1984, 392.

[14] G. Vandersanden, 'A Desired Birth: The Court of First Instance of the European Communities', 21 *Georgia Journal of International and Comparative Law* (1991), 51 at 61.

[15] For judicial discussion of Article 215 see for instance Case 90/78, *Granaria* v *Council and Commission* [1979] ECR 1081; Cases 116 and 124/77, *Amylum* v *Council and Commission* [1979] ECR 3497.

[16] 999 UNTS 171.

[17] 999 UNTS 302.

[18] 213 UNTS 221.

[19] D. W. Bowett, *The Law of International Institutions*, 317, 4th edn (1982).

[20] Vandersanden, 21 *Georgia Journal of International Law and Politics* (1991), 56.

[21] By the Hague Convention, 187 CTS 410. See also the Hague Convention of 1907, 54 LNTS 435.

[22] 479 UNTS 39, Articles 16–18.

[23] 3 *I.L.M.* (1964), 1116. For discussion see T. Maluwa, 'The Peaceful Settlement of Disputes among African States, 1963–1983: Some Conceptual Issues and Practical Trends' 38 *I.C.L.Q.* (1989), 299.

[24] 21 *I.L.M.* (1982), 59.

[25] G. J. Naldi, *The Organization of African Unity*, 131 (1989).

[26] WHA Res. 46/40 (1993), joined by the UN General Assembly's request in UN GA Res. 49/75K, 49 UN A/PV (1994).

[27] Some organisations give a right of appeal to the ICJ from decisions of their organs. Article 84 of the Chicago Convention on Civil Aviation, 1944 provides for disputes on interpretation or application of the Convention or its Annexes to be decided by the Council subject to appeal either to an *ad hoc* arbitral tribunal or to the ICJ. India instituted an appeal against ICAO Council decisions in respect of its dispute with Pakistan in 1971. The Court considered that the Council had jurisdiction to make its decisions and rejected India's appeal. See *Appeal Relating to the Jurisdiction of the ICAO Council*, I.C.J. *Rep.* 1972, 46.

[28] *Certain Expenses of the United Nations*, I.C.J. *Rep.* 1962, 151 at 168. See further E. Osieke, 'The Legal Validity of *ultra vires* Decisions of International Organisations', 77 *A.J.I.L.* (1983), 239 at 255, who argues that *ultra vires* acts are not void *ab initio* but voidable (i.e. valid until declared unlawful).

[29] *Ibid.*, 197. See also dissenting opinion of Judge Bustamente, 304; and dissenting opinion of Judge Morelli, 217.

[30] Schermers, *Institutional Law*, 324.

[31] GA Res. 2145, 21 UN GAOR Supp. (No. 16) (1966).

[32] *Legal Consequences for States of the Continued Presence of South Africa in Namibia (South West Africa) Notwithstanding Security Council Resolution 276 (1970)*, I.C.J. *Rep.* 1971, 16 at 21–2, 45. See further M. Bedjaoui, *The New World Order and the Security*

Council: Testing the Legality of its Acts, 24–5 (1994).

[33] *Ibid.*, 51–3.

[34] *Ibid.*, 294.

[35] G. P. McGinley, 'The ICJ's Decisions in the Lockerbie Cases', 22 *Georgia Journal of International and Comparative Law* (1992), 577 at 598.

[36] *Lockerbie* case, *Libya* v *UK*, I.C.J. *Rep.* 1992, 3 at 11.

[37] SC 3033 mtg, 47 UN SCOR (1992).

[38] *Lockerbie* case, *Libya* v *UK*, I.C.J. *Rep.* 5–7.

[39] See Article 41 of the ICJ Statute.

[40] *Lockerbie* case, *Libya* v *US*, I.C.J. *Rep.* 1992, 114 at 126.

[41] See dissenting opinion of Judge Bedjaoui, *ibid.*, 153.

[42] *Application of the Convention on the Prevention and Punishment of the Crime of Genocide, Provisional Measures, Order of 13 September 1993*, I.C.J. *Rep.* 1993, 325 at 332.

[43] *Ibid.*, 439–42.

[44] *Lockerbie* case, *Libya* v *US*, 126–7.

[45] T. M. Franck, 'The "Powers of Appreciation": Who is the Ultimate Guardian of UN Legality?', 86 *A.J.I.L.* (1992) 519. For further discussion see: B. Graefrath, 'Leave to the Court What Belongs to the Court: The Libyan Case', 4 *European Journal of International Law* (1993), 184; E. McWhinney, 'The International Court as Emerging Constitutional Court and the Co-ordinate UN Institutions (Especially the Security Council): Implications of the Aerial Incident at Lockerbie;, 30 *Canadian Yearbook of International Law* (1992), 261; M. W. Reisman, 'The Constitutional Crisis in the United Nations', 87 *American Journal of International Law* (1993), 83; G. Watson, 'Constitutionalism, Judicial Review, and the World Court', 34 *Harvard International Law Journal* (1993), 1.

[46] *Lockerbie* case, *Libya* v *US*, I.C.J. *Rep.* 1992, 138 (separate opinion).

[47] *Ibid.*, 142 (separate opinion).

[48] *Ibid.*, 143 (dissenting opinion).

[49] *Ibid.*, 165–6, 176 (dissenting opinion). Judge Oda based his separate opinion on the fact that the Court could not challenge the Council's competence to determine a 'threat to the peace' and take action under Chapter VII, *ibid.*, 129.

[50] See for instance L. N. Brown and T. Kennedy, *The Court of Justice of the European Communities*, ch.7, 4th edn (1989).

[51] See also Articles 177, 184, 228(6). The other treaties of the Communities, the ECSC and Euratom, also provide for judicial review.

[52] Case 190/84, [1986] ECR 1017 at 1339.

[53] But see the Court's somewhat restrictive approach to the *locus standi* of individuals and companies. Brown and Kennedy, *The Court of Justice*, 133–6.

[54] See for example: Cases 8–11/66, *Noordwijks Cement Accord*, [1967] ECR 75; Case 22/70, *Commission* v *Council* [1971] ECR 263.

[55] D. Freestone and J. S. Davidson, *The Institutional Framework of the European Communities*, 143–4 (1988). Case 9/56, *Meroni* v *High Authority* [1958] ECR 133; Case 24/62, *Germany* v *Commission* [1963] ECR 63; Case 138/79, *Roquette Frères* v *Council* [1980] ECR 3333; Case 139/79, *Maizena GmbH* v *Council* [1980] ECR 3393.

[56] Brown and Kennedy, *The Court of Justice*, 146. 'There is no theoretical limit to the general principles'. The ECJ has used concepts of due process, good faith, fairness, *audi alterem partem*, non-discrimination and even 'fundamental human rights enshrined in the general principles of Community law and protected by the Court' even though the Treaty

contained no provisions relating to human rights – Freestone and Davidson, Institutional Framework 146–7. Case 29/69, *Stauder* v *City of Ulm* [1969] ECR 419.

[57] Brown and Kennedy, *The Court of Justice*, 120–1.

[58] O. Due, 'A Constitutional Court for the European Communities', in T. F. O'Higgins and D. O'Keefe (eds), *Constitutional Adjudication in European Community and National Law*, 8 (1992).

[59] I.C.J. *Rep.* 1949, 182. See also the advisory opinion *Effect of Awards of Compensation made by the UN Administrative Tribunal*, I.C.J. *Rep.* 1954, 4.

[60] But see M. Rama-Montaldo, 'International Legal Personality and the Implied Powers of International Organizations', 44 *B.Y.B.I.L.* (1970), 111 at 130–1, where he makes the tenuous distinction between non-expressed rights derived from the international personality of an organization and non-expressed rights which can only be inferred from the purposes and functions of each organization. In the *Reparation* case he sees the Court drawing this distinction 'between the right to present an international claim and the right to assert certain rights by means of an international claim. The former arises from legal personality. The latter is related to functions and implied powers'. He does not state from which express provisions the latter right is derived.

[61] I.C.J. *Rep.* 1949, 198.

[62] Schermers, *Institutional Law*, 208–11.

[63] Bowett, *International Institutions*, 337.

[64] See Article 236 of the Treaty of Rome as repealed by Article N on the Treaty on European Union (the Maastricht Treaty).

[65] Freestone and Davidson, *Institutional Framework*, 71. But see Schermers, *Institutional Law*, 209. Case 8/55, *Fédération Charbonnière de Belgique* v *High Authority* [1956] ECR 245 at 292.

[66] I.C.J. *Rep.* 1971, 46–7, 49–50.

[67] *Ibid.*, 52.

[68] Bowett, *International Institutions*, 337–8.

[69] *Ibid.*, 338.

[70] I.C.J. *Rep.* 1962, 163–4.

[71] *Ibid.*, 177.

[72] F. Seyersted, *United Nations Forces*, 133–4 (1966).

[73] *Ibid.*, 155.

[74] Bowett, *International Institutions*, 338.

[75] Rama-Montaldo, 44 *B.Y.B.I.L.* (1970), 143, 154.

[76] *Ibid.*, 122.

[77] But see Rama-Montaldo's attempt to limit implied powers to the concept of functional necessity rather than to the purposes of the organisation, 44 *B.Y.B.I.L.* (1970), 152–5. See also P. H. F. Bekker, *The Legal Position of Intergovernmental Organizations*, 69, 76–7, 82–4.

[78] But see Rama-Montaldo's critique of Seyersted, 44 *B.Y.B.I.L.* (1970), 118–22.

6

Universalism, regionalism and decentralisation

This chapter will contain an analysis of the structure of international organisations and the relationship between them. This will entail looking at organisations of general competence, primarily the League of Nations and the United Nations in terms of powers, practice and effectiveness. The basic theme will be an assessment of whether the international legal and political order has been best served by universal organisations. The examination will include a comparison between the League and the UN to see if the drafters of the Charter made sufficient improvements for the world's second attempt at universalism. The chapter will also contain an overview of organisations of regional competence, not simply to describe them briefly but to assess whether regionalism is the more productive method of improving and developing the international legal order. This will entail an assessment of whether any such development has occurred as well as a comparison between universalism and regionalism. Furthermore, an assessment will be made of the impact on world order of organisations set up to deal with particular issues or problems. Decentralisation will be discussed as a concept in general terms and will be accompanied by only brief illustrations of organisations and bodies of limited competence.

Universalism

The significance of universal organisations, namely those institutions open to all States, is summarised by Professor Schermers in his seminal work on international institutions:

> If public international organizations are seen as the first step in creating an administration above the level of the national State, universal organizations are the beginnings of world government. In that respect their position will become stronger, the closer they come to universality. Rules made by a really universal organization would be rules of world law. By marshalling more States the organization obtains a greater control over dissident Members of the world community. Participation on a world scale would minimize the opportunity for non-Members to band together to thwart the purpose of the organization.[1]

The rationalists would argue that such aims are achievable by universal organisations of general competence, in other words those institutions which have general competence over global affairs whether they be economic, social or security. World government could only be achieved if these functions were brought under one authority, albeit with delegation to subsidiary bodies. In this section the two main examples of this type of organisation – the universal and general – will be examined. However, it must not be forgotten that many functional organisations dealing with specific problems are open to all States and are in that sense universal. Indeed, the functionalist would argue that world order is best achieved by such organisations, although they do admit that such a system may evolve to the extent that such organisations are brought under the umbrella of a world authority. The extent to which functional organisations, and regional organisations are subordinate to the current world Organisation, the United Nations, will be the subject of later sections in this chapter.

An examination of global organisations of general competence must commence with an account of the League of Nations. The significance of the League has been clearly stated by F. P. Walters:

> Although the League's span of life was short and troubled, its success transitory, and its end inglorious, it must always hold a place of supreme importance in history. It was the first effective move towards the organization of a world-wide political and social order, in which the common interests of humanity could be seen as served across the barriers of national tradition, racial difference, or geographical separation.[2]

In order to analyse the contribution of the League to world order it is necessary to examine the main areas of operation, namely security, disarmament and economic and social affairs,[3] not only in terms of powers and structure but also, apart from collective security which will be dealt with in chapter 7, briefly in terms of practice and effectiveness. A comparative analysis of each area with the powers and practice of the United Nations will be undertaken.

Collective security

The League's failures in the related areas of collective security and disarmament inevitably led to its demise. The principal organ of the League, the Council, consisting of permanent[4] and non-permanent members, was vested with an array of powers designed to achieve international peace and security. The Covenant contained a *partial* prohibition on the right to resort to war and a *quasi*-centralisation of coercion. These two factors undermined the League's effectiveness along with the absence of many key countries, particularly the United States, and the requirement for unanimity in Article 5 of the Covenant.

By Article 10 of the Covenant, members of the League undertook 'to respect and preserve as against external aggression the territorial integrity and existing political independence of all Members of the League'. When combined with the obligations in the Preamble 'not to resort to war', this provision could have been construed as a total prohibition on war. Indeed, Article 11(1) seemed to complement a ban on war by supporting the idea of collective security in stating that 'any war or threat of war ... is hereby declared a matter of concern to the whole League, and the League shall take any action that may be deemed wise and effectual to safeguard the peace of nations'.

Unfortunately, subsequent provisions effectively undermined any purported ban on war by allowing for the lawful resort to war in certain circumstances. Article 12(1) obliged members to submit their disputes to arbitration or to the Council and not 'to resort to war until three months after the award by the arbitrators or the report by the Council'. Article 13(4) obliged Members to carry out arbitral awards and not to 'resort to war against a Member of the League which complies with' such an award. Article 15 obliged States to submit all disputes to the Council which by paragraph 4 was empowered to make recommendations for the settlement of the dispute. Article 15(6) then stated that '... the Members of the League agree that they will not go to war with any party to the dispute which complies with the recommendations of the [Council's] report'. However, if this report was not unanimous then Article 15(7) reserved the right of member States 'to take such action as they consider necessary for the maintenance of right and justice'.

Hence Articles 12, 13 and 15 preserved the rights of States to go to war, all that was imposed were certain procedural requirements. The obligation in Article 10 not to resort to aggression, albeit ambiguous in itself, was undermined. This was reinforced by Article 16(1) which stated that 'should any Member of the League resort to war in disregard of its covenants under Articles 12, 13 or 15, it shall *ipso facto* be deemed to have committed an act of war against all the other Members of the League...'. No mention was made of the breach of the obligation contained in Article 10. Article 16(1) went on to oblige member States to sever 'all trade or financial relations' with the transgressor State. It is noticeable that the Council itself is not empowered to 'decide' to impose sanctions against the aggressor State, in other words there is no co-ordination and control of the sanctions regimes. Furthermore, Article 16(2) stated that 'it shall be the duty of the Council in such case to recommend ... what effective military, naval or air force the Members of the League shall severally contribute to the armed forces to be used to protect the Covenant of the League'. Military coercion is not centralised under the Covenant in that member States are under no obligations either to undertake military action against an aggressor or to contribute forces to the League.

The demise of the League and the creation of its successor, the United Nations,[5] gave the world's leaders a second chance to create an organisation to maintain international peace and security. The UN Charter appeared to remedy the defects of the Covenant, namely partial prohibition of war, quasi-centralisation of coercion, and the requirement of unanimity. In addition the United Nations' membership has grown to include most of the world's States and all the world's major powers.

The 'primary responsibility' for the maintenance of international peace and security[6] lies with the Security Council. This was originally composed of eleven members, but in 1966 this was increased to fifteen to reflect the increase in membership of the UN. There are five permanent members, the United States, the United Kingdom, France, China (the People's Republic since 1971), and from 1992, Russia, as successor to the Soviet Union. The requirement of unanimity found in the League's Covenant is not to be found in the UN Charter. Instead, Article 27 states that procedural matters, such as adopting items for the agenda,[7] shall be decided by 'an affirmative vote of nine members', while substantive matters shall be decided by 'an affirmative vote of nine members including the concurring votes of the permanent members; provided that, in decisions under Chapter VI, and under [Article 52(3)], a party to a dispute shall abstain from voting'. While not requiring unanimity for the whole of the Council, there has to be unanimity among the permanent members which reduces the chances of the Council acting to maintain international peace and security. (The development and use of the veto has been examined in chapter 3.)

Article 2(4) of the UN Charter states:

> All Members shall refrain in their international relations from the threat or use of force against the territorial integrity or political independence of any State, or in any other manner inconsistent with the Purposes of the United Nations.

The only exceptions admitted to this prohibition, not simply on war but on any threat or use of force, are a narrowly defined right of self-defence in response to an 'armed attack' contained in Article 51, and the Security Council deciding to use armed force against a transgressor under Article 42. Furthermore, unlike the Covenant of the League of Nations, the United Nations Charter does not tie together its prohibition on war or the use of force with the effective functioning of its collective machinery for the settlement of disputes. Unlike Article 10 of the Covenant, Article 2(4) of the Charter is entirely divorced from the provisions of Chapters VI and VII which endow the Security Council with its powers. Indeed, it could be stated that Article 2(4) has become in effect a *conditio sina qua non* for the effective maintenance of peace by the United Nations, in complete contrast to the League system, where the effective functioning of the machinery for the settlement of disputes was a precondition for the prohibition of war.[8]

The final improvement on the defects of the Covenant can be found in Chapter VII of the UN Charter which provides for a much more centralised system of enforcement to enable the Council to deal with disputes or situations which constitute a 'threat to the peace', 'breach of the peace', or 'act of aggression', within the meaning of Article 39. Article 41 does not simply oblige members to impose sanctions against transgressors, but empowers the Council to impose mandatory economic sanctions against a State by a binding decision within the terms of Article 25 of the UN Charter. It is the Council which imposes the obligation and supervises compliance with it, it is not simply a treaty obligation with no supervision or control. The centralisation of sanctions is accompanied by the even more ambitious provisions of the Charter which provide for the centralisation of military coercion, by in effect, creating a UN army which the Council may decide to use against transgressing States. Article 42 provides that the Council 'may take such action by air, sea, or land forces as may be necessary to maintain or restore international peace and security'. By the provisions of Article 43, members are obliged to negotiate agreements to provide armed forces to be made available to the Security Council. The direction and control of the armed forces does not lie with the contributing States, but with the Military Staff Committee of the Council and the Security Council itself, according to Articles 46 and 47. These provisions represent a much higher degree of centralisation than that found in Article 16 of the Leagues' Covenant which was based entirely on voluntary contributions. The question whether the UN has developed these radical provisions in practice will be reviewed in chapter 7. Suffice it to say for the moment that the drafters of the UN Charter certainly appeared to have remedied many of the defects of the Covenant.

Disarmament

For any system of collective security to work, there must be some degree of central control over the level of armaments in the world. Unfortunately neither the League nor the UN has developed any such capability. In many ways the UN Charter is *less* fulsome in its coverage of disarmament than its predecessor. Article 8 of the Covenant stated that 'the Members of the League recognise that the maintenance of peace requires the reduction of national armaments to the lowest point consistent with national safety and the enforcement by common action of international obligations'. The provision goes on to condemn the 'manufacture by private enterprise' of arms and its 'evil effects', and obliges the Council to formulate plans for the reduction of each Members' level of armaments.

Despite the impressive-sounding nature of this provision, and the establishment of subsidiary bodies such as the Temporary Mixed Commission for the Reduction of Armaments and a Disarmament Conference, the League's attempts to reduce the level of armaments completely failed simply because national interests prevailed.[9]

> Generally, the League failed to secure any meaningful arms control because of basic disagreement amongst the great powers: Germany demanded arms equality, France demanded security through arms superiority over Germany, and Britain called for direct and general reductions in armaments of all states. The United States created further difficulty by actively supporting a direct and universal arms reduction while refusing to join in any security guarantee system that many states regarded as a *sine qua non* to arms control. Discussions also broke down over specifics involving the composition, nature, size and types of forces to be reduced and the means of inspection and enforcement, the very same kinds of question that have also stymied UN disarmament efforts ...[10]

The UN Charter also obliges the Security Council to formulate plans for the reduction in armaments 'in order to promote the establishment and maintenance of international peace and security with the least diversion for armaments of the world's human and economic resources'. In fact the General Assembly has taken on the responsibilities of the United Nations in the field of disarmament, for the Security Council has abstained in general from exercising its competence as regards disarmament given to it under Article 26, although it has made a recent specific exception for Iraq in 1991. Article 11(1) of the Charter empowers the Assembly to 'consider the general principles of co-operation in the maintenance of international peace and security, including the principles governing disarmament and the regulation of armaments, and may make recommendations with regard to such principles to the Members or to the Security Council or to both'.

In practice the Assembly has elevated disarmament from the relatively low-key treatment given to it under the Charter, to it being one of the most important areas of UN work. The work on disarmament is not only done in the regular and special sessions of the Assembly, but also by bodies set up or brought under the auspices of the United Nations, for example the Disarmament Commission and the Conference on Disarmament.

The Assembly has interpreted its powers under Article 11(1) widely to go beyond the recommendation of mere principles to resolutions establishing bodies to study the problem and to provide the machinery for the negotiation of disarmament. Indeed, it was remarkable that during the period of over forty years of superpower arms build-up in the Cold War, the discussions and agreements on disarmament, either inside or outside the United Nations, continued. To this extent the General Assembly proved an effective organ, not for achieving disarmament, but for maintaining a dialogue over levels and regulation of armament particularly in the period of *détente* in the 1970s.[11]

However, the next decade saw the return of the Cold War, which meant that disarmament talks, once again, were dominated by the spirit of confrontation.[12] The Twelfth and Fifteenth Special Sessions on disarmament in 1982 and 1988 produced no new concrete proposals or recommendations. Again we saw the schism in the Assembly which so often put the Western States in the minority, a trend that seems to have continued with the end of the Cold War, although often the division is on the most contentious issue of nuclear weapons, between those nuclear States unwilling to make concessions on the one hand, and those that say they are, and the vast majority of non-nuclear States, on the other.[13]

The Assembly has certainly expressed support for the several bilateral agreements between the superpowers for nuclear weapons reduction, for instance the Treaty on the Elimination of Intermediate Range and Shorter Range Missiles of 1987,[14] but it has also recently made several encouraging, if small, initiatives in the area of disarmament. One small step was taken at the Assembly's 46th session in 1991 when it adopted a resolution without a vote on the issue of conventional arms. The resolution was inspired by the realisation that the end of the Cold War was not going to lead to a reduction in local or regional conflicts. The resolution invited member States to provide the Secretary General with annual reports from 1 January 1992, on their conventional arms inventories and the export or import of battle tanks, armoured combat vehicles, large-calibre artillery systems, combat aircraft, attack helicopters, warships and missiles, as well as calling on steps to eradicate the illicit trade in all kinds of weapons.[15] The Secretary General's first report on the item of 'transparency of arms' showed that many States were willing to provide this data.[16] Such information is essential in order to prevent another arms race where secrecy over military expenditure and capability results in States arming themselves to a higher level than is necessary for defensive purposes simply because they have little idea of their potential enemy's level of armaments.

Further UN progress in disarmament was in evidence in 1992 when the Assembly welcomed the Convention on the Prohibition of the Development, Production, Stockpiling and Use of Chemical Weapons and on their Destruction, negotiated in the forum of the Disarmament Conference.[17] When the Convention comes into force it will establish an International Organisation for the Prohibition of Chemical Weapons, with powers to inspect State parties' compliance with the terms of the Treaty, without giving much prior notice.[18]

From these recent developments, one can see the Assembly, whilst not moving entirely away from rhetorical confrontation between non-nuclear and nuclear States in the area of nuclear weapons, is moving positively towards arms control in the area of conventional weapons, although the voluntary register is only a small step; and is moving even further in the area of chemical weapons, not only by sponsoring a Convention, but also by insisting on enforcement mechanisms within a treaty system.[19] Such steps must be contrasted with the League's abject failure despite the greater emphasis given to disarmament in the Covenant.

Economic and social matters

It is in the area of co-operation in economic and social matters that the League made the most impact. From the rather modest provisions of the Covenant,[20] a host of institutions were established to deal with common problems. For the first time, international society tackled a whole range of issues such as slavery, drugs trafficking, refugees, labour conditions, health regulations, navigation aids, communications and many others, all 'necessary ... in the complex life of a modern world'.[21] The leading institutions included the Economic and Financial Organisation which mainly compiled studies and gave advice to governments on economic matters. This represented a great leap forward in information available, although its advice was often ignored by countries wanting to make short-term gains. The Communications and Transit Organisation went further and drafted several treaties, for instance in 1923 it concluded a treaty on the International Regime of Maritime Ports[22] and another on the International Regime on Railways.[23] The Health Organisation also successfully drafted conventions aimed at controlling communicable diseases and improving public health. Again its creation and success were evidence of the fact that such problems could not be dealt with by States' acting alone. Many of these institutions and the other League bodies such as the Refugee Organisation, and the massively successful ILO, were continued in UN bodies such as the Economic and Social Council (ECOSOC) – examined next – and specialised agencies examined in later sections and elsewhere.

The UN Charter of 1945 put more emphasis on international Economic and Social Co-operation in Chapter IX. Article 55 of which reads:

> With a view to the creation of conditions of stability and well-being which are nec-essary for peaceful and friendly relations among nations based on respect for the principle of equal rights and self-determination of peoples, the United Nations shall promote:
>
> (a) higher standards of living, full employment, and conditions of economic and social progress and development;
> (b) solutions of international economic, social, health and related problems; and international cultural and educational co-operation; and
> (c) universal respect for, and observance of, human rights and fundamental freedoms for all without distinction as to race, sex, language, or religion.

Article 56 pledges all members 'to take joint and separate action in co-operation with the Organization for the achievement of the purposes set forth in Article 55'. Article 57 provides that the various inter-governmental organisations set up to deal with 'economic, social, cultural, educational, health and related fields', the 'specialized agencies', shall be brought into a relationship with the UN through agreements with ECOSOC examined below. Articles 58 and 59 of the UN Char-ter empower the UN to recommend methods of co-ordinating the specialised agencies as well as initiating negotiations for the establishment of any new spe-cialised agencies required to fulfil any of the purposes enumerated in Article 55. Article 60 provides that responsibility for the discharge of the functions of the UN under Chapter IX of the Charter shall be placed on the General Assembly, and 'under the authority of the General Assembly', ECOSOC. The existence of a sep-arate organ to deal with economic and social matters was an improvement on the League and represented, at least on paper, a greater degree of centralisation and co-ordination in this area.

ECOSOC consists of 54 members of the UN elected by the General Assem-bly.[24] The aim is to ensure representation of a broad cross-section of economic and social interests, though in practice this has neither prevented the five permanent members of the Security Council from always being elected, nor, more generally, has it stopped ECOSOC from being 'dominated by the richer states'.[25] ECOSOC decisions are adopted on a simple-majority vote.[26] ECOSOC has a variety of func-tions and powers: it can initiate 'studies and reports with respect to international economic, social, cultural, educational, health and related matters'; it can make recommendations on such matters to the General Assembly, to member States and to the specialised agencies; it can also make recommendations 'for the pur-pose of promoting respect for, and observance of, human rights'; it can also prepare draft conventions and call international conferences.[27] Further, according to Article 63, ECOSOC may enter into agreements with the specialised agencies, and is empowered with the task of co-ordinating the activities of those agencies (this will be looked at in a later section). As well as furnishing information to the Security Council and performing such functions as requested by the General Assembly of the UN, ECOSOC 'may, with the approval of the General Assembly, perform services at the request of Members of the United Nations and at the request of the specialized agencies'.[28]

The ill-defined role of ECOSOC, particularly as regards the specialised agencies, has led, as we shall see, to an ominous lack of central co-ordination between ECOSOC and the specialised agencies. 'The system lacked any central brain, and remained very weak in its co-ordination mechanism ... the immediate reason for this was that the United Nations system was pluralistic; its decentralized character allowed the member states to avoid the problems which would arise if the instruments of collectivity were to be strengthened'.[29] The problem of decentralisation was compounded by the splintering of the effort towards a common goal on development due to the fact that developing States, dissatisfied with the domination of the world's financial and economic organisations by the developed States, and using the powers of ECOSOC to call for conferences and to perform services, used their voting power in the UN General Assembly in 1962,[30] to establish the United Nations Conference on Trade and Development (UNCTAD) as a subsidiary organ of the Assembly under Article 22 of the Charter rather than a specialised agency.[31] 'UNCTAD's activities spanned the spectrum of concerns of [the] developing countries': international commodity trade, market access for exports of developing countries, international monetary and financial reform and institutional change. By 1979, UNCTAD had effectively adopted the agenda of the New International Economic Order, meant to redress the North–South imbalance, which had been put forward by the General Assembly of the UN in 1974.[32] Furthermore, various funds, set up by ECOSOC to assist developing countries, were brought together by the Assembly in 1965, in line with the Jackson report,[33] to form the UN Development Programme (UNDP),[34] the aim of which was 'to co-ordinate the activities of the older institutions with regard to the development of the Third World'.[35]

With the development of UNCTAD and UNDP, any semblance of central control by ECOSOC was lost. Although, as shall be seen in a later section, ECOSOC has 'failed ... to co-ordinate the activities of the specialised agencies',[36] those agencies are at least required to report to ECOSOC under the terms of Article 64 of the UN Charter. In effect UNDP and UNCTAD have become 'major rivals of ECOSOC as candidates for the role of policy maker and co-ordinator of the system'.[37] A report by the UN's Joint Inspection Unit in 1985 contained a scathing attack on the system, condemning: the lack of an integrated or even co-ordinated approach despite constant repetition to the contrary by the General Assembly; 'inadequate analysis of the role assigned to the United Nations system in the general scheme of technical assistance requirements of the various countries'; 'absence of a unified concept of development'; 'lack of satisfactory machinery at the centre of local levels to ensure the preliminary work of co-ordination of contribution of the various agencies'; 'the vagueness of the terms of reference' of the various organisations and bodies concerned with the area, in particular the 'similarity of jurisdiction between organs as important as the Economic and Social Council, UNCTAD, the Second and Third Committees of the General Assembly' which 'have created in the United Nations system a state of confusion'.[38] The further lack of co-ordination with other international economic institutions such as the World Bank and the IMF has led to overlap, inefficiency and fragmentation of the system. Reform has been limited and further diffusion of control continues with Conferences of the Environment in 1992 and on World Population in 1994.[39]

As primary organ responsible for development matters, the UN General Assembly has attempted to address the problems of the UN system. Recently it has recognised that the system is inefficient and in many ways fails the developing countries. Its first real attempt to reorganise the system occurred in 1977,[40] but 'governmental and bureaucratic inertia ... prevented ECOSOC from revitalising itself'.[41] In 1989, in examining the operational activities of the UN system in the field of development, the Assembly stated the fundamental characteristics of the system to be:

> their universality, voluntary and grant nature, neutrality and multilateralism, and ability to respond to the needs of the developing countries in a flexible manner, and that the operational activities of the United Nations system are carried out for the benefit of the developing countries, at the request of those countries and in accordance with their own policies and priorities for development.

In several ways these aims are incompatible and have led to the confusion and failure of the system. The voluntary nature of funding for the various funds and programmes[42] has led richer States to donate less than is necessary for an effective system, a fact recognised by the same resolution when it urged:

> developed countries, in particular those countries whose overall performance is not commensurate with their capacity, taking into account established official development assistance targets, and present levels of contributions to substantially increase their development assistance, including contributions to operational activities of the UN system.

Putting emphasis on the development plans of the recipient government de-emphasised the need for a more objective assessment by the UN, and encouragement of multilateralism undermined the need for a more co-ordinated UN effort. The resolution itself seems to put primary emphasis on UNDP 'as the central funding mechanism for the United Nations system of technical co-operation, the full potential of which has not yet been realised', and yet ECOSOC is the organ to oversee implementation of proposed reforms. Furthermore, the Assembly calls for a further decentralisation of the system by moving manpower and activities away from the headquarters of the various agencies to the individual activities and countries. Although clearly put forward as a method of making better use of the limited resources, the emphasis on decentralisation undermines the stated need of 'all organs and organizations of the [UN] system' to achieve 'greater integration in programme and project formulation and implementation of technical co-operation among developing countries'.[43]

Later resolutions of the Assembly make it clear that the aim is to decentralise the activities of the various agencies in this area, to remove bureaucracy and to make more efficient use of limited resources by emphasising a more co-ordinated response, in the form of 'resident co-ordinators', in the particular country concerned rather than co-ordination at a more remote level at UN headquarters.[44] The creation of field offices in certain countries in 1993 was further aimed at enhancing the activities of the UN at country level.[45] Co-ordination of aid and activities at the individual country level may well improve the system in the short term and reflect the philosophy of decentralisation prevalent in the donor States, but overall and long-term improvement of the system requires a rationalisation of the Funds and Programmes at the UN level. The call for reform along decentralised lines has continued in resolutions from ECOSOC.[46]

In many ways, although there are far greater resources put into economic and social matters, the UN system has not progressed, in terms of greater effectiveness and co-ordination, from its solid base in the League of Nations, where 'the tendency ... had been to centralise its functional agencies'.[47] With the current emphasis on decentralisation due to financial constraints the system will probably continue to fragment and fail developing countries.

Decentralisation: the UN specialised agencies

The founders of the UN were faced with a choice between a rationalist conception of world organisation, with 'one central organization embracing all activities',[48] or a functional conception with specialised agencies dealing with problems of common concern. Although the functional approach was clearly favoured, the founders still created a central political organisation, the United Nations, not simply to deal with peace and security (in the shape of the Security Council), but also to become involved in the areas covered by the specialised agencies (via the General Assembly and ECOSOC). The legal relationship between the UN and the specialised agencies will be examined in the next section. The relative failure of the system can possibly be put down to the fact that the founders should have either opted for complete functional decentralisation, or complete central control.[49] The unhappy halfway house adopted in the UN Charter has meant that attempts at reform have either been to increase central co-ordination or to decentralise further – the end result has been to create further confusion. Furthermore, the evidence is that the political atmosphere of the General Assembly and ECOSOC has spread to some of the specialised agencies, undermining their ability to deal, as they were intended, with serious global problems in a practical and non-political way.

In November 1975, the then US Secretary of State, Dr Kissinger, gave notice that the US intended to withdraw from the ILO, a threat which was carried out two years later. In his letter to the Director General of the ILO, Dr Kissinger stated that one of the reasons for withdrawing from the Organisation was 'the increasing politicization of the Organization'.

> In [the early 1970s] the ILO has become increasingly and excessively involved in political issues which are quite beyond the competence and mandate of the organization. The ILO does have a legitimate and necessary interest in certain issues with political ramifications. It has major responsibility, for example, for international action to promote and protect fundamental human rights, particularly in respect of freedom of association, trade union rights and the abolition of forced labour. But international politics is not the main business of the ILO. Questions involving relations between States and proclamations of economic principles should be left to the United Nations and other international agencies where their consideration is more relevant to those organizations' responsibilities. Irrelevant political issues divert the attention of the ILO from improving the conditions of workers – that is, from questions on which the tripartite structure of the ILO gives the organization a unique advantage over the other, purely governmental, organizations of the United Nations family.[50]

The 'politicization' of the ILO resolutions can be found in its 1974 resolution which led, in part, to the US withdrawal. This resolution was directed at the continued Israeli occupation of Arab territories, declaring that any occupation of territory was a violation of human and trade union rights. It condemned Israeli violation of trade union freedom in its occupied territories and called on the Director General of the ILO to use all means to end the violation.[51] Although directed at trade union rights issues, the resolution is clearly a continuation of the condemnatory approach of the majority of States in the UN General Assembly, which has consistently called for the end of Israeli occupation.[52] The ILO's resolution adds nothing to the substance of the Assembly's resolutions and distracts it from its principal norm creating activities.[53]

Similar problems of politicisation led to the withdrawal of the United States and the United Kingdom from UNESCO in 1984 and 1985.[54] UNESCO was created in 1945 as the principal specialised agency having the purpose of promoting international collaboration through education, science and culture. Admittedly, UNESCO has used its power of recommendation to carry on the political agenda of the majority of States, by selectively and rather ineptly condemning South Africa, Israel and other pariah States, by, for instance, adopting resolutions on archaeology in Jerusalem which amounted to an attack on the occupying power.[55] Although clearly undermining the credibility and effectiveness of UNESCO,[56] it is somewhat hypocritical of the West to accuse the Non-Aligned majority of abusing the voting power in certain specialised agencies, whilst they use their weighted-voting power in the economic and financial organisations, namely the IMF and the World Bank, to deny access to the facilities those organisations provide for certain pariah States (in this case from the perspective of developed countries).[57] For instance in 1981 the US managed to reduce a proposed IMF credit to Grenada of $9m to $3m by arguing 'that the construction of the international airport in Grenada would hurt the balance of payments of Grenada'.[58] Although the US's arguments seem to bring the issue within the IMF's mandate, certainly more clearly than the blundering attempts of the developing States to use UNESCO's power to condemn Israeli occupation, the motivating factor behind the US argument was the fear that the airport on Grenada was to be used by the Cuban military, fears which gave rise, in part, to the military action against Grenada in 1983. Furthermore, as well as refusing credit and resources for certain States, the increasing reaction by right-wing Western governments against a collective approach to global problems and an increasing emphasis on regional and bilateral approaches, has resulted in a decreased commitment to the Bretton Woods economic and financial organisations as a whole.[59]

Furthermore, the constitutions of the ILO and UNESCO, in particular, invite the discussion of issues wider than simply the development of standard working conditions or the level of primary education in Africa.[60] The Preamble of the constitution of the ILO starts off by stating that 'universal and lasting peace can be established only if it is based upon social justice' and that 'conditions of labour exist involving such injustice, hardship and privation to large numbers of people as to produce unrest so great that the peace and harmony of the world is imperilled'.

UNESCO's constitution also makes an explicit link between its primary area of work and wider political issues, particularly peace and security, by declaring in its Preamble, *inter alia*, that 'since wars begin in the minds of men, it is in the minds of men that the defences of peace must be constructed', and further that 'a peace based exclusively upon the political and economic arrangements of governments would not be a peace which could secure the unanimous, lasting and sincere support of the peoples of the world, and that peace must therefore be founded, if it is not to fail, upon the intellectual and moral solidarity of mankind'. The explicit link between peace and security and education, science and culture is made in Article 1 which defines UNESCO's purposes. In many ways, it is not possible to accuse the majority in UNESCO or the ILO of acting *ultra vires* when they adopt resolutions which concentrate on security issues rather than labour or education issues, particularly if the doctrine of inherent powers is accepted whereby the organisation is acting lawfully if its acts within the purposes of the organisation as long as it does not breach one of the express provisions of its constituent document.[61] Furthermore, the political condemnations by UNESCO and the ILO only take up a small part of its time and resources. Over one third of UNESCO's budget is expended on education programmes designed to improve the quality of education in developing countries. Other areas include scientific cooperation on research and projects. Social sciences, culture and communications are also centres of activities, programmes and research, co-ordinated and financed by UNESCO.

It would be misleading to overstate the case against specialised agencies on the ground that they have become over-politicised and therefore less effective. In several of the so-called technical agencies such as the WMO, UPU, and ITU, the focus is indeed mainly on resolving common problems such as improving weather predictions, the world postal service, and telecommunications between States. However, even in these more technical tasks, for instance the allocations of radio frequencies to States and the allocation of slots for communications satellites in the lucrative geostationary orbit (tasks performed by the ITU), it would be unrealistic to expect political matters to be put to one side by States. The realist would argue that no matter how technical a matter is, a member State will generally only support action to tackle a global problem either if it is in its best interests to do so, in the short or long terms, or if such acts do not affect its vital interests.

International organisations, whether their tasks are overtly political or not, will, according to the realist, simply reflect the political and ideological battles taking place in the world. The political tensions in the ITU are expressed in the following comment:

> There also remains the tension between the developed and developing world: between for example equitable access to radio frequency spectrum and the GSO [geostationary orbit], and a rational, efficient and economic use of those resources, an argument of particular importance when technology advances so rapidly and can often be constrained by regulation, especially by *a priori* planning which sets aside large amounts of scarce resources for possible future development which may in fact not happen.[62]

In relation to the GSO, the developing States increasingly used their voting power in the ITU's administrative conferences to push through an allotment plan, which came into force in 1990, for the orbit in relation to certain satellite services, to replace the 'first-come, first-served' philosophy advocated by the developed States, whose use of the orbit was already high.[63] The fact that politics intrudes into every aspect of international regulation, perhaps reflects the critical lawyers' contention that there is in reality no line between law and politics.

The basic political division in the international community is between the rich North and the poor South, between developed and developing countries. This was so even in the Cold War, where, security issues apart, the North–South gap, dominated many of the agendas of the specialised agencies from the mid-1960s. The South's desire for a greater share of the world's wealth produced many new organs created or taken on board by the UN General Assembly, initially as subsidiary organs although subsequently they have developed an autonomy, though no international personality.[64] UNCTAD and UNDP have already been mentioned[65] as organs where the developing countries, using the 'one-State, one-vote' principal, could attempt to counterbalance the weighted-voting systems which favoured the developed countries in the Bretton Woods organisations (IMF and IBRD).

Furthermore, the desire of developing countries to have organisations, as opposed to organs, where their views could be properly represented, led to the UN Industrial Development Organisation (UNIDO), set up as an independent organ of the General Assembly in 1966, becoming the sixteenth UN-specialised agency in 1985 after its Treaty was adopted in 1979,[66] its primary objective being the promotion and acceleration of industrial development in the developing countries. The developing countries in UNIDO 'are usually interested in receiving the largest possible help with their industrialization from the developed countries and paying as little compensation as possible'. 'In contrast, Western countries tend to preserve and maintain their superior positions in industrial production', although they may relinquish to the developing countries 'the less profitable old industries, usually material and energy intensive, which sometimes present a threat to the environment'. As a result of this conflictive, rather than co-operative approach, the developing countries share of manufacturing industry has increased only slightly, raising the question of whether UNIDO's conversion into a specialised agency was really necessary. Western dissatisfaction with the Organisation led to cutbacks in funding, both in terms of non-payment of assessed contribution and little voluntary donation, although the evidence is that technical co-operation programmes in developing countries is increasing slightly.[67] Further, there is strong evidence to show that the World Bank's use of credit to aid development, including industrial development, in developing countries, far outweighs UNIDO's attempts to generate industrial development through technical assistance programmes and industrial projects funded by the Organisation.[68] In the battle between the Western-dominated World Bank and the developing States'-centred UNIDO, the World Bank inevitably wins out with the result that developing countries are saddled with increasing amounts of unpayable debt, instead of receiving assistance for industrialisation funded collectively.[69]

Relationship between the UN and its specialised agencies[70]

The formal links between ECOSOC and the specialised agencies are provided for in Articles 63 and 64. While Article 64 provides that ECOSOC 'may take appropriate steps to obtain regular reports from the specialised agencies', Article 63 creates the basis of a much stronger link by providing:

1. The Economic and Social Council may enter into agreements with any of the agencies referred to in Article 57, defining the terms on which the agency concerned shall be brought into a relationship with the United Nations. Such agreements shall be subject to approval by the General Assembly.
2. It may co-ordinate the activities of the specialized agencies through consultation with and recommendations to such agencies and through recommendations to the General Assembly and to Members of the United Nations.

The agreements between ECOSOC and the specialised agencies generally contain very similar provisions, although there is a marked difference 'notably in the greater degree of autonomy possessed by the Fund, Bank and Finance Corporation'.[71] For example a comparison can be drawn between the UN and the WHO's agreement of 1948,[72] and that between the UN and the IMF of 1947,[73] to illustrate how the Western-dominated Bretton Woods organisations secured greater autonomy and independence from the UN than the other agencies.

Article 1 of the WHO Agreement simply states that the UN 'recognizes the World Health Organization as the specialized agency responsible for taking such action as may be appropriate under its Constitution for the accomplishment of the objectives set forth therein.' In contrast, Article 1 of the IMF Agreement states, *inter alia*, that 'the Fund is a specialized agency ... having wide international responsibilities ... in economic and related fields ... By reason of the nature of its international responsibilities ... the Fund is, and is required to function as, an independent international organization'. Article 2 of both Agreements provides, in similar terms, for reciprocal representation at the meetings of the other Organisation without any voting rights. Article 3 contains significant differences. Whereas the WHO is obliged to include on its agenda items proposed by the UN (and vice versa), the IMF is simply under an obligation to 'give due consideration to the inclusion in the agenda of items proposed by the United Nations' (and vice versa). The freedom to ignore the political will of the UN in the case of the IMF is further enhanced by Article 4 of its agreement with the UN which provides that 'any formal recommendations made by either organization after ... consultation will be considered as soon as possible by the appropriate organ of the other'. The more extensive Article 4 of the WHO's agreement with the UN provides, *inter alia*, that the WHO 'agrees to arrange for the submission, as soon as possible ... of all formal recommendations which the United Nations may make to it' to the appropriate organ of the agency. Further, the WHO agrees to report to the UN on the implementation or otherwise of its recommendations and more generally to co-operate with the other specialised agencies under the co-ordination of the UN. Article 5 of the WHO agreement provides that the WHO shall produce regular reports on its activities to the UN, whereas the equivalent provision of the IMF Agreement simply provides for the 'exchange of information and publications of mutual interest', despite the provisions of Article 64 of the UN Charter. Although most of the other provisions of the Agreement are similar (including the power to request advisory opinions of the International Court of Justice), it is noticeable that the WHO Agreement contains a provision for the closer co-operation on budgetary matters (Article 15), and holds out the future prospect of a unified civil service (Article 12), whereas the Fund Agreement makes the independence of the Fund on budgetary and administrative matters crystal clear (Articles 10(3) and 12).

Professor Bowett assesses the Agreements between the UN and its specialised agencies in fairly optimistic terms:

Clearly these agreements provide a useful basis for co-ordination. The submission of reports by the agencies, the examination of these reports by the Council and the power to make recommendations to the agencies are useful factors is securing co-ordination and avoiding duplication.[74]

This seems an unduly positive analysis of the Agreements: first, because, as Professor Bowett recognises, these powers apply to the specialised agencies with the exception of the Bretton Woods bodies, which do not have to report to ECOSOC and simply have to 'consider' the recommendations of the UN body. Second, the other agencies, although under a more onerous obligation to report on whether an ECOSOC recommendation has been adopted or not, have, in practice, carved out a huge degree of autonomy subject to little control by ECOSOC due to that organ's concern more with voting victories than effective co-ordination of what is a huge and unwieldy system.[75] Even in the post-Cold War era, ECOSOC often uses its recommendatory powers to condemn particular States along the lines of the General Assembly, rather than concentrating on development and assistance matters.[76]

The system has failed to produce the necessary degree of co-ordination because the member governments, from developed and developing countries alike, could not identify a common purpose and therefore could not produce a common policy in relation to the Specialized Agencies on the basis of which they could impose some co-ordination on them.[77]

Neither in theory nor in practice are the specialised agencies of the UN 'agents' of the world body in the proper sense of the word. None subject themselves to the authority of the UN and some, the Bretton Woods bodies, are virtually completely independent, with the result that in most economic and social matters there is a system of decentralisation. Professor Bowett counters that:

There are, however, additional means of co-ordination. The first ... is the Administrative Committee on Co-ordination (ACC) which, comprising the Secretary General and the administrative heads of the agencies, directly and through its sub-committees, can review the whole field of operations of the various organisations in the light of the need for co-ordination, fixing priorities and enabling a concentration of effort and resources. ECOSOC has itself established a Committee for Programme and Co-operation which holds joint meetings with the ACC. And, of course, on the technical assistance side, all agencies are represented on the Inter-Agency Consultative Board of UNDP.[78]

The evidence is that this proliferation of bureaucratic machinery has 'made the problem somewhat worse by effectively weakening further still the co-ordinating role which Article 63 of the Charter gave to ECOSOC'. The ACC,[79] established as early as 1947 by ECOSOC,[80] has simply become a forum for the heads of the agencies to safeguard the autonomy and independence of those bodies.[81]

As has been stated above, the General Assembly recognised this problem in the mid-1970s, and established an *Ad Hoc* Committee on the Restructuring of the

Economic and Social Sectors of the United Nations,[82] whose report was endorsed by the Assembly in 1977.[83] The report, although remaining effectively unimplemented, in many ways, tried to re-establish the hierarchy, with the General Assembly concentrating on 'over-all strategies, policies and priorities for the system as a whole in respect of international co-operation, including operational activities, in the economic, social and related fields', with a balanced and efficient distribution of agenda items between its Second (Economic and Financial) and Third (Social, Humanitarian and Cultural) Committees. Under the general direction of the Assembly, ECOSOC should concentrate on fulfilling its role 'as the central forum for the discussion of the international economic and social issues', 'to monitor and evaluate the implementation of over-all strategies, policies and priorities established by the General Assembly', and 'to ensure the over-all co-ordination of the activities of the organization of the United Nations system'. To this end ECOSOC should rationalise the system of subsidiary bodies and 'refrain from establishing new bodies'. At the lowest level the resolution states that

> All United Nations organs and programmes, the specialized agencies, the General Agreement on Tariffs and Trade, the International Atomic Energy Agency and *ad hoc* world conferences should co-operate in whatever measures are necessary for the effective discharge of the responsibilities of the General Assembly and the Economic and Social Council and should, in accordance with the Charter of the United Nations and within the scope of their respective basic instruments, give full and prompt effect to their specific policy recommendations.

The resolution finally states the need for effective, integrated and co-ordinated action at the country level. As has been seen, these calls are still being made in the 1990s. The attempt in 1977, to establish a clear chain of authority, from the Assembly to ECOSOC and then to the agencies, although a worthy ideal, has proved impossible in practice. The General Assembly and ECOSOC are still too much concerned with political points scoring than creating workable policies for development; the specialised agencies are too autonomous to be subject to tighter control by ECOSOC, particularly the Bretton Woods Organisations. Furthermore, organisations such as the IAEA and GATT (now the WTO), are not *de facto* specialised agencies of the UN as suggested by the resolution. They are independent organisations, which, if they so choose, can co-ordinate with the UN in certain activities. The Institutional, Procedural and Legal Sub-Committee of the Preparatory Committee of the WTO expressly stated in November 1994 that while it was necessary to have effective co-operation between the WTO and the UN, there were no grounds for establishing institutional links between the two Organisations.[84] With the WTO's emergence as a new international organisation on 1 January 1995, it is interesting to note that it specifically rejects the idea of coming within the UN family. Unlike the IMF and the World Bank, the Trade Organisation appears unprepared even to negotiate an agreement under Article 63 of the UN Charter, allowing it a great deal of autonomy. Rather than closer co-ordination of functional organisations under world authority, the move is, in effect, towards greater decentralisation and further lack of co-ordination.

Models of regionalism

The debate over whether the international order was best served by the centralisation of decision making in a global organisation or in regional bodies, came to the fore on the demise of the League of Nations. Most of the leaders of the Great Powers were in favour of a supreme world organisation, at least in security matters, seeing that the failure of the League was not because of the fact that it was meant to be global but due to the deficiencies of the Covenant. Only Churchill, in 1943, argued for stronger regional Councils, although even he admitted that they must be subject to the World Council.

> Churchill stressed the regional principle because he believed the experience of the League of Nations had demonstrated that 'it was only the countries whose interest were directly affected by a dispute could be expected to apply themselves with sufficient vigour to secure a settlement'. The major powers, he thought, should be represented on all the regional councils in which they were directly interested: the United States, he hoped in all three; the Soviet Union probably in both the European and Pacific; while Canada 'would naturally' represent the Commonwealth in the Western Hemisphere Council. But the Prime Minister also emphasized that 'the last word would remain with the Supreme World Council, since any of the issues that the Regional Councils were unable to settle would automatically be of interest to the World Council ... The central idea of the structure was that of a three-legged stool – the World Council resting on three Regional Councils.[85]

It will be seen that in many matters the world Organisation and the regional bodies overlap, there is generally no *de jure* priority,[86] although practical matters, including the purposes and effectiveness of the organisations in question, may mean that, *de facto*, certain issues are left to the UN or to the regional body. In some matters though there is *de jure* priority for the UN, in particular, Article 53(1) of the UN Charter states that 'no enforcement action shall be taken under regional arrangements or by regional agencies without the authorization of the Security Council'.[87] Furthermore, the UN Charter asserts the supremacy of the United Nations when there is a conflict between treaty obligations, Article 103 providing:

> In the event of a conflict between the obligations of the Members of the United Nations under the present Charter and their obligations under any other international agreement, their obligations under the present Charter shall prevail.

This provision is effective because of the near universal membership of the UN. As Professor Schermers states:

> Establishment of the priority of the law of one organization over that of another by a constitutional rule of the superior organization will be effective when all Members of

the inferior organization are, simultaneously, Members of the superior one. When this is not the case, the other Members of the inferior organization may object to such priority.[88]

This will apply to other organisations where questions of priority may arise, for instance between two regional organisations. Often, however, the constitutions of the organisations will be silent on the point and then hierarchy follows 'from factual circumstances'. Professor Schermers cites the example of the WEU and NATO where all members of the WEU are members of NATO. Since both bodies operate in the same field, that of defence, there is potential for overlap, although the stronger and more effective organisation, NATO, has so far in practice been the supreme organisation of the two,[89] although with the enhancement of the WEU by the Maastricht Treaty of 1992, and the possible expansion in membership to include non-NATO members, the situation may begin to reverse in the future.

Questions of priority and co-ordination of organisation in the areas of security, human rights and the environment will be returned to in chapters 7 to 10, for the moment it is necessary to look further at the arguments for stronger regionalism and the different stages of development achieved by regional bodies.

Regionalism can be seen to be in opposition to the functionalist theory of decentralisation, which does not permit the evolution of functional organisations to be restricted to a particular region. It has been illustrated above that decentralisation suffers from lack of integration and lack of commitment by States to deal with problems beyond their interests. Regional bodies and organisations are far more likely to be able to adopt an integrated approach in dealing with particular tasks. Paul Taylor gives the example of the Commonwealth, 'where despite a surprising durability, regimes have nevertheless been weakened, compared with the European Community, where they have been strengthened'. He cites problems of communication, transaction costs, and the inability to internalise markets in organisations not based upon a specific region, as factors which encourage the growth of regional organisations.[90]

In many ways arguments in favour of regionalism are also in opposition to the rationalist conception of world government, which puts forward 'a view of the organic unity of space-ship earth' and so 'to allow any intermediate level of competence is seen as permitting an unacceptable compromise with the integrity of the essential whole'.[91] Theoretical arguments apart, there is strong evidence to suggest that global, universal organisations have failed many of the developing States, while the rich States simply desire a continuation of the *status quo* in relation to the developing countries, particularly in the global economic organisations. This has led developing States to form regional organisations so that they can attempt to redress the imbalance in the global system.[92] Furthermore, the desire in the West to go beyond the *status quo*, in terms of greater economic growth in the already rich countries, has led to the development of regional organisations amongst developed countries. Regionalism is thus set to expand as 'the result of attempts to solve practical problems within' the regions 'and to achieve

security against military attack and economic domination in relations with out-
siders'.[93]

Furthermore, once a process of regionalisation has been started upon, it is difficult to stop further integration.

> ... as the scope of integration is increased the chances of that scope being extended
> are enhanced by the fear of any one partner that, unless they accept this, a more pro-
> gressive coalition of their partners could emerge. This integrative dynamic therefore
> contains elements both of economic self-interest and of political fear. Its underlying
> condition is probably the appearance in the state of the widespread conviction that
> the benefits arising from the integration are real and important, and that the costs of
> even partial exclusion would be considerable, resulting not only in economic dis-
> advantage but also political enfeeblement.[94]

It is unlikely that a regional organisation, such as the European Union, where this
dynamic forces reluctant States such as the United Kingdom to agree to greater
integration, will become more and more powerful and swallow up so many States
that it becomes, in effect, a global organisation. Expansion of membership will
slow down because 'the costs in terms of the draining of the resources of the
regional organisations are likely to increase with expansion', due to the fact that
'the core states are likely to be richer than the later applicants, and because the
latter are likely to seek the help of the former with their economic development'.
Eventually, the costs of expansion will exceed the benefits.[95] Following this line
of argument, predicated as it is on economic integration within regions, the world
will eventually evolve into a number of stable but competing regional bodies.[96]
The question remains whether such a system would be more stable than the current one, or indeed one based wholly on world government or on functional
decentralisation. Proponents of regionalism hypothesise that a 'multi-bloc'
system would be more orderly and stable than the current one, or indeed any of
the alternatives. Amongst other reasons, regionalists argue that although conflict
would not be eliminated it would be much reduced because of the hypothesis that
regional 'integration is normally followed by an inward or "selfish" orientation
rather than by outward aggression'.[97]

Regionalism in practice

Whether such models will become reality remains uncertain, though there is evidence that regional integration is speeding up around the world,[98] although there
is a vast difference between the integration achieved in one region when compared to another. The European Union is the most advanced regional organisation, in terms of integration. The nature and purposes of the Organisation have
been discussed elsewhere[99] and there is little scope in a book of this nature to
develop an extensive analysis of Community Law.[100] Nevertheless, the main features of the Union as an international organisation can be outlined. First of all,

confusion as to the number of organisations operating under the umbrella of the European Union needs to be cleared up. Professor Hartley provides a succinct summary:

> The Maastricht Agreement brought about important changes of a conceptual kind, which some regard as paving the way for a federal Europe. The European Economic Community (EEC) was renamed the European Community (EC) and a new entity was created, the European Union. This is 'founded on the European Communities, supplemented by the policies and forms of co-operation' established by the Maastricht Agreement. The latter are two in number: 'common foreign and security policy' and 'co-operation in the fields of justice and home affairs'. The European Union (EU) thus comprises three legal persons – the EC, the ECSC and Euratom – together with two 'policies and forms of co-operation'.[101]

Although 'there are still three Communities ... there is only one set of institutions', namely the Council, the Commission and the Parliament 'each containing inter-governmental and federal elements, though the former is more noticeable in the case of the Council and the latter in the case of the Commission'.[102] Whereas the Communities, namely the EC, ECSC and Euratom, have advanced down the road of supranationalism towards federalism with common institutions, the new areas of co-operation added by the Maastricht Treaty of 1992, namely defence and security, and justice and home affairs,[103] are dealt with on an inter-governmental level in the Council which has the responsibility for all decisions. The Commission has no significant role in these areas. In addition, the European Court is excluded from reviewing European Union actions in these fields, in effect confining the Court's constitutional role, essential for a federal system, to the three Community Treaties. Furthermore, decisions on defence and security matters are made unanimously following a recommendation by the European Council (replacing EPC), allowing for member States to protect their vital interests, and legislation is only permissable by recourse to the European Community Treaty and institutions.

It is clear that although the EC has advanced a long way towards federalism in the area of coal and steel, atomic energy and economic matters, the other elements of the European Union have not developed beyond the level of an autonomous international organisation. Furthermore, the weakest aspect of the nascent federal structure in the *EC* institutions, is the Parliament.

> [T]he powers of the European Parliament fall short of those normally enjoyed by the legislature of a federation. Nevertheless, they are gradually increasing – whenever a new amendment to the Community treaties is adopted, the Parliament gains some additional powers – and the days are long past when it could be dismissed as no more than a 'talking shop'.[104]

Nevertheless, until there is an increase in the powers of the Parliament, which at the moment has limited joint legislative capacity with the Council (the Council still has by far the greatest capacity to enact Community legislation); and until the federal elements of the Community extend to the areas of defence, security, justice and home affairs, it is only possible to state that the European Union, as an international organisation has elements of federalism but is not yet a federal system.

Whereas the European Union is probably the most advanced regional organisation, there are others at a stage lower than the Union, but still significantly developed. The Organisation of American States is perhaps the best example, and will be the one briefly discussed here. Since its origins in the First International Conference of American States of 1890, thereby making it the oldest regional organisation, the OAS has developed significantly by expanding its treaty base and institutional structure. In some ways this makes the OAS similar to the EU although the major difference lies in the fact that the OAS does not possess significant legislative powers. The OAS bears very few of the hallmarks of a supranational, let alone federal, organisation, although as we shall see in chapter 8, it does have limited mandatory powers in the field of collective security.

The modern-day OAS is based on the Charter of the Organisation adopted at Bogotá in 1948. This Charter has been modified on several occasions in order to strengthen the institutions and purposes of the Organisation. Nevertheless, as Heidi Jiminez points out in a very helpful note on the OAS Charter (as consolidated by these amendments):

> In retrospect, however, these amendments revealed a structural weakness in the Charter itself, namely the possibility of different legal regimes applying simultaneously to individual Member States, conditioned solely by their ratification of any of the Protocols of amendment.[105]

The problem of different regimes applying to different members of a regional organisation is not applicable to the EU because treaty amendments there can only be carried out by unanimity, in other words upon ratification by all member States. In the case of the OAS, on the other hand, the principle of consent as embodied in Article 145 of the OAS Charter means that if two-thirds of the members have ratified the amendment to the Treaty then the amendment is only binding on those members, the unamended text remains in force for the other members. Although the amendments do not have the effect of splitting the Organisation into smaller splinter organisations, the unequal number of ratifications for each undermines the cohesiveness and effectiveness of the Organisation.

The amending instruments are the Protocol of Buenos Aires of 1967, which significantly enhanced the institutional structure of the OAS. Of the thirty-five OAS member States, it appears that only Cuba has not ratified the 1967 Protocol. The 1985 Protocol of Cartagena de Indias, contained significant amendments to the purposes of the OAS, particularly as regards support for the principle of representative democracy. This Protocol has received the requisite number of ratifications to enter into force, although a number of OAS members have yet to accept the obligations therein, including Cuba, Guatemala, Haiti, Peru and the United States. The remaining two amendments to the OAS Charter, the 1992 Protocol of

Washington and the 1993 Protocol of Managua, have not yet entered into force, each having received five ratifications, including that of the United States.

As regards the OAS Charter as amended by the 1967 and 1985 protocols, Article 2 proclaims the purposes of the OAS as: the strengthening of peace and security in the Continent; the promotion and consolidation of representative democracy with due respect for the principle of non-intervention; the solution of political, juridical and economic problems; the promotion of cultural, economic and social development; and the restriction of conventional armament to allow for greater economic and social development. Article 3 contains the principles of the OAS and includes, *inter alia*, clause 3(d) added by the 1985 Protocol. It states that the 'solidarity of the American States and the high aims which are sought through it require the political organization of those States on the basis of the effective exercise of representative democracy'. The support for democracy introduced by the 1985 protocol, was intended to be further enhanced by the 1992 Washington Protocol which provides for a new Article 9 in the OAS Charter. This provision would allow for the suspension of a 'Member of the Organization whose democratically constituted government has been overthrown by force'.[106]

In terms of organs and institutional structure, the OAS tends to parallel the UN. The Charter provides for a General Assembly which decides on general policies, co-ordination and budgets;[107] a Meeting of Consultation of Ministers of Foreign Affairs to deal with security and defence matters;[108] and a permanent Council of the Organisation with responsibility for peaceful relations and for carrying out the decisions of the Assembly.[109] Furthermore, the Charter provides for an Inter-American Economic and Social Council whose purposes parallel those of the Economic and Social Council of the UN.[110] The parallels with the UN are taken even further by Articles 131 to 133 which provide that the specialised agencies of the OAS, namely 'organizations established by multilateral agreements and having specific functions with respect to technical matters of common interest to the American States',[111] shall enter into relations with the OAS by means of an agreement, and should take into account any recommendations made by any of the OAS organs as well as furnishing reports to the Assembly.

Given the problems of co-ordination and integration encountered by the decentralised UN system of specialised agencies, it was inevitable that the OAS, similarly structured, would encounter similar difficulties. In order to combat this and to create an organisation 'more functionally effective in its delivery of technical co-operation services', and increase 'contributions to collaborative efforts combating critical poverty throughout the region', the General Assembly of the OAS adopted the Managua Protocol of 1993 which, when in force, will create a new Inter-American Council for Integral Development, replacing the Inter-American Economic and Social Council and the Inter-American Council for Education, Science and Culture. Whereas the present Inter-American Economic and Social Council simply recommends programmes and promotes co-ordination,[112] the new Council for Integral Development will 'formulate and recommend to the General Assembly a strategic plan which sets forth policies, programs and courses of action in matters of co-operation for integral development', as well as co-ordinating and assigning responsibilities for the execution of programmes to subsidiary bodies and organisations, in co-operation with other international organisations and UN agencies.[113] When, and if, the amendment comes into force, the new Council will be much more directive, controlling and co-ordinating responses to economic and social development problems, an aspect so far lacking at the international level in the United Nations.

Chapter VII of the OAS Charter contains provisions on integral development. These provisions illustrate the lack of legislative competence possessed by the OAS as compared to the EU, in that the provisions simply emphasise the promotion of economic and social co-operation and development. The statement of principles on these matters are wide ranging, including an 'equitable distribution of national income'; 'adequate and equitable systems of taxation'; 'modernization of rural life''; 'accelerated and diversified industrialization'; 'stability of domestic price levels'; 'fair wages'; 'proper nutrition', and 'adequate housing'.[114] The aims are high indeed but the powers of the Organisation are not commensurate with the task. Changes in the structure of the Organisation to be introduced by the Managua Protocol when it comes into force, for the more effective delivery of assistance, should improve the situation, but do not provide for a regional organisation which can decide on economic policy and effectively implement its decisions by means of legislation binding on and within member States. The sheer economic disparity between the richest and poorest American nation makes economic integration an improbability.

Interestingly, though, the OAS Charter does provide in Article 41 that:

> The Member States recognise that integration of the developing countries of the Hemisphere is one of the objectives of the inter-American system and, therefore, shall orient their efforts and take the necessary measures to accelerate the integration process, with a view to establishing a Latin American common market in the shortest possible time.

The possibility of the OAS developing in the direction of the EC is envisaged in the OAS Charter. In practice such developments have not taken place within the OAS framework itself but by various treaties agreed by a number of members which operate outside the Organisation but within the region.[115]

For instance, the Latin-American Integration Association (ALADI), which replaced the Latin-American Free Trade Association (LAFTA) in 1980,[116] has eleven State parties, and has the aim of renewing the Latin American integration process, with the long-term objective of establishing a common market. In view of the economic disparity between its members the Organisation divides its membership into three categories, distinguished by their degree of economic development, with provision for differential treatment. The move from LAFTA to ALADI also signified a development from a simple conference towards an autonomous international organisation, with permanent organs adopting decisions and recommendations generally by majority vote. The Organisation has been active in moving towards the aim of a common market with the establishment of a regional tariff preference mechanism, and a programme to eliminate non-tariff barriers and correct trade imbalances.[117] Whether this Organisation will reinvent itself again to become more of a legislative organisation along the lines of the EU remains to be seen, though an evolutionary trend can clearly be discerned.

Similar trends can be seen in other sub-regional organisations in the Americas, for instance the Andean Group of five States established in 1969,[118] promised moves towards greater integration and established a Commission and Junta of State representatives to carry it out. The prospect of economic integration seems closer with the establishment of an Andean Parliament in 1979,[119] directly elected by the peoples of the Andean countries, with a mandate not only to achieve economic integration but also to protect human rights, social justice and democracy. The Andean Tribunal of Justice also established in 1979 has a mandate to establish rules of community law and interpret the Cartagena Agreement which established the Andean Group in 1969. A further evolutionary step towards greater integration in the economic field was taken by the Andean Group in 1992 with the establishment of an Andean Common Market.[120] Other sub-regional groups have simply established free-trade agreements without any significant institutional structures, although the impact of the agreement in the international economic sphere can be great. The most recent free-trade agreement links the developed economies of the United States and Canada, with the expanding economy of Mexico. The North American Free Trade Agreement (NAFTA), agreed between the three States in December 1992,[121] establishes a free-trade area between the parties, as well as various mechanisms such as binational and arbitral panels, to enable the parties to settle disputes over the implementation of the Agreement.[122] However, the Agreement also has within it the seeds of further institutional development towards an autonomous international organisation in that it establishes a supervisory Free Trade Commission and a Secretariat.[123]

Other regions of the world, for example the Middle East and South East Asia,[124] have a similar plethora of regional and sub-regional organisations, though they tend to be less developed than the American organisations. For example one of the principal regional organisations in South East Asia,[125] the Association of South East Asian Nations (ASEAN), which has seven member States (Vietnam joining in 1995), lays down its purposes in paragraph 2 of the Bangkok Declaration 1967,[126] namely to accelerate economic growth, social progress, peace and stability and 'to collaborate more effectively for the greater utilization of their agriculture and industries, the expansion of their trade ... the improvement of their transportation and communication facilities and the raising of the living standards of their people'. The aims and purposes are certainly wide enough to allow for economic integration in the future, although as yet the organisation operates on the basis of co-operation and consensus within its simple structure of an annual Ministerial Meeting, a more regular Standing Committee, and various permanent functional committees. The lack of legislative capacity has inhibited the development of the Association, although after a very cautious start, important decisions have been made on a variety of matter ranging from the 1983 ASEAN Customs Code of Conduct, the 1981 ASEAN Food Security Reserve, the 1981 ASEAN Minerals co-operation Plan, to the 1977 ASEAN Preferential Trading Arrangements.[127]

Concluding remarks

As regards general universal organisations, although there has been an increase in competence and centralisation, at least in the powers vested in the UN as compared to the League, the performance of the UN in economic and social matters has been disappointing when compared to its predecessor. The generally unco-ordinated growth in agencies and bodies has not been matched by an improvement in the development of poorer countries. The UN does not show significant signs of governmental activity in economic and social matters, its actions being characterised as a compromise between the revolutionary attitude of the developing States and the realist approach of the developed States. In disarmament matters, it does provide a forum for debate and limited compromise. However, in the area of collective security the UN not only has crude governmental powers, it has also started to exercise them in the post-Cold War era (see chapter 7).

There is little evidence that the functionalist vision has been fulfilled, although the fact that the UN is co-ordinator for many of the agencies tends to dilute the pure approach envisaged by Professor Mitrany. Nevertheless, it appears from the practice of 'technical' organisations such as the ITU, as well as organisations such as the ILO and UNESCO dealing in 'class' matters, to use Marxist terminology, that politicisation of functional organisations is inevitable. When universal standards are being set or the world's resources being discussed or, in a limited way, reallocated, by international organisations, there is going to be confrontation between North and South, between those States that have and those that have not. In the 'one State, one vote' organisations such as UNIDO, the South will inevitably win the vote, although it will rarely win extra resources, whereas in the Bretton Woods Organisations with their weighted-voting mechanisms, the North inevitably wins out. The result is not really a compromise along Marxist lines but a continuation of a system dominated by the richer States along realist lines, leading to continued injustice and inequality identified by the critical lawyers. Indeed, when examining the legal and practical relationship between the UN and the functional organisations, the divide, between the Northern-dominated institutions on economic, trade and financial matters, and those concerned with social and humanitarian matters which tend to be dominated by the South, is made even more apparent in that the former are subject to little or no formal control by the majority in the UN.

With the failure of the universal organisations, whether general or functional, to make an impact on the economic development of the majority of States, there has been a trend towards regionalism, not only by richer countries wanting to create larger markets, but for poorer countries whose united economic strength may enable them to survive and perhaps even grow. Regionalism will not result in the strongest region swallowing up others to produce a world government, but will, more likely, result in competing regional groupings, although there is growing evidence that within these, sub-regional groupings will be formed between States of similar wealth. Regionalism and sub-regionalism are really incompatible with pure rationalism which sees the development of regional governments as a step towards world government, and functionalism which concentrates on the solution of common problems without regard to State or regional frontiers. In many ways it illustrates the realist view that organisations reflect the world's balance of power, which with the end of the Cold War, is moving towards competing *economic* regional organisations. However, in the three areas to be examined in chapters 7 to 10, namely security, environmental protection and human rights, the activities of the UN are still significant, if not paramount.

Notes

[1] H. G. Schermers, *International Institutional Law*, 29, 2nd edn (1980).

[2] F. P. Walters, *A History of the League of Nations* 1, (1952).

[3] The League's mandate system and the UN's trusteeship system will not be analysed.

[4] Article 4(1) of the Covenant. The original permanent members of the Council were: the British Empire, France, Italy (until 1927) and Japan (until 1933). Additional permanent members: Germany (1926–35) and the USSR (1934–9).

[5] For a comprehensive examination of the background and drafting process see R. B. Russell and J. E. Muther, *A History of the United Nations Charter* (1958).

[6] Article 24(1) of the UN Charter.

[7] See further S. D. Bailey, *The Procedure of the UN Security Council*, 199, 2nd edn (1988).

[8] L. M. Goodrich, E. Hambro, and P. S. Simons, *Charter of the United Nations*, 43–4, 3rd edn (1969).

[9] See Walters, *History of the League*, chs 18, 31, 41, 44, 51, 61.

[10] J. C. Plano and R. E. Riggs, *Forging World Order: The Politics of International Organization*, 28 (1967).

[11] See in particular GA Res. S-10/2, 10 UN GAOR SS Supp. (No. 4) 3 (1978).

[12] J. P. Cot and A. Pellet, *La Charte des Nations Unies*, 272 (1985).

[13] See for example GA Res. 48/75, 48 UN GAOR (1993); GA Res. 49/73, 49 UN A/PV (1994).

[14] 12 *United Nations Disarmament Yearbook*, (1987), Appendix 7.

[15] GA Res. 46/36 L, 46 UN GAOR Supp. (No. 49) 73 (1991).

[16] UN doc. A/48/344 (1993). See further GA Res. 49/66, 49 UN A/PV (1994).

[17] GA Res. 47/39, 47 UN GAOR (1992).

[18] 32 *I.L.M.* (1993), Article 8.

[19] Contrast the UN-sponsored 1972 Convention on the Prohibition of the Development, Production and Stockpiling of Bacteriological (Biological) and Toxin Weapons and on their Destruction, 1015 UNTS 187. But see B. Simma (ed.), *The Charter of the United*

Nations, 247 (1994).

²⁰ Articles 23 and 24.

²¹ Walters, *History of the League*, 176.

²² 58 LNTS 285.

²³ 47 LNTS 55.

²⁴ Article 61 of the UN Charter.

²⁵ P. Taylor, 'The Origins and Institutional Setting of the UN Special Conferences', in P. Taylor and A. J. R. Groom (eds), *Global Issues in the United Nations' Framework*, 19 (1989).

²⁶ Article 67 of the UN Charter.

²⁷ Article 62 of the UN Charter.

²⁸ Articles 65 and 66 of the UN Charter.

²⁹ P. Taylor, *International Organizations in the Modern World*, 115 (1993). See also the report of Sir Robert Jackson, *Study of the Capacity of the United Nations Development System* (1969).

³⁰ GA Res. 1785, 17 UN GAOR Supp. (No. 17) (1962).

³¹ G. Sen, 'UNCTAD and International Economic Reform', in Taylor and Groom (eds), *Global Issues*, 245 at 247.

³² *Ibid.*, 249.

³³ See above n. 29.

³⁴ GA Res. 2029, 20 UN GAOR Supp. (No. 14) (1965).

³⁵ Taylor, *International Organization*, 118.

³⁶ *Ibid.*, 127.

³⁷ *Ibid.*, 129.

³⁸ Joint Inspection Unit, *Some Reflections on Reform of the United Nations*, prepared by Maurice Bertrand, JIU/REP/85/9, (1985).

³⁹ Taylor, *International Organization*, 133–9.

⁴⁰ GA Res. 32/197, 32 UN GAOR (1977).

⁴¹ D. Williams, *The Specialized Agencies and the United Nations: The System in Crisis*, 52 (1987).

⁴² Specialised agencies themselves derive the majority of their funds from the assessed contributions of member States. Contributions to funds and programmes – for instance those administered by UNDP are voluntary and are decreasing in real terms. Williams, *Specialized Agencies* 44.

⁴³ GA Res. 44/211, 44 UN GAOR (1989).

⁴⁴ GA Res. 47/199, 47 UN GAOR (1992).

⁴⁵ ECOSOC Res. 1993/7, 22 July 1993.

⁴⁶ ECOSOC Res. 1994/33, 28 July 1994.

⁴⁷ D. Williams, *Specialized Agencies*, 19.

⁴⁸ Schermers, *International Institutional Law*, 837.

⁴⁹ See further, J. Harrod, 'United Nations Specialized Agencies: From Functionalist Intervention to International co-operation?', in J. Harrod and N. Schrijver (eds), *The UN Under Attack*, 130 (1988).

⁵⁰ UN doc. A/C.5/1704 (1975).

⁵¹ *Record of Proceedings*, ILC, 59th session, 808 (1974).

⁵² For example, GA Res. 3414, 30 UN GAOR Supp. (No. 34) 6 (1975).

⁵³ See further L. Emmerij, 'The International Labour Organization as a Development Agency', in J. Harrod and N. Schrijver (eds), *The UN Under Attack*, 111.

[54] For reasons for US withdrawal see 84 *Dept of State Bulletin* (1984), 41.

[55] Williams, *Specialized Agencies*, 57.

[56] M. Mourik, 'UNESCO: Structural Origins of Crisis and Needed Reforms', in Harrod and Schrijver (eds.), *The UN Under Attack*, 123.

[57] But see H. O. Ruding, 'The Development and Future Role of the International Monetary Fund and the World Bank', *ibid.*, 57.

[58] Williams, *The Specialized Agencies*, 67.

[59] *Ibid.*, 12–13.

[60] *Ibid.*, 1.

[61] See chapter 5.

[62] S. White, S. Bate and T. Johnson, *Satellite Communications in Europe*, 63 (1994).

[63] M. Benko and K-U. Schrogl, *International Space Law in the Making*, 166–8 (1993).

[64] Schermers, *Institutional Law*, 840.

[65] Other such organs, though not operating in the economic sphere, include the UN Children's Fund (UNICEF), the UN High Commissioner for Refugees (UNHCR) and the UN Environment Programme (UNEP).

[66] UKTS 67 (1991), Cmnd 1666.

[67] Y. Lambert, *The United Nations Industrial Development Organization*, 23, 35, 57, 114–6, 123–6 (1993).

[68] *Ibid.*, 127.

[69] M. Bertrand, *The Third Generation World Organisation*, 128–30 (1989).

[70] There are also specialised agencies within some of the regional organisations, see Schermers, *Institutional Law*, 848–51.

[71] D. W. Bowett, *The Law of International Organizations*, 66, 4th edn (1982).

[72] Reproduced in H. F. Panhuys *et al.*, *International Organization and Integration*, 601 (1968).

[73] 16 UNTS 328.

[74] Bowett, *International Institutions*, 68.

[75] Taylor, *International Organization*, 127–9.

[76] See for example ECOSOC Res. 1993/13 on women and children under apartheid, and ECOSOC Res. 1993/15 on the situation of and assistance to Palestinian women, both adopted on 27 July 1993. The purpose of these resolutions was to condemn South Africa and Israel rather than deal effectively with specific matters of social concern.

[77] Williams, *Specialized Agencies*, 117.

[78] Bowett, *International Institutions*, 68.

[79] On the Committee for Programme and Co-ordination see ECOSOC Res. 920 (44) (1962). See further ECOSOC Res. 1472 (48) (1970).

[80] ECOSOC Res. 13 (3) (1946). See further ECOSOC Res. 1643 (51) (1971).

[81] M. Hill, 'The Administrative Committee on Co-ordination', in E. Luard (ed.), *The Evolution of International Organisations*, 104 (1966).

[82] GA Res. 3362 (S-7), 7 UN GAOR SS (1975).

[83] GA Res. 32/197, 32 UN GAOR (1977).

[84] 112 *Focus: GATT Newsletter* (1994 Nov.), 8.

[85] Russell and Muther, *History of the United Nations*, 107 (1958).

[86] See for instance the somewhat contradictory provisions of the UN Charter relating to the peaceful settlement of disputes, Article 33 and 52.

[87] See further chapter 7.

[88] Schermers, *Institutional Law*, 850.

[89] *Ibid.* See also Article 8 of the NATO Treaty, which may also establish *de jure* priority for NATO.

[90] Taylor, *International Organization*, 17–8.

[91] *Ibid.*, 7.

[92] *Ibid.*, 11, 29.

[93] *Ibid.*, 34.

[94] *Ibid.*, 36.

[95] *Ibid.*, 37.

[96] R. D. Masters, 'A Multi-Bloc Model of the International System', 55 *American Political Science Review* (1961), 780 at 797.

[97] *Ibid.*, 783.

[98] Taylor, *International Organization*, 43–4.

[99] See in particular chapter 2.

[100] See generally S. Weatherill and P. Beaumont, *EC Law: The Essential Guide the Legal Workings of the European Community* (1993).

[101] T. C. Hartley, *Foundations of European Community Law*, 8, 3rd edn (1994), referring to Articles A, J, K of the Maastricht Treaty.

[102] *Ibid.*, 9.

[103] Titles 5 and 6 of the Maastricht Agreement.

[104] Hartley, *Foundations*, 37.

[105] H. V. Jiminez, *Introductory Note on the Organization of American States: Integrated Text of the Charter as Amended by the Protocol of Buenos Aires and Cartagena de Indias; the Protocol of Amendment of Washington and the Protocol of Amendment of Managua*, 33 *I.L.M.* (1994), 981.

[106] *Ibid.*, 1005.

[107] Article 53 of the OAS Charter.

[108] Article 60 of the OAS Charter.

[109] Article 90 of the OAS Charter.

[110] Articles 93 and 94 of the OAS Charter. See also Articles 111 112, and 104 which create an Inter-American Commission on Human Rights, a Secretariat and an Inter-American Juridical Committee.

[111] Article 129 of the OAS Charter.

[112] Article 94 of the OAS Charter.

[113] New Article 94 introduced by the Washington Protocol, 33 *I.L.M.* (1994), 1010. Not yet in force.

[114] Article 33 of the OAS Charter. See also the new Article 33 in the Washington Protocol of 1992, 33 *I.L.M.* (1994), 1007. Not yet in force. The new Article 33 stresses the eradication of extreme poverty, as do the proposed amendments to Article 2 (see para.(g)) and Article 3 (see para. (f)).

[115] See generally, Bowett, *International Institutions*, 225–9.

[116] 20 *I.L.M.* (1981), 672.

[117] 29 *Yearbook of International Organizations: Vol 1* (1992–3), 07910. 1 *Europa World Yearbook*, 36th edn (1995), 181–2.

[118] 8 *I.L.M.* (1969), 910.

[119] 18 *I.L.M.* (1979), 1203.

[120] 29 *Yearbook of International Organisations: Vol 1* (1992–3), 00314, 00324. 1 *Europa World Yearbook*, 36th edn (1995), 104–5.

[121] 32 *I.L.M.* (1993), 289.

[122] Articles 101, 102, 1901, 2008 of NAFTA.

[123] Articles 2001 and 2002 of NAFTA.

[124] See generally Bowett, *International Institutions*, 229–36.

[125] See also the Colombo Plan for Co-operative Economic Development in South and South East Asia, 1950. The Constitution of the Colombo Plan was adopted in 1977, see P. G. J. Kapteyn *et al.*, *International Organization and Integration: Volume 2.B–2.J.*, doc. 2.F.1.a. (1983).

[126] *Ibid.*, doc. 2.F.2.

[127] 29 *Yearbook of International Organisations: Vol 1* (1992–3), 01146. 1 *Europa World Yearbook*, 36th edn (1995), 109–12.

7

Collective security and the UN

The book will now turn to substantive areas to analyse how the various bodies interact and how, in the first place, they deal with disputes that threaten international peace, regional peace and indeed internal peace, looking in particular at the issue of enforcement. The next two chapters follow the rationalist contention that keeping the peace should be the primary purpose of the international legal order. The question of whether it achieves such an aim will be considered.

The concept of collective security

Collective security can be defined as:

> ... the proposition that aggressive and unlawful use of force by one nation against another will be met by the combined strength of all other nations. All will co-operate in controlling a disturber of the peace. They will act as one for all and all for one. Their combined strength will serve as a guarantee for the security of each.[1]

A true collective security system, whether international or municipal, principally involves the provision of a police force which is largely independent of any of members or groups that make up society.[2] This signifies that no State nor group of States should be able to dominate a collective security system.

Furthermore, a collective security system is normally designed not merely to take defensive force on a par with the collective defence organisations examined in chapter 8, it can enforce the peace by removing not only aggressors but also *situations* that threaten the peace. 'Collective measures' or 'enforcement action',[3] taken for the maintenance or restoration of international peace and security, do not have to conform with those principles operating to limit the right of self-defence, whether individual or collective.[4] However, this does not mean that the enforcement action can be unlimited in scope, it must be proportional to the ends aimed at, namely the maintenance or restoration of international peace and security.[5] On occasions this may entail action that is limited to defensive force, such as repelling an aggressor, on other occasions it may be offensive action, such as the removal of the aggressor, or the removal of a situation that threatens international peace.

The carnage and destruction of the Great War forced the world to attempt its first real effort at providing collective security. President Wilson, the major force behind the League, had a vision of collective security very close to that outlined above. Furthermore, he saw the League replacing the inherently unstable balance-of-power system that had collapsed in 1914.[6] It is interesting to note at this stage, that the world's second attempt at collective security embodied in the United Nations, frozen for forty years during the Cold War between the superpowers, was largely replaced in that period by a balance-of-power system based on collective defensive alliances. The concept of collective defence, being derived from the balance-of-power system, proved more acceptable to States than collective security. Despite the term, a State acting in *collective* defence of another usually does so out of *national* self-interest, whereas a collective security system requires a State to act for the benefit of all States to maintain or restore international peace and security. This perhaps explains why the idea of collective security has made only tentative inroads in international relations and why the concept of collective defence, derived from the old balance-of-power system, has dominated the search for world peace. Nevertheless, with the end of the Cold War in the late 1980s, the world has seen a revitalisation of collective security, particularly in the global body.

In essence collective security means the centralisation of the use of force in international affairs. As a corollary, States must give up a great deal of their individual freedom to use force. However, even in a municipal system, individuals still have the right to act in self-defence until the State acts to protect them. The right of self-defence for States has been preserved in international law in Article 51 of the UN Charter, until the UN Security Council takes measures to restore international peace and security. However unlike the tightly-defined municipal law concept of self-defence, international law allows a right of self-defence that is, relatively speaking, much wider. This is particularly so as regards the concept of collective self-defence and its institutionalisation in defensive alliances, examined in chapter 8.

The League of Nations and collective security

In chapter 6 it was pointed out that the League of Nations suffered from several defects, including the partial prohibition of war and the minimal centralisation of coercion. However, it may be argued that although the Covenant did not totally prohibit war, the loopholes were actually reasonably well defined and relatively quite limited.[7] Certainly, the major hostilities of the period, such as the Japanese conquest of Manchuria in 1931–32, and the Italian conquest of Abyssinia in 1935–36, could not be categorised as exploitations of the Covenant's loopholes, in fact they could only be described as wholesale breaches of the obligations in the Covenant to which the League responded ineffectually.

However, the loopholes in the Covenant did suggest that embarking on a war was simply a question of procedural formalities, and that despite the vague wording of Article 10, there was no substantive prohibition in the Covenant outlawing war. States like Italy, Japan and eventually Germany were not inhibited by a set of procedures. The point is that the loopholes created an inherently unstable edifice. States did not exploit the loopholes, instead they simply knocked down the structure of the League.

The League of Nations had failed to keep world peace primarily because the idea of collective security was far weaker than the individual State's desires to protect their national interests. As has been pointed out, one of the statesmen behind the creation of the League, President Wilson, saw the Organisation replacing the previous balance-of-power system with a centralised body which comprised powerful States acting in concert as the trustees of world peace. Paradoxically, it was the United States' refusal to join which could be said to be a primary example of a powerful State believing that collective security was not in its best interests.

Although the Covenant of the League of Nations did contain innovative provisions for collective security and provided for the imposition of embargoes and possibly collective military sanctions against offending States,[8] the League was doomed to failure because sovereign States continued to see national interests as paramount over collective interests despite the horror of the First World War, a situation exacerbated by the requirement in Article 5 of the Covenant of unanimity for most substantive decisions of the Council or Assembly of the League. Overriding considerations of national power resulted in the dilution of the League's powers to such an extent that the question of imposition of sanctions under Article 16 became not one for the consideration of the Council or Assembly, but for each individual member, evidenced by the piecemeal and ineffective sanctions imposed against Italy after its invasion of Abyssinia in 1935.[9] The failure to impose any sort of collective measures against aggressors meant the inevitable demise of the League.[10]

The competence of the UN Security Council

In chapter 6 it was noted that Article 24 of the UN Charter confers on the UN Security Council primary responsibility for the maintenance of international peace and security. In order to fulfil this responsibility the Charter confers on the Security Council an impressive array of powers in Chapters VI and VII. Chapter VI contains mainly recommendatory powers enabling the Security Council to encourage the pacific settlement of disputes, whereas Chapter VII contains a mixture of recommendatory and mandatory enforcement powers to enable the Council to take action with respect to threats to the peace, breaches of the peace or acts of aggression.

Generally, for the Security Council to utilise the recommendatory powers under Chapter VI it must determine that the conflict, whether principally internal or international must endanger international peace.[11] There is limited jurisprudence on the meaning of a 'danger' to international peace. Early discussion in 1946 on the Spanish Question revealed some concern as to the nature of disputes to be dealt with under Chapter VI when a sub-committee established by the Security Council determined that the existence and activities of the Franco regime in Spain endangered international peace and security.[12]

Despite this early practice the Council has developed the practice of utilising the powers of Chapter VI when it is politically desirable to do so without the need for a formal determination of a danger to international peace. Though this flexibility has a certain anti-formalist appeal enabling the Council to deal with any sort of dispute or situation under the provisions of Chapter VI, it does prevent the Council from being held accountable for simply ignoring certain conflicts, or from dealing with conflicts under Chapter VI of the Charter which should be dealt with under Chapter VII.[13]

Chapter VII of the UN Charter contains the enforcement powers of the Security Council. The 'gateway' provision to Chapter VII is Article 39 of the Charter which states:

> The Security Council shall determine the existence of any threat to the peace, breach of the peace or act of aggression and shall make recommendations, or decide what measures shall be taken in accordance with Articles 41 and 42, [economic sanctions or military measures] to maintain or restore international peace and security.

The term 'threat to the peace' is the most flexible of the jurisdictional concepts contained in Article 39 and one that enlarges the UN's ambit of competence compared to the League. Early practice indicates that a determination of a threat to the peace was a precursor to a later determination of a breach of the peace, in other words a threat to the peace was less serious.[14]

However, even in the early practice of the Security Council there were signs that the concept of a threat to the peace was much wider. The Spanish Question of 1946 raised the issue as to whether the remaining European Fascist regime of General Franco in Spain constituted a threat to the peace. In the end the Council failed to adopt a resolution as it split on whether the regime was a threat, and so ripe for sanctions under Article 41, or whether, as was suggested by its sub-committee, it was a potential threat to be dealt with under the recommendatory powers of Chapter VI.[15] The debate revealed that it is possible to view the situation within one country as being a threat to the peace. This certainly applies to internationalised civil wars such as found in the Congo between 1960–64. In 1961 the Security Council found the situation in that country was a threat to international peace and security.[16] Indeed, recent Council practice indicates that basic civil wars can constitute a threat to international peace, when it made such a determination in relation to the initial internal conflict in Yugoslavia in 1991,[17] and in relation to the civil wars in Somalia[18] and Liberia in 1992.[19]

The concept of a threat to the peace was developed in the Council's actions towards the racist regime in Southern Rhodesia between 1965 to 1979. The Council condemned the Unilateral Declaration of Independence by the Smith regime in November 1965, called for an oil embargo in the same month, then in April 1966 found that the breach of that embargo constituted a threat to the peace, and finally in December 1966 found that the 'present situation in Southern Rhodesia', as a whole, constituted 'a threat to international peace and security'.[20]

Although a serious civil war was developing in Southern Rhodesia, a war that involved surrounding States supporting the guerrillas, the basis of the finding of a threat to the peace appears to be the denial of self-determination to the black majority in that country. This conclusion is further strengthened by the Security Council's determination in 1977 that 'having regard to the policies and acts of the South African Government, ... the acquisition by South Africa of arms and related materiel constitutes a threat to the maintenance of international peace and security';[21] and by its condemnation in 1991 of 'the repression of the Iraqi civilian population in many parts of Iraq, including most recently in Kurdish populated areas, the consequences of which threaten international peace and security',[22] although in this situation it was the genocidal acts of the Iraqi regime, rather than the denial of Kurdish self-determination, that constituted the threat.

From this practice, which has mushroomed since the end of the Cold War, it can be seen that the Council developed the concept of a threat to the peace to cover civil conflicts but generally only if members of the Council could be persuaded that such conflicts have international repercussions, either in the form of a spillover of refugees or, more straightforwardly, in terms of regional or international peace. The latter qualification is so flexible as to make the concept of a threat to *international* peace a political decision rather than a legal requirement. The fact that the term 'threat to the peace' is in many ways simply used as a key word to unlock the gates to Chapter VII is shown by the recent extension of the concept in Council practice to cover the support for terrorism in the case of Libya,[23] and the denial of democracy in the case of Haiti.[24] Such developments reflect Western domination and it may simply be a matter of time before the Security Council finds other situations or countries a threat to the peace – for example drug-exporting countries, enabling it to apply the enforcement provisions of Chapter VII to a wider range of pariah States. Nevertheless, since the concept of a threat to the peace has not been defined in the Charter, and the International Court of Justice appears unwilling to review its use,[25] it is open to development by the Security Council and therefore there appears to be no legal limitation on the political extension of this concept.

Whilst the concept of a threat to the peace has been developed by the Council to cover intra-State violence and breaches of fundamental international laws, the concept of a 'breach of the peace' is applicable to inter-State uses of force. Logically, it can be argued that a breach of the peace is the correct finding for a less serious use of force, one not amounting to an armed attack, whilst 'aggression' is applicable to the serious uses of force.[26] However, in practice, the Council has used both terms for serious breaches of Article 2(4). Indeed, it has used the term 'breach of the peace' when dealing with full-scale attacks of one State by another, whilst it appears to have reserved the term 'aggression' for what could be called 'acts', as opposed to 'wars', of aggression, principally confining such determinations to *ex post facto* condemnations of Israeli and white South African attacks on neighbouring States.[27] The Council has found that there has been a breach of the peace on the following occasions: when North Korea invaded South Korea in 1950;[28] when Argentina invaded the Falklands/Malvinas islands in 1982;[29] in the Gulf War between Iraq and Iraq *seven* years after Iraq had invaded Iran;[30] and in 1990 when Iraq invaded Kuwait.[31]

'It would seem logical that any resort to armed force would come within the meaning of the phrase' breach of the peace.[32] Even if the phrase is defined more narrowly as referring to international and not internal peace, it appears, at the very least, incongruous, that a body established with primary responsibility for international peace and security has found a breach of the peace on only four occasions. The conflicts between Ethiopia and Somalia in 1977; Tanzania and Uganda between 1978–9; India and Pakistan between 1947–9 and again in 1965 and 1971; Vietnam and Cambodia in 1978; China and the Soviet Union in 1969; India and China in 1962; the Arab–Israeli Wars of 1948–9, 1956, 1967 and 1973; the Israeli invasions of Lebanon in 1978 and 1982; the Soviet armed interventions in Hungary 1956, Czechoslovakia 1968 and Afghanistan in 1979; the United States' incursions into Guatemala 1954, the Dominican Republic 1965, Grenada 1983 and Panama 1989, are just some of the most obvious breaches of international peace in the sense of direct inter-State armed conflict, on which the Council failed to make a determination under Article 39, or, in some instances, did not even discuss the matter. Bearing in mind the fact that we are only discussing the assertion of jurisdiction over a conflict by the Security Council, irrespective of whether the Council has adopted measures, it seems that the Council has so far failed to address many issues of inter-State peace, suggesting that it has failed in its collective security task. With the increasing trend after the Cold War of utilising the concept of 'threat to the peace' more readily, it was hoped that a similar trend might develop as regards breaches of international peace. However, the Council's reluctance to deal with these issues, unless they involve the interests of the powerful States, is shown by its failure, for example, to become involved in the solution of the conflict between Ecuador and Peru which broke out in February 1995.

The competence of the UN General Assembly

In 1945, when the UN Charter was drafted, there was a split between the Great Powers and the smaller States at the San Francisco conference as to the role and powers of the General Assembly. The Great Powers wanted it simply as a meeting place for the world community without granting it any real power, whereas the smaller States insisted that it be given more extensive powers. The result, in the best traditions of treaty drafting, was a compromise between those provisions which grant the Assembly wide powers and those that attempt to restrict it.

Article 10 allows the Assembly to 'discuss any questions or any matters within the scope of the present Charter' and 'make recommendations to the Members of the United Nations or to the Security Council or both on any such questions or matters'. Article 14 states that the Assembly 'may recommend measures for the peaceful adjustment of any situation, regardless of origin, which it deems likely to impair the general welfare or friendly relations among nations, including situations resulting from a violation of the provisions of the present Charter, setting forth the Purposes and Principles of the United Nations'. Both these very wide *recommendatory* powers are explicitly stated to be subject to Article 12(1), which provides that '[w]hile the Security Council is exercising in respect of any dispute or situation the functions assigned to it in the present Charter, the General Assembly shall not make any recommendation with regard to that dispute or situation unless the Security Council so requests'. This provision has been ignored in practice mainly because of the uncertainty as to what is meant by the Security Council performing its 'functions'.

The only other provision in Chapter IV of the UN Charter which attempts to restrict the Assembly's powers is Article 11(2) which provides, in part, that any question 'on which action is necessary, shall be referred to the Security Council'. The World Court in the *Expenses* case seemed to favour the view that the word 'action' in this provision referred to mandatory enforcement action which only the Security Council could order under Chapter VII, and did not in any way restrict the recommendatory power of the Assembly.[33] This interpretation is reinforced by Article 11(4) which states that the provisions of Article 11 do not limit the Assembly's recommendatory powers contained in Article 10.

Whatever the legal niceties of Chapter IV, the practice of the Assembly, during the period of Western domination (1945–55), through the years in which the Non-Aligned and Socialist majority were dominant, to the rather subdued post-Cold War Assembly, shows that the Assembly has developed its competence to deal with issue of peace and security. Apart from principles governing disarmament, it has developed a wide competence in recommending peaceful solutions, a subsidiary competence in peacekeeping matters, as well as a quasi-judicial capacity under which it condemns breaches of international law, all of which it has utilised extensively.

In addition, there was an early attempt to recognise that the Assembly had competence in the field of enforcement. With the Soviet Union's veto seriously debilitating the Security Council, the United States, wanting to use its dominant position within the Organisation in that first decade, and realising that the Security Council's action in Korea was only due to the Soviet absence at the time, proposed the Uniting for Peace Resolution, which was duly adopted by the pro-Western majority in the General Assembly in November 1950.[34] The resolution stated that although the initiative for the creation of a collective security system was with the Security Council, the Assembly desired that in the meantime the UN should have the means for maintaining international peace and security.

The Assembly resolved if the Council failed to act it would 'consider the matter immediately with a view to making appropriate recommendations to members for collective measures, including, in the case of a breach of the peace or act of aggression, the use of armed force when necessary'.

The Soviet Union stated that the resolution was *ultra vires*, arguing that collective action was solely within the province of the Security Council.[35] However, the resolution recognised the primary responsibility of the Security Council, and only granted the Assembly the power to *recommend* collective measures. Given that the Charter does appear to grant the Assembly wide recommendatory powers as regards peace and security, in addition to the fact that the World Court in the *Expenses* case recognised that the Assembly possessed significant subsidiary powers,[36] it can be argued that the resolution is *intra vires*, and that the only powers exclusively within the domain of the Security Council are the *mandatory* ones granted by Articles 40, 41 and 42.

Paradoxically, the Uniting for Peace Resolution, whilst being accepted in practice as a procedure of moving items from the Security Council's agenda to the General Assembly's (meeting in Emergency Special Session), has failed to make the intended impact in the realm of collective security in its proper sense. No UN enforcement action has been authorised by it, although it was used to authorise the first UN peacekeeping force, the United Nations Emergency Force (UNEF I) in the Sinai, in 1956, and it did take over as the mandating body for the UN Operation in the Congo (ONUC) in 1960, which came close to being an enforcement action.

Despite the fact that it has failed to develop a recommendatory power in the field of military action, the Assembly has developed an ability to call for sanctions against several member States, principally South Africa, Southern Rhodesia, Portugal and Israel.[37] It must be stressed, however, that these are *voluntary* sanctions, not *mandatory* ones.

Although the General Assembly cannot be said to have performed the tasks of the Security Council, it did develop a wide subsidiary competence, which helped maintain a minimal UN involvement in many conflicts during the Cold War period when there was a stalemate in the Council.

The competence of the UN Secretary General

From the relatively narrow provisions of the UN Charter concerning the office of Secretary General, the various holders of this post have developed an impressive set of powers to be used in the peaceful settlement of disputes and situations. Article 97 states that the Secretary General 'shall be the chief administrative officer of the Organization'. However, unlike the Secretary General of the League of Nations, who was simply a 'civil servant', the Secretary General is granted somewhat wider powers in the Charter. Article 98 provides that the Secretary General 'shall perform such other functions as are entrusted to him' by the Security Council, General Assembly, Economic and Social Council and the Trusteeship Council. Under this provision the Secretary General carries out the mandates granted to him by the Security Council or the General Assembly. This may range from sending a fact-finding mission, to offering his good offices, to the organisation and emplacement of a peacekeeping force.

The only autonomous power granted to him in the Charter is contained in Article 99 which provides that '[t]he Secretary General may bring to the attention of the Security Council any matter which in his opinion may threaten international peace and security'. Given the importance of the concept of a 'threat to the peace' in the workings of the Security Council, particularly as regards internal conflicts, this is potentially a very important provision. However, it has been little used by the office holders.[38]

Nevertheless, despite the fact that the Charter explicitly only grants the Secretary General the autonomous power to bring to the attention of the Security Council threats to international peace, over the years the office holder has developed an impressive set of autonomous or inherent powers, such as good offices, mediation, even arbitration and fact finding. These powers have developed either with the acquiescence of the Security Council and General Assembly, or sometimes with their active encouragement in the sense that it has been recognised that the Secretary General has inherent powers not dependent on a specific mandate from one of the other principal organs of the United Nations.[39]

The Secretary General's autonomous powers seem to have stretched as far as to allow the office holder, on his own authority, to send a fact-finding mission to a conflict, they have not extended as far as the authorisation of an observer force or peacekeeping force, that still has to be mandated by the Council or the Assembly, with the former dominating the peacekeeping function.[40]

Limitations upon the activities of the UN

Being a political organisation, the United Nations' activities are subject to the will of the political majority, and in the case of the Security Council, the permanent membership. The fact that the Security Council has a smaller membership, with a privileged sub-group within it, means that the political influences within it are different from those operating on the plenary body, the General Assembly. During the first decade of the UN's life, the Organisation as a whole was dominated by the West. This domination was felt in the Assembly, particularly in the expansion of the Assembly's powers in the field of peace and security, by, for example, the Uniting for Peace Resolution. The Western majority wished to expand the subsidiary role of the Assembly during the first ten years because the executive organ, the Security Council, was hamstrung by the Soviet Union, in the minority in both organs, using its veto. Indeed, the Security Council was paralysed, in the main, for the first forty years of its life by the vetoes of the permanent members. The West's use of the Assembly declined after the first decade when the dominance of that organ passed into the hands of the Non-Aligned majority with the advent of wide-scale decolonisation in the late 1950s. Although naturally the Non-Aligned majority continued to develop the Assembly's competence in the field of peace and security, the Assembly could not possess the same powers as the Security Council, in particular it had no power to enforce the will of the world community through the use of mandatory sanctions, and it had limited capacity, without the consent of the permanent members, to take military action.

In addition to the power of the veto, reviewed in chapter 3, there was another provision of the Charter that attempted to put the interests of individual States above those of the collectivity. Article 2(7) attempted to embed the principle of sovereignty in the UN, under the guise of removing from the purview of the United Nations, matters which were within the 'domestic jurisdiction of any State', except when the Security Council was considering 'the application of enforcement measures under Chapter VII'.

A very narrow reading of this provision would mean that all internal matters would be beyond the purview of the Security Council, the General Assembly or the Secretary General, unless the Security Council was utilising its enforcement powers under Chapter VII.[41] However, in practice all three 'organs' of the United Nations concerned with international peace and security have taken a narrow view of what is 'essentially within the domestic jurisdiction of any State'. As international law has developed since 1945 a number of what, *prima facie*, appear to be domestic matters have now been deemed to be of international concern and so susceptible to Security Council recommendations under Chapter VI, or similar General Assembly resolutions, as well as good offices moves by the Secretary General, or constituting threats to the peace within Chapter VII. It will be seen in the sections below that the denial of the right to self-determination, the widespread denial of human rights and civil wars, are amongst those issues that the United Nations has concerned itself with.

It is now necessary to turn to an overview of the practice of the UN, particularly the Security Council as the primary organ responsible for maintaining international peace and security. Its three areas of practice, peaceful settlement, peacekeeping and enforcement, will be considered in order to assess the effectiveness of the UN in the realm of collective security.

Peaceful settlement by the UN

The Council's powers of peaceful settlement are contained in Chapter VI. The basic provision in this chapter is the power to call upon States to settle their disputes by peaceful means, contained in Article 33(2). Clearly this power should be used to try to prevent disputes erupting into armed conflicts. It has occasionally been used in this way, for instance in 1982, with the invasion of the Falkland Islands imminent but not yet under way, the Council made a statement calling on Britain and Argentina to search for a diplomatic solution and refrain from the threat or use of force.[42] Although the warning was ignored, the call for a peaceful solution had more chance of being heeded than if it had been sometime after the conflict erupted. Indeed, when Argentina did invade the Islands, the Council immediately condemned the invasion as a breach of the peace under Chapter VII of the Charter.

Unfortunately during most of the Cold War period, the Council used its power under Article 33 simply as a token gesture with no real attempt to provide a solution to the conflict. The war between Iran and Iraq broke out on 17 September 1980, eleven days later the Security Council called on the parties to refrain from the use of force and to settle their dispute by peaceful means.[43] The fact that the war had already started meant that the Council should have been dealing with it as a breach of the peace under Chapter VII, an event which did not occur until July 1987. The end of the Cold War has not seen an end to this failure of preventive diplomacy. Indeed, there was no attempt by the Council to warn Iraq against invading Kuwait in 1990, its response, although much more forceful than in the Falklands Conflict or the Gulf War, only occurred *after*, the invasion of Kuwait.

The Council has the power, contained in Article 34, to despatch a fact-finding body to conflict zones. This power was little used during the Cold War, and again was often simply used as a panacea to disguise the lack of greater Security Council involvement. Indeed, the power was most often used to send a fact finding team to investigate *faits accomplis*, for example mercenary aggressions, when there was little prospect of the Council taking further action.[44] The end of the Cold War has seen a greater use of fact finding. Nevertheless, fact finding by the Security Council is not undertaken as a matter of course, it often relies on a patchwork of sources including established peacekeeping or observation teams, the Secretary General and his staff, and the occasional formal fact finding body mandated by a Security Council resolution. Whatever the source, fact-finding can only be undertaken with the consent of the State or States involved in the dispute. Although the Security Council has not attempted to invoke a mandatory power to send a fact-finding mission into a State, in the Gulf Conflict, after the cease-fire in March 1991, Iraq was subjected to very intrusive missions to ensure its compliance with the cease-fire resolutions on disarmament. Although Iraq consented to them, when it agreed to the permanent cease-fire in Security Council resolution 687 on 3 April 1991, it really had little choice given the threat of further military actions against it.

Without a mandatory power to order a State to accept a fact-finding mission, and in view of the fact that the Gulf Crisis was exceptional in the sense that military action *preceded* the missions when normally they should be one of the first steps taken by the Council, fact finding is not going to be properly institutionalised. Unfortunately, the codification of fact-finding principles by the General Assembly in 1992 did not question the requirement of State consent.[45] The fact is that even when States consent to such missions, they are often too late to contribute to prevent a conflict breaking out, and if a conflict is already under way, they do little towards its peaceful settlement. The sending of a fact-finding mission in May 1992 to the disputed enclave of Nagarny Karabakh, which is in Azerbaijan but is claimed by Armenia, was endorsed by the Security Council months after the dispute, which had been a long-running dispute between Soviet Republics, had become internationalised with the break up of the Soviet Union in December 1991.[46]

Article 36(1) of the UN Charter provides that the 'Security Council may, at any stage of the dispute', the continuance of which is likely to endanger international peace and security, 'or of a situation of like nature, recommend appropriate procedures or methods of adjustment'. The Council has used this provision to suggest methods of settlement or to support plans arrived at by the parties to a conflict sometimes with the good offices of the Secretary General and, recently, quite often with the utilisation of a peacekeeping force. During the Cold War, however, there was a tendency for the Security Council to adopt recommendations for the settlement of disputes, without envisaging any mechanism for their implementation. Many of these resolutions suffered from lack of clarity, an inevitable result of the political compromise necessary for their adoption. Resolution 242 for instance, adopted on 6 November 1967, five months after the Israeli seizure of the Occupied Territories following the Six-Day War, recommended a framework of principles to govern settlement of the Middle East Question including 'withdrawal of Israeli armed forces from territories occupied in the recent conflict.' The fact that this principle does not make it clear whether withdrawal should be from 'some' or 'all' the Occupied Territories has, in some ways, exacerbated the problem.

UN peacekeeping

Peacekeeping developed out of the need for the UN to observe the cease-fires it managed to broker in the first decade of its life. Conflicts arose as areas of the world were reshaped politically and sometimes physically after the Second World War. The struggle for decolonisation led to the need for observers in Indonesia in 1947, as that country struggled for independence from the Netherlands. Decolonisation also led to conflicts between newly independent States over disputed areas such as that over Kashmir, claimed by both India and Pakistan. The initial conflict ended in stalemate in July 1949, with the signing of the Karachi Agreement between India and Pakistan detailing a cease-fire.[47] This bilateral accord granted observation functions to the UN Military Observer Group in India and Pakistan (UNMOGIP), established by the Security Council.[48] This team of between forty and one hundred unarmed observers has reported on the cease-fire ever since, its presence contributing to relative stability in the area, though it was powerless to prevent major breaches of the cease-fire in 1965[49] and 1971.

The emergence of the State of Israel in 1948 was another significant factor in the genesis of peacekeeping. The first Arab–Israeli War that erupted out of this reshaping of the Middle East was eventually ended with acceptance of Security

Council resolutions calling for a cease-fire. The detailed functions of the UN observer force emerged out of the armistice agreements of 1949 between Israel on the one hand and Jordan, Syria, Egypt and Lebanon on the other. The functions of the UN Truce Supervision Organisation (UNTSO) were recognised by the Security Council in 1949, although the force had been *in situ* since 1948, to supervise the Truce negotiated by the Truce Commission with the authority of the Security Council.[50] This haphazard emergence of UNTSO's mandate was illustrative of the way peacekeeping developed in the formative years, with the Council responding to the requirements of the parties to the dispute rather than taking the initiative. Indeed, UNTSO has remained in the Middle East, its force of two to six hundred unarmed observers performing various functions in the region, observing cease-fires after the 1956, 1967, and 1973 Wars, as well as observing Palestinian and Israeli withdrawal from Beirut in 1982–83. UNTSO is another force that the Security Council has found essential to keep in a very volatile region of the world.

Peacekeeping took a major stride in 1956, when the Suez Crisis led to the establishment of the first full peacekeeping force, the First UN Emergency Force in the Middle East (UNEF I). This differed from the observation teams, already mentioned, in three ways. First of all the force was much larger, UNEF I comprised over six thousand troops at its height. Second, those troops had arms although only of a light nature, and finally the functions of the force were not only to observe and report on the situation, but also to secure and supervise the cessation of hostilities including the withdrawal of the armies of the United Kingdom, France and Israel.[51] Once this was achieved then the force was to act as a buffer between Israel and Egypt. However, the force was emplaced only after the belligerents had accepted the cease-fire and had agreed to withdraw. Although actively involved in separating the former warring parties, UNEF I was not empowered to keep them apart if major hostilities broke out again, being armed for the purposes of defence rather than enforcement.[52]

Peacekeeping follows from the parties to the conflict accepting a cease-fire or a withdrawal, and then consenting to the presence of a force on their soil. The principle of consent was graphically illustrated in 1967, when Secretary General U Thant ordered the withdrawal of UNEF I, after President Nasser of Egypt made it clear that Egypt's consent had been withdrawn. Although it may be argued that the General Assembly, as the author of UNEF's mandate, was responsible for its status and therefore it, not the Secretary General, had the power to withdraw the force, U Thant's decision *vis-à-vis* Egypt was essentially correct.[53] Indeed, it is highly likely that at least some contributing States would have withdrawn their troops if U Thant had not withdrawn UNEF I.[54] Nevertheless, the withdrawal of UNEF I and the ensuing Six-Day War illustrated the limitations of peacekeeping. It was somewhat ironic that the fourth major Arab–Israeli conflict, the Yom Kippur War of 1973, made States realise once again the usefulness of peacekeeping, when the Security Council created UNEF II,[55] which successfully supervised the renewed cease-fire between Israel and Egypt between 1973 and 1979 when the Camp David Accords finally established peace between the two States.

Although the UN Charter does not expressly provide for the emplacement of non-aggressive, consensual peacekeepers, their creation by the Security Council and the General Assembly can readily be encompassed by the UN Charter as the World Court recognised in the *Expenses* case.[56] Article 36 or Article 40 can be used as a basis for peacekeeping, in that peacekeepers traditionally oversee provisional measures such as a cease-fire and withdrawal, and more recently oversee the implementation of a peaceful solution agreed to by the parties.

Generally speaking, inter-State forces such as UNEF, UNMOGIP, UNIIMOG (emplaced between Iran and Iraq 1988–91) and UNDOF (in place on the Golan Heights between Israel and Syria since 1974), have the traditional tasks of supervising a cease-fire, and a withdrawal to positions occupied before the conflict started, both of which have already been consented to by the parties. An examination of inter-State forces reveals that they are almost always successful within the limited objectives of their mandates. In the case of intra-State peacekeeping forces the mandates sometimes have to be different to cope with the more difficult situation. The difficulties of peacekeeping in a civil war-type situation results in the principles of peacekeeping, namely consent, neutrality and limited self-defence, being much harder to achieve as the UN's experience in the Congo between 1960–64 illustrates.

The UN Operation in the Congo (ONUC) was initially sent under the authority of the Security Council at the request of the government of the Congo in July 1960, to provide assistance to that government until the Congolese security forces could fulfil their tasks following the breakdown of order on Belgian decolonisation.[57] By the time ONUC arrived it was in a precarious position, with fighting continuing in the Congo, rival governments being established, and the attempted secession of the Katanga region of the country with the active assistance of Belgian troops and mercenaries. A simple UNEF-type mandate and operation was clearly insufficient to prevent the collapse of the Congo altogether, which led the General Assembly,[58] and then the Security Council[59] to adopt resolutions which seemed to authorise the offensive use of force by the almost twenty thousand-strong UN force. Although ONUC, in the main, tried to keep within the principles of peacekeeping, particularly in the period before the adoption of Resolution 161, namely by negotiating cease-fires and by not overtly siding with any one of the factions, it eventually had to use force to subdue the Katangese rebellion in April 1961, again in December 1961, and between December 1962 and January 1963.[60] It is very difficult to see ONUC as a true peacekeeping operation, in that it was authorised to use force beyond that necessary for strict self-defence, it was not impartial in the conflict, it received little co-operation, and although it did have the formal consent of the central government, the fact was that for a period until August 1961 there was no real government in the Congo. On the other hand, ONUC was not clearly an enforcement action as undertaken by the UN force in Korea for instance, a view reinforced by the International Court in the *Expenses* case.[61]

The UN has utilised this rather dangerous combination of peacekeeping and enforcement in subsequent conflicts, principally in Bosnia where UNPROFOR has been present since 1992,[62] and Somalia where UNOSOM was emplaced between 1992 and 1995.[63] Although the UN's actions in the Congo were successful they have failed in Bosnia and Somalia leading to question marks being raised against using peacekeeping forces in an aggressive way, indeed whether such a use is compatible with the neutral nature of peacekeeping.[64]

Whereas the 'quasi-enforcement' approach to peacekeeping appears to undermine the credibility of the UN's role as a peace broker, the 'integrated and pacific' approach, which has also developed since the end of the Cold War, can be seen as a natural development of the principles of peacekeeping, namely those of neutrality, co-operation and consent. This method has involved bringing pressure to bear on the parties to a conflict not only to get them to accept a peacekeeping force to keep them apart, but also to accept a recommendation for settlement either by the Security Council, the General Assembly, the Secretary General or by outside States, bodies or individuals. Thus the force not only performs traditional functions such as supervising a cease-fire but also supervises the implementation of the peaceful solution to the conflict. More precisely, there are normally two or three separate forces or one force with two or three distinct elements, namely a traditional peacekeeping component, perhaps a civilian police element when necessary, and finally a civilian component, normally an election supervision division, to oversee the implementation of the agreed settlement process. Whilst the peacekeeping element is derived from Article 40, the police and election elements designed to help the parties towards the agreed solution are more obviously derived from Articles 36 and 37 of Chapter VI.

The origins of this approach can be traced back to the Cold War period, when the Netherlands and Indonesia sought and were granted General Assembly approval for the creation of a UN Temporary Executive Authority (UNTEA) and a UN Security Force (UNSF) on West Irian in 1962. This precedent has since been used by the Security Council during the changes in the geopolitical shape of the world with the end of the Cold War. The approach was first applied in Namibia. The 1978 mandate of the UN's Transition Assistance Group (UNTAG)[65] foresaw the creation of a unique force, combining traditional peacekeeping, the supervision of a cease-fire between, and the partial withdrawal of, South West African People's Organisation (SWAPO) guerrillas and South African troops; with a pacific solution to South Africa's occupation of Namibia, namely the policing and supervision of free and fair elections leading to an independent Namibia. Unfortunately, UNTAG was planned at the end of the period of *détente* in the 1970s. The decade that followed was dominated by the stepping up of the Cold War by both superpowers preventing any de-escalation in the civil wars in which they were involved. It was not until December 1988, that South Africa consented to the Namibian peace plan as a result of a superpower-sponsored package, which linked South African withdrawal from Namibia to Cuban withdrawal from Angola. After an inauspicious start, UNTAG performed its tasks effectively, supervising elections which led to the independence of Namibia on 21 March 1990.

The UN operation in Central America, particularly in Nicaragua, represented a further development of the peacekeeping function by the Organisation. Whilst UNTAG was concerned with bringing about a State's independence and could be seen as part of the UN's deep-rooted desire to end colonialism in all its forms, the operation in Central America was concerned with an already independent State. Again the initiative came from the parties to the conflict, benefitting from the thaw in East–West relations, when Guatemala, El Salvador, Honduras, Nicaragua and Costa Rica, signed the Guatemala Accords in August 1987.[66] The Agreements provided for a process of national reconciliation in each country leading to the ending of civil wars, and for a process of free elections in each country. Nicaragua became the first State in which this process was attempted and to facilitate it the parties requested UN supervision of the electoral process, as well as a UN multinational force to prevent cross-border attacks, weapons infiltration or any external involvement in the country's elections. To this end, the Security Council endorsed the Secretary General's establishment of a UN Observer Mission to Verify the Electoral Process in Nicaragua (ONUVEN), and a one thousand-strong UN Observer Group in Central America (ONUCA).[67] Both these forces contributed to the ending of the civil war in Nicaragua, the peaceful elections which ended in a surprise defeat for the Sandinistas on 25 February 1990, and the demobilisation of the Contras.

The Security Council has persisted with this approach with varying degrees of success – in El Salvador,[68] Western Sahara,[69] Cambodia,[70] Angola,[71] Mozambique,[72] Liberia,[73] and in Rwanda.[74] The operations have ranged from relative successes in El Salvador and Cambodia, to abject failures in Angola and more particularly in Rwanda, where the peace process collapsed with the genocidal actions of the Hutu government against the Tutsi minority in April 1994. Nevertheless, despite these serious setbacks, the Security Council appears ready to continue with this approach and to this end authorised a larger, seven thousand-strong, peacekeeping force (UNAVEM III) for Angola to try to rescue the peace plan in February 1995.[75]

Enforcement by the UN: economic sanctions

Article 41 of Chapter VII of the United Nations' Charter reads,

> The Security Council may decide what measures not involving the use of armed force are to be employed to give effect to its decisions and it may call upon the Members of the United Nations to apply such measures. These may include the complete or partial interruption of economic relations and of rail, sea, air, postal, telegraphic, radio, and other means of communication, and the severance of diplomatic relations.

The powers contained in Article 41 were intended to allow for the imposition of mandatory enforcement measures following a finding of a 'threat to the peace', 'breach of the peace' or 'act of aggression', by the Security Council under Article 39. However, on many occasions, the Council has been unwilling to take mandatory action with the consequence that it has settled for a call for voluntary measures or sanctions. Although the Charter base for such powers is inconclusive there is no doubt that the Council has developed such a power, the evolution of which lies in political compromise. Voluntary sanctions, as the term implies, are breached with impunity and so are relatively ineffective except for a certain symbolic role.

The UN Security Council has only used the weapon of mandatory sanctions once against an *aggressor*, a State breaching inter-State peace. In the case of Iraq, sanctions were first imposed by Resolution 661 of 6 August 1990, following Iraq's refusal to comply with the Council's mandatory cease-fire and withdrawal call in resolution 660 of 2 August 1990, the day of its invasion of Kuwait. Sanctions in this case were imposed very quickly and, as the terms of resolution 661 show, they were comprehensive. Resolution 661 prohibited the import of goods from, and the export of goods to, Iraq and Kuwait, except for 'supplies intended strictly for medical purposes, and, in humanitarian circumstances, foodstuffs', as well as a freeze on financial arrangements with Iraq and its overseas assets. The Council also decided to establish 'a Committee of the Security Council consisting of all the members of the Council', to examine reports on the progress of implementation of sanctions by member States. In analysing these reports, Bethlehem concludes that support for resolution 661 reached well over eighty per cent of the membership of the UN. Many non-members responded positively, although at least one, Switzerland, stated that it was not under a legal obligation to impose sanctions against Iraq.[76]

The sanctions regime against Iraq appeared relatively watertight. As Bethlehem states,

> From the outset, Iraq appeared to be uniquely placed to be influenced by sanctions: it was a one product economy that had recently emerged from a punishing war against Iran; the movement of its principal export commodity, oil, was relatively easy to track and interdict; Iraq imported between 60–70% of its basic food requirements; with the possible exception, in the early stages of the crisis, of Jordan, it could not count on support from any of its immediate neighbours to circumvent sanctions; in an unprecedented show of solidarity, virtually the entire international community had condemned the Iraqi action which had been the cause of the crisis. In short, if sanctions as a means of enforcing international law were not to succeed here, they would not be likely to succeed elsewhere.[77]

Indeed, the Security Council adopted a series of resolutions to fine-tune the embargo,[78] including, the authorisation given to mainly Western navies in the Gulf to intercept suspected sanctions-breaking ships. Sanctions were imposed in August 1990; by January 1991, when the UN-authorised military campaign started against Iraq, sanctions did not appear to have weakened Iraq's resolve to hang on to Kuwait, although they may have affected Iraq's military capacity to resist the overwhelming military action launched against it. Nevertheless, question marks must be raised against the effectiveness of sanctions. Sanctions were continued against Iraq by resolution 687 of 3 April 1991 after military action successfully ousted Iraq from Kuwait. The purpose of the continuing sanctions regime was to secure Iraq's compliance with the resolution's provisions on disarmament and compensation, although the hidden agenda must have been to undermine the regime of Saddam Hussein. Resolution 687 provides for a review of the sanctions regime against Iraq 'every sixty days in the light of the policies and practices of the Government of Iraq'. The sanctions remain in place.

If we look to the effectiveness of sanctions, a fundamental flaw can perhaps be perceived. The aim of sanctions was expressly stated not to be to starve the people of Iraq into submission, but initially to weaken Iraq's hold on Kuwait and then, following its defeat in Kuwait, to force it to comply with its obligations to disarm and to compensate States and individuals for its aggression. This was made clear from the outset by Resolution 661 adopted on 6 August 1990 and elaborated upon by Resolution 666 of 13 September 1990. The latter resolution outlined a mechanism whereby the Sanctions Committee would monitor the food situation in Iraq and make determinations of how particular needs ought to be met. The Committee struggled to achieve the aim of not using 'starvation as a weapon'.[79] Nevertheless, whereas some States, including the United States, thought that the sanctions regime prohibited foodstuffs unless there was clear evidence of humanitarian need, other States on the Council, particularly Cuba, argued that there was a general humanitarian need in Iraq, and therefore all foodstuffs should be allowed into Iraq without any particular proof being required.[80] It appears that the direct effect of sanctions was not on the regime's grip on Kuwait, and when removed from that country in March of 1991, on its grip over its own people, but upon the Iraqi people themselves, significant elements of which, it appears from independent reports, suffered and continue to suffer from malnutrition and an increase in diseases.[81]

The Security Council was not unresponsive to these negative effects. In Resolution 687, 3 April 1991, which contained the terms of settlement imposed on Iraq, the Security Council formalised the 'no-objection' procedure which had come to replace the necessity for proof of humanitarian need in the Council's Sanctions Committee. This meant that the export of foodstuffs or other materials or supplies for essential civilian needs was permitted as long as the Committee was notified, and there were no objections to the cargoes in that Committee. In addition to this *prima facie* right to export foodstuffs to Iraq, the Council permitted, by Resolution 706 of 15 August 1991, Iraq to sell $1.6 billion of oil to allow for the purchase of foodstuffs and medicine for its civilian population in general. The Security Council established the mechanisms for the sale and the transfer of funds in Resolution 712 of 19 September 1991, but Iraq has so far refused to export any oil, complaining of violations of its economic sovereignty. Without this income Iraq is unable to purchase the foodstuffs it requires and must depend on the provision of charitable aid. Indeed, the UN is funding, in part, its humanitarian activities in Iraq, by the seizure of Iraqi funds abroad and the selling of Iraqi petroleum deposits outside Iraq.[82]

Iraq must blame itself for the suffering of its people, not only by the fact that it has not taken advantage of the Security Council's offer, but also by its unwillingness to comply fully with Resolution 687. In addition, one must not forget that it was Iraq which had clearly violated international law in August 1990. Nevertheless, it appears that the sanctions regime is not a sufficiently sharp weapon to point directly at those responsible for the invasion, namely the Iraqi regime of Saddam Hussein. The ordinary Iraqi citizens appear to be the ones suffering, more particularly those elements, the Kurds in the north and the Shiahs in the south, that revolted against the regime and are now suffering themselves from an internal embargo imposed by the Iraqi government as punishment.

It is possible to argue that the sanctions weapon, although a blunt instrument and not capable of removing aggression, is more suitable to remove threats to the peace in that they are directed at those who must change the internal situation, both rulers and ruled. However, the Iraqi experience shows that the people who suffer the most are those who are not responsible for the unlawful acts, namely the ordinary citizens. Furthermore, the effect is not only on the citizens of Iraq or the target State, but also on the peoples and governments of States that have traditionally traded with the target State. The sanctions regime against Iraq illustrates that the Security Council was really powerless to address the immediate economic plight of other States such as Jordan, even though Article 50 of the UN Charter provides that such States have 'the right to consult the Security Council with regard to a solution of those problems'.[83] Whether or not sanctions provoke a change in the Iraqi regime, either by fostering discontent in the population, or by eventually forcing the regime to fundamentally change the system in a way acceptable to the Security Council, the sanctions experiment against Iraq, appears to suggest that economic coercion is not an effective alternative to military coercion *per se*, and that sanctions alone are not an adequate enough weapon on which to base a system of collective security.

Other than Iraq, the Security Council has deployed the mandatory sanctions weapon in the following instances of *threats to the peace*: comprehensive regimes against Southern Rhodesia from 1968–79, Yugoslavia (Serbia and Montenegro) from 1992, and the Bosnian Serbs from 1994; more selective regimes against Libya from 1992, Haiti 1993–94, and UNITA held areas of Angola from 1993; and arms embargoes against South Africa between 1977–94, and against Somalia and Liberia from 1992. It is clear from this list that during the Cold War the Council was greatly reluctant to use its full powers under Article 41, but with the freeing of the Council from the chains of the superpower veto, the Council has used the power contained in Article 41 quite frequently. The fact that the Council has increased the use of its mandatory powers to impose sanctions indicates that it feels that they are effective in a collective security role. The purpose here will be to review the use and effectiveness of sanctions to combat and control threats to the peace.

There have been varying assessments of the effectiveness of the mandatory economic measures imposed against Rhodesia. The figures produced by the Security Council's Committee established to monitor reports on the effect of the sanctions regime suggest that, after initially struggling, from 1968 the Rhodesian economy improved.[84] This data provides *prima facie* evidence to deny the effectiveness of economic measures.[85] Nevertheless, there is evidence to suggest that after 1974 with the combined effects of Mozambique's independence (Portugal, the colonial power, was a major sanction breaker), the guerrilla war and the sanctions regime, the Rhodesian domestic situation as a whole began to decline. Although the application of sanctions did not immediately achieve the primary goals of the Security Council of either ending UDI by forcing Smith to negotiate or ruining the Rhodesian economy and thus forcing internal change, it did help to achieve certain subsidiary goals which must be viewed as a success. These were namely, the limitation of the conflict mainly to Rhodesian soil, the prevention of foreign military intervention to end UDI, and the eventual encouragement of the white regime to negotiate.

Some more recent, and yet incomplete, sanctions regimes will now be considered. Although the evidence on the effectiveness of these embargoes is preliminary it might be suggested that the sanctions experiences against Rhodesia and Iraq show that the only potentially successful method of ensuring that the weaknesses of the relatively strong target State's economy are exposed is to impose an immediate comprehensive embargo. Limited embargoes are insufficient because even if they are aimed at those areas of weakness the other unsanctioned areas of the economy will develop to compensate. Nevertheless, there are humanitarian considerations to be taken into account when a full embargo is imposed. (As discussed in the Iraq case in the preceding section.)

The use of an arms embargo against South Africa was questionable because South Africa's strong economy and natural resources supply, enabled it to produce its own weapons. However, an effectively policed arms embargo may be successful against a country totally dependent on outside States providing arms, particularly when there is no real prospect of that country being able to produce its own arms, as with the arms embargo against war-torn Somalia imposed by the Council in Resolution 733 of 23 January 1992. However, the resolution contained no machinery for the monitoring of arms shipments, and without that the Council is simply relying on members' sense of obligation towards a mandatory decision of the Council. The Council's mandatory arms embargo against Liberia imposed by Resolution 788 of 19 November 1992 seems to have had a greater impact on the peace process in that ravaged country, although by far the major factor seems to be the military activities of the ECOWAS 'peacekeeping' force, reviewed in chapter 8, which is exempted from the embargo. The effect of a mandatory oil and arms embargo against another extremely poor country, Haiti, by Resolution 841 adopted on 17 June 1993 seems to have been more dramatic, with the military regime agreeing to the restoration of democracy under the deposed President on

2 July 1993. However, there was a subsequent lack of implementation of the agreement with the result that the Security Council reimposed the oil and arms embargo in October 1993, accompanied by the authorisation to member States to stop suspected sanctions-breaking ships.[86] Although sanctions were further expanded in May 1994,[87] it required the threat, in July 1994,[88] of a UN-authorised United States' military operation, for the military dictatorship in Haiti to step down in October 1994, consenting to a US and then a UN force to oversee the return to democracy. Sanctions were lifted on 16 October 1994.[89] Again it seems that sanctions alone, without the threat or use of military force, were inadequate for the tasks.

Nevertheless, these instances provide limited evidence that sanctions imposed to combat internal situations designated threats to the peace can be effective if the target State is very weak, and that it does not necessarily require a comprehensive embargo to make these effective. Indeed, a comprehensive embargo against a State whose population is below the poverty line would seem inhumane in the extreme. A slightly different approach has been taken as regards the civil war in Angola following the breakdown in the peace process, with the Security Council imposing a mandatory arms and oil embargo only against UNITA-held areas of Angola.[90] This approach was later adopted in September 1994 when the Security Council imposed a more comprehensive regime against the Bosnian Serbs.[91] In these cases, sanctions are directed at the faction responsible for the continuation of the internal conflict, but this more 'just' approach is only possible in a State which is not only divided politically or ethnically but also geographically.

A more comprehensive embargo was imposed against the remnants of the war-torn State of Yugoslavia by Resolution 757 of 30 May 1992. The Council condemned the continued intervention by Yugoslavia (Serbia and Montenegro) and Croatia in the former Yugoslav Republic, and emerging State, of Bosnia, and determined that the situation there constituted a threat to international peace and security. Despite the fact that both Serbia and Croatia were intervening in Bosnia in support of the factions there, the Security Council implicitly blamed Serbia when it imposed mandatory sanctions against it on the import or export of commodities except for 'supplies intended for medical purposes and foodstuffs' notified to the Council's Committee on Sanctions against Yugoslavia, established by resolution 724 of 15 December 1991, as well as a freeze on financial and other transactions with Yugoslavia (Serbia and Montenegro).

The resolution built on the mandatory arms embargo imposed against the whole of Yugoslavia by resolution 713 of 25 September 1991. Clearly the aim of the arms embargo resolutions against Somalia, Haiti, Liberia and the former Yugoslavia, was to prevent the escalation of the civil wars which would occur if outside States supplied arms to one faction or the other. One problem with this approach is that it leaves the most poorly-armed faction, in the latter instance, the Muslims in Bosnia, in a very vulnerable position. An attempt to lift the arms embargo to allow the Bosnian Muslims to receive arms was defeated on 29 June

1993 by a vote of six in favour to none against with nine abstentions in the Security Council.[92]

The aim of the more comprehensive sanctions regime against Serbia is to prevent its forces assisting the Bosnian Serbs in their struggle to gain more territory in Bosnia. Unlike the arms embargo which is to prevent escalation, the aim of the regime against Serbia is to punish it for its intervention and support for the policy of ethnic cleansing, and to coerce it into withdrawing its military support for the Bosnian Serbs, as well as forcing that faction to agree to the proposals for the peaceful settlement of the conflict in Bosnia.[93] The evidence is that the sanctions are having a dramatic effect in Serbia and Montenegro with hyper-inflation, unemployment and many shortages as the embargo is tightened by those States surrounding Serbia, and by the presence of NATO forces in the Mediterranean.[94] Sanctions seemed to have led, in part, to Serbia's agreement to close its border with Bosnia in return for the suspension of some of the economic sanctions against it in September 1994.[95]

One final point to note in this catalogue of UN sanctions regimes is the mandatory arms and air embargo imposed against Libya in Resolution 748 of 31 March 1992. This followed a determination by the Council that Libya's support for terrorism constituted a threat to international peace and security and was designed to coerce Libya into not supporting terrorism, in particular, to hand over the two suspected of the Lockerbie bombing. So far the resolution has not had its desired effect. In response, the Security Council ordered States to freeze Libyan assets abroad and also not to supply any oil-related equipment.[96] Again the Council is adopting an incremental approach but has so far stopped short of a mandatory oil embargo. One of the problems being that to have sanctions regimes in place against two of the world's major oil producers, Iraq *and* Libya, might severely disrupt the World's economy.

Enforcement by the UN: military measures

As with the UN's use of sanctions, the use of military force to achieve collective security goals has an uneven track record, although the evidence seems to suggest that military measures are more effective in removing aggressors, illustrated by the limited success against North Korea in 1950, and the greater success against Iraq in 1991. The evidence is less clear-cut as regards threats to the peace where there is not often a clear 'enemy', although the threat of force against the military rulers in Haiti was successful in removing them without the need to use force in 1994. In other cases of threats to the peace, particularly in Bosnia and Somalia, the use of force has proved ineffective, in particular in Somalia where UNOSOM II was withdrawn in March 1995 leaving the civil strife to continue in that country.

Although the effectiveness of military measures will be further considered in this brief review, it is necessary to concentrate on a more important issue of principle – namely whether the military actions authorised by the UN fulfil the principle of collective security and thereby reinforce the UN claims to world government or do they constitute unacceptable delegations of power to dominant States?

The Organisation's collective security role was premised, in 1945, on the ability of its primary organ, the Security Council, ultimately to use military measures to enforce the peace. The Council's ultimate weapon and deterrent was contained in Article 42.

> Should the Security Council consider that measures provided for in Article 41 would be inadequate or have proved to be inadequate, it may take such action by air, sea or land forces as may be necessary to maintain or restore international peace and security. Such action may include demonstrations, blockade, and other operations by air, sea, or land forces of Members of the United Nations.

Article 43 of the Charter provides a specific mechanism whereby the power granted to the Security Council could be made operative – by in effect creating a standing UN army which could be ordered by the Security Council to deal with threats to or breaches of the peace. This did not come about because of the pressure of the Cold War. Instead, the Council has simply recommended military action in certain instances and has relied on States voluntarily offering their services.

Nevertheless, it would appear legally acceptable for the Council to use the power granted to it in Article 42 without the mechanisms that were designed to make the imposition of military coercion a practical option. If an alternative practical option emerges such as an *ad hoc* coalition prepared to act under UN authority, then there would be a presumption that the action is lawful.

Although it may be argued that the creation of a UN army is not necessary to make the Council's military option under Article 42 a practicality, the Charter does strongly indicate that UN control of such military operations is an essential prerequisite for the legality of military action by the Security Council. This appears to be made clear by Articles 46 and 47(3) which provide that 'plans for the application of armed force shall be made by the Security Council with the assistance of the Military Staff Committee', and 'the Military Staff Committee shall be responsible under the Security Council for the strategic direction of any armed forces placed at the disposal of the Security Council ...'. It can be argued that strategic control by the Military Staff Committee and overall political control by the Security Council appear necessary for the achievement of the collective security concept, in that they embody the centralisation of the collective use of force. This argument can be used to criticise the Security Council's practice in the use of the military option, when it has simply delegated authority and control to a State or group of States.

A counter-argument would be to state that if the Security Council simply authorises a State to use force to achieve an objective within the ambit of the UN's security role, despite the fact that it is being performed by one State, it is still a *collective* use of force, in that it is being performed to carry out the collective will of the Security Council on behalf of the United Nations. This is all the more so when the Security Council authorises a group of States to carry out such a function.

The answer lies somewhere between these poles. It probably would be too formalistic and bureaucratic to require control by UN Committee, though it must be said that enforcement of sanctions is put under the control of a Committee of the Security Council. Nevertheless, a complete delegation of control of a military operation to a member State or a collection of States would lack that degree of centralisation legally necessary to designate a particular military action as a *United Nations* military action, as opposed to a unilateral or multilateral, and probably illegal, use of force outside the umbrella of the UN. The minimum legal requirement for a military action to be a UN military action, is first of all a resolution authorising the use of force, and second, that resolution and subsequent resolutions should specify clearly the extent, nature and objectives of the military action. Problems of lack of continuous control can be overcome by a clear and unambiguous mandate at the outset. If States using force under this authority then wish to use more or less force, they must seek a change in mandate from the Security Council.

Such a legal requirement ensures that the UN Security Council is in control of military operations undertaken under its authority, it does not prevent dominant groups within the Security Council using that organ to achieve their ends as well as the UN's. Use of centralised power to achieve the ends of a dominant individual or group within any society is not necessarily unlawful, if that power is channelled correctly through the institutional structures. Current dominance by the West in the Security Council does not mean that when the West uses that organ to protect Western interests it is automatically a misuse of power as long as the military action achieves the collective security purposes of the Organisation as well.

The result, however, is an erratic collective security system, stuttering into life only when the interests of the West are affected, but is that not better than none at all? Indeed, arguments of self-interest may embarrass the West into agreeing that the Council can be used to fulfil purposes beyond narrow Western interests – witness the increasing use of NATO under the authority of the UN in Yugoslavia and UN-authorised actions in war-torn Somalia. However, in these conflicts there are some doubts about the commitment of the powerful States to the resolution of the crisis.

The initial failure of UN operations to provide humanitarian assistance to the starving people of Somalia in 1992 led to the Secretary General outlining the options the Council had in order to create conditions for uninterrupted delivery of relief supplies to Somalia.[97] The final choice from these options vividly illustrates the changing nature of UN operations in civil conflicts, away from simple humanitarian provision towards enforcement. The options were: first, a continued deployment of UNOSOM under the existing principles of peacekeeping. The Secretary General stated that this option 'would not in present circumstances be an adequate response to the humanitarian crisis in Somalia'. Second, to abandon the use of international military personnel to protect humanitarian relief, withdraw UNOSOM's military elements and leave humanitarian agencies to negotiate with faction leaders. This option was favoured by some of the humanitarian agencies but the Secretary General stated that he was 'more than ever convinced of the need for international military personnel to be deployed in Somalia'. Finally, that force should be used either by UNOSOM, in a limited area or country wide, or by a group of States under Security Council authorisation.[98]

As regards the last option, while favouring the development of enforcement action under the command and control of the United Nations in the future, the Secretary General recognised that at the current time, the UN did not have the capacity to mount such an operation within the time frame required. Dr Ghali concluded that the only option was to resort to Chapter VII of the Charter. Again although stating a preference for UN command and control of such an operation, he stated that a Council-authorised operation undertaken by member States would be acceptable as long as the aims of the operation were precisely defined and limited in time to enable post-conflict peacekeeping and peacemaking.

The Secretary General concluded that the US Secretary of State had informed him that if the Council would authorise the use of force to ensure aid delivery, the United States was willing to lead such an operation.[99]

On 3 December 1992, the Council unanimously adopted Resolution 794 'under Chapter VII', authorising the 'Secretary General and Member States co-operating to implement the offer' by the United States 'to use all necessary means to establish as soon as possible a secure environment for humanitarian relief operations in Somalia', after determining that the 'magnitude of the human tragedy caused by the conflict in Somalia, further exacerbated by the obstacles being created to the distribution of humanitarian assistance, constitutes a threat to international peace and security'. The Council demanded that the parties comply with a cease-fire and co-operate with the force to be established. The resolution contained very little concerning the command and control of the force, indeed it implicitly left it to the United States by authorising 'the Secretary General and the Member States concerned to make the necessary arrangements for the unified command and control of the forces involved, which will reflect the offer' made by the United States. The resolution did not mention a time frame nor specific tasks for the US-led Unified Task Force (UNITAF) beyond the establishment of a 'secure environment for humanitarian relief operations in Somalia'.

Under the initial phase of 'Operation Restore Hope', UNITAF was composed of twenty-eight thousand US personnel, later to be supplemented by seventeen thousand personnel from twenty other States. UNITAF was emplaced on 9 December 1992 and it immediately adopted a fairly aggressive stance towards disarming the various factions in the country and in opening up humanitarian aid routes. It was not afraid to use substantial force beyond that required for self-defence. The United States started to reduce its troop commitment in February 1993, even before the Security Council approved the Secretary General's proposal[100] for a twenty-eight thousand-strong UN force (UNOSOM II) under Chapter VII of the Charter on 26 March 1993. Resolution 813 authorised the use of force if necessary to ensure the delivery of humanitarian assistance, but also stressed the need to restore peace, to disarm factions, and to protect relief workers, suggesting the possible wider use of force. The force would also be responsible for returning hundreds of thousands of refugees, clearing land mines, setting up a police force, and helping to rebuild the economy.

UNITAF handed over responsibility, effectively for the policing of Somalia, on 4 May 1993. The new force attempted to continue the aggressive approach of the US led force and is so doing lost any semblance of neutrality in the conflict, by taking forceful actions against one of the factions, the Somali National Alliance, and under Security Council authority, seeking the arrest of that faction's leader for attacks against UNOSOM II.[101] The UN effectively became one of the factions in a civil war on which it could not impose its will. In this 'no-win' situation the UN force ignominiously withdrew from Somalia in March 1995.

The collective action in Somalia not only illustrates the dangers of a peace-keeping force being converted or being supplemented by an enforcement action, it also highlights the problem of using volunteers to enforce the will of the international community: that those volunteers may withdraw their services as with the withdrawal of the US forces from UNITAF and their replacement by what was essentially a peacekeeping force with an enforcement mandate. This cannot be prevented unless the Security Council binds the States to act, a power envisaged in the original Charter scheme but not activated, as also evidenced by the US withdrawal from the NATO naval patrol in the Adriatic in November 1994. Although the sanctions against the former Yugoslavia are mandatory and binding on all States including the US, the request that they be enforced by NATO and WEU warships was simply a recommendation,[102] not binding on the US or any other contributing State.

However, in all instances when the Security Council has authorised the use of force by a State or group of States on behalf of the UN – Korea, the Gulf, Somalia, Yugoslavia, Haiti, Rwanda – there has been a legal defect, namely insufficient centralisation of the aims and objectives of the authorisation.

For instance, its authorisations of naval forces to take necessary measures to enforce sanctions regimes against Rhodesia in 1966,[103] Iraq in 1990,[104] and Yugoslavia in 1993, did not specify what levels of force were to be used, for example firing across the bows or firing at the suspected sanctions-breaking ship. This raises question marks about whether the authorisation to use force was adequately centralised. Despite the lack of centralisation in these limited naval operations, there is no evidence to suggest that the States concerned, in any way interpreted the language of the enabling resolutions to enable them to pursue national aims beyond those stated by the Security Council. There is of course a far greater danger of this happening when the Security Council authorises the full scale use of force against an aggressor.

In the case of Korea in 1950, the Council recommended 'that the Members of the United Nations furnish such assistance to the Republic of Korea as may be necessary to repel the armed attack and to restore international peace and security in the area'.[105] The Secretary General wished for some form of central UN control of this force,[106] but the United States rejected this idea. Instead, as we all know, the US commanded and dominated the force which appeared to be following the war aims of the United States, not the UN, when it crossed the 38th parallel. Insufficient centralisation either of objectives or of control undermined the credibility and the legality of the operation, even though the US-led force eventually managed to combat the North Korean aggression.

In the Gulf War, there were similar doubts about the legality of the extent of delegation to the United States, although the operation itself was confined to defensive action – the removal of Iraq from Kuwait.[107] Resolution 678 of 29 November 1990, authorised member States 'to use all necessary means to uphold and implement Security Council resolution 660 and all subsequent resolutions and to restore international peace and security in the area' unless Iraq withdrew before 15 January 1991.

The unnecessarily ambiguous language of this resolution seems to breach the legal requirement of UN control of the operation. The Coalition actions were not supervised by the Council, the Coalition simply reported on its activities. Nevertheless, it can be argued that the need for greater UN control of the operation does not necessarily signify that the operation was contrary to the UN Charter. The use of force needs to be assessed to see if it achieved those aims set out in resolution 678 as restrictively interpreted above. The Coalition of forces operating under the umbrella of the UN, but not on this occasion using its flag as in Korea, started its air campaign against Iraq on 16 January 1991 soon after the deadline in resolution 678 ran out. The ground offensive started on 24 February 1991 and was successful in achieving the liberation of Kuwait within five days. It appears that, individual actions in the campaign apart, which must be judged by the laws of war,[108] the Coalition did adopt a reasonable interpretation of Resolution 678 limiting the military action to the enforcement of Resolution 660 and other resolutions of the Security Council aimed at securing the withdrawal of Iraq from Kuwait. Although the air campaign did penetrate deep into Iraq and was aimed at industrial as well as military targets, and the ground offensive included a large part of southern Iraq involving a temporary occupation of part of the south after the war, these actions appeared necessary to achieve the successful liberation of Kuwait without the need for a long drawn-out and even more destructive war between Iraq and the Coalition.

The campaign against Iraq was limited to UN objectives, it was not hijacked for Western purposes beyond those that coincided with Western purposes. Although it is probable that the Security Council could authorise an offensive war involving the overthrow of a regime, such as that in Iraq, with a record of aggression, such an aim should be clearly spelt out in the enabling resolutions. Nevertheless, the defeat of Iraq enabled the Security Council to impose a temporary cease-fire on Iraq in mandatory resolution 686 of 2 March 1991, which, *inter alia*, forced Iraq to rescind its annexation of Kuwait, accept its liability for damages caused by its aggression, release third State nationals and prisoners of war, return all property seized in Kuwait, and to provide information on all mines and weapons left in Kuwait. Iraq complied and also agreed to the even more stringent mandatory resolution providing for a permanent cessation of hostilities, Resolution 687, adopted on 3 April 1991 which obliged Iraq to compensate for its aggression, imposed some disarmament provisions, and provided for the demarcation of the boundary between Iraq and Kuwait as well as continuing the sanctions regime. The Security Council, in effect, decided that it would maintain pressure on the Iraqi regime by the use of sanctions rather than the use of force.

Despite the success of the operation in the Gulf, question marks hang over the extent that the UN simply delegated its power to a group of willing volunteers. In order to combat these doubts it must be admitted that whereas the prevention of aggression is indeed a legitimate and ultimate aim of a collective security system, the methods of achieving it need to be clearly stated and approved if the action itself is going to comply with the principle of collective security and also the rule of law.

Similar accusations of lack of centralisation of the use of force can be found in the resolutions authorising NATO air strikes: against warplanes violating the air space above Bosnia,[109] and the protection of so-called safe areas,[110] where the resolutions again use the elliptical phrase 'necessary measures'. However, in practice a large measure of UN control of NATO airstrikes has emerged, with NATO strikes only taking place at the request, or with the consent, of UNPROFOR – the so-called 'dual key' approach.[111]

As regards the Security Council authorisation for the United States to use force in Haiti in 1994, the resolution simply said that the Council 'acting under Chapter VII of the Charter ... authorises Member States to form a multinational force under a unified command and control and, in this framework, to use all necessary means to facilitate the departure from Haiti of the military leadership ...' and to create the conditions for the restoration of democracy.[112] This is arguably an unacceptable delegation of power to the United States shown by the fact that the removal of the military dictatorship was finally achieved by US negotiators led by Jimmy Carter and had nothing to do with the UN.[113]

There are, undoubtedly, problems with relying on a system of volunteers to uphold collective security ideals, not the least of which is the erratic nature of such a method in that aggression will only be met by force when there are volunteers to be found. States will generally only volunteer when it will serve their purposes as well as the UN's. Political considerations apart, the legality of these UN-authorised operations is still a matter of heated debate, but there are now, within UNs terms, several precedents for recommendatory military action, and it is arguable that the Security Council has by its practice,[114] established a power to authorise States to take 'necessary measures' with regard to a particular conflict or situation. On the other hand, it is arguably legally unacceptable to imply a power which goes against the express provisions of the Charter which clearly envisage collective security in the form of the centralisation of armed force. In this respect the Council authorisations to use force to date, when there is often neither a clear and relatively precise enabling resolution nor UN control of these operations, undermine the constitutionality of the resolutions in this crucial area of UN practice. Nevertheless, as the number of precedents increase, the line between illegality and legality will be crossed.

Although there some doubts about the constitutionality of UN military operations, there has been an increase in the number of successes since the end of the Cold War. However, the inconsistent responses of the world community, inevitable in a system which relies simply on the recommendation of military action, illustrates that as yet the UN cannot claim to embody the collective security ideal.

Concluding remarks

A comparison between the failed attempt at creating a collective security system in the League of Nations, and the partially successful and still developing UN experiment, reveals a process of evolution along rationalist lines, which holds out the prospect of a 'minimal' world government in the area of collective security. There are numerous weaknesses in the UN system, most of which have been detailed in this chapter.

In the area of peaceful settlement and peacekeeping there is a large element of collectivity in the resolutions and operations adopted and undertaken. However, although peacekeeping is important, it is not a coercive power and cannot form the basis of a collective security system. Indeed, there are strong arguments for keeping peacekeeping, as a neutral and consensual method of pacific settlement, separate from enforcement which puts the UN in a position of the 'enemy' of the target State.

Nevertheless, a collective security system must have teeth if it is to be effective. In intractable conflicts, not susceptible to pacific settlement, coercive measures, distinct and entirely separate from peacekeeping, must be undertaken. The defect in the UN system is that once the move is made away from pacific settlement and peacekeeping towards enforcement action, the greater the lack of collectivity. Military authority is simply delegated to one or more powerful States. Economic sanctions have less of this stigma in that they do entail a collective obligation not to trade with the target State, although the most recent sanctions regimes have, in the main, been imposed at the instigation of the West, and more particularly, the regimes have relied on Western military power to make them effective. Furthermore, there is evidence that sanctions are not, *per se*, an effective alternative to military coercion, which places greater emphasis on military enforcement action where Western domination is even more predominant.

A critical evaluation, which would categorise most other visions of world order, from rationalist to functionalist, as reinforcing Western liberal ideology, might well admit that the UN is utilising governmental powers in the post-Cold War era. The UN, from a critical perspective, might be seen as furthering Western ideology by, for example, using the neutralist terminology of peacekeeping, to impose Western-style democracies on developing States through the brokerage, and supervision, of elections; or, more overtly, furthering Western causes by selectively using the enforcement powers of the Security Council.

As this chapter has shown, enforcement actions are dominated by the militarily powerful Western States, particularly the United States, leading to the subversion of the collective security ideal. However, in the case of peacekeeping, although the use of elections has been the dominant method which has sometimes been used prematurely in countries not yet ready, either politically or economically, for such an exercise, it still can be seen as a continuation of the traditional non-aligned method of peacekeeping, favouring neither left nor right, but allowing the people to decide. The result is a democracy but not necessarily a Western 'capitalist' democracy. This aspect of peacekeeping is not dominated by the powerful States, indeed in many ways, it can be seen as a genuine 'collective' effort, authorised by the Security Council, but often supported by the majority in the General Assembly as well. If military enforcement operations were to have evolved in a similar collective fashion, as envisaged in the UN Charter, the UN would be in a better position to portray itself as a successful and equitable collective security system. Nevertheless, as the following chapter shows, the UN is still the dominant organisation in the area of collective security.

Notes

[1] K. P. Sakensa, *The United Nations and Collective Security*, 4–5 (1974).

[2] L. A. Mander, *Foundation of a Modern World Society*, 59 (1948).

[3] See Articles 1(1), 2(5), 2(7), 50, 53 of the UN Charter.

[4] Y. Dinstein, *War, Aggression and Self-Defence*, 2nd edn (1994).

[5] J. N. Singh, *Use of Force under International Law*, 82 (1984).

[6] H. Notter, *Origins of the Foreign Policy of Woodrow Wilson*, 328–29 (1937).

[7] C. H. M. Waldock, 'The Regulation of the Use of Force by Individual States in International Law', 81 *Hague Recueil* (1952), 455 at 471.

[8] Articles 10, 11 and 16 of the Covenant.

[9] See F. S. Northedge, *The League of Nations: its life and times*, ch. 10 (1986).

[10] On the limited development of military measures, see F. Seyersted, *United Nations Forces*, 28–9 (1966).

[11] See Articles 34 and 36 of the UN Charter.

[12] Report of the Sub-Committee on the Spanish Question, 1 UN SCOR Special Supp. (No. 2) (1946).

[13] See N.D. White, *Keeping the Peace: The United Nations and the Maintenance of International Peace and Security*, 38–44 (1993).

[14] SC Res. 54, 3 UN SCOR Resolutions 22 (1948), re the first Arab–Israeli conflict.

[15] SC 45–8 mtgs, 1 UN SCOR (1946).

[16] SC Res. 161, 16 UN SCOR Resolutions 2 (1961).

[17] SC Res. 713, 46 UN SCOR Resolutions (1991).

[18] SC Res. 733, 47 UN SCOR Resolutions (1992).

[19] SC Res. 788, 47 UN SCOR Resolutions (1992).

[20] SC Res. 216, 217, 20 UN SCOR Resolutions 8 (1965); 221, 232, 21 UN SCOR Resolutions 7 (1966).

[21] SC Res. 418, 32 UN SCOR Resolutions 5 (1977).

[22] SC Res. 688, 46 UN SCOR Resolutions (1991).

[23] SC Res. 748, 47 UN SCOR Resolutions (1992).

[24] SC Res. 841, 48 UN SCOR Resolutions (1993).

[25] See chapter 5.

[26] See GA Res. 3314, 29 UN SCOR Supp. (No. 31) 142 (1974).

[27] Condemnations of South African 'aggression' include: SC Res. 387, 31 UN SCOR Resolutions 10 (1976) re Angola; SC Res. 466, 35 UN SCOR Resolutions 17 (1980) re Zambia; SC Res. 568, 40 UN SCOR Resolutions 20 (1985) re Botswana. Condemnations of Israeli 'aggression' include: SC Res. 573, 40 UN SCOR Resolutions 23 (1985) re PLO base in Tunis; SC Res. 611, 43 UN SCOR Resolutions 15 (1988), re assassination of Abu Jihad.

[28] SC Res. 53, 5 UN SCOR Resolutions (1950).

[29] SC Res. 502, 37 UN SCOR Resolutions 15 (1982).

[30] SC Res. 598, 42 UN SCOR Resolutions 5 (1987).

[31] SC Res. 660, 45 UN SCOR Resolutions 19 (1990).

[32] L. M. Goodrich, E. Hambro and P. S. Simons, *The Charter of the United Nations*, 296, 3rd edn (1969). See further B. Simma (ed.), *The Charter of the United Nations*, 609 (1994).

[33] *Certain Expenses of the United Nations*, I.C.J. *Rep.* 1962, 151 at 163.

[34] GA Res. 377, 5 UN GAOR Resolutions 10 (1950).

[35] GA 299 mtg, 5 UN GAOR (1950). See Articles 11(2) and 12 of the UN Charter.

[36] I.C.J. *Rep.* 1962, 162–5.

[37] GA Res. 1663, 16 UN GAOR Supp. (No. 17) 10 (1961); GA Res. 2107, 20 UN GAOR Supp. (No. 14) 62 (1965); GA Res. 2151, 21 UN GAOR Supp. (No. 16) 68 (1966); GA Res. 39/146, 39 UN GAOR Supp. (No. 51) 50 (1984).

[38] See for example SC 873 mtg, 15 UN SCOR (1960), re the Congo. See further, B. Simma (ed.), *Charter*, 1048–57.

[39] See the General Assembly's Declaration on the Prevention and Removal of Disputes and Situations which may Threaten International Peace and Security and the Role of the United Nations in this Field, GA Res. 43/51, 43 UN GAOR Supp. (No. 49) 276 (1988).

[40] See R. Lavalle, 'The "Inherent" Powers of the UN Secretary General in the Political Sphere: A Legal Analysis', 37 *N.I.L.R.* (1990), 22.

[41] D. R. Gilmour, 'The Meaning of "Intervene" within Article 2(7) of the United Nations Charter', 16 *I.C.L.Q.* (1967), 330 at 349.

[42] SC 2349 mtg, 37 UN SCOR (1982).

[43] SC Res. 479, 35 UN SCOR Resolutions 23 (1980).

[44] See for example the special mission to Benin, 32 UN SCOR Special Supp. No.3 (1977), followed by a general condemnation of mercenary aggression, SC Res. 419, 32 UN SCOR Resolutions 18 (1977).

[45] GA Res. 46/59, 46 UN GAOR (1992).

[46] 29(3) *UN Chronicle*, (1992), 35.

[47] UN doc. S/1430 (1949).

[48] SC Res. 47, 3 UN SCOR Resolutions 17 (1948).

[49] See also the UN India–Pakistan Observation Mission (UNIPOM), 1965–66, established to oversee the cease-fire line beyond Kashmir, R. Higgins, *United Nations Peacekeeping: Documents and Commentary*, Vol. 2, 419–70 (1970).

[50] SC Res. 73, 4 UN SCOR Resolutions 7 (1949); SC Res. 54, 3 UN SCOR Resolutions 22 (1948).

[51] GA Res. 998, 1 UN GAOR ESS Supp. (No. 1) 2 (1956).

[52] UN docs A/3289 and A/3302 (1956).

[53] UN doc. A/6370 (1967). But see J. I. Garvey, 'United Nations Peacekeeping and Host State Consent', 64 *A.J.I.L.* (1970), 241.

[54] Higgins, *Peacekeeping*, Vol. 1, 339 (1969).

[55] SC Res. 340, 28 UN SCOR Resolutions 12 (1973).

[56] I.C.J. *Rep.* 1962, 151. For a discussion of this case, see chapter 2 under the section 'Judicial consideration'.

[57] SC Res. 143, 15 UN SCOR Resolutions (1960).

[58] GA Res. 1474, 4 UN GAOR ESS Supp. (No. 1) 1 (1960). It could be said that this added nothing more to the mandate than indicated in previous Council resolutions – SC Res. 143, 146, 15 UN SCOR Resolutions (1960).

[59] SC Res. 161, 169, 16 UN SCOR Resolutions (1961).

[60] UN doc. S/5240 (1963).

[61] I.C.J. *Rep.* 1962, 177.

[62] SC Res. 743, 47 UN Resolutions SCOR (1992). Although States are authorised to render assistance to UNPROFOR in the form of enforcement in order to facilitate the delivery of humanitarian assistance – SC Res. 770, 47 UN SCOR Resolutions (1992) – UNPROFOR has, in the main, adopted a consensual approach to peacekeeping. However, the deployment of the Rapid Reaction Force in July and August 1995 marks a move towards enforcement – SC Res. 998, 50 UN S/PV (1995).

[63] SC Res. 751, 47 UN SCOR Resolutions (1992).

[64] See N. D. White, 'U.N. Peacekeeping: Development or Destruction?', 12 *International Relations* (1994), 129.

[65] SC Res. 435, 33 UN SCOR Resolutions 6 (1978).

[66] 26 *I.L.M.* (1987), 1164.

[67] SC Res. 637, 644, 44 UN SCOR Resolutions (1989).

[68] SC Res. 693, 46 UN SCOR Resolutions (1991).

[69] SC Res. 690, 46 UN SCOR Resolutions (1991).

[70] SC Res. 717, 46 UN SCOR Resolutions (1991).

[71] SC Res. 696, 46 UN SCOR Resolutions (1991).

[72] SC Res. 797, 47 UN SCOR Resolutions (1992).

[73] SC Res. 866, 48 UN SCOR Resolutions (1993).

[74] SC Res. 872, 48 UN SCOR Resolutions (1993).

[75] SC Res. 976, 50 UN S/PV (1995).

[76] D. Bethlehem, (ed.), *The Kuwait Crisis: Sanctions and their Economic Consequences*, xxxiv–xxxvi (1991). UN doc. S/21585 (1990).

[77] Bethlehem, *Kuwait Crisis*, xliii.

[78] SC Res. 666, 669, 670, 45 UN SCOR Resolutions 22, 24 (1990).

[79] Provisional Record of the 5th meeting of the Sanctions Committee, 31 August 1991, USSR. Bethlehem, *Kuwait Crisis*, 797.

[80] See for example the argument between Cuba and the United States over a cargo of powdered milk, *ibid.*, 809–10.

[81] UN doc. S/22799 (1991).

[82] SC Res. 778, 47 UN SCOR Resolutions (1992).

[83] On this see SC Res. 669, 45 UN SCOR Resolutions 24 (1990). Bethlehem, *Kuwait Crisis*, ch. 3.

[84] See UN doc. S/12265 (1975).

[85] J. A. Sigmon, 'Dispute Resolution in the United Nations: An Inefficient Forum?', 10 *Brooklyn Journal of International Law* (1984), 437 at 450.

[86] SC Res. 874, 875, 48 UN SCOR Resolutions (1993).

[87] SC Res. 917, 49 UN SCOR Resolutions (1994).

[88] SC Res. 940, 39 UN SCOR Resolutions (1994).

[89] SC Res. 948, 49 UN SCOR Resolutions (1994).

[90] SC Res. 873, 48 UN SCOR Resolutions (1993).

[91] SC Res. 942, 49 UN SCOR Resolutions (1994).

[92] The UN General Assembly requested that the Security Council lift the arms embargo against the Bosnian Muslims in GA Res. 48/88, 48 UN GAOR (1993), by 109 votes to 57.

[93] See further SC Res 820, 48 UN SCOR Resolutions (1993).

[94] SC Res. 787, 47 UN SCOR Resolutions (1992).

[95] SC Res. 943, 49 UN SCOR Resolutions (1994).

[96] SC Res. 883, 48 UN SCOR Resolutions (1993).

[97] UN doc. S/24868 (1992).

[98] 30(1) *UN Chronicle* (1993), 13–16.

[99] UN doc. S/24868 (1992).

[100] UN doc. S/25168 (1993).

[101] SC Res. 837, 48 UN SCOR Resolutions (1993).

[102] SC Res. 787, 47 UN SCOR Resolutions (1992).

[103] SC Res. 221, 21 UN SCOR Resolutions 5 (1966).

[104] SC Res. 665, 45 UN SCOR Resolutions 21 (1990).

[105] SC Res. 83, 5 UN SCOR Resolutions 5 (1950).

[106] T. Lie, *In the Cause of Peace*, 334 (1954).

[107] It has been argued that the UN authorisations in the cases of Korea and Kuwait were simply calling for or endorsing collective defence operations under Article 51 of the UN Charter – Simma (ed.), *Charter*, 611.

[108] N. D. White and H. McCoubrey, 'International Law and the Use of Force in the Gulf', 10 *International Relations* (1991), 347 at 359–73.

[109] SC Res. 816, 48 UN SCOR Resolutions (1993).

[110] SC Res. 836, 48 UN SCOR Resolutions (1993).

[111] Security Council resolutions authorise NATO airstrikes 'subject to close co-ordination' with the UN Secretary General and UNPROFOR. See for example SC Res. 958, 49 UN SCOR Resolutions (1994), which authorised NATO airstrikes against Serb airbases in Croatia. They do not explicitly state that UN consent is necessary before each strike.

[112] SC Res. 940, 49 UN SCOR Resolutions (1994).

[113] See also SC Res. 929, 49 UN SCOR Resolutions (1994), authorising the French humanitarian operation in Rwanda.

[114] See Article 31(3)(b) of the Vienna Convention on the Law of Treaties 1969.

8

Regionalism and collective security

It is true to say that the United Nations is the predominant actor in the field of peace and security. As this chapter will show, regional, defence and security organisations perform a subsidiary, sometimes peripheral role, particularly in the area of peacekeeping. It is clear that in a formal legal sense, according to the letter of the UN Charter and the constituent treaties of these organisations, in the areas of peaceful settlement, peacekeeping and collective defence, these organisations have freedom of action, whilst in certain types of enforcement action, the Security Council has formal supremacy. Whether this is the position in the practice of these bodies will be the subject of this chapter. First to be considered will be the legal positions of these types of organisations.

Regional organisations

Supporters of regional organisations, principally the Latin American States and the League of Arab States, lobbied at San Francisco to remove regional organisations operating in the security field from the purview of the United Nations. Their view received some support in that Article 51 of the UN Charter permitted regional organisations to act in collective self-defence against aggression without authorisation from the Security Council. Further support for regional organisations can be seen within Chapter VIII, Article 52 of which permits regional organisations to undertake pacific measures to settle disputes and consensual peacekeeping within their region without authorisation from the Security Council. However, Article 52(4) makes it clear that attempts at pacific settlement by regional organisations do not preclude parallel and perhaps conflicting action by the Security Council.[1]

As regards the division of collective security responsibility the UN Charter is quite clear. Article 53(1) provides,

> The Security Council shall, where appropriate, utilize such regional arrangements or agencies for enforcement action under its authority. But no enforcement action shall

be taken under regional arrangements or by regional agencies without the authorization of the Security Council ...

Enforcement actions designed to restore or maintain international peace and security appear to be those measures contained within Chapter VII of the Charter, namely economic or military coercion which may be used not only in a defensive way, but also offensively to remove threats to, and breaches of, the peace. Article 53 seems to make it clear that any use of such measures must have their basis in a Security Council resolution. When a regional organisation such as the Organisation of American States (OAS), or indeed a *prima facie* collective defence pact such as the North Atlantic Treaty Organisation (NATO), is planning an action which is not entirely defensive, they must have the approval of the Security Council for such an operation. Such a provision represents a triumph for the globalists over the regionalists in the realm of collective security and has presented a problem to regional organisations such as the OAS wishing to take coercive action within their regions.

Defence and security organisations

Article 51 of the UN Charter, which preserves the 'right of individual and collective self-defence if an armed attack occurs against a member of the United Nations, until the Security Council has taken measures necessary to maintain international peace and security ...', was introduced, in part, to preserve the autonomy of the emerging Inter-American security system and to prevent its paralysis by the veto in the Security Council of the United Nations. In the original Dumbarton Oaks proposals, the Security Council was required to authorise enforcement action by regional organisations. Working on the assumption that this provision could possibly cover defensive actions taken by such organisations, the Latin American States, supported by France and the United States, insisted on the insertion of Article 51, which preserved the regional organisations' ability to take collective defensive action until the Security Council took measures – in other words the veto could not prevent the operation of collective self-defence by such organisations, although Security Council authorisation was still required for enforcement action. The right of collective self-defence was defined by the Chairman of the relevant Committee at San Francisco.

> ... an aggression against one American state constitutes an aggression against all other American states and all of them exercise their right of legitimate defense by giving support to the state attacked, in order to repel such aggression. That is what is meant by collective self-defense.[2]

However, whereas the Inter-American system involved the development of a complex treaty network of which collective self-defence was just a part, the non-fulfilment of the collective security provisions in the UN Charter due to the Cold War, led to the emergence of pacts based entirely on collective self-defence.

The defensive alliances which gave rise to NATO and the Warsaw Pact seemed to provide the post-war world with a kind of security, at least in terms of East–West relations, so that it appeared that the collective security system of the UN had been replaced to a large extent by a system of collective defence and mutual deterrence. Nevertheless, it is correct to say that collective defence and collective security are not one and the same thing,[3] and that it was somewhat fortuitous that a system of collective defence did provide an alternative method of keeping a limited peace, in terms of preventing a third world war, during the Cold War. Legally speaking, collective defence is undertaken solely in response to an armed attack, whilst a collective security system is concerned with the much wider issue of preserving international peace and security by dealing, *inter alia*, with threats to the peace as well as breaches of it.

The leading example of a defensive pact is NATO. The North Atlantic Treaty Organisation came into force on 24 August 1949. The Treaty has sixteen parties drawn principally from Western Europe and North America.[4] Unlike regional organisations such as the OAS, which has a defensive pact built in, NATO has none of the economic and social trappings of such bodies. The defensive right is contained in Article 5.

> The parties agree that an armed attack against one or more of them in Europe or North America shall be considered an attack against them all; and consequently they agree that, if such an armed attack occurs, each of them, in exercise of the right of individual or collective self-defence recognized by Article 51 of the Charter of the United Nations, will assist the party or parties so attacked by taking forthwith, individually, and in concert with the other parties, such action as it deems necessary, including the use of armed force, to restore and maintain the security of the North Atlantic area.
>
> Any such armed attack and all measures taken as a result thereof shall immediately be reported to the Security Council. Such measures shall be terminated when the Security Council has taken the measures necessary to restore and maintain international peace and security.

This provision follows Article 51 of the UN Charter quite closely with its requirements of an armed attack, its duty to report to the Security Council, and the temporary nature of defensive action in the face of Security Council measures. The subservience of NATO to the UN is reinforced by Article 7, which reaffirms the primary responsibility of the Security Council for the maintenance of international peace and security.

Neither NATO nor the Warsaw Pact were called into operation during the Cold War in that there were no actions in collective self-defence following an armed attack against parties to these treaties. Nevertheless, NATO has been used in the post-Cold War era by the Security Council, to undertake limited enforcement action in Bosnia. It appears that NATO is simply being used by the UN as a convenient 'sub-contractor', able and willing to undertake the limited aerial enforcement mandate given to it.[5] Since the individual member States of NATO could have volunteered to undertake the mandate, it follows that the UN Security Council can use NATO in this fashion. What is clear is that NATO could not act in this way without Security Council authorisation, the basis of which lies in Articles 39 and 53 of the UN Charter.

With the collapse of the Warsaw Pact and the emergence of the Common-wealth of Independent States (CIS), more emphasis has been placed on the pan-European security body, the Conference on Security and Co-operation in Europe (CSCE), renamed the Organisation on Security and Co-operation in Europe (OSCE) in December 1994.[6] The essence of this security organisation appears simply to take effective collective action in the fields of peaceful settlement,[7] and peacekeeping,[8] by utilising individual members existing powers. Since it has not yet claimed enforcement powers, the question of it coming under the umbrella of the UN Security Council has not yet arisen. If such a power were claimed as the Organisation continues its rapid evolution, then it would formally be subject to the limitation of Article 53 of the UN Charter. The first step in this direction, how-ever, has been taken by the CSCE claiming to be a regional arrangement under Chapter VIII of the Charter, at its Helsinki meeting in 1992, although the Con-ference only envisaged peacekeeping operations at that stage.[9]

Peaceful settlement and peacekeeping

Regional organisations possess similar powers to the UN in the area of pacific set-tlement. Article 3(3) of the Charter of the OAU, for instance, provides that the member States agree to the 'peaceful settlement of disputes by negotiation, medi-ation, conciliation or arbitration'. Unlike the UN, the Organisation of African Unity (OAU) is a much looser knit organisation relying primarily on informal diplomacy and the good offices of the OAU's Secretary General, despite the fact that the OAU Charter deliberately restricts the Secretary General to the role of an administrator.[10] As was stated in chapter 5, the OAU has, since 1964, established a Commission of Mediation, Conciliation and Arbitration.[11] However, this organ has not become operational reflecting the unwillingness of African States to submit to formal dispute resolution mechanisms and also the limited budget of the African Organisation. In an attempt to start a culture of institutional pacific set-tlement, the OAU Heads of State at their twenty-ninth summit in Cairo in June 1993 proposed the establishment of the African Mechanism Apparatus for Pre-venting, Managing and Resolving African Crises, a body with a specific mandate to prevent and resolve disputes and conflicts as well as undertaking peacekeeping tasks.[12]

The OAS is a much more developed regional organisation and has, as part of its Treaty make-up, the *Pact* of Bogotá or American Treaty on Pacific Settlement of 1948,[13] which is concerned solely with the settlement of disputes by peaceful means and provides for procedures of good offices, mediation, investigation, con-ciliation, judicial settlement and arbitration. However, there is a contrast between theory and practice. In practice the OAS does not use this Treaty but uses the organs of the OAS created by the *Charter* of Bogotá of 1948. These are: the Inter-

American Conference which 'has the authority to consider any matter relating to friendly relations among the American States';[14] the Meeting of Consultation of Ministers of Foreign Affairs which considers urgent matters of peace and security; the Council which is permanently in session and has as a subsidiary organ, the Inter-American Committee on Peaceful Settlement, which has the mandate to assist in the pacific settlement of disputes through recommendations of settlement as well as mediation and inquiry;[15] and the Secretary General who has developed a good-offices function like his UN counterpart, and also since 1985 possesses the power to bring to the attention of the Council or the Assembly 'any matter which in his opinion might threaten the peace and security of the hemisphere'.[16]

Furthermore, dispute resolution mechanisms and procedures can be found in the leading defence organisation's make-up. In 1956 the primary organ of NATO, the North Atlantic Council, made a clear commitment to the peaceful settlement of disputes among members by resolving that when disputes cannot be settled by direct negotiation, they should be submitted to NATO's good-offices procedure through NATO's Secretary General.[17] The European Union (EU) and OSCE are quickly developing fact finding and good-offices abilities after the end of the Cold War, both organisations being involved in attempted peaceful settlement in the former Yugoslavia,[18] and the OSCE in negotiating cease-fires and proposed settlements in the rebellious Russian republic of Chechenia in 1995.

Several international organisations have, like the UN, developed the power to deploy peacekeeping forces. Although the express power to do this is not contained in the constituent document, these organisations have developed the practice as an implied or inherent power in order to facilitate their peaceful settlement powers. If a peacekeeping operation conforms to the legal principles of peacekeeping, namely, consent, co-operation, neutrality and limited use of force for defensive purposes, then it can be lawfully undertaken by regional, defence or security organisations, or indeed on a collective or individual *ad hoc* basis. Consensual, non-offensive operations do not breach the ban on the use of force contained in Article 2(4) of the UN Charter, nor are they actions which require authorisation by the Security Council under Article 53.

Examples of international organisations creating peacekeeping forces include: an Arab League force emplaced in Kuwait in 1961; the Commonwealth Force in Southern Rhodesia pursuant to the Lancaster House Agreement of 1979; and an unsuccessful OAU force emplaced in Chad to oversee a cease-fire in 1981. Although by no means a complete list, these three instances of peacekeeping by regional organisations illustrate the principles and practice in this area. More recent examples not detailed here include a CIS force in Georgia emplaced in July 1994,[19] and the EU administration of Mostar in Bosnia starting in December 1993. In addition, there have been several joint peacekeeping efforts in recent years with both the UN and the regional body involved. For example, the UN and the OAS have shared responsibility for the fraught passage of Haiti from dictatorship to democracy, starting with the elections of 1991.

The Arab League's peacekeeping involvement in Kuwait arose from the independence of that country from the United Kingdom on 19 June 1961.[20] Six days later, Iraq reasserted its claim to sovereignty over Kuwait. This was accompanied by implicit threats to use force so that on 30 June, the rulers of Kuwait requested British and Saudi Arabian assistance, under the provisions of the agreement by which Kuwait achieved independence, six thousand British and Saudi Arabian troops arrived within a week. It was explicitly stated by Britain in the UN Security Council that the forces were only to be employed in a combat role if Kuwait were to be attacked from across the border.[21]

On 20 July 1961, the Council of the Arab League adopted a resolution, in the absence of the Iraqis who had walked out in protest before the vote was taken, which authorised the members of the Arab League to assist Kuwait 'for the preservation of its independence' upon withdrawal of British troops. The force consisted of troops from several Arab States and was expressly stated to be acting under the Arab League's Joint Defence and Economic Co-operation Treaty of 1950[22] (to which Kuwait had quickly adhered), which provides for collective self-defence in the face of aggression, as well as the Pact of the Arab League of 1945 (to which Kuwait had been admitted, again in the absence of Iraq), which allows the Council to take measures necessary to combat aggression.[23] By the middle of October 1961, the Arab League force was in place and the British forces had been removed. By January 1963 the Iraqi threat had receded and the force was reduced to one simply of observation. The installation of a new regime in Iraq in February 1963 led Kuwait to request the final withdrawal of League troops.

The precise basis of the Arab League Force in Kuwait remains unclear. It seems to be an action in preparation for self-defence and therefore not requiring UN Security Council authorisation under Article 53 of the UN Charter. However, while still not needing Council authorisation, in many respects the force performed a peacekeeping role with the consent of the government of Kuwait. It did not have Iraqi consent, but neither was it in fact pitted against the Iraqis as a belligerent. It acted in many ways as a buffer force, observing the continuation of peace between the two countries. Although neither the Arab League Pact nor the later Defence Treaty explicitly envisaged the creation of a peacekeeping force by the Arab League, it can be argued that such a power can readily be implied for a regional organisation concerned with peace and security, just as such a power has been established by the UN in practice. The successful performance of the Arab League in Kuwait in 1961, in what was essentially an inter-State conflict, where it did comply with the requirements of its own treaties as well as the UN Charter, must be contrasted with the League's performance in the internecine conflict in Lebanon starting in 1976 (reviewed below). This contrast highlights the difficulty of peacekeeping in internal conflicts.

Nevertheless, there are precedents for successful peacekeeping operations in civil wars by bodies outside the UN. The internecine conflict in Southern Rhodesia was brought to an end by the Lancaster House Agreement of 15 December 1979 which: defined the terms of a constitution for an independent Republic of Zimbabwe; arrangements for the immediate pre-independence period during which the country would return to the status of a British dependent territory under a Governor, while elections were held; and finally, the details of a cease-fire to end the fighting in the guerrilla war.

The cease-fire agreement entered into by the parties to the conflict stated that the British government was responsible for the establishment of a monitoring force under the Command of the Governor's Military Adviser, 'to assess and monitor impartially all stages of the inception and maintenance of the cease-fire by the forces'. The Commanders of the Rhodesian security forces and those of the Patriotic Front forces undertook to co-operate fully with the Commonwealth Force. The agreement also provided that 'members of the monitoring force will carry weapons for their personal protection and will be provided with vehicles and aircraft carrying a distinctive marking'.[24] In a statement accompanying the cease-fire agreement, the Chairman of the conference, Lord Carrington, stated that the force would be twelve hundred strong and would contain troops from Australia, New Zealand, Kenya, Fiji and the United Kingdom. His statement also made it clear that the Commonwealth Force's role was one of peacekeeping not enforcement.

> It is impossible for any external authority or force to guarantee that a cease-fire will be effective. Only the parties themselves can ensure this. The purpose of [the agreement] is to help the forces to initiate and maintain a cease-fire through arrangements by which they can be separated from their present inter-locked positions ... The task of a monitoring force is not and cannot be to compel either side to maintain a cease-fire, or in any sense to guard the forces of one side or the other. Its task is to observe and report on the manner in which the forces maintain the cease-fire agreement and thus to give an assurance that it will not be possible for any force to conduct any activities in breach of the cease-fire ...[25]

The cease-fire became effective on 29 December 1979 and despite breaches was held sufficient for the election process to be held, supervised by Rhodesian and British police as well as British election officials at the end of February 1980. A Commonwealth Observer Group (COG) and British election observers pronounced that, despite intimidation and irregularities, the election result, by which Robert Mugabe's Zimbabwean African National Union (ZANU) party came to power, fairly reflected the wish of the Zimbabwean electorate. The Commonwealth Monitoring Force (CMF) withdrew in March 1980.[26]

The CMF was clearly a peacekeeping force, and despite the fact that the Commonwealth has no express power to create such a force, again, it can be seen as a necessary implied power for an international body concerned with the peace and security of its members. The establishment of a stable, if subsequently undemocratic Zimbabwe, showed the positive aspect of a combination of peacekeeping and pacific settlement, an approach which has been widely used by the United Nations in recent years. It also shows the benefits of a combined approach over a simple traditional peacekeeping force such as United Nations Interim Force in Lebanon (UNIFIL) in Lebanon or the OAU's force in Chad.

The OAU force in Chad in 1981 to 1982[27] was again authorised by a regional organisation not having specific competence to create a peacekeeping force but was accepted as coming within the implied powers of such a body. The Chairman of the OAU, President Moi of Kenya, specified two conditions before the OAU force was to be sent to the civil war in Chad. They were: the invitation of the government of Chad, and the withdrawal of Libyan troops present in the country since 1980 at the request of the President of Chad.

The mandate of the OAU force was unclear. The enabling resolution of the Assembly of the OAU defined the function of the force as ensuring 'the defence and security of the country whilst awaiting the integration of Government Forces'. President Moi envisaged a far greater role, namely the supervision of free and fair elections in Chad. Both of these aims are within the ambit of peacekeeping and the emphasis throughout was on the neutrality and impartiality of the force, but it appeared that the President of Chad saw the force simply as an arm of his government to be used in fighting against the rebels.

In addition, the OAU force was poorly organised, lacked logistical support, and was not properly financed, the OAU having no experience in peacekeeping and limited resources. Six States originally volunteered to provide ten thousand troops, but after withdrawals, a force of only just over three thousand arrived in Chad. Western financial help and a fund established by the Security Council of the United Nations,[28] helped to finance the operation.

It was clear that the rival Chadian forces were unwilling to negotiate a cease-fire (a normal precondition for the emplacement of a peacekeeping force), let alone a peaceful solution. In this atmosphere Nigeria withdrew half its contingent leaving a force which was increasingly, and inevitably, becoming involved in the fighting. When the Chadian capital fell to the rebel forces in June 1982, the Chairman of the OAU ordered the withdrawal of the force by the end of the month.

The OAU operation in Chad was a failure not only because it was badly organised and poorly resourced, but also because of the inherent difficulty of peacekeeping in an internecine conflict, where the parties had not yet agreed to a cease-fire. The tendency in this situation is for the peacekeeping force to become embroiled in the conflict, in effect, becoming an enforcement action. The force then loses its neutrality and becomes the enemy for at least one of the factions. The involvement of the ECOWAS force in Liberia detailed below illustrates the problems of this type of operation.

Economic sanctions

The brief review of the principal peacekeeping forces authorised by regional organisations illustrates that compared to the UN's activities, other organisations contribution to this aspect of collective security is small. The same can be said of the practice of other organisations in the area of the imposition, as opposed to the recommendation, of economic sanctions. Articles 8, 17 and 20 of the 1947 Rio

Treaty[29] permit the OAS to impose mandatory sanctions. One of the problems with this is whether such a power requires the authorisation of the UN Security Council under Article 53(1) of the UN Charter as a type of enforcement action.

Early practice of the OAS on this issue occurred when it imposed a limited sanctions regime against the Dominican Republic in 1960 for subversive activities against Venezuela, and in 1962 against Cuba for subversive activities against other Latin American countries. Both cases revealed the uncertainty that exists over the interpretation of Article 53. Both cases were debated in the UN Security Council and the organ was divided between Eastern bloc States and their sympathisers stating that mandatory sanctions were enforcement measures within the meaning of Article 53 and so required Security Council authorisation, whilst Western States and their supporters argued to the contrary stating that only military measures could be so construed.[30]

Despite these early instances of the OAS using or considering using its sanctioning machinery, since the late 1960s to the late 1980s, when the Organisation ceased to be dominated by the United States, the use of sanctions by the OAS has been strictly limited. However, the most striking use in recent times does suggest a change in approach by the OAS. The imposition of sanctions against Haiti in 1991 suggests that with the collapse of the Soviet Union and the demise of the Communist bloc, opposition to the imposition of economic sanctions without the prior authorisation of the UN Security Council seems to have disappeared, or at least no State has overtly objected to it. The military coup in Haiti on 30 September 1991 was quickly followed by the imposition of sanctions under the Rio Treaty by an *ad hoc* Meeting of Ministers of Foreign Affairs of the OAS on 8 October consisting of: a trade embargo, the freezing of Haitian government assets, the banning of arms sales, and the diplomatic isolation of the military junta that had overthrown the democratically elected government of President Aristide.[31] Although the UN Security Council did not comment on the legality of the OAS action, the UN General Assembly approved, without dissent, the OAS resolution imposing sanctions against the regime.[32]

When the sanctions were initially imposed the expectations were that they would have an instant effect on the nation's poor economy which was heavily dependent on the United States, one of the proposers of the resolution. However, the embargo failed to produce any concessions. Instead, it provided opportunities for the pro-coup élite and sections of the army to make profits by smuggling, although there was evidence of devastating effects on the welfare of the general population. In light of this, the OAS Foreign Ministers, acting again under the Rio Treaty, tightened the sanctions regime on 17 May 1992. The new sanctions barred ships from ports in the region from delivering oil and other commercial cargoes to Haiti, banned commercial air flights from transporting goods, and ended the issue of travel visas.[33] Again this resolution was welcomed by the General Assembly of the UN in a resolution adopted by consensus.[34] Although the sanctions did not have immediate effect, eventually they did force the junta into an agreement negotiated under UN/OAS auspices, but only after the Security Council itself had imposed an oil and arms embargo in June 1993.[35] Furthermore, the agreement was only finally implemented in 1994 under the threat of UN-authorised force.[36]

The OAS is one of the rare international organisations the constitution of which permits for the imposition of binding sanctions, and its practice has been to impose sanctions against its own members, although Article 28 of the 1948 Charter of the OAS does seem to envisage external sanctions at least if an American State is subject to an armed attack by a non-member.[37] Another organisation that has the power to impose sanctions according to its Treaty make-up is the European Union. However, the EU has gone further by imposing sanctions against non-members, not only non-member States committing aggression against member States (Argentina in 1982),[38] but also non-member States committing aggression against non-members (Iraq), and threats to the peace in non-member countries (South Africa and Yugoslavia). The constitutional basis of this power has received review in chapters 2 and 4.

In the case of South Africa, the informal group of EC Foreign Ministers known as the European Political Co-operation (EPC) met on 10 September 1985 in an attempt to draw up a list of economic sanctions covering arms, oil, military co-operation and sport, to try to bring an end to the state of emergency and widespread civil unrest in that country.[39] The UK opposed the proposal, and despite the fact that the other members agreed to the imposition of sanctions, without approval by the Council of Ministers and implementation in the form of a binding regulation or decision under Articles 113 and 189 of the Treaty of Rome,[40] the sanctions were not binding on the UK, even though that country appeared to accept the limited package of measures agreed to by the other States on 25 September 1985.[41] The EPC again met on 15 to 16 September 1986 and agreed on a more extensive package of measures against South Africa, consisting of a ban on the imports of South African iron, steel and gold coins, and an end to new investment there. Germany refused to agree to a ban on South African coal imports and the then British Prime Minister, Mrs Thatcher, seemed to undermine the EPC agreement by stating she had serious doubts about the value of sanctions.[42] At this stage the Council of the EC adopted regulations and decisions making the ban on investments, gold coins, and iron and steel binding on all members of the EC.[43] The arms and sports boycotts were not enacted as binding community legislation, but it must be remembered that EC members were bound by the UN arms embargo.

With the South Africa government promising reform in 1990 and lifting the state of emergency in June of that year, the United Kingdom was the first to announce it was revoking the EC's ban on new investments in February 1990. This was followed by the Council lifting its investment ban on 25 February 1991,[44] after the South African government had repealed some of its apartheid legislation. This was followed by the lifting of the other binding sanctions covering iron and steel and gold coins on 15 April 1991 and 22 January 1992, as well as the voluntary embargoes on oil and sport despite objections by the African National Congress.[45]

Despite the fact that the EU sometimes simply agrees on sanctions without enacting them as binding regulations of the Community or, as in the case of South Africa, takes a mixed and incremental approach to sanctions, it has the power to make them binding from the outset, and has used that power recently in the imposition of trade sanctions against Iraq and Yugoslavia. In the case of Iraq the EPC decided to impose a trade embargo against the country on 4 August 1990 two days prior to the Security Council resolution which imposed mandatory sanctions.[46] This was followed on 8 August by the EC Council of Ministers imposing a trade embargo by binding regulation under Article 113 of the Treaty of Rome.[47]

The increasing interaction between Western regional organisations in the realm of collective security is illustrated by the EC's imposition of sanctions against Serbia and Montenegro. Interestingly, the initiative for the imposition of these trade sanctions in the period before the Security Council adopted Resolution 757 of 30 May 1992, came from a NATO summit of 8 November 1991 which decided to impose sanctions,[48] despite the fact that the NATO Treaty does not literally grant this power. Article 2 does speak of developing economic collaboration between the State parties to the NATO Treaty, but this seems far removed from the imposition of economic sanctions against a State which is neither a member of NATO, or is attacking a member of NATO.

The formal decision by the Council of the EC on economic sanctions against Yugoslavia was made on 11 November 1991. The regulation suspended the economic co-operation agreements between the EC and Yugoslavia.[49] The EPC was pushing for a complete and binding trade embargo against Serbia and Montenegro when the Security Council adopted Resolution 757. The EC followed Resolution 757 and adopted a complete trade embargo between the EC and the two Republics of Serbia and Montenegro.[50] This was a binding decision on all members of the EC.

The power to impose mandatory sanctions against States appears very limited in regional or defence organisations. The main examples appear to be the OAS and the EU. In both organisations there appears to be evidence that such a power can be an effective one in relation to internal conflicts. In Haiti it led to moves towards the restoration of democracy, and in Yugoslavia it has caused severe economic hardship in Serbia although it has not yet brought an end to the conflict in Bosnia. Furthermore, the 'carrot and stick' approach to sanctions against South Africa taken by the EC does seem to have influenced the accelerating reform process in that country. In all these instances the Security Council of the UN also imposed mandatory sanctions. Member States of the UN are bound to comply with Security Council resolutions imposed under Article 41 of the UN Charter by means of Articles 25 and 103, and although it is debatable whether the regional organisations themselves are bound by Security Council resolutions, the point seems rather moot if the members of those organisations are members of the UN, as they most invariably are.

Military measures

There is a larger body of practice in this area, indeed an amount to rival that of the UN, suggesting that in this most crucial area of collective security, it is unclear whether the UN is not only the more effective body, but also whether in fact it is supreme as suggested by Article 53 of the UN Charter. Nevertheless, the practice of both the UN and other organisations in this area is still quite limited considering the number of conflicts requiring some sort of military intervention under the auspices of an international organisation, suggesting that even if dealt with altogether international organisations have not established an effective collective security system, with a workable military deterrent.

One of the major regional users of military force is the OAS, which during the 1960s was used to further the political objectives of the United States. The emplacement of Soviet missiles in Cuba in 1962 led to the imposition of a quarantine around Cuba in 1962. To justify imposing a quarantine, the United States relied mainly on the recommendation it obtained from the OAS,[51] which called 'for the immediate dismantling and withdrawal from Cuba of all missiles and other weapons with any offensive capacity'. It further recommended that the members of the OAS 'take all measures, individually and collectively, including the use of armed force' to ensure that Cuba could not receive any more missiles from the Soviet Union, in accordance with Articles 6 and 8 of the Inter-American Treaty of Reciprocal Assistance (the Rio Treaty). President Kennedy put great emphasis on this resolution when he imposed the quarantine a few hours later on the 22 October 1962.[52]

The quarantine appeared to be a either a threat of force, or indeed, a use of force contrary to Article 2(4) of the UN Charter that did not come within one of the exceptions to the ban on the use of force, namely self-defence in response to an 'armed attack' within the meaning of Article 51 UN Charter, given that there was no armed attack by Cuba against the United States. Indeed, the United States put greater effort into justifying the quarantine under the provisions of Chapter VIII of the UN Charter. The US State Department employed quite ingenious arguments in an attempt to circumvent the restriction on regional organisations contained in Article 53, namely the necessity for Security Council authorisation of any enforcement action.

The fact that the OAS had imposed economic sanctions against some of its members in the past was pointed to as evidence that the Organisation had developed regional autonomy in the sphere of enforcement action.[53] This view, while controversial at the time, seems to have been subsequently accepted as regards *economic* enforcement action, but not necessarily *military* enforcement action, as illustrated by the OAS/UN practice as regards Haiti when economic sanctions were imposed by the OAS prior to the UN Security Council, but military force was only authorised by the Security Council in July 1994. However, the OAS countries did discuss the use of military force under the auspices of the Organisation in May 1994 but only three States were in favour of it.[54]

It could be argued that whatever the position as regards sanctions, military action, which is not undertaken in self-defence nor as part of a peacekeeping operation, would appear to be enforcement action requiring Security Council authorisation, whether the regional organisation orders military action or simply recommends it. From the viewpoint of the target State, it does not matter whether the resolution authorising the military action is a recommendation or a decision. Such issues are more important as regards the constitution of the Organisation. In the *Expenses* case, the World Court dismissed the argument that UNEF I and ONUC were enforcement actions by stating that peacekeeping operations were founded on the consent of the host State.[55] It follows that, formally speaking, non-consensual military action is enforcement action requiring Security Council authorisation. The United States' contention that an OAS *recommendation* to use force against Cuba escaped that requirement,[56] must be doubted.

Being imposed at the height of the Cold War, and being directed at the Soviet Union as much as at Cuba, the quarantine was unlikely to be the subject of a Security Council resolution authorising it or condemning it. Despite this the State Department contended that the fact that the Security Council did not adopt a resolution signified that it had acquiesced, which was to be construed as authorisation in accordance with Article 53.[57] The logic of this argument would allow the United States to use its veto in the Security Council to block any resolution being adopted on a proposed military operation by the OAS, so freeing the regional organisation to use force. There appears to be no doubt that a literal analysis of the word 'authorisation' in Article 53 cannot readily encompass acquiescence, and so the US's policy-based interpretation appeared dubious in the extreme. Nevertheless, as we shall see, there has been further Security Council practice in the case of Liberia which suggests that acquiescence may be sufficient to satisfy Article 53, leading to the conclusion that Article 53's requirement of authorisation of military measures may have been reinterpreted by subsequent practice, although there probably needs to be more practice on this issue. Nevertheless, there are signs that the formal supremacy of the Security Council established in Article 53 is being eroded not only in the area of sanctions but also military measures.

However, some military operations by regional organisations do not undermine the normativity of Article 53, for example in the Dominican Republic. The United States originally claimed that its military intervention in the Dominican Republic in 1965 was carried out to protect American citizens in that strife-torn country.[58] The American army had established a neutral zone in the capital by the end of April 1965 and had by that time effectively altered the course of the civil war in favour of the right-wing faction. There was little doubt that the initial American intervention was contrary to Article 2(4) of the UN Charter. However, the American force was then formally replaced by an OAS-negotiated Inter-American Force, although still mainly composed of US troops. The OAS force was emplaced after a cease-fire at the request of the various factions. It was intended to be neutral and to facilitate the parties bring about the restoration of democracy.[59] The Inter-American Force appeared to be a peacekeeping force within the accepted definition, in that it was not only sent at the request of the belligerents but also was not authorised to take any offensive military action to enforce the peace. Peacekeeping forces merely facilitate the carrying out of measures agreed to by the parties to the conflict. True peacekeeping operations are neither enforcement actions within the meaning of Article 53, nor uses of force within the meaning of Article 2(4). It follows that they can be created and emplaced by regional organisations without breaching either of those provisions. It follows that the OAS operation in the Dominican Republic was lawful, but this could not somehow retroactively legalise the initial unlawful intervention by the United States.[60]

However, the fact that a military force claims to be 'peacekeeping' or meets some of the requirements of such a force, should be viewed cautiously. One aspect of peacekeeping is that it requires the prior consent of the parties to the conflict. In the case of the military action in Grenada in 1983, the United States relied on the argument that the decision to take collective action by the Organisation of Eastern Caribbean States (OECS) did not require authorisation by the Security Council under Article 53 of the UN Charter because it had been undertaken at the request of the lawful governmental authority in Grenada.[61] However, the action was not claimed by the United States to be one of peacekeeping, nor one of collective self-defence under Article 51, instead it was said to be a military action to restore internal order. There is little doubt that the person from whom the request was made, the Governor General, did not have the requisite constitutional authority to make such a request.[62] Besides which, a request for forcible intervention to restore order would appear to be a invitation for enforcement action requiring authorisation by the Security Council under Article 53, even though the Governor General requested what he termed a 'peacekeeping' force for this purpose.[63] The US-dominated military action forcibly restored order on the island, rather than simply overseeing an agreement by the parties and so could not be categorised as a peacekeeping operation.

Nevertheless, this amounted to another example of Article 53 being eroded in reality, again with the United States using a regional organisation it could dominate, though by this time it could not use the OAS, but a little-known sub-regional body. Although the main examples of the use of regional organisations for enforcement purposes come from the Americas, other organisations have used military coercion even though their charters do not appear to grant such powers and despite the fact that no Security Council authorisation was secured under Article 53 of the UN Charter.

The establishment of a small Symbolic Arab Security Force by the Arab League in June 1976, followed by the creation of a much larger Arab Deterrent Force (ADF) of thirty thousand troops mainly from Syria in October 1976 in response to the civil war in Lebanon,[64] is another example of a regional organisation attempting peacekeeping operations in an environment unsuited to such actions, with the result that the operation became one of military intervention or enforcement.

Although there were aspects of the mandate of the ADF which appeared to be based on the peacekeeping concept, such as supervision of a cease-fire, withdrawal of troops and the collection of the weaponry belonging to the parties to the internal conflict, other aspects seemed to grant the force much wider powers of enforcement, such as maintaining internal security and assisting the Lebanese authorities to take over public utilities.[65] Although it is possible to argue that the UN gave a similarly wide mandate to ONUC in the Congo, that operation in reality became one of enforcement.[66] In addition, if the performance of the Arab League Force is examined it can be seen that it became increasingly ruthless in its actions and was unafraid to use military coercion beyond that required in strict self-defence. Furthermore, even when the Lebanese government withdrew its consent to the ADF in 1982, the force, which was by then entirely composed of Syrian troops, remained and increasingly aligned itself with the pro-Syrian factions in Lebanon.[67] The situation seemed to be a reverse of the Dominican Republic situation in 1965. In that case, the United States' military intervention was then succeeded by an OAS 'peacekeeping' operation, while in the case of Lebanon in 1976, the initial Arab League peacekeeping initiative was gradually replaced with Syrian military intervention.

Neither the Pact of the Arab League of 1945,[68] nor the Treaty of Joint Defence and Economic Co-operation of 1950,[69] drawn up by some of the members of the Arab League, contained any explicit reference to the creation of peacekeeping or coercive military operations. Although it is possible to argue that the power to create peacekeeping forces can be implied from the provisions of a treaty creating a regional organisation, one of the purposes of which is to co-ordinate the policies of the members 'in order to achieve co-operation between them and to safeguard their independence and sovereignty',[70] it does not appear legitimate to imply a power to undertake military enforcement action in an internal conflict. Whereas peacekeeping would appear to be *intra vires* a regional body, military enforcement does not appear so, unless the charter or pact explicitly recognises the power. The Treaty of Joint Defence does not envisage military enforcement action, being based on Article 51 of the UN Charter.[71] Even if it were possible to imply the power to take enforcement action from the wording of Article 3 of the Treaty on Joint Defence, which provides that 'in the event of a threat of war or the existence of an international emergency, the Contracting States shall immediately proceed to unify their plans and defensive measures, as the situation may demand', then formally the military action should still be authorised by the UN Security Council under Articles 53 and 103 of the UN Charter.

Similar formal legal difficulties can be seen in the activities of the Economic Community of West African States (ECOWAS) in the civil war in Liberia. The civil war started in 1989 when the National Patriotic Forces of Liberia (NPFL), rebelled against the corrupt and incompetent regime of Samuel Doe. In July 1990, the Liberian government accepted a peace proposal put forward by ECOWAS, primarily an economic regional organisation, consisting of a cease-fire, the deployment of a regional peacekeeping force, and the immediate formation of a government of national unity. Despite the fact that this proposal was rejected by the NPFL, on 25 August 1990, a four thousand-strong peacekeeping force known as the ECOWAS Monitoring Group (ECOMOG), arrived in Liberia. The NPFL saw this as military intervention on behalf of the beleaguered government. Although ECOMOG attempted to tread the neutral tightrope of a true peacekeeping force it slowly became embroiled in the civil war, particularly after the death of President Doe in September 1990. At the time of Doe's death the NPFL controlled ninety per cent of Liberia and it is arguable that ECOWAS should have accepted the NPFL as the *de facto* government of Liberia, although, it should be pointed out, the NPFL did not control the capital Monrovia. Instead, ECOMOG started an offensive against the NPFL as well as increasing the already large Nigerian element of the force. The new Nigerian commander of the force was ordered to take offensive action against the rebels by the Nigerian government. Parallels can easily be drawn with the Syrian involvement in the ADF in Lebanon.

Various cease-fires were agreed to by factions culminating in the Yamoussoukro IV Accords of 30 October 1991,[72] which also detailed procedures for disarmament of the various factions, the restructuring of ECOMOG to make it less dominated by Nigeria, the surrendering of territory to ECOMOG by the NPFL, and the holding of elections. The cease-fire did not hold, and this led to fighting between the expanded nine thousand-strong ECOMOG force and other rebels factions against the NPFL during 1992.

At this stage the UN Security Council became involved, adopting Resolution 788 on 19 November 1992, which imposed a mandatory arms embargo against the whole of Liberia, except for ECOMOG. The resolution also expressed support for the Yamoussoukro IV Accords, whilst recalling the provisions of Chapter VIII of the UN Charter and commending 'ECOWAS for its efforts to restore peace, security and stability in Liberia'. From January 1993, ECOMOG went on the offensive against the NPFL pushing them back from the capital with the help of an extra five thousand troops. On 26 March the Security Council adopted Resolution 812 which threatened further measures if the peace accords were not complied with. The parties finally agreed to the implementation of the Liberian Peace Agreement on 25 July, which contained provisions for the involvement of UN observers in the disarmament and elections process. In Resolution 856 of 10 August 1993, the Security Council agreed to dispatch an advance team of thirty military observers to pave the way for the emplacement of a UN Observer Mission for Liberia (UNOMIL) to help implement the Peace Agreement, alongside ECOMOG.[73]

It can be seen from this account that during its long involvement in Liberia, ECOMOG had overstepped the boundary between consensual and neutral peacekeeping and military enforcement action. It appears that the ECOWAS 1981 Protocol on Non-Aggression and Mutual Assistance in Defence Matters does permit for limited enforcement action, although not in the case of purely internal conflict, and only as 'justified by the legitimate defence of the territories of the Community'.[74] It is highly questionable whether the conflict in Liberia justified ECOWAS intervention given these limitations. Despite this, the UN Security Council has apparently retrospectively endorsed the action as coming within the provisions of Chapter VIII of the UN Charter in Resolution 788. The Security Council did not authorise the action from the outset, possibly because it initially was sent as a peacekeeping force. However, the lax approach of the UN Security Council is again illustrative of the disregard of the literal meaning of Article 53.

Further relaxation of the terms of Article 53, in this case the meaning of 'regional arrangements or agencies', can be seen in the involvement of NATO in Bosnia. The use of NATO in Bosnia is an example of the UN being prepared to sanction military enforcement action by a *defence* organisation, even though that body is apparently not acting within the powers of its own constituent treaty. In Resolution 770 of 13 August 1992, the Security Council, 'acting under Chapter VII of the Charter of the United Nations', called 'upon States to take nationally or through regional agencies ... all measures necessary to facilitate in co-ordination with the United Nations the delivery by relevant United Nations humanitarian organisations and others of humanitarian assistance to Sarajevo and wherever needed in other parts of Bosnia ...'. The phrase 'all measures necessary' has been used in the past by the Security Council to authorise military operations. Furthermore, the Council, in Resolution 781 of 9 October 1992 imposed a no-fly zone over Bosnia. Authorisation to enforce this no-fly zone was granted by the Security Council in Resolution 816 of 31 March 1993. Safe havens were established by Resolutions 819 of 16 April 1993, 624 of 6 May, 836 of 4 June, and 844 of 22 June under UNPROFOR protection. Limited use of air power by member States was also authorised by Resolution 836. Limited coercion has been used by NATO under these provisions, instances being: the NATO threat of air strikes against the Bosnian Serbs surrounding Sarajevo in February 1994 if they failed to withdraw their heavy weapons; the shooting down of four Serb warplanes by NATO planes above Bosnia in the same month; the bombing by NATO planes of Serb airbases in Croatia in November 1994;[75] and the further bombing of Serb ammunition dumps near Pale, the Bosnian-Serb 'capital', in May 1995.[76] It appears from this precedent that the Security Council is able to use NATO, if NATO's members are willing, to carry out enforcement measures. Legally, Article 53 states that NATO cannot initiate enforcement action by itself, only action in collective self-defence.

Concluding remarks

The above review shows a disparity between the literal meaning of the constituent treaties of the UN and of regional, defence and security organisations, and their interpretation by the subsequent practice of those organisations.

NATO, a defence organisation, has flexed its muscles in anger for the first time, in Bosnia, its apparent disregard of its own treaty being 'cured' by the authorisation of the Security Council. This appears to be an example of the UN treating a defence organisation as a regional organisation for the purposes of Chapter VIII.

However, when it comes to regional organisations proper undertaking enforcement action, there appears to be a trend towards increased autonomy, certainly in the case of economic sanctions. In addition, the above examples illustrate that Article 53 does not necessarily operate as an effective constraint on military action by regional organisations and that they have, in practice, carved out an autonomous role in this area. However, the fact that in some of these cases (Cuba and Grenada) members of the regional organisation have made strenuous efforts to explain the compatibility of their action with Article 53 of the UN Charter, suggests that it is still recognised, at least in some organisations, as a legal constraint. Nevertheless, further indications of the relaxation of the formal supremacy of the UN in collective military measures, is shown by the Liberian situation, when the UN retrospectively endorsed the regional body's military operations.

However, recent practice raises doubts about the capacity of *regional* organisations to maintain *global* security. Economic and military measures often require global compliance and co-operation to make them effective. Most regional organisations, showing their inherent inward-looking nature, appear only willing to deal with conflicts in their own hemisphere, with only the EU taking more consistent action against non-members. Recent conflicts in Haiti, Liberia and the former Yugoslavia for example, have not been dealt with solely by the relevant regional body, but have required the substantial involvement of the UN as well. It appears that while there is strong, though preliminary, evidence that regionalism is predominant in matters of economic integration between States, where it is 'natural' for competing trading blocs to be established; in security matters, which inherently require global co-ordination, the universal body is the most significant actor. Thus while its formal supremacy is being eroded by limited regional practice in the area of enforcement, the UN still remains the most important actor, though organisations as a whole have a significant way to go before an effective and equitable collective security system is established.

Furthermore, while the UN's formal, though not necessarily practical, supremacy in military and economic matters is under pressure from regional organisations, its formal *equality* with regional bodies in the area of the pacific settlement of disputes is ignored in practice, with the UN's peacekeeping burden, in particular, far outweighing that carried by regional organisations.

Such contradictions between the literal meaning and the interpretation of the constituent treaties of organisations, is a result of the clash between regionalism and universalism. The founders of the UN attempted to resolve the problem in 1945, but the literal wording of the UN Charter has not been able to stand the pressure of subsequent developments. States are more willing to allow the often more effective universal body to be involved with peaceful settlement, which, by its consensual nature, does not encroach on their sovereignty, but are not willing in practice to allow the world body complete supremacy in enforcement matters, which can amount to a direct attack on sovereignty, preferring instead regional bodies in which they have more control. Furthermore, the powerful States who, though willing to use the global coercive competence of the UN Security Council when it suits their purposes, still fall back on their own regional organisations when politically desirable to do so and to avoid deadlock in the UN Council. Thus for powerful States, it is not always a question of protecting their sovereignty from coercive measures but of using universal or regional organisational power to further their own interests, to the detriment of less powerful States.

Such tremendous political pressures have inevitably warped the original Charter scheme for collective security, which simply indicated universal supremacy in enforcement matters and equality in others. The UN, although losing its formal supremacy, is however, still the most important actor in the realm of collective security. Regional organisations have, by their sporadic practice, carved out a large amount of autonomy, but are only willing to use their powers to protect their own interests, not those of the global community. Such a self-interested attitude, with the limited exception of the EU, undermines the collective security ideal.

Notes

[1] But see Article 52(2).

[2] UNCIO, vol. 12, 687.

[3] R. Higgins, *The Development of International Law through the Political Organs of the United Nations*, 209 (1963).

[4] 34 UNTS 243. Parties: Belgium, Canada, Denmark, France, Germany, Greece, Iceland, Italy, Luxembourg, Netherlands, Norway, Portugal, Spain, Turkey, UK, USA. In 1966 France unilaterally withdrew from its Treaty commitments without withdrawing from the Treaty itself. In January 1994 NATO offered the former Eastern bloc States 'partnership for peace' accords, guaranteeing military co-operation but not full membership. Eighteen States had signed accords by May 1994. *Keesing's* (1994), 40034. Russia agreed to partnership for peace in May 1995, *The Times*, 12 May 1995.

[5] See N. D. White, 'The Legitimacy of NATO Action in Bosnia', 144 *New Law Journal* (1994), 649.

[6] 15 *Human Rights Law Journal* (1994), 449.

[7] The CSCE adopted a Convention on Conciliation and Arbitration within the CSCE, 31 *I.L.M.* (1993), 551.

[8] The CSCE agreed in principle to send a peacekeeping force to Nagorny Karabakh in December 1994, *Keesing's* (1994), 40338.

[9] 31 *I.L.M.* (1992), 1385 at 1392, 1400.

[10] 479 UNTS 39, Articles 16–18.

[11] 3 *I.L.M.* (1964), 1116.

[12] *Keesing's* (1993), 39500, 39725.

[13] 30 UNTS 55.

[14] 119 UNTS 4, Article 33.

[15] See C. Sepulveda, 'The Reform of the Charter of American States' 137 *Hague Recueil* (1972), 83.

[16] See J. G. Merrills, *International Dispute Settlement*, 210, 2nd edn (1991).

[17] *Ibid.*, 208.

[18] See H. McCoubrey and N. D. White, *International Organizations and Civil Wars*, 92 (1995).

[19] See SC Res. 937, 49 UN SCOR Resolutions (1994).

[20] A full analysis of the situation is contained in H. A. Hassouna, *The League of Arab States and Regional Disputes*, ch. 6 (1985).

[21] SC 957 mtg, 16 UN SCOR (1961).

[22] 157 BFSP 669.

[23] Article 6, 70 UNTS 238.

[24] 19 *I.L.M.* (1980), 401–3.

[25] *Ibid.*, 404.

[26] *Keesing's* (1980), 30365–78.

[27] G. J. Naldi, *The Organization of African Unity*, 27–9 (1989).

[28] SC Res. 504, 37 UN SCOR Resolutions 16 (1982).

[29] The Inter-American Treaty of Reciprocal Assistance, 21 UNTS 77. See chapter 4.

[30] See M. Akehurst, 'Enforcement Action by Regional Agencies with Special Reference to the O.A.S.', 45 *B.Y.B.I.L.* (1967), 175 at 188–92.

[31] *Keesing's* (1991), 38522. UN doc. S/23127 (1991). OAS doc. MRE/RES.2/91.

[32] GA Res. 46/7, 46 UN GAOR (1991).

[33] *Keesing's* (1992), 38905. OAS doc. MRE/RES.3/92. 86 *A.J.I.L.* (1992), 667.

[34] GA Res. 47/20, 47 UN GAOR (1992).

[35] SC Res. 841, 48 UN SCOR Resolutions (1993).

[36] SC Res. 940, 49 UN SCOR Resolutions (1994).

[37] See chapter 4.

[38] EC Regulation 877/82, *OJ* 1982 L102/1.

[39] *Bull.EC* (1985/9) para.2.5.1.

[40] S. Bohr, 'Sanctions by the United Nations Security Council and the European Community', *European Journal of International Law* (1993), 256 at 266.

[41] *Bull.EC* (1985/9) para.2.3.30.

[42] *Bull.EC* (1986/9) paras. 2.4.1., 2.4.2, 2.4.3.

[43] EC Decision 86/459, *OJ* 1986 L268/1; EC Regulation 3302/86, *OJ* 1986 L 305/6.

[44] EC Decision 91/114, *OJ* 1991 L59/18; *Bull.EC* (1991/1/2) para.1.3.32.

[45] *Keesing's* (1985), 33898; (1986), 34597–8; (1990), 37234, 37910; (1991), 38132.

[46] UN doc. S/21444 (1990).

[47] EC Regulation 2340/90, *OJ* 1990 L213/1.

[48] *Bull.EC* (1991/11) para.1.4.4.

[49] EC Regulation 3300/91, *OJ* 1991 L 315/1.

[50] EC Regulation 1432/92, *OJ* 1992 L 151/4.

[51] SC 1022 mtg, 17 UN SCOR (1962).

[52] 57 *A.J.I.L.* (1962), 512.

[53] A. Chayes, 'Law and the Quarantine of Cuba', 41 *Foreign Affairs* (1963), 552 at 556.

[54] 1 *Europa World Yearbook*, 36th edn (1995), 206.

[55] *Certain Expenses of the United Nations*, I.C.J. Rep. 1962, 151, 170, 177.

[56] L. C. Meeker, 'Defensive Quarantine and Law', 57 *A.J.I.L.* (1963), 515 at 521.

[57] *Ibid.*, 515.

[58] UN doc. S/6310 (1965).

[59] SC 1202 mtg, 20 UN SCOR (1965), US.

[60] Akehurst, 45 *B.Y.B.I.L.* (1967), 213.

[61] D. R. Robinson, 'Letter from the Legal Adviser', 18 *International Lawyer* (1984), 382 at 384.

[62] W. C. Gilmore, *The Grenada Intervention*, 73 (1984).

[63] *Ibid.*, 65.

[64] For a thorough review see I. Pogany, *The Arab League and Peacekeeping in the Lebanon* (1987).

[65] *Ibid.*, appendix 3.

[66] N. D. White, *Keeping the Peace: The United Nations and the Maintenance of International Peace and Security*, 233–41, 2nd edn (1993).

[67] Pogany, *Lebanon*, ch. 8.

[68] 70 UNTS 238.

[69] Above, n. 22.

[70] Article 2 of the Pact of the Arab League.

[71] Article 2.

[72] UN doc. S/24811 (1991).

[73] *Keesing's* (1993), 39258, 39306. The peace process remains unimplemented – see SC Res. 972, 50 UN S/PV (1995).

[74] M. Weller (ed.), *Regional Peacekeeping and International Enforcement: The Liberian Crisis*, 19–24 (1994). Article 4(b) of the 1981 Protocol does provide that member States shall take appropriate measures 'in the case of internal armed conflict within any Member State engineered and supported actively from outside likely to endanger the security and peace in the entire community ...' Measures include military measures with the authority of the state concerned. However, Article 18(2) provides that 'Community forces shall not intervene if the conflict remains purely internal'. The further limitation on ECOWAS intervention is provided by Article 15(1) which provides that intervention 'shall in all cases be justified by the legitimate defence of the territories of the Community'.

[75] SC Res. 958, 49 UN SCOR Resolutions (1994).

[76] The deployment, under UN authorisation, of the Rapid Reaction Force, consisting of troops from NATO-member countries, in July and August 1995, is a further move towards enforcement action – SC Res. 998, 50 UN S/PV (1995).

9

The promotion and protection of human rights

In chapters 7 and 8 the struggle of the United Nations and regional organisations to fulfil the function of collective security became apparent. Although organisational activity in this area has increased dramatically with the end of the Cold War, there appears to be some distance to cover before there is sufficient centralisation of coercion and submission to the collective will for there to be a rudimentary form of world government in this area. However, it is probably true to say that the world community has made more advances in the area of collective security than in the tasks of protecting human rights and the environment, the topics of the next two chapters.

One rationalist approach to the evolution of international law and the role of international organisations is to see, as a basic stage, the setting of *standards* in treaties and customs, these standards being upheld by simple condemnation. Condemnation in its crudest form will be in a haphazard unfocused fashion by individual States; eventually this may take the form of collective condemnation in institutional settings – this is really the next stage of development in that the standards of international law are upheld by organisations. In effect, the organisations *supervise* the implementation of standards although they have little power if a State chooses to ignore the supervision. The final stages are the application of *mandatory* decisions, and if necessary, the effective *enforcement* of those standards by international organisations when a State has breached them. Whereas, in the area of collective security, organisations do possess mandatory and enforcement powers, although as we have seen they are imperfectly formed, in human rights there is generally standard setting and supervision with the development of mandatory, though not enforcement, powers in the European and American systems, whilst in the area of the environment there is only limited organisational development beyond standard setting. Nevertheless, both areas are developing rapidly as the following two chapters show.

The UN and human rights

The development of human rights standards within the United Nations is even more remarkable when the meagre coverage of the subject in the UN Charter is considered. In 1945, the United Nations' primary function was to establish a collective security system, the Security Council being granted mandatory enforcement powers in that area. Despite the fact that the Organisation arose from the ashes of a war fought against human rights-abusing States, the UN Charter devoted little to the protection of human rights. The Preamble included the phrase 'to reaffirm faith in fundamental human rights, in the dignity and worth of the human person, in the equal rights of men and women and of nations large and small'. Article 1(3) stated that one of the purposes of the UN was to achieve 'international co-operation in solving international problems of an economic, social, cultural or humanitarian character, and in promoting and encouraging respect for human rights and for fundamental freedoms for all without distinction as to race, sex, language, or religion'. The fact that these provisions did not create an immediate obligation on members to protect human rights, only an obligation on the UN to promote increased respect for human rights, is highlighted further by Articles 55 and 56 of the UN Charter.

> 55. With a view to the creation of conditions of stability and well-being which are necessary for peaceful and friendly relations among nations based on respect for the principle of equal rights and self-determination of peoples, the United Nations shall promote:
> (a) higher standards of living, full employment, and conditions of economic and social progress and development;
> (b) solutions of international economic, social, health, and related problems; and international cultural and educational co-operation; and
> (c) universal respect for, and observance of, human rights and fundamental freedoms without distinction as to race, sex, language, or religion.
> 56. All Members pledge themselves to take joint and separate action in co-operation with the Organization for the achievement of the purposes set forth in Article 55.

Furthermore, Article 62 provides that ECOSOC may make recommendations or prepare draft conventions for the 'purpose of promoting respect for, and observance of, human rights and fundamental freedoms for all'. Despite the fact that these provisions do not appear to impose obligations directly on member States, the International Court of Justice has, in the *Namibia* advisory opinion, stated that South Africa had breached the UN Charter by its policy of race discrimination.[1]

While it is true to say that a number of the UN specialised agencies, namely the ILO, FAO, WHO and UNESCO, promote the protection of human rights by setting standards, either in the form of recommendations, regulations or treaties, in specific areas such as rights in the workplace, freedom from hunger, right to health and right to education,[2] the initial responsibility for developing a range of human rights standards to fill the gaps in the UN Charter fell to the General Assembly, ECOSOC, and the Commission on Human Rights established by ECOSOC in 1946.[3]

In fact the General Assembly referred to ECOSOC the issue of drafting a declaration on human rights in its first session in 1946. It only took two years for the

Universal Declaration of Human Rights[4] to be adopted by the UN General Assembly in 1948.[5] This document can be considered the first step towards the development of a body of 'international constitutional law', the aim of which is to protect the individual from abuse by his or her government.[6] It contained a list of twenty-seven rights and freedoms, protecting both civil and political rights and freedoms (principally rights to life, privacy, a fair trial, free movement, freedom of thought and religion, freedom of expression and peaceful assembly, and the right to take part in government; and freedoms from slavery, torture, discrimination, and arbitrary arrest); and economic, social and cultural rights (rights to social security, work, rest and leisure, adequate standard of living, education, and to participate in the cultural life of the community). Although the declaration was in the form of a non-binding General Assembly resolution, it soon became part of the legal language of States and international organisations.[7] By the time of the UN Conference in Teheran in 1968,[8] it was deemed to be an obligation for all the members of the international community.[9] Traditional international lawyers would argue that this was the completion of a process of the declaration from recommendation of an international organisation to customary international law, or from non-source to source of international law. It is equally possible to see the Declaration, which filled in a vital gap in the UN Charter and international law, as an early example of the quasi-legislative capacity of the General Assembly.

Looking at the latest UN Conference on Human Rights, held in Vienna, June 1993, it might appear that the United Nations has progressed little beyond the simple setting of human rights standards in the Universal Declaration. The Vienna Declaration and Programme of Action are clearly founded on the UN Charter and the UN Declaration on Human Rights, although notable attempted additions are the more controversial third-generation rights to democracy and development. The Conference emphasised that 'the Universal Declaration of Human Rights, which constitutes a common standard of achievement for all peoples and all nations, is the source of inspiration and has been the basis for the United Nations in making advances in standard setting ...'. As far as the role of international organisations is concerned, the Vienna Declaration simply advocates that the various international, regional, and non-governmental organisations, should increase their activities and co-ordination (at the UN, co-ordination should be undertaken by the Centre for Human Rights examined below), while recognising that these institutions 'play a vital role in the formulation, promotion and implementation of human rights standards'. The Vienna Declaration centres on the development and implementation of standards deriving from the Universal Declaration by international organisations. There is no suggestion of the world community attempting to enforce these standards by coercive means,[10] although the most concrete proposal for the advancement of institutional promotion and protection of human rights, the creation of a UN High Commissioner for Human Rights, with an essentially promotional mandate, was adopted by the UN General Assembly in 1993.[11]

UN-sponsored treaties

The Vienna Declaration tends to concentrate on the reinforcement of established standards and the setting down of new ones rather than the increasingly elaborate structure of institutions that have been set up to deal with human rights. One such area of development in the past has been the establishment of organs under the provisions of binding treaties developed at the UN for protecting *specific* human rights. However, initial human rights treaties sponsored by the UN General Assembly concentrated on the setting of standards rather than the creation of machinery to try to ensure the implementation of those standards.

This is illustrated by the Convention on the Prevention and Punishment of the Crime of Genocide of 1948,[12] which arose from the outrage caused by the atrocities of the Second World War. The Convention defined the offence of genocide with reasonable clarity in Article 2 and designated it an international crime in Article 1. The standard having been set, the Convention simply obliges State parties to enact the necessary legislation to give effect to the provisions of the Genocide Convention. There is little attempt in the Convention to create any machinery to monitor the implementation by States of its provisions. Article 9 of the Convention states that disputes between the contracting parties regarding the Convention including disputes over the 'responsibility of a state for genocide ... shall be submitted to the International Court of Justice at the request of the parties to the dispute'. This provision was little used until the government of Bosnia requested provisional measures from the World Court on 20 March 1993 for alleged acts of genocide by Yugoslavia (Serbia and Montenegro) against the people and State of Bosnia.[13]

Without conclusively determining the existence of acts of genocide in Bosnia nor whether Serbia could be held responsible for it, the Court, on 8 April 1993, indicated that Yugoslavia should 'take all measures within its power to prevent the commission of the crime of genocide' as well as ensuring that any paramilitary group 'which may be directed or supported by it' 'do not commit any acts of genocide, of conspiracy to commit genocide, of direct and public incitement to commit genocide, or of complicity in genocide, whether directed against the Muslim population of Bosnia and Herzegovina or against any other national, ethnical, racial or religious group'.[14] Whether the Court will conclusively determine that Serbia is guilty of genocide remains to be seen.

Limited supervision of the provisions of the Genocide Convention are matched by a narrow approach to jurisdiction over persons, 'whether ... constitutionally responsible rulers, public officials or private individuals',[15] allegedly guilty of genocide. Persons charged with genocide are to be tried under the principle of territorial jurisdiction in the State in which the act was committed. There is no attempt to recognise universal jurisdiction enabling alleged perpetrators to be tried in whichever country they are arrested, although such jurisdiction probably exists under customary international law.[16] However, Article 6 of the Genocide Convention does refer to 'such international penal tribunal as may have jurisdiction with respect to those contracting parties as may have accepted its jurisdiction'. Although no such tribunal has yet been established in the literal sense of Article 6, there are recent examples of tribunals, examined below, established by the UN Security Council to try individuals guilty of genocide and other international crimes in specific conflicts.

In contrast to early UN-sponsored human rights treaties, later ones dealing with specific human rights, not only laid down standards, but included provisions creating the machinery necessary for overseeing the implementation of these standards. Such an approach can also be found in the International Covenants on Human Rights finally adopted by the General Assembly in 1966, examined below. The early move towards greater institutional protection of human rights can be found in the International Convention on the Elimination of all Forms of Racial Discrimination 1966,[17] which, *inter alia*, established a Committee on the Elimination of all Forms of Racial Discrimination, consisting of eighteen independent experts. The Committee receives periodic reports from the parties on the issue of the implementation of the Convention. In addition, there are little-used systems providing for inter-State claims, whereby one State can complain of another State's non-implementation of the convention, and an optional system, which has only recently been activated, for petitions to the Committee by individuals.[18] The Committee has no power to make binding decisions in any of these matters, its competence being limited to recommendations and suggestions.[19]

A similar structure is to be found in later UN-sponsored human rights treaties such as the Convention against Torture and other Cruel, Inhuman or Degrading Treatment or Punishment 1984,[20] which not only treats torture as a crime of universal jurisdiction in Article 5(2), but also establishes a Committee against Torture consisting of ten independent experts with competence to hear State party reports on implementation and State party complaints on non-implementation by other parties, and under Article 22, an optional procedure whereby individual petitions can be heard. Again there are no powers given to the Committee to make binding decisions let alone enforce its findings. For example, in *Qani Halimi-Nedzibi* v *Austria* where Article 12 of the Convention had been found to be breached,[21] the Committee simply requested that the State party ensured that similar violations do not occur in the future as well as reporting back to the Committee on any relevant measures taken by the State in conformity with the Committee's views. However, in another case, *Balabou Mutombo* v *Switzerland*,[22] the Committee stated that Switzerland had 'an obligation to refrain from expelling' the complainant who ran the real risk of torture on return to his native Zaïre. It appears that the Committee was not attempting to make a binding decision, it was simply using stronger language to remind the State party of its obligations under the Convention, in this case Article 3.

Although the later Conventions prohibiting racial discrimination and torture are an improvement over the simple standard setting of the early Genocide Convention, the lack of mandatory and enforcement powers leaves the Committees to act as mere 'watchdogs', relying on publicity and pressure, as well as treaty obligations, to ensure compliance with the treaties. Furthermore, not all recent treaties go as far in the empowerment of the supervisory body. The Convention on the Rights of the Child of 1989,[23] contains very thorough standards regarding the treatment of children, but creates a Committee on the Rights of the Child only empowered to hear State reports and to make suggestions and recommendations thereon,[24] there being no provision for State complaints or the right of individual petition. The failure to extend the rights of the child to include complaint to an impartial body undermines the completeness of these rights. Indeed, even under the treaties which do contain the right of individual petition, the optional procedure still places the ultimate control over the exercise of the right at the behest of the State. The fundamental contradiction at the heart of human rights law, is that, despite appearances, it does not grant full rights to individuals on the international plane. The granting of those rights is still under the sovereign command of the State, which has the option of not ratifying the treaty at all, or of ratifying the treaty but not agreeing to the optional system (if one is present) allowing individuals within their domains to complain of abuse.

UN Commission on Human Rights

The lack of proper redress for human rights abuses could be overcome if there were a procedure for individuals to complain to an international organisation outside of any specific human rights treaty framework. At this point it is necessary to look at the UN Commission on Human Rights, which now consists of fifty-three representatives from member States. Despite the highly politicised atmosphere inherent in a UN organ consisting of member States, as opposed to independent experts, the Commission has had major successes such as the Universal Declaration on Human Rights and the International Covenants on Human Rights examined below. Despite the fact that the Commission's mandate extends to considering questions of human rights violations within specific countries,[25] the political atmosphere in the Commission has led to selective condemnations.

> There is no doubt that the special procedures which are focused on *country situations*, inasmuch as they are contentious and denunciatory, carry heavy political overtones. With the exception of such persistent situations as those prevailing in Southern Africa, in the territories occupied by Israel and in Chile, there appears now to be a growing reluctance among the UN membership to make country situations the object of public scrutiny. The country approach seems to be on the retreat, and instead the so-called *thematic approach* has come into favour in the most recent years.[26]

Whilst organs created under specific treaties can only supervise State parties' compliance with their treaty obligations, the UN Commission can supervise all States that are members of the UN irrespective of their human rights treaty commitments. Unfortunately, it has a rather limited approach as regards condemnation of States in the field of human rights. Furthermore, in 1946 it adopted a policy of not even considering petitions from individuals alleging that their rights were being violated by their governments.[27] This over-sensitivity to the sovereignty of member States was relaxed slightly in 1959, when ECOSOC made available to the members of the Commission the communications received for individuals, and gave copies to the UN member States mentioned in any complaints (the author remaining anonymous), but it was made clear that the Commission could not take any action on any complaints.[28]

Much greater strides towards treating human rights breaches as creating a right to be heard if not a right of redress were taken in 1967, when ECOSOC authorised its Sub-Commission on the Prevention of Discrimination and Protection of Minorities to examine information regarding gross violations of human rights and to report to the Commission thereon.[29] Further advances were made in 1970 when ECOSOC finally established a procedure for reviewing petitions received from individuals from any member State of the UN.[30] The supervising body under this procedure is the Sub-Commission, a body of twenty-six people serving in their individual capacities, not as representatives of States.[31] The Sub-Commission examines, in private, communications received by the UN Secretary General from individuals or non-governmental organisations with a view to referring to the Commission 'situations which appear to reveal a consistent pattern of gross and reliably attested human rights violations'. If a situation is referred to it by Sub-Commission, the Commission may appoint an *ad hoc* committee to investigate the allegations with the consent of the State in question. The Sub-Commission then reports and makes recommendations to the Commission. Although many States have been subject to this review procedure, it is limited in its impact by the control of governments within their own jurisdictions. The procedure is not really about upholding individual rights but is a means of indicating major human rights-abusing States. Investigation is only carried out with State consent and if the Sub-Commission decides to criticise a State, the Commission itself might not adopt its recommendations because of political factors. Furthermore, action under this procedure remains confidential until such a time as the Commission makes a recommendation to ECOSOC. Although an improvement on the previous system, the UN Commission's protection of human rights is at a low level. Professor Harris provides a sober evaluation of its impact:

> Whereas the Commission's enforcement work … is undoubtedly worthwhile in the sense that it results in reports evidencing state conduct and requires states to defend themselves at Commission sessions, there are limits to its value. Although attention may be focused beneficially on situations of real concern for human rights, politics clearly influence the choice and treatment of particular cases. There are no mandatory powers to hear witnesses or enter territory to conduct investigations. Where infringements of human rights are found, the Commission's powers are restricted to persuasion, public criticism and, in the most serious cases, attempts at isolation of the offending state; there are no legally binding sanctions available.[32]

Although Professor Harris labels aspects of the Commission's work as 'enforcement', this author believes that they are more correctly seen as supervision. Enforcement implies positive coercion beyond simple condemnation, a facet which is singulary lacking in the area of human rights.

Lack of mandatory powers and lack of coercive powers can be seen in the other main organs of the United Nations concerned with human rights. The Centre for Human Rights, for instance, which the Vienna Declaration of 1993 identified as playing an 'important role in co-ordinating system wide attention for human rights', is simply that section of the UN Secretariat which administers the UN's involvement in human rights,[33] it has no proactive role. Even one of the most successful UN organs, in this case an organ created under Article 22 of the UN Charter as a subsidiary organ of the General Assembly in 1950,[34] the United Nations High Commissioner for Refugees, essentially has a supervisory role, as recognised in Article 35 of the 1951 Convention Relating to the Status of Refugees.[35] Furthermore, the UNHCR is dependent upon State consent embodied in paragraph 8 of the Statute of the UNHCR contained in the 1950 General Assembly resolution. Although paragraph 1 of the Statute states that the High Commissioner 'shall assume the function of providing international protection ... to refugees', paragraph 8 makes it clear that this shall be done only with State consent, there being no mandatory or coercive powers to ensure protection of the refugees. It follows that it is not possible to speak in absolute terms of refugees having 'rights' on the international plane, and that the status of the refugee in international law is limited by State sovereignty and the lack of international institutional protection when faced with an intransigent government.[36]

The machinery of the International Covenants

In some ways the creation of a treaty framework protecting the list of human rights to be found in the Universal Declaration can be seen as an attempt to create a system of human rights' supervision independent of the United Nations, with its bedrock of State sovereignty and its political machinations. The two treaties: the International Covenant on Civil and Political Rights[37] and the International Covenant on Economic, Social and Cultural Rights,[38] adopted by the UN General Assembly in 1966 were the product of a drafting process started in the Commission on Human Rights in 1947. The treaties themselves did not enter into force until 1976. The treaties split the list of human rights contained in the Universal Declaration, the strongest justification for this being that civil and political rights (so-called first-generation human rights) had an absolute character requiring immediate State compliance, whilst economic and social rights (so-called second-generation human rights) were relative, depending upon the development of the State in question. Such arguments are reflected in the obligations on State parties to the two covenants contained in Article 2(1) of each with civil and political rights being subject to an absolute and immediate obligation, whilst economic and social rights are subject to a qualified and progressive obligation.[39] In reality the driving force behind the division was the ideological divide between the West, which naturally advocated civil and political rights, and the Socialist bloc which advocated economic and social rights. The division into two inevitably weakened the covenants, which, even with the end of the Cold War, have not been ratified by the full membership of the UN.

The system of supervision established for the two Covenants differs, the institutional framework being much more advanced in the case of the Treaty protecting civil and political rights. Article 28 of the Covenant establishes a Human Rights Committee consisting of eighteen independent experts. The Committee's primary function as regards all State parties is, according to Article 40 of the Covenant, to review State reports, in practice every five years, on the 'measures they have adopted which give effect to the rights' contained in the Treaty. Part of the review process involves the public questioning of State representatives on aspects of their reports. Obviously the problem with this procedure is that abusing governments may well attempt to hide their abuses in their reports, and so an informal procedure has developed whereby individual members of the Committee receive reports from NGOs operating in the field of human rights. The Committee will conclude its cross-examination of a State representative with an often critical series of concluding observations,[40] as well as transmitting to the State parties general comments on overall compliance with the Treaty. However, the Committee has, until recently, interpreted Article 40(4) as not allowing it to make any country-specific reports, a severe limitation on the reporting process. Clearly the system mainly relies on States taking on board any comments made during the oral hearings and any applicable aspects of the general comments and incorporating them into their domestic legislation and procedures for protecting human rights before the next report has to be submitted in five years. This method of supervision can only be labelled one of 'implementation' in a very broad sense indeed,[41] depending upon a very haphazard system of fact finding beyond those facts presented by the government of a State. There appears to be no real method of ensuring compliance with the Committee's views beyond relying on the next round of reports.

The Covenant also provides, in Article 41, for an optional system of application by States to the Committee alleging violation by another State of its obligations under the Treaty. No applications have been made so far. More successful has been the First Optional Protocol to the International Covenant on Civil and Political Rights which has over sixty-five State parties.[42] Under Article 1 of this Protocol State parties recognise 'the competence of the Committee to receive and consider communications from individuals subject to its jurisdiction who claim to be victims of a violation by that State Party of any of the rights set forth in the Covenant'.[43] This system has proved a greater success with the Committee receiving 587 communications under the Protocol in the period 1977–94; 193 of these have resulted in a Human Right's Committee report, the majority of which have contained a finding that the Covenant has been breached.[44] Nevertheless, the

Committee itself has recognised its limitations in protecting human rights under the optional protocol:

> ... the Committee is neither a court nor a body with a quasi-judicial mandate, like the organs created under ... the European Convention on Human Rights ... Still, the Committee applies the provisions of the Covenant and the Optional Protocol in a judicial sprit and performs functions similar to those of the European Commission on Human Rights, in as much as the consideration of applications from individuals is concerned. Its decisions on the merits ... are, in principle, comparable to the reports of the European Commission, non-binding recommendations. The two systems differ, however, in that the Optional Protocol does not provide explicitly for friendly settlement between the parties, and, more importantly, in that the Committee has no power to hand down binding decisions as does the European Court of Human Rights. State parties to the Optional Protocol endeavour to observe the Committee's views, but in case of non-compliance the Optional Protocol does not provide for any enforcement measures or for sanctions.[45]

Furthermore, 'compliance with the HRC's views has been disappointing although some states have shown a willingness to co-operate with the HRC and give effect to its views'.[46] Overall, bearing in mind that only about one third of the world's States are parties to the protocol, the Human Rights Committee presents a very limited avenue of redress for individuals who have suffered human rights abuses, and compares unfavourably to the more established regional systems in this respect.

The International Covenant on Economic, Social and Cultural Rights, has even more limited institutional machinery for attempting to ensure compliance with its provisions. The Treaty itself in Articles 16 to 22 places responsibility for overseeing the implementation of rights contained therein on ECOSOC. The failure of ECOSOC or its Working Group, consisting of State representatives, led to the creation by ECOSOC,[47] with effect from 1987, of a Committee on Economic, Social and Cultural Rights modelled on the Human Rights Committee in terms of composition. The Economic and Social Rights Committee's competence is much more straightforward, in that it simply reviews State reports submitted on a five-yearly basis according to Articles 16 and 17 of the Treaty. Like the Human Rights Committee, the Economic and Social Rights Committee has had tremendous problems with State parties not submitting reports.[48] The Committee examines reports in public hearings along the lines of the Human Rights Committee and makes critical comments in its concluding observations.[49] The Committee may also make 'suggestions and recommendations of a general nature on the basis of its consideration of' national reports. This reporting process has the same defects as for the Covenant on Civil and Political Rights, although strangely, the Economic and Social Rights Committee has developed more formal procedures than the Human Rights Committee for receiving factual information from non-governmental sources – NGOs and the UN-specialised agencies,[50] although the Human Rights Committee has recently formalised the receipt of NGO information. A member of the Committee has assessed the reporting procedure as follows:

In general terms, the potential effectiveness of the reporting procedure clearly lies less in the formal exchanges between the Committee and the state party and more in the mobilization of domestic political and other forces to participate in monitoring government policies and providing a detailed critique (assuming that one is warranted) of the government's own assessment of the situation.[51]

The fact that the system relies on the marshalling of domestic public opinion in a criticised State surely depends on whether public opinion plays a formal or informal role is lobbying a government to change its policy: a role that it often singularly lacking in a major human rights-abusing State.[52]

Collective security and human rights

It can be seen that although there has been a proliferation of the institutional machinery for attempted human rights protection under the auspices of the UN, the bodies established all have significant weaknesses, in particular the lack of any mandatory and enforcement powers which would enable us to speak of human *rights* in a fuller sense. In reality the only occasions in which human rights standards have been enforced by the international community is when coercive measures have been applied under the collective security umbrella, reviewed in chapters 7 and 8, for example the imposition of sanctions against Southern Rhodesia where the denial of self-determination constituted a threat to international peace. It was seen in those chapters that where there is sufficient collective will serious and widescale abuses of human rights can constitute a threat to the peace and so be dealt with under the collective security powers of the organisations.

Another related development is the establishment by the UN Security Council of judicial tribunals with powers of enforcement, presumably derived from a combination of Article 29 and Chapter VII (Article 41 perhaps) of the UN Charter,[53] based loosely on the precedent of the Nuremberg Tribunal which tried major Nazi war criminals after the Second World War.[54] The Security Council established an international tribunal for the prosecution of persons responsible for serious violations of humanitarian law committed in the territory of the former Yugoslavia since 1991.[55] Imprisonment of individuals convicted of war crimes, crimes against humanity, acts of genocide, or breaches of the Hague or Geneva Conventions, will take place in consenting member States. A similar tribunal was established in November 1994 for the purpose of prosecuting persons responsible for committing genocide and other serious violations of international humanitarian law committed in Rwanda during 1994.[56] It is only in these few, though serious, cases that it can be said that the UN has attempted enforcement of international human rights standards.

Nevertheless, considering the limited coverage of human rights in the UN Charter, the development of standard setting and supervision, and the fact that many States are at least called to account for some of their human rights practices, is a remarkable achievement for the world Organisation. Turning now to look, albeit briefly at the main regional organisations, it will become apparent that, in some instances, further progress towards international institutional protection of human rights has been made.

European organisations and human rights

There are several organisations covering, wholly or partly, the protection of human rights in Europe. The main one examined in the next section is the Council of Europe and the human rights treaties produced by it. However, it is also necessary to mention briefly the CSCE (now OSCE) and the EU as institutions also concerned with human rights.

As was noted in chapter 2, the CSCE, deriving from the Helsinki Final Act of 1975, is a pan-European political process designed during a period of *détente* to encourage political dialogue between East and West. Its main concern was with security, although in 'Basket 1' of the non-binding Final Act, respect for human rights and fundamental freedoms was one of the guiding principles governing relations between States. An increasing list of human rights to be protected and an increasingly complex diplomatic, not legal, method of monitoring compliance was agreed to in the Vienna, Copenhagen and Paris conferences of 1989–90.[57] The value of the CSCE process as regards protection of human rights has been stated to be 'marginal' given the political, not legal, nature of the obligations, and by the fact that with the end of the Cold War many of the former Eastern bloc States are now ratifying the European Convention on Human Rights, which has a much more developed *legal* system for ensuring compliance with the Treaty.[58]

Nevertheless, for those States outside the Convention system, and for promoting a diplomatic dialogue between European States, Russia, the United States and Canada, the CSCE remains a significant, and increasingly institutionalised,[59] forum. Indeed, in Budapest in December 1994, the CSCE renamed itself the Organisation on Security and Co-operation in Europe (OSCE), emphasising its permanency and move towards being a fully-fledged, inter-governmental organisation.[60] In its Prague Document of January 1992, the CSCE Council of Ministers decided that 'in order to develop further the CSCE's capability to safeguard human rights, democracy and the rule of law through peaceful means, that appropriate action may be taken by the Council' or the Committee of Senior Officials, 'if necessary in the absence of the consent of the State concerned in cases of clear, gross and uncorrected violations of relevant CSCE commitments'. However, 'appropriate action' was stated to consist of 'political declarations and other political steps to apply outside the territory concerned', although such decisions may be taken on the basis of 'consensus minus one' thereby preventing the abusing country vetoing the proposed action.[61] Further, and more intrusive, human rights mechanisms and institutions were created by the Helsinki Document of

1992, namely an Office for Democratic Institutions and Human Rights whose activities 'may contribute to early warning in the prevention of conflicts';[62] and a CSCE High Commissioner on National Minorities,[63] allowing the CSCE to 'have an early presence on the ground before conflicts escalate'.[64] Furthermore, the CSCE seems to envisage fact finding, not necessarily with the consent of the State concerned. The earlier CSCE document, concluded at Vienna in 1990,[65] makes it clear that 'a rapporteur can be sent on a mission to address a particular, clearly defined question on its territory relating to the human dimension even *without* the agreement of the State concerned'.[66] Human rights missions were sent to Yugoslavia in 1991 to 1992 on the basis of these commitments, and many of the new members of the Conference have CSCE missions of one sort or another on their territories,[67] illustrating that successful fact finding and monitoring can take place without any formal treaty commitment, indeed without any requirement of formal consent, although this is often given.

The Council of Europe, progenitor of the Conventions of human rights, was originally viewed in 1949 as the first step towards greater European integration. Instead, the Council's human rights system developed alongside the functionally evolving European Community, although increasingly, the two systems have co-ordinated. In particular the Maastricht Treaty of 1992, in Article F, lays down that the EU 'shall respect fundamental rights as guaranteed by the European Convention of Human Rights and Fundamental Freedoms ... 1950 and as they result from the constitutional traditions common to the Member States, as general principles of Community law'. In fact, the European Court had already developed a substantial body of law which takes account of the European Convention on Human Rights as well as insisting that Community Law should be applied consistently with the European Convention.[68] Professor Hartley concludes that 'all the Member states' of the EU are parties to the European Convention 'and there is no doubt that the rights protected by it are Community human rights'.[69]

The Council of Europe

It can be seen that for the EU and to a lesser extent the OSCE, the European Convention of Human Rights is the defining law on human rights in Europe. Its creator, the Council of Europe, was established in 1949, affirming its devotion 'to the spiritual and moral values which are the common heritage of the peoples and the true source of individual freedom, political liberty and the rule of law, principles which form the basis of all genuine democracy'.[70] The Organisation primarily consists of a Committee of Ministers, composed of representatives of member States, which acts as the executive organ, and a Parliamentary Assembly consisting of members appointed by each national parliament, with delegations ranging from three to eighteen roughly corresponding to the size of the members' populations, which acts as the deliberative or plenary body. The treaty-drafting competence of the Council of Europe is invested in the Committee of Ministers by

Article 15(a) which provides that 'on the recommendation of the [Parliamentary Assembly] or on its own initiative, the Committee of Ministers shall consider the action required to further the aim of the Council of Europe, including the conclusion of conventions ...'. The Statute of the Council of Europe itself contains greater obligations as regards human rights than the UN Charter does. Article 3 provides that 'every Member ... must accept the principles of the rule of law and the enjoyment by all persons within its jurisdiction of human rights and fundamental freedoms ...', without specifying the types of human rights to be protected. Furthermore, the Council's commitment to human rights is illustrated in Article 8 which provides that if any member seriously violates Article 3 then it may be suspended and requested to withdraw. If the State in question refuses to withdraw, the Committee of Ministers may decide that it has ceased to be a member of the Council.

The lack of a list of specific human rights and the need for a more effective monitoring procedure, when combined with the anti-Communist nature of the Organisation, resulted in the rapid development of the European Convention for the Protection of Human Rights and Fundamental Freedoms,[71] signed in 1950 and entering into force in 1953. This Treaty, the backbone of the European human rights system, protected first-generation civil and political rights. The reasons for its rapid development by the Council is explained by Dr Beddard:

> The Committee on Legal and Administrative Questions agreed unanimously that initially only those rights and freedoms could be guaranteed which were defined and accepted, after long usage, by democratic regimes. Other rights and freedoms, including social rights, were to be defined and protected in the future, but it was necessary to begin with accepted, widely agreed principles, and to seek to guarantee, first of all, political democracy. The next step in the quest for European union would then be the co-ordination of national economies, and not until after that stage had been reached could any attempt be made to generalize human rights.[72]

The initial lack of enthusiasm for a treaty on second-generation human rights did not prevent the Council sponsoring the European Social Charter,[73] which was signed in 1961 and entered into force in 1965. However, as shall be seen, the obligations and monitoring procedures of this Treaty have resulted in the following bleak assessment: 'whereas the Convention is firmly established as the jewel in the Council of Europe crown, the Charter has led a twilight existence',[74] mostly due to a lack of political will on the part of the members. When it was proposed to include a 'Social Chapter' in the Maastricht Treaty of 1992, recognising much less extensive individual rights than the Social Charter, the UK felt unable to agree to it with the result that it was included as a separate Agreement on Social Policy to which the UK is not a party.[75] Whereas the UK is prepared to be a party to the institutionally weak Social Charter of the Council of Europe, it was not prepared to be a party to treaty obligations, with the possibility of them being implemented by the supranational European Organisation.

The Social Charter itself does not clearly impose an absolute and immediate obligation on State parties, Article 20 adopting an unusual approach by placing parties under an obligation to pursue the policy of realising the nineteen economic and social rights listed in Part 1, but also giving the parties a choice of which rights to protect from at least ten of the Articles detailing the rights in Part 2, with five at least chosen from a basic list of core rights. Despite this obligation being placed upon the parties, most of the rights are still to be protected progressively, making it difficult to identify any definite breaches of the Treaty. In addition, allowing the State parties to select the rights they wish to protect devalues them as substantive legal rights, and allows States to avoid areas of economic and social concern on political grounds. This problem is further exacerbated by the inadequacy of the supervisory system when compared to the system under the European Convention on Human Rights. State parties are obliged to submit reports concerning the implementation of the rights which have been accepted under Article 20 as well as on the status of those non-accepted rights to the Committee on Independent Experts, nominated by the parties. The Committee of Experts' reports are taken on board by the Parliamentary Assembly of the Council of Europe, but less so by the more powerful State-representative Committee of Ministers, which is empowered to make recommendations to a particular contracting party based upon a determination that the Charter has been breached.[76] Attempts to improve the system and empower the Committee of Experts were made in 1991,[77] with the introduction, *inter alia*, of the possibility of oral hearings, an increase in the role of NGOs, as well as relaxing the voting rules in the Committee of Ministers.

As with the International Covenant on Economic, Social and Cultural Rights, there is no means of ensuring that an individual who has suffered from an alleged breach of the Social Charter can complain to the Committee, let alone receive redress if a breach is proven. In these circumstances it seems a little premature to call those 'aims', 'policies', or 'goals', human *rights* in the full sense. However, when we turn to the European Convention of Human Rights and Fundamental Freedoms, it can be seen that the process of institutionalising civil and political rights has been much more thorough, though the individual still does not possess these rights on the international plane as a full subject of international law. Article 25(1) states:

> The [European Commission on Human Rights] may receive petitions addressed to the Secretary General of the Council of Europe from any person, non-governmental organisation or group of individuals claiming to be the victim of a violation by one of the High Contracting Parties of the rights set forth in this Convention, *provided that the High Contracting Party against which the complaint has been lodged has declared that it recognises the competence of the Commission to receive such petitions.* Those of the Contracting Parties who have made such a declaration undertake not to hinder in any way the effective exercise of this right.[78]

The fact that all State parties to the European Convention have made such declarations[79] means that individuals within the member States do have a right of action, but not *per se*, it depends on the grant of their governments. Contrast this with Article 24 of the Convention which provides that any State party 'may refer to the Commission … any alleged breach of the provisions of the Convention' by another party. Clearly, as with all human rights conventions, the complainants in the main are going to be individual victims of abuses, not States as the small number of cases referred to the Commission under Article 24 shows.

> It should be noted that the inter-state procedure is not predicated upon the alleged violation of one of the substantive rights protected by the Convention, but can be invoked in relation to any provision of the Convention. Even if an alleged violation does infringe or violate one of the ECHR's substantive rights, it is not necessary for the complaining state to demonstrate that it has a special interest in, or relationship to, the victim. In a technical sense, all that states are concerned with here is ensuring that other parties observe their obligation under the Convention. It has been apparent, however, that in the small number of inter-state cases brought to date, the majority have been motivated by political hostility.[80]

The lack of collective will on the part of States in the most established human rights treaty is disappointing, but illustrates the need for implementation systems based not on inter-State claims but on reporting and individual applications. Professor Kirgis states that 'on only two occasions in the first 38 years – once against Greece and once against Turkey – was [Article 24] used as a kind of *actio popularis*, on behalf of non-nationals of the complaining states'.[81] Both actions were brought by Denmark, Norway, Sweden and the Netherlands: one concerning the imprisonment and torture of political prisoners by the Greek military regime in 1970, and the other concerning alleged torture and mistreatment of prisoners in Turkey in 1982.[82]

There is a little-used system of reporting under Article 57 of the Convention which states that 'on receipt of a request from the Secretary General of the Council of Europe any High Contracting Party shall furnish an explanation of the manner in which its internal law ensures the effective implementation of any of the provisions of this Convention.' Professor Kirgis reports that this power has only been used by the Secretary General on five occasions,[83] and therefore, in reality, the enforcement system depends on Article 25. Nevertheless, the number of barriers contained in Article 27 of the Convention to the admissibility of individual applications means that the Commission, screens out ninety-six per cent of petitions by individuals.[84] Of those that are allowed to proceed, 'the Commission's role is to examine complaints of alleged breaches of the Convention, to establish the facts and to try to obtain a friendly settlement of cases, failing which it expresses its opinion as to whether there has been a violation of the Convention'.[85] If the recommendatory powers of the Commission are insufficient to settle the matter, the Commission or a State involved in the case,[86] and under Protocol 9[87] of 1990 an individual, can refer the case to the European Court of Human Rights, but only if the respondent State has accepted the compulsory jurisdiction of the Court under Article 46(1).[88]

If the individual wins his or her case before the European Court of Human Rights the decision is final and, by Article 53, the State parties 'undertake to abide by the decision of the Court in any case to which they are parties.' The Court can award damages,[89] though it, in the main, simply declares the Convention has been breached, it being upon the State then to take the necessary action to remedy the breach. The decisions of the Court are not only binding, Article 54 further provides that 'the judgment of the Court shall be transmitted to the Committee of Ministers which shall supervise its execution'. Although no specific powers have been granted to the Committee to enforce judgments, the system appears to have worked in the main without the need for coercive measures. However, this may well be because of the relatively homogenous character of many of the State parties, although Turkey and several Eastern European States have ratified the Convention. Furthermore, the evidence is that the system does not work as well when confronted with recalcitrant States:

> Much of the work of the Convention's institutions has been directed towards resolv-
> ing deficiencies in the domestic law of state parties, rather than dealing with the gross
> violations of human rights which its drafters originally appeared to envisage. None
> the less, the ECHR has on occasion had to deal with the eruption of totalitarianism
> ... in *Denmark, Norway, Sweden and The Netherlands* v *Greece*, which ... high-
> lighted some of the weaknesses of the Convention's protective system.[90]

Despite Greece's withdrawal from the Convention, the junta remained responsible for its breaches of the Treaty as identified by the Court, yet there was no way under the Convention of actually protecting human rights or remedying the breaches. Thus although the system is an improvement on the simple supervisory procedures of the UN system, in that individuals rights are normally upheld by the institutions and remedied by the States, the system will break down in the face of a major and widespread violation of human rights. The Committee of Ministers, although empowered to supervise execution of the judgments of the Court, does not have any real powers of enforcement.[91]

The European system for human rights protection continues to develop, the latest Protocol (No. 11) to the European Convention of Human Rights of May 1994 will, when it comes into force one year after ratification by all parties to the main Convention, remove the Commission, and simply have a permanent European Court of Human Rights operating within a more elaborate chamber system, performing the functions of the Commission and the old Court.[92] This will stream-line the system which has become too cumbersome with the increasing number of applications and the increasing number of parties to the Convention. Furthermore, Protocol 11 will make the jurisdiction of the Court compulsory, removing the need for declarations by State parties recognising its jurisdiction.

It cannot be doubted that the European Convention on Human Rights has created one of the most successful human rights systems in the world. Despite the fact that the institutions created are not supranational in any sense of the word, as noted by the Secretary General of the Council of Europe, 'the Convention and its organs are not judicially superior to national systems and cannot intervene directly in them',[93] State party compliance with the decisions of those organs has been remarkably high.[94] Overall, the system 'has provided an extremely useful and potent mechanism of last resort for large numbers of individuals whose grievances have not been redressed by the relevant institutions in their own states'.[95]

American organisations and human rights

The inter-American human rights system is, after the European system, one of the most-advanced regional systems, with an institutional structure that has, like the United Nations, expanded from a narrow treaty base. Unlike the European system which is separate from the European Union, the inter-American system at least started as an aspect of the work of the Organisation of American States (OAS).

The early parallels with the UN's treatment of human rights can be seen in the fact that the OAS Charter contains very little reference to human rights. Under Article 3(k) of the amended OAS Charter 'the American States proclaim the fundamental rights of the individual without distinction as to race, nationality, creed, or sex'.[96] Like the UN Charter, and the Statute of the Council of Europe, there is no list of human rights in the Treaty. This was remedied at the Bogotá conference of 1948, at which the OAS Charter was agreed, when States adopted a non-binding resolution entitled the American Declaration on the Rights and Duties of Man.[97] This document strongly parallels the Universal Declaration on Human Rights with the major exception of a large number of Articles detailing duties (for example duty to vote if eligible, duty to pay tax), as well as rights. Although technically non-binding, the American Declaration, like the Universal Declaration has taken on a normative status, illustrating the quasi-legislative capacity of the OAS, as recognised in the decisions of the institutions that have subsequently developed as part of the inter-American system.[98]

The lack of a human rights supervisory body for the OAS was remedied in 1959, when a Meeting of Consultation of OAS Ministers of Foreign Affairs adopted a resolution creating the Inter-American Commission on Human Rights, to be composed of seven members serving in their individual capacities, with the mandate of promoting respect for human rights.[99] Although the Statute of the Commission limited the Commission to 'advisory and recommendatory functions',[100] the Commission rapidly developed a capacity for investigations of human rights abuses within OAS countries as well as a power to make recommendations to governments. These implied powers, however, were severely limited by the fact that State consent was required to undertake investigations, and by the fact that the Commission did not feel it had the competence to hear individual petitions alleging human rights abuses. However, if a large number of communications were received by it, indicating widespread human rights abuse by a particular State, it, like the UN Commission of Human Rights, has quite often undertaken country studies. Davidson records that the Commission's first country studies involved Cuba, Haiti and the Dominican Republic in the early 1960s. Only the latter permitted the Commission to undertake on-site investigations, in the case of Cuba and Haiti it relied mainly on statements. On-site investigations have proved the most useful, for example the Commission actually found a number of 'disappeared' individuals in jail when visiting Argentina.[101] The application of the Commission's findings and recommendations depends on the publicity given to the Commission's reports, and whether its recommendations are taken on board in a condemnatory resolution of the OAS General Assembly, a fact more likely now that the region has moved from its 'totalitarian phase' to its 'democratic phase'.[102]

The Commission's lack of capacity to hear individual petitions was remedied in 1965 by the Second Special Inter-American Conference,[103] which adopted a resolution entitling the Commission to receive complaints from individuals, to seek information and to make recommendations to States. Although a significant step in the development of human rights protection, the right of individual petition to the Commission was in fact of limited value in that the Commission, like the Human Rights Committee under the International Covenant, has only recommendatory powers. Furthermore, unlike the system under the European Convention of Human Rights, there is no provision within the OAS Charter for a final, binding determination by a human rights court, or the possibility of an award of damages against the offending State.

By the time the Inter-American Commission on Human Rights was formally incorporated into the OAS structure as one of the principal organs of the OAS by the Protocol of Buenos Aires which entered into force in 1970, the OAS member States had adopted the American Convention on Human Rights in 1969.[104] Article 111 of the current integrated OAS Charter declares that 'there shall be an Inter-American Commission on Human Rights, whose principal function shall be to promote the observance and protection of human rights and to serve as a consultative organ of' the OAS. Furthermore, it provides that the American Convention on Human Rights 'shall determine the structure, competence, and procedure of this Commission ...'. It is to the American Convention and its development of the Commission and the creation of a Court that this analysis now turns. However, it must not be thought that the Convention system replaces the system of human rights protection developed under the OAS Charter. In effect there are two parallel and overlapping systems, 'a dual legal basis' for human right protection,[105] one for OAS members States and one for those member States which have become parties to the Convention. The Commission is used under both systems. As was pointed out in chapter 6 the OAS is characterised by the development of several overlapping legal regimes with varying State participation, resulting not only from the Convention on Human Rights but also from the various amendments to the OAS Charter, which have not all been uniformly ratified.

The American Convention on Human Rights was adopted at the end of the Inter-American Specialised Conference on Human Rights held at San José. It entered into force in 1978. The Convention covers the normal first-generation human rights but like its European counterpart, the Inter-American system of human rights protection has moved towards the protection of second-generation human rights with the adoption of the Protocol of San Salvador in 1988, which obliges State parties progressively to achieve the realisation of the rights contained therein, in contrast to the absolute and immediate obligations in the Convention itself. The Protocol, however, is not yet in force.[106]

In many ways the institutions created by the American Convention for the protection of human rights parallel the European Convention system, at least until the latest reform of the latter. The existing Commission is recognised under Article 34, and under Article 41 is empowered with the functions of promoting and defending human rights, developing awareness of human rights, and making recommendations to States and to prepare studies and reports. Unlike the European Commission, the Inter-American Commission has a 'unique' competence as regards receiving complaints from individuals, and other non-State entities.[107] Article 44 provides:

> Any person or group of persons, or any nongovernmental entity legally recognized in one or more member state of the Organization, may lodge petitions with the Commission containing denunciations or complaints of violation of this Convention by a State Party.

Unlike the European Convention, individuals automatically have the right of complaint to the Commission. In contrast, as regards inter-State complaints, Article 45(1) provides that 'any State Party may ... declare that it recognises the competence of the Commission to receive and examine communication in which a State Party alleges that another State Party has committed a violation of human rights set forth in this Convention'. Furthermore, such complaints may only be instituted on the basis of reciprocity, in other words if both State have made such declarations.

The political sensitivity of many American States with poor human rights records explains why there is such a restricted inter-State complaint mechanism, but it does not directly explain the empowerment of individuals to make complaints without any 'optional' procedure under the Convention. The answer to this apparent paradox is partly provided by lack of competence given to individuals to seize the Inter-American Court. If the complaint, whether by a State or by an individual, is deemed admissible by the Commission, the Commission is empowered to attempt friendly settlement and to make recommendations to the government concerned.[108] At the end of this procedure, which includes the possibility of onsite investigation with the consent of the State concerned, Article 61(1) provides that, either the Commission or the concerned State can refer the case to the Inter-American Court. Article 62 then states that contentious proceedings can only be initiated before the Court if the State party or parties concerned have accepted its jurisdiction in such matters. Thus although individuals have the right of access to the Commission with its *recommendatory* powers, they have no right of access to the Court with its *mandatory* powers – in other words the State parties still have ultimate control over the work of the most significant institution created by the Convention. A contrast must be made with the Protocol 9 of the European Convention which allows access to the European Court of Human Rights for individuals from States that have ratified the protocol. Furthermore, Protocol 11, when it comes in to force, will make the European Court's jurisdiction compulsory for States.

The political sensitivity of many American States to human rights issues has meant that the Inter-American Court of Human Rights only utilised its contentious jurisdiction on three occasions during the 1980s. Although it has used its advisory jurisdiction under Article 64 on more occasions during this period, the limited jurisprudence of the Court is a significant defect in the system.[109] The advisory jurisdiction of the Court is only triggered at the request of the State or an empowered organ of the OAS, and its decisions under this head are not binding. In effect, this elaborate system of human rights protection, which has, as its ultimate deterrent, the binding power of the Court in a contentious case is in the main avoided because of the unwillingness of the States to submit to the possibility of 'the binding adverse decision that could result'.[110]

Article 63(1) of the Convention states that:

> If the Court finds that there has been a violation of a right or freedom protected by this Convention, the Court shall rule that the injured party be ensured the enjoyment of his right or freedom that was violated. It shall also rule, if appropriate, that the consequences of the measure or situation that constituted the breach of such right or freedom be remedied and that fair compensation be paid to the injured party.

Further, Article 68(1) states that 'the State Parties to the Convention undertake to comply with the judgment of the Court in any case to which they are parties'. In the few instances the Court has been asked to make a binding judgment, it has made statements offering a certain encouragement to States to allow the Court to be able to exercise its power more often. In the *Velásquez Rodríguez* case,[111] the Court stated that:

> The international protection of human rights should not be confused with criminal justice. States do not appear before the Court as defendants in a criminal action. The objective of international human rights law is not to punish those individuals who are guilty of violations, but rather to protect the victims and to provide for the reparation of damages resulting from the acts of the States responsible.[112]

In the case the Court went on to award the next of kin of Velásquez, for whose disappearance the Honduran government was held responsible, full damages, calculated along delictual lines, namely to put the next of kin into the position they would have been in had the Convention not been breached – covering the loss of earnings of the 'disappeared', as well as emotional loss suffered by his wife and children as a result of the disappearance.[113] Although Honduras did pay compensation to the next of kin following this case,[114] there is no mandatory enforcement mechanism, Article 68(2) simply stating that compensatory damages '*may* be executed in the country concerned in accordance with the domestic procedure governing the execution of judgments against the state'.[115] In effect, though the Court's judgments in contentious cases are binding there is no enforcement mechanism as such to ensure that they are complied with. Political pressure may be brought to bear on the recalcitrant State by the OAS General Assembly adopting a condemnatory recommendation upon receipt of a report from the Court on non-compliance with its judgment.[116]

Although there are great similarities between the European and Inter-American human rights systems, the European one seems to have been more successful, at least in granting relief to individual victims of human rights. The relative homogeneity of most of the States in the region can partly explain this, though as has been pointed out that system cannot cope with major violations of human rights, a factor more evident in the Inter-American system, with its vast disparities between States not only in wealth but also in human rights protection. In the Inter-American system, with much greater widescale human rights abuse occurring, it is unfortunate that this results in the greater negative impact of sovereignty, preventing human rights from being protected. It may be that now the region is entering a 'democratic phase', the protection of human rights will be made easier and the Court made more use of. There are early signs that this is happening,[117] although given the Court's record so far, and the statements it has made in those cases, it would be difficult to agree that the Court has become 'a kind of international criminal court competent to judge some of the most heinous crimes committed by, or with the acquiesence of, States in the hemisphere'.[118] The Court has itself stated that it does not operate as a criminal court, and the constraints of State sovereignty have meant that it has only a limited impact on the protection of human rights in the region.

The OAU and the protection of human rights

Africa has undergone a much more recent process of regional organisation. The OAU itself was not established until 1963. The OAU Charter does make limited reference to the Universal Declaration of Human Rights in its Preamble and in Article 2.[119] However, it was not until 1981 that the African Charter on Human and Peoples' Rights was adopted, entering into force in 1986.[120] The tardiness of this process, when compared to the European and Inter-American systems, is explained by Dr Naldi:

> Decolonization was still in its infancy and the young states jealously guarded their independence. The international protection of human rights was seen by some as a legacy of imperialism or as an excuse to interfere in their internal affairs. Yet the need for their protection was self-evident. The atrocities committed by Idi Amin in Uganda (1971–79), Bokassa in the Central African Empire (1966–79), and Nguema

in Equatorial Guinea (1969–79), and the prevailing situation in Southern Africa made the strengthening of civil and human rights imperative.[121]

Tentative steps were taken by various bodies to develop mechanisms for human rights protection, including a call in 1972 to create an African human rights commission made by the UN Commission on Human Rights.[122] This process finally led to the adoption of the African Charter in 1981. It has a number of distinctive features when compared to its European and Inter-American counterparts.

First of all as regards the number and type of rights protected, it is probably true to say that the African Charter is the most comprehensive in that it covers not only traditional 'Western' first-generation rights, but also second- and third-generation rights, as well as containing a significant section on duties. The Preamble to the African Charter makes it plain why all three generations of rights are protected in the same Treaty:

> *Convinced* that it is henceforth essential to pay a particular attention to the right to development and that civil and political rights cannot be dissociated from economic, social and cultural rights in their conception as well as their universality and that the satisfaction of economic, social and cultural rights is a guarantee for the enjoyment of civil and political rights.

As well as the right to development, third-generation rights protected by the treaty include: a people's rights to self-determination, to natural resources, peace and security, and a satisfactory environment. In addition, all the rights are subject to the same obligation contained in Article 1 whereby State parties 'shall recognize the rights, duties and freedoms enshrined in this Charter and shall undertake to adopt legislative or other measures to give effect to them'. The Charter reflects the African view that collective rights are as important as civil and political rights.

Furthermore, the traditional African approach to law is said to explain why, when looking at the institutional mechanisms created by the Charter to protect human rights, there is no judicial organ. Africans prefer to settle their disputes by reconciliation rather than relying on confrontation in the court room.[123] Nevertheless, the absence of a court with the capacity to make binding determinations that there have been breaches of the Treaty, as in the European and Inter-American systems, severely weakens the protection afforded by the African Charter.

The Charter relies on a sole supervisory organ to ensure implementation of its provisions, the African Commission on Human and Peoples' Rights. Its mandate, contained in Article 45, includes: the collection of documents, the undertaking of studies, the making of recommendations to governments, the formulation of principles on which governments may base their legislation, the development of co-operation with other African and international institutions involved in the protection of human rights, and the interpretation of the provisions of the African Charter. As well as a rather ambivalent supervisory function under Article 62, the Commission has jurisdiction to hear inter-State complaints under Articles 47 and 49, as well as other communications not from State parties, but from individuals and presumably NGOs as well, under Article 55. Although there is no 'optional' mechanism whereby States have to indicate their willingness to be the subject of the complaint procedure, this apparent dent in the domination of the sovereign State is counterbalanced by the weakness of the Commission's powers.

As regards inter-State disputes, the procedure is essentially directed at friendly settlement, any adverse report must be taken on board by the recommendatory powers of the Assembly of the OAU Heads of State and Government,[124] in effect placing ultimate supervision in the hands of one of the OAU's politicised organs. Similarly, the investigation and report on individual communications seems to be restricted, like the UN ECOSOC's procedure, to those which 'reveal the existence of a series of massive violation of human rights', in which case the Commission 'shall draw the attention of the Assembly of Heads of State and Government to these special cases'.[125] The reason behind this appears to be the view that the African States were more worried about the gross violations that have occurred in Africa rather 'than the "peripheral" violations which occur within the European context'.[126] Nevertheless, it is true that if the African States really wanted to submit themselves to proper institutional review of their human rights records, they would have granted the Commission greater powers of investigation and condemnation, as well as creating a court with the power to make binding decisions. Furthermore, they should have produced a greater openness in the activities of the Commission. Instead Article 59(1) states that 'all measures taken within the provisions of the present chapter shall remain confidential until such a time as the Assembly of Heads of State and Government shall otherwise decide', thus almost always depriving 'the system of one of the most valuable sanctions available in the human rights field – the sanction of publicity'.[127] As it is, the continuing massive human rights violations, for example in Rwanda in 1994 and Burundi in 1995, remain virtually untouched by the African human rights mechanisms.

Concluding remarks

In essence this chapter has been an examination of the development of international institutions for the protection of human rights. There has been a remarkable expansion in the number of institutions, both at the international, regional and non-governmental level.[128] The emergence of these bodies since 1945 can be seen as following a rationalist rather than a functionalist evolutionary path. However, the fact remains that the further development of these institutions is blocked by the positivist/realist attitudes of most nation States, evidenced by the continued wariness of most governments to permit intrusive human rights protection by international organisations. The evolution of standard setting, supervision, and the partial development of judicial organs with mandatory powers, has not yet progressed to the further step of enforcement. Most of the organisations examined still depend on *political* pressure to achieve results, which may not always be present when upholding breaches of the international *law* of human rights.[129] Both international and regional organisations fall foul of this weakness, particularly when faced with widespread human rights abuses, although there is an increasing, though limited, use of enforcement action being taken under collective security provisions. Furthermore, all the systems fail to treat human rights as full legal rights, belonging to individuals, giving them real protection and redress, suggesting that there may be some truth in the view of the critical school, that 'rights' are simply granted as a panacea disguising the continued dominance and oppression by the nation State. Even in the most advanced system, where individuals can and do obtain redress from the European Court of Human Rights, adequate protection is only accorded to 'Western' civil and political rights, the granting of which simply reinforces the ideology of those States.

However, despite the flawed nature of human rights, and the imperfect protection afforded, there is little doubt that the development and application of human rights standards has reduced, though by no means eliminated, oppression. Turning to a comparison of the effectiveness of universal and regional organisations in this area, it can be seen that, unlike the collective security system, which is dominated by the UN, there is much greater regional input into the promotion and protection of human rights. This is partly explained by the desire of each regional organisation to foster and protect its own ideological approach to human rights, and partly by the fact that regional organisations can probably put greater pressure to bear on recalcitrant States. However, as with the collective security system, which required a universal organisation to deal with global threats and local threats inadequately dealt with by the regional organisation, it is the UN which provides the backbone of the system. The UN has made the greatest inroads into universalising human rights, particularly important when there are numerous States which are not members of regional organisations with a human rights component. UN standard setting, though not perfect – as exemplified by the existence of the two separate International Covenants – has established certain universal norms, such as those prohibiting genocide and torture. Regional organisations' human rights protection has added to this universalisation, but without the UN, there would simply be a series of isolated regional legal systems, each with their own, sometimes widely differing, approaches to the protection of human rights.

Notes

[1] *Legal Consequences for States of the Continued Presence of South Africa in Namibia (South West Africa) Notwithstanding Security Council Resolution 276 (1970)*, I.C.J. *Rep.* 1971, 16 at 57.

[2] J. S. Gibson, *International Organizations, Constitutional Law and Human Rights*, 44 (1991).

[3] ECOSOC Res. 9 (2) (1946).

[4] See generally, A. Eide *et al.*, *The Universal Declaration of Human Rights: A Commentary* (1992).

[5] GA Res. 217A (3), 3 UN GAOR Resolutions 71 (1948).

[6] Gibson, *International Organizations*, 110.

[7] See for instance GA Res. 265 (3), 3 UN GAOR Resolutions 15 (1949) re treatment of

people of Indian origin in South Africa.

[8] UN doc. A/CONF. 32/41.

[9] See also Section 7 of the Helsinki Declaration 1975, I. Brownlie, *Basic Documents on Human Rights*, 396, 3rd edn (1992).

[10] *World Conference on Human Rights*, 26, 30, 32, 42, 45, 47–9 (UN Publication, 1993).

[11] GA Res. 48/141, 48 UN GAOR (1993). See generally P. Alston, 'Critical Appraisal of the UN Human Rights Regime' in P. Alston (ed.), *The United Nations and Human Rights*, 1 (1992).

[12] 78 UNTS 277.

[13] *Case Concerning Application of the Convention on the Prevention and Punishment of the Crime of Genocide (Bosnia Herzegovina v Yugoslavia (Serbia v Montenegro). Request for Provisional Measures*, I.C.J. *Rep.* 1993, 3 at 14–17.

[14] *Ibid.*, 24.

[15] Article 4 of the Genocide Convention.

[16] But see I. A. Shearer, *Starke's International Law*, 213, 11th edn (1994).

[17] 640 UNTS 133.

[18] Articles 8, 9, 11, 14 of the Convention against Racial Discrimination. The first petition by an individual under Article 14 was *Yilmaz-Dogan v Netherlands*, CERD Report, 43 UN GAOR, Supp. (No. 18) 59 (1988).

[19] For an analysis of the Committee see D. J. Harris, *Cases and Materials on International Law*, 678–82, 4th edn (1991).

[20] 24 *I.L.M.* (1985), 535.

[21] 2(1) *International Human Rights Reports* (1995), 190.

[22] 1(3) *International Human Rights Reports* (1994), 122. See also *Khan v Canada*, 15 *Human Rights Law Journal* (1994), 426 at 433.

[23] 28 *I.L.M.* (1989), 1488.

[24] Articles 43–5. For recent examples see 1(3) *International Human Rights Reports* (1994), 162–92.

[25] ECOSOC Res. 1102 (40) (1966); ECOSOC Res. 1235 (43) (1967).

[26] T. Van Boven, 'Political and Legal Control Mechanisms: Their Competition and Coexistence', in A. Eide and B. Hagtvet (eds), *Human Rights in Perspective*, 44 (1992). Themes covered in the 1993 Commission session included racism, the right to development, disability, disappearances, torture, HIV and human rights, child labour, and street children, see 1(1) *International Human Rights Reports* (1994), 196–237.

[27] Approved in ECOSOC Res. 75 (V), (1947).

[28] ECOSOC Res. 728F (28) (1959).

[29] ECOSOC Res. 1235 (42) (1967). On the Sub-Commission generally, see A. Eide, 'The Sub-Commission on Prevention of Discrimination and Protection of Minorities', in Alston (ed.), *United Nations*, 211.

[30] ECOSOC Res. 1503 (48) (1970).

[31] But see H. Tolley, *UN Commission on Human Rights*, 166–7 (1987).

[32] D. J. Harris, *International Law*, 604. Harris notes the limited nature of public criticism under the Resolution 1503 procedure.

[33] Gibson, *International Organizations*, 199–201.

[34] GA Res. 428 (V), 5 UN GAOR Supp. (No. 20) (1950).

[35] 189 UNTS 150.

[36] G. S. Goodwin-Gill, *The Refugee in International Law*, 131 (1983).

[37] 999 UNTS 171.

[38] 993 UNTS 3.

[39] P. Sieghart, *The International Law of Human Rights*, 25–6 (1983).

[40] See for example 2(1) *International Human Rights Reports* (1995), 161–213.

[41] D. McGoldrick, *The Human Rights Committee*, 500 (1991).

[42] 999 UNTS 302.

[43] On the meaning of 'victim' see *Aumeeruddy-Cziffra* v *Mauritius* 1 *Selected Decisions of the Human Rights Committee* (1981), 67.

[44] Report of the Human Rights Committee, 49 UN GAOR Supp. (No. 40), vol. 1, 63 (1994). For examples of recent decisions see 1(3) *International Human Rights Reports* (1994), 14–118.

[45] HRC Report, 44 UN GAOR, Supp. (No. 40) 14 (1989). But see HRC Report, 45 UN GAOR Supp. (No. 40) Annexe 11 (1990), on the adoption of measures to monitor compliance with the Committee's view under the First Optional Protocol, in particular the appointment of a special rapporteur.

[46] McGoldrick, *Human Rights Committee*, 500.

[47] ECOSOC Res. 1985/17.

[48] Harris, *International Law*, 669.

[49] See for example 1(3) *International Human Rights Reports* (1994), 142–58.

[50] ECOSOC Res. 1987/5; Rule 69, Committee on Economic, Social and Cultural Rights Provisional Rules of Procedure, UN doc. E/C.12/1990/4.

[51] P. Alston, 'U.S. Ratification of the Covenant on Economic, Social and Cultural Rights: The Need for an Entirely New Strategy', 84 *A.J.I.L.* (1990), 365 at 371.

[52] F. L. Kirgis, *International Organizations*, 911, 2nd edn (1993).

[53] UN doc. S/25704 (1993), para. 28.

[54] 41 *A.J.I.L.* (1947), 172.

[55] SC Res. 808, 48 UN SCOR Resolutions (1993). See also SC Res. 780, 47 UN SCOR Resolutions (1992), establishing a Commission of Experts. On the tribunal's first indictment, see 15 *Human Rights Law Journal* (1994), 480.

[56] SC Res. 955, 49 UN SCOR Resolutions (1994). This resolution was clearly stated to be adopted under Chapter VII of the UN Charter. See also SC Res. 935, 49 UN SCOR Resolutions (1994) establishing a Commission of Experts.

[57] A. H. Robertson and J. G. Merrills, *Human Rights in Europe*, 252–60, 3rd edn (1993).

[58] R. Beddard, *Human Rights and Europe*, 38, 3rd edn (1993).

[59] See D. McGoldrick, 'The Development of the Conference on Security and Co-operation in Europe (CSCE) after the Helsinki 1992 Conference', 42 *I.C.L.Q.* (1993), 411.

[60] 15 *Human Rights Law Journal* (1994), 449. According to the Budapest Declaration, the CSCE Council becomes the Ministerial Council, the Committee of Senior Officials becomes the Senior Council, and the Permanent Committee becomes the Permanent Council.

[61] 31 *I.L.M.* (1992), 976 at 989–90.

[62] McGoldrick, 42 *I.C.L.Q.* (1993), 424.

[63] See Chapter 2 of the Helsinki 1992 Document, 31 *I.L.M.* (1992) 1385.

[64] McGoldrick, 42 *I.C.L.Q.* (1993), 424. On the further strengthening of these institutions by the Budapest Declaration of December 1994, see 15 *Human Rights Law Journal* (1994), 449 at 459.

[65] See 28 *I.L.M.* (1989), 527; 29 *I.L.M.* (1990), 1305; and 30 *I.L.M.* (1991), 1670.

[66] McGoldrick, 42 *I.C.L.Q.* (1993), 431.

[67] McGoldrick, 42 *I.C.L.Q.* (1993), 432.

[68] N. Grief, 'The Domestic Impact of the European Convention on Human Rights as Mediated through Community Law', *Public Law* (1991), 555.

[69] T. C. Hartley, *The Foundations of European Community Law*, 146, 3rd edn (1994).

[70] 87 UNTS 103.

[71] 213 UNTS 222.

[72] Beddard, *Human Rights in Europe*, 22.

[73] 529 UNTS 89.

[74] D. J. Harris, 'A Fresh Impetus for the European Social Charter', 41 *I.C.L.Q.* (1992), 659.

[75] Hartley, Foundations, 9.

[76] Robertson and Merrills, *Human Rights in Europe*, 351–2.

[77] 31 *I.L.M.* (1992), 155. Harris, 41 *I.C.L.Q.* (1992), 659.

[78] Author's italic.

[79] See 15 *Human Rights Law Journal* (1994), 114.

[80] S. Davidson, *Human Rights*, 103–5 (1993). See *Greece* v *UK* 2 YB 182; *Austria* v *Italy* 6 YB 742; *Ireland* v *UK* 21 YB 602, Eur.Ct.H.R., Series A, No. 25; and *Cyprus* v *Turkey* 18 YB 82, 20 YB 98.

[81] Kirgis, *International Organizations*, 1040.

[82] 12 YB (special Volume); 8 EHRR 205.

[83] Kirgis, *International Organizations*, 1039.

[84] Davidson, *Human Rights*, 111.

[85] *The Council of Europe and the Protection of Human Rights*, (Pamphlet of the Directorate of Human Rights of the Council of Europe, 1990), 10.

[86] Article 48.

[87] In force with thirteen ratifications out of the thirty parties to the Convention. 15 *Human Rights Law Journal* (1994), 115.

[88] Again all State parties have recognised the compulsory jurisdiction of the Court. There is provision in the Convention for the Committee of Ministers of the Council of Europe to make binding decisions if the question is not referred to the Court in 3 months or the respondent State has not accepted the jurisdiction of the Court – Article 32. See also Protocol 10, 15 *Human Rights Law Journal*, (1994) 115.

[89] See for example *Oberschlick* v *Austria*, Eur.Ct.H.R., Series A, No. 204; *Ringeisen* v *Austria*, Eur.Ct.H.R., Series A, No. 15.

[90] Davidson, *Human Rights*, 101.

[91] See A. G. Mower, *Regional Human Rights*, 160–1 (1991).

[92] For text of protocol 11 see 15 *Human Rights Law Journal* (1994), 86. For discussion see A. R. Mowbray, 'A New European Court of Human Rights', *Public Law* (1994), 539.

[93] *Tenth Anniversary of the Entry into Effect of the European Convention of Human Rights* 10 (Council of Europe, 1963).

[94] Mower, *Regional Human Rights*, 165.

[95] Davidson, *Human Rights*, 120.

[96] 33 *I.L.M.* (1994), 981 at 990.

[97] Res. 30, Final Act of the 9th International Conference of American States, Bogotá, Columbia, 1948, 48. I. Brownlie, *Basic Documents on Human Rights*, 488, 3rd edn (1992).

[98] See for example the Advisory Opinion of the Inter-American Court of Human Rights of 14 July 1989 (OC-10/89), Inter-American Court of Human Rights, Series A, *Judgments and Opinions*, No. 10.

[99] Res. 7, 5th mtg of Consultation 1959, OAS doc. OEA/Ser.C/II.5.

[100] Davidson, *Human Rights*, 129.

[101] *Ibid.*, 133–4.

[102] *Ibid.*, 134.

[103] Res. 22, Second Special Inter-American Conference, 1965. OAS doc. OEA/Ser.C/I.13, 32–4.

[104] 9 *I.L.M.* (1970), 673. About two-thirds of the OAS membership are parties to this Treaty.

[105] Mower, *Regional Human Rights*, 48.

[106] PAUTS 69.

[107] See Inter-American Court of Human Rights judgment in *Government of Costa Rica (in the matter of Viviana Gallardo et al.)*, No.G. 101/81, 1981. 20 *I.L.M.* (1981), 1424.

[108] Articles 48–51. See further the advisory opinion of the Inter-American Court in *Certain Attributes of the Inter-American Commission on Human Rights*, 1(2) *International Human Rights Reports* (1994), 196.

[109] Mower, *Regional Human Rights*, 118–21.

[110] Kirgis, *International Organization*, 1007.

[111] Inter-American Court of Human Rights, 1988, Series C, *Decisions and Judgements*, No. 4.

[112] See further on 'moral damages', *Aloeboetoe et al.* v *Surinam*, 1(2) *International Human Rights Reports* (1994), 208 at 219–20. S. Davidson, 'Remedies for Violations of the American Convention on Human Rights', 44 *I.C.L.Q.* (1995), 405.

[113] 11 *Human Rights Law Journal* (1990), 127.

[114] *Annual Report of the Inter-American Court of Human Rights* (1991), OAS doc. OAS/Ser.L/5/3.25, 9 (1992).

[115] Author's italic.

[116] Article 65.

[117] See the *Aloeboetoe* case above and *Gangaram Panday* v *Surinam*, 15 *Human Rights Law Journal* (1994), 168. Other cases are pending.

[118] C. M. Cerna, 'The Structure and Functioning of the Inter-American Court of Human Rights (1979–1992)', 63 *B.Y.B.I.L.* (1992), 135 at 168.

[119] 479 UNTS 39.

[120] 46 *I.L.M.* (1982), 58. The OAU has added further human rights treaties, principally the African Charter on the Rights and Welfare of the Child 1990, OAU doc. CAB/LEG/153/Rev. 2. Not yet in force.

[121] G. J. Naldi, *The Organization of African Unity*, 108 (1989).

[122] Res. 24, (39) (1972).

[123] K. M'Baye, 'Introduction to the African Charter on Human and Peoples' Rights', International Commission of Jurists, *The African Charter on Human and Peoples' Rights: A Legal Analysis*, 27 (1985).

[124] Articles 52 and 53.

[125] Article 58.

[126] Davidson, *Human Rights*, 161.

[127] *Ibid.*

[128] As regards the work of NGOs see, for example, H. Thoolen and B. Verstoppen, *Human Rights Missions: a Study of the Fact Finding Practice of Non-Governmental Organizations* (1986).

[129] But see T. Van Boven, '"Political" and "Legal" Control Mechanisms: Their Competition and Coexistence', in A. Eide and B. Hagtvet, *Human Rights in Perspective: A Global Assessment*, 58 (1992).

10

Environmental matters

The development of legally-binding environmental standards by international organisations is a recent phenomenon. Indeed, the formalist/realist grip on international law, still, to a large extent, denies the existence of a body of international environmental law, seeing it as a vain attempt to limit the freedom of States; or, alternatively, grudgingly accepts it as 'soft law', which has a limited impact on the practice of States.[1] Although there is an increasing amount of organisational practice in the area of the setting and implementation of environmental standards, it seems to be admitted that the institutions involved in the area have limited, 'realistic' aims. States accept the limitations imposed by human rights standards and organisational supervision of them, because in the main these do not impinge on their ultimate concerns of 'national security and maintaining economic growth'.[2] However, these national interests would certainly appear to severely restrict the development of relatively powerful autonomous or supranational organisations whose aim is to protect the environment, and furthermore would seem to restrict the development of a human right to a decent environment. The evidence is that international organisations dealing with the environment are dominated by States, the individual generally having no power to enforce environmental standards on the international stage.[3]

Given the dominance of sovereign concerns in this area it is argued that 'organized international responses to shared environmental problems will occur through co-operation among States, not through the imposition of government over them', so that these basic institutions will 'promote change in national behaviour that is substantial enough to have a positive impact, *eventually*, on the quality of the natural environment'.[4] This 'realist' assessment of the role of international organisations in environmental law belies the fact that 'co-operation' between States on environmental matters may be something of a charade. Taking a critical approach, it can be seen that international environmental law and the role of international organisations in the area are beset by a serious contradiction which will prevent the achievement of anything more than a superficial attempt to protect the environment, or more accurately will result in what Marxists would label an ambiguous compromise. The contradiction is between the developing States' desire for industrial and economic development, and the developed States desire to temper industrial development, particularly in the 'dirty' industries established in the developing world, with greater environmental protection, as a gradually deteriorating environment has an adverse effect on the high standards of living in these countries. With this flaw at its heart, it can be argued that environmental law and institutional activity in the area are doomed to failure. Indeed, it has been argued that in the period between the Stockholm Declaration of 1972, which marked the beginning of legal and institutional developments in the area, and the Rio Declaration of 1992, when the world was faced with mounting evidence of long-term environmental degradation, environmental concerns have been subordinated to development concerns as the majority of developing States' desire for industrial development is married to the still rampant consumer economies of the developed world.

> The new discourse of 'integration' suggests that there is no longer any conflict between environmental protection and economic development, and that the latter has become a necessary complement, condition even, of the former. This obfuscates the very real and increasing conflict between the dominant view of 'development' and prevailing patterns of economic growth on the one hand, and the imperatives of environmental protection on the other. It ambiguously stands as much for the subordination of environmental policies to economic imperatives in the eyes of some, as for the converse to others. The opportunities it presents to subordinate environmental law are reflected in several provisions of the Rio Declaration and the other instruments adopted at [the UN Conference on Environment and Development 1992].[5]

It is to the ambiguous role of international organisations in the development of environmental law and the protection of the environment that this analysis now turns.

International organisations and the environment

Beginning with the UN's involvement in attempting to protect the environment in 1972, international organisations have quickly moved towards the setting of standards, sometimes in the form of binding treaty commitments, but usually in the form 'of framework or "umbrella" treaties or of non-binding declarations, codes, guidelines, or recommended principles'. Such soft laws are 'clearly not law in the sense used by [Article 38 of the Statute of the ICJ] but none the less they do not lack all authority'.[6] This formalist approach to international law does illustrate the weakness of environmental law and of the organisations which have helped to develop it or have been created by it.

In fact compared with human rights law, international organisations have mainly been occupied with the setting of standards for the protection and improvement of the environment, and the laying down of basic legal principles governing States' rights and duties in the environmental field, a task which is far from completed. Basic definitions are lacking:

> ... we can see that what 'pollution' means is, like the term 'environment', signifi-
> cantly dependent on context and objective. While it is possible to talk of an obliga-
> tion to prevent pollution, or to protect the environment, such an obligation has a very
> variable content, and there is little point attempting a global definition.[7]

Furthermore, the content and ambit of crucial concepts developed in international organisations, such as the 'common heritage of mankind', are unclear; the views of States, varying with their political stance on whether resources should be shared, benefits redistributed and technology transferred from the North to the South, and whether such a concept is simply applicable to resources or areas beyond national jurisdiction such as the deep-sea bed and the moon, or does it extend to areas within national boundaries, such as the Amazon rain forest. Although it appears to be gradually accepted that the application of the concept of the common heritage to areas entail some sort of trusteeship, or stewardship, with responsibility towards present and future generations, it is still unclear as to which areas the common heritage concept is applicable, and furthermore its content may vary considerably depending on the various interests of States most directly concerned either in the exploitation or conservation of the area in question.[8]

Having said that, other areas of environmental law as developed by international organisations have become accepted as clear international legal principles. Principle 21 of the United Nations' Conference on the Human Environment held in Stockholm in 1972, although not presented at the time as a binding commitment,[9] has been accepted as an international legal principle, with its simple statement that States have 'the responsibility to ensure that activities within their jurisdiction or control do not cause damage to the environment of other States or of areas beyond the limits of national jurisdiction'.[10] The 'no harm' principle, which acts as a definite limitation upon the sovereignty of a State to do what it likes within its own territory, is in many ways the bedrock of international environmental law. However, its use either to prevent harm or to remedy harm caused has proved limited, as the Chernobyl nuclear catastrophe of 1986 shows, illustrating the limitations of the law and the institutions designed to help implement it.

In general, international organisations have not moved in a significant way towards the supervision or enforcement of environmental laws such as Principle 21 or of standards laid down in so-called soft-law instruments, the only exceptions being the European Union, reviewed more fully later in this chapter, and to a much more limited extent the Security Council of the United Nations. The latter body has held Iraq 'liable under international law for any direct loss, damage, *including environmental damage and the depletion of natural resources*, or injury to foreign Governments, nationals and corporations, as a result of Iraq's unlawful invasion and occupation of Kuwait' in August 1990, in a binding 'Chapter VII' resolution adopted after the end of the military conflict in April 1991.[11] The further possible extension of the collective security umbrella to cover environmental matters was flagged by the special Security Council summit of world leaders held in January 1992 which declared that 'non-military sources of instability in the economic, social, humanitarian and ecological fields have become *threats to the peace* and security'.[12] As in the area of human rights, the collective security machinery of international organisations may provide an avenue for enforcing environmental laws, but only in extreme situations amounting to threats to international peace.

The United Nations

Unlike the protection of human rights, which received brief but express mention when the UN Charter was adopted in 1945, that document fails to mention protection of the environment. Nevertheless, the UN has developed competence in the area, utilising an inherent powers approach to its express social and humanitarian jurisdiction, to the extent that, as has already been stated, the Security Council has equated certain types of environmental degradation with threats to the peace thereby opening up the possibility of enforcement action by the UN. Apart from the role of the UN's specialised agencies, reviewed below, the competence of the UN in this area is divided between the General Assembly, ECOSOC and the United Nations Environment Programme (UNEP), with the latter performing the active role.

UNEP was established pursuant to the 1972 Stockholm Conference, which had been called for by the General Assembly.[13] The 1972 Conference not only adopted a declaration of general principles, some of which, as has been seen, have become part of customary international law, but also laid down an action plan on environmental policy, and established a UN Environment Fund based upon voluntary contributions from States.[14] Instead of being established as an autonomous specialised agency, UNEP was created by a General Assembly resolution of 1972,[15] presumably under Article 22 of the UN Charter which allows the Assembly to establish subsidiary organs. Nevertheless, the result of the Assembly's resolution was to establish a subsidiary organ 'with an "autonomous" status ... equipped with separate budgets, secretariats and organs',[16] something of a 'half-way house' between a subsidiary organ and a specialised agency. The resolution was not adopted by consensus but by an overwhelming majority of States who were 'convinced of the need for prompt and effective implementation by Governments and the international community of measures designed to safeguard and enhance the environment for the benefit of present and future generations of man', requiring the establishment of 'a permanent institutional arrangement within the United Nations system for the protection and improvement of the environment'. As well as a Secretariat serving 'as a focal point for environmental action and co-ordination within the' UN headed by an Executive Director, the Assembly established the Governing Council of UNEP consisting of fifty-eight members elected by the Assembly, on the basis of achieving a certain number of members from each region.[17] This body is responsible for: promoting international co-operation, laying down policy guidance, reviewing reports on implementation of UNEP environmental programmes received from the Executive Director of UNEP, keeping under review the 'world environmental situation', and promoting knowledge about environmental problems. The Governing Council is under a duty to report annually to the Assembly via ECOSOC.

Advances have been made by UNEP in its areas of responsibility as well as the development of principles of international environmental law, both soft and hard,[18] its approach being:

> [b]ased on first formulating the scientific positions, then developing legal strategies, and in the process building political support with an important role accorded to the negotiation of 'soft law' guidelines, principles etc. In the support-building process many compromises have to be arrived at especially in the interests of maintaining the 'sustainable development policy' propounded by the World Commission on Environment and Development. Thus the conventions are replete with constructive ambiguities in relation both to definitions and terms and the more controversial issues are generally left to the 'soft law' processes, the procedures and status of which are often made deliberately obscure.[19]

In the soft-law area, only the World Charter for Nature adopted by the UN General Assembly in 1982[20] following a UNEP special session, seems to be of a peremptory character,[21] other declarations and principles adopted by UNEP and the Assembly, on mining, pollution, waste management and chemicals, seem to attempt to place no real obligations on States.[22] Ambiguous treaties negotiated and drafted by UNEP include the 1985 Vienna Convention for the Protection of the Ozone Layer.[23] Although the work of UNEP has been of great significance in setting standards, the compromise necessary to accommodate the polarised positions of the North and those of the South have undermined its effectiveness. Furthermore, UNEP has none of the review and supervisory functions possessed by human rights bodies for example, in that although it can review environmental implementation in a general sense there is no duty on States to report to UNEP on progress achieved in implementing the standards laid down by UNEP. Furthermore, although the resolution provided for an Environmental Co-ordination Board to attempt to 'provide for the most efficient co-ordination of United Nations Environment programmes', this was soon made redundant and the job given to the largely discredited UN's Administrative Committee on Co-ordination (ACC), reviewed in chapter 6.

It is somewhat ironic that the United Nations desire to hold another international conference on the environment at Rio in 1992 in order to improve international protection of the environment, resulted in further obfuscation of the core issues and a lack of concrete obligations imposed on States. Both UNEP and ECOSOC called on the General Assembly to convene a UN Conference on Environment *and Development* in 1989.[24] The content of the General Assembly's resolution, which was adopted without a vote, reveals the major difficulty, if not impossibility, of such a conference agreeing on significant environmental controls. The Assembly begins by recognising that despite Stockholm and UNEP there was a 'continuing deterioration of the state of the environment and the serious degradation of the global life support systems' which, if allowed to continue, 'could disrupt the ecological balance, jeopardize the life-sustaining qualities of the earth and lead to an ecological catastrophe'. The Assembly also recognised the 'global character of environmental problems, including climate change, depletion of the ozone layer, transboundary air and water pollution, the contamination of the oceans and the seas and degradation of land resources ...'. As well as attempting to direct the conference towards the adoption of measures for the protection of the environment, the Assembly disabled its potential impact by, on the one hand, condemning economic development and its accompanying pollution in industrialised countries, while, on the other, encouraging development, alongside environmental protection, in developing countries. The overall aim of the conference, according the Assembly, should have been to 'elaborate strategies and measures to halt and reverse the effects of environmental degradation in the context of strengthened national and international efforts to promote sustainable and environmentally sound development in all countries'. One possible way of squaring the circle would be for the advanced nations to fund 'clean' development in developing countries, while at the same time cleaning up their own industries and cutting back on consumer demand. Although this is suggested in the Assembly's resolution,[25] its naïvety is revealed in the negotiations and outcome of the UN Conference, also known as the Earth Summit in Rio in June 1992.

The Earth Summit produced two treaties for formal ratification by States, the Framework Convention on Climate Change,[26] which as the title suggests contains vaguely-worded guiding principles and even vaguer commitments regarding the stabilisation of greenhouse gases;[27] and the Convention on Biological Diversity,[28] which again is another framework treaty the aim of which is to create general obligations for the conservation of ecosystems, of species, and diversity of species. Although both treaties are beset by compromise and ambiguity they do create institutions to promote compliance, and financial mechanisms to ease the burden on developing States. These institutions and mechanisms will be reviewed later.

In addition to two formal treaties, the Rio Conference produced two non-binding declarations and a programme of action known as Agenda 21. One of the declarations was a statement of principles on the management, conservation and sustainable development of all types of forest. Despite the fact that the Statement of Principles on Forests restates Principle 21 of the Stockholm Declaration, which might suggest that States which severely deplete forests within their own jurisdiction may be responsible for the consequent deterioration in the climates of other countries, the statement then makes it clear that 'states have the sovereign and inalienable right to utilize, manage and develop their forests in accordance with the development needs and level of socio-economic development and on the basis of national policies consistent with sustainable development ...'.[29] The more significant Rio Declaration on Environment and Development[30] encapsulates the greater emphasis on sovereignty and development than that found twenty years earlier at Stockholm. The subjugation of environment to development is present in the majority of the principles contained in the document, for example, Principle 4 states that 'in order to achieve sustainable development, environmental protection shall constitute an integral part of the development process and cannot be considered in isolation from it'. Principles that seem to support environmental protection are ambivalent, for instance Principle 11 states that:

> [s]tates shall enact effective environmental legislation. Environmental standards, management objectives and priorities should reflect the environmental and developmental contexts to which they apply. Standards applied by some countries may be inappropriate and of unwarranted economic and social concern to other countries, in particular developing countries.

Turning to Agenda 21, the same emphasis on economic issues is found. Instead of emphasising the need for environmental standards to be set and implemented by all States irrespective of development, the Agenda generally waters down environmental standards by making them relative to socio-economic factors.[31] More significant for the development of international organisations in the field of environmental protection, Agenda 21 addresses 'International Institutional Arrangements'.[32] As well as urging UNEP and the UN Development Programme to develop and expand their activities in the environmental and developmental fields, Agenda 21 urges the creation of a further institution within the UN framework, the aim of which would be to 'rationalize the intergovernmental decision-making capacity for the integration of environment and development and to examine the progress in the implementation of Agenda 21 at the national, regional and international levels'. Such a commission would be created under Article 68 of the Charter and would report to ECOSOC and the Assembly, identified as the 'supreme policy-making forum that would provide overall guidance to Governments, the United Nations system and relevant treaty bodies'.

The General Assembly recommended the creation of a Commission on Sustainable Development 'as a functional commission of' ECOSOC.[33] The Commission consists of fifty-three State representatives elected by ECOSOC and has, in essence, a monitoring brief, namely to: monitor progress in the implementation of Agenda 21 by examining reports from organisations and bodies concerned with environment and development; significantly to 'consider information provided by Governments ... in the form of ... national reports regarding the activities they undertake to implement Agenda 21 ...'; to review Agenda 21 commitments such as the transfer of technology; to review the progress towards the UN target of 0.7 per cent of GNP of the developed countries for development assistance; and to receive and analyse reports from NGOs. The Commission's mandate contains a significant breakthrough in the monitoring and supervision of standards, namely by providing for a State reporting system. However, this advance is checked by the wider range of activities to be monitored in the 'integrated' areas of environment and development. In the Commission on Sustainable Development's report on its second session of 1994,[34] the Commission had received a number of communications by a number of governments and organisations on a voluntary basis. However, this encouraging sign was offset by the fact that development assistance was down by ten per cent, and that there was scant evidence of any transfer of environmentally-sound technology from North to South as advocated by Agenda 21. Overall, the report and the subsequent Assembly resolution emphasise the lack of financial commitment by the richer nations to achieve the goals set out in Agenda 21.[35]

The UN's specialised agencies

The above section illustrates that the UN's approach to environmental issues has been to create various highly political institutions such as UNEP to attempt to set and monitor environmental standards. The end result has been a bureaucratisation and politicisation of the area to the extent that it has now become established that the state of the environment is linked to development, increasingly with developmental issues taking precedence as the majority of developing States on these bodies make their presence felt. The fact that the majority has to make concessions to the developed States in order to get the desired consensus in these bodies has resulted in a *mélange* of principles which can best be described as 'soft law', at worst, no law at all.

The functionalist would argue that this is an inevitable result of empowering a political body, such as the UN, with the solution of these problems. Organisations which have emerged to deal with particular common areas may be better able to focus on setting, *inter alia*, environmental standards in those specific areas so that instead of attempting to achieve global consensus on environmental principles and ending up with ambiguous and possibly dangerous concepts such as 'sustainable development' which is at the heart of Agenda 21,[36] there emerges a series of concrete and practical principles and standards in those areas of greatest concern. The UN's specialised agencies have had some such success. Inevitably there are going to be areas such as greenhouse gases and biodiversity which escape the net of the agencies, although there are several UN-sponsored treaties, reviewed at the end of this chapter, dealing with these areas, most of which contain monitoring machinery.

As regards the specialised agencies, on the success side, the IMO for instance has produced fairly widely ratified conventions such as the International Convention for the Prevention of Pollution of the Sea by Oil of 1954.[37] UNESCO is responsible for the Convention for the Protection of the World Cultural and Natural Heritages 1972,[38] including environmentally significant areas. The WHO's International Heath Regulations cover such things as water quality and have had a major impact in the setting of environmental standards on matters directly relating to health.[39] The WMO provides essential information on climate and weather indicative of man-made changes in the environment. On the negative side men-

tion can be made that the FAO's Committee on Fisheries has been less successful in developing global mechanisms for fish stock conservation.[40]

The World Bank

Concentrating further on the negative impact of the specialised agencies on matters of environmental concern, the role and work of the World Bank is worthy of
some attention. In the case of this particular specialised agency, the world community's attempt to achieve a compromise between development and environmental protection can be seen to have evolved in a different, though no less
environmentally detrimental, way.

> Through the gun sights of an eco-activist few international institutions appear in
> greater need of greening than the World Bank. The Bank and the affiliated interna-
> tional institutions known as the Bretton Woods group, have been accused of
> bankrolling ecological and economic disaster in the developing world, by promoting
> developmental projects that have denuded forests, depleted soils, and increased
> dependence on unsustainable energy sources. Gestures by the bank to introduce
> greener policies in response to these criticisms have been met with deep scepticism
> and accusations of superficial 'greenwashing'.[41]

World Bank projects 'are often massive infrastructure or industrialization programs',[42] and have a 'failure rate staggering even by internal assessments',[43] leading inevitably to ecological and social damage. The World Bank's drive to fund
development at any cost was tempered to some extent in the late 1980s by green
guidelines,

> [d]esigned to incorporate environmental considerations into loan decisions. These
> measures focus on mitigating negative effects of loans for traditional development
> projects in all areas including, among others, the power sector and agriculture. How-
> ever, environmental considerations rarely, if ever, prevent the World Bank from
> making a loan, limiting the ultimate benefit of the new guidelines.[44]

However, a much more positive greening occurred in 1991 with the establishment
of the Global Environmental Facility (GEF)[45] established by the World Bank,
UNDP and UNEP, with the aim of funding environmental projects in the developing world.

The GEF marks a tentative move towards co-operation between the UN and the
World Bank, which traditionally have been separated since the World Bank was
established in 1947.[46] Before the GEF was created, the UN's development of an
environmental competence was entirely divorced from the Bank's concern with
economic issues. Furthermore, the 'one dollar, one vote' power structure of the
Bank is contrasted with the UN's 'one State one vote' principle, leading to diver-
gent agendas in each organisation, with the developed States dominating the Bank
and the developing States the UN, at least in the Assembly, UNDP and UNEP.[47]

Inevitably the World Bank came in for some criticisms at the UN Conference in Rio in 1992. The Rio Declaration was indirect but clear in Principle 7, when it stated that 'the developed countries acknowledge the responsibility that they bear in the international pursuit of sustainable development in view of the pressure their societies place on the global environment and of the technologies and *financial resources* they command'.[48] Furthermore, in Chapter 38 of Agenda 21, the recommendations on the Commission on Sustainable Development states that the Commission should monitor reports on the implementation of Agenda 21 from organisations 'including those relating to finance'.

The developed States which dominate the World Bank not only agreed to the Rio Declaration and Agenda 21, they had already agreed to the establishment of the GEF, allowing for a greater UN (i.e. developing States) say in the World Bank. Although initial reports of the GEF are discouraging, with control still firmly in the hands of developed countries,[49] the incorporation of the GEF into the Framework Convention on Climate Change adopted at Rio in 1992 is a more positive sign. The activities of the GEF under the Convention are controlled by the Conference of the Parties, which is dominated by the developing States. Indeed, the Convention in Article 11 simply states that a 'financial mechanism', to fund projects to address climate change, 'shall function under the guidance of and be accountable to the Conference of the Parties, which shall decide on its policies, programme priorities and eligibility criteria'. The GEF is simply appointed as the financial mechanism on an 'interim basis' by Article 21(3), reviewable after four years according to Article 11(4).

Although the limitations on the World Bank's autonomy in the funding of development projects in the form of greater UN control over the GEF, both within the context of the Climate Convention and beyond, is to be welcomed, the problem of the ambiguity of the commitments under the Climate Change Convention, Agenda 21 and the Rio Declaration, remain. Simply adding these into the criteria, the World Bank should consider if funding projects in the developing world does not necessarily produce environmental benefits, in particular, there being little explanation of what is meant by the concept identified as the most fundamental at Rio, 'sustainable development', beyond it being the amalgamation of development and environment. Indeed, as has already been pointed out, 'sustainable development' can be seen as either an ambiguous compromise between North and South, incorporating the North's environmental concerns and the South's developmental concerns, or it can be viewed as a much more dangerous concept which actually encourages the belief 'that continued economic growth and development, as well as population growth, can take place in a manner that will bring the global population to an acceptable overall standard of living, without damaging the life support system so much that it prevents this goal from ever being attained'. This does not appear to be based on scientific evidence. Behind 'sustainable development' is simply the *belief* 'that science and engineering can overcome our environmental problems and allow us to continue expanding resource extraction and use, producing products and raising the material standard of living of the earth's people indefinitely, even as the population increases'.[50] Principle 12 of the Rio

Declaration embodies this fundamental contradiction, by attempting to reconcile environmental protection and economic growth. It reads: 'States should co-operate to promote a supportive and open international economic system that would lead to economic growth and sustainable development ...'.

International organisations are simply not going to be effective in protecting the environment if the basic goals and principles are unattainable. It has been mooted that the more recently established European Bank for Reconstruction and Development (EBRD), which started operating in 1991, 'to provide assistance to the emerging market economies in Central and Eastern Europe', will have a more 'pro-active role in safeguarding the environment, focusing on environmental issues when evaluating loans'.[51] The basis for this assertion is that, unlike the World Bank, concern for the environment is written into the constitution of the EBRD, Article 2 providing that the Bank will 'promote in the full range of its activities environmentally sound and sustainable development'.[52]

Regional organisations

Although the EBRD's constitution incorporates the unattainable concept of 'sustainable development', the Bank also intends to base its environmental policy on more concrete principles, namely those of the European Union.[53] Like the UN Charter, the Treaty of Rome of 1957 contained no explicit reference to environmental protection, being based firmly on the principle of freedom of trade and the creation of a common market. Nevertheless, emerging environmental movements in some continental European States which pointed to the detrimental effect on the environment of the Community's policies on development, agriculture, transport and energy, combined with a desire to create uniform regulations and thereby prevent trade barriers, led to a drive, following the UN Conference at Stockholm, to introduce uniform environmental regulations into the Community. This led to the adoption of hundreds of pieces of binding EC environmental legislation.[54]

Finally, the Single European Act of 1986 introduced an express Chapter into the Treaty, governing environmental protection. The emergence of environmental concerns challenging the traditional *raison d'être* of the EC, led to a potential conflict between trade and the environment. This was further exacerbated by the amendments to the Treaty of Rome introduced by the Maastricht Treaty of 1992 which increased the importance of environmental considerations in the Treaty obligations. The Maastricht Treaty even amended the most basic principle of the Community, namely the creation of a common market, in Article 2, by insisting on 'sustainable and non-inflationary growth respecting the environment'. Article 130r.1 as introduced by the Single European Act and added to by Maastricht, states that:

Community policy on the environment shall contribute to pursuit of the following objectives:

263

  - preserving, protecting and improving the quality of the environment;
  - protecting human health;
  - prudent and rational utilization of natural resources;
  - promoting measures at international level to deal with regional or worldwide environmental problems.

Although the institutions of the Community are required to instigate this commitment, there are provisions in the remainder of Article 130r which may permit them to prefer to encourage trade over the environment when taking account of 'the potential benefits and costs of action or lack of action', and 'the economic and social development of the Community as a whole and the balanced development of the regions'.

Although economic growth remains the paramount consideration of the Community,[55] there has been significant greening of the Treaty both in the form of substantive obligations and the increase in qualified voting on the matter, and by the interpretation put on some of the other fundamental provisions of the Treaty by the European Court. In particular Article 30 of the Treaty of Rome, which guarantees free movement of goods between member States by banning 'quantitative restriction on imports and all measures having equivalent effect', has been interpreted by the Court as not necessarily prohibiting the restriction by member States of the free movement of goods on environmental grounds 'provided that there was no Community legislation regulating the issue; that the measure applied equally to domestic and imported products; and that the measure was proportional to the objective to be achieved'.[56]

As in many other areas, the EU with its mandatory, cohesive legislation and developed institutional structures, leads the way in enforceable environmental legislation on the international plane. However, at the heart of the EU's policy on the environment there still exists that potentially fatal flaw – the incompatibility of continued economic growth, and there are no signs that the EU is about to abandon this, with protective measures that will actually stop or reverse environmental damage. Indeed with the EU's potential expansion further east, its contribution to environmental depletion will continue apace. However, the following brief review will show that the EU, out of all the organisations, has made the most inroads into attempting to curb the damage done to the environment by free trade and continued economic growth, reflecting, to a large extent, the environmental fears of the developed world.

In contrast, the OAU's environmental policy is limited; that Organisation, consisting of developing States, is more concerned with development. Nevertheless, given the African preference for collective rights, there has been some rhetorical support for environment protection, most recently in the 1986 Banjul Charter, which in Article 24 states that 'all peoples shall have the right to a satisfactory environment favourable to their development'. As has been seen in chapter 9, this right is afforded little protection under the weak enforcement machinery of the African Charter on Human and Peoples' Rights, besides which the right is only a relative one in that it is conditioned by developmental issues.

Nevertheless, unlike the EU, environmental considerations did make an early mark in the life of the African Organisation with the adoption in 1968 of the African Convention for the Conservation of Nature and Natural Resources.[57] However, this Treaty has 'lain dormant',[58] although it is still the centrepiece of the OAU's environmental policy alongside its support for the World Charter for Nature, and the adoption of the Lagos Plan of Action in 1980, following a joint OAU and UN Economic Commission for Africa (ECA),[59] summit. The Lagos Plan was essentially an economic blueprint until the year 2000, although it did identify many areas of environmental concern: 'health, sanitation, provision of safe drinking water, deforestation, soil degradation, desertification, drought, marine pollution, conservation of marine resources, problems of human settlements planning, mining development, air and water pollution control …'.[60] The lack of any real progress in many of these areas is a product of the fact that many African nations have had to ignore environmental problems and concentrate on development, or more accurately, survival. In addition, the OAU, unlike the EU, has no enforcement powers so that its environmental recommendations are ignored. In addition, the formal treaty commitments of the 1968 treaty have a very limited impact in the absence of any effective monitoring machinery.

The almost total lack of impact of the African regional Organisation in the area of the environment is mirrored in regional organisations whose membership is drawn from developing countries, simply because their overriding concern is with development. Like the OAU, there has been limited, almost token environmental legislation coming from these regional bodies, for example the 1940 Convention on Nature Protection and Wild Life Preservation[61] sponsored by the OAS's predecessor, the Pan American Union; and ASEAN's Agreement on the Conservation of Nature and Natural Resources, 1985.[62] In contrast, the EU and even the Council of Europe, in the shape of the sponsorship of the European Convention on Human Rights and its judicial mechanisms,[63] have become much more concerned with environmental matters over the recent past, reflecting the developed world's fear that environmental degradation is threatening its dominance, indeed, existence.

Trade and other organisations

There are many other organisations involved in environmental matters, ranging from: functional organisations such as the IAEA, whose standard-setting competence, reviewed in chapter 4, is of tremendous importance in limiting nuclear, and therefore environmentally catastrophic, accidents; to primarily security organisations such as NATO[64] and the OSCE. The 1975 Helsinki Final Act which set up the latter conference/organisation recognised the duty not to degrade the environment, and designated the UN's Economic Commission for Europe (ECE)[65] as the mechanism to formulate measures regarding pollution and the environment. The

CSCE had significant input into the ECE's 1991 Convention on Environmental Impact Assessment in a Transboundary Context.[66]

Economic and trade organisations have also developed an environmental competence. The OECD established an Environment Committee in 1970, which makes recommendations on a wide range of matters from waste disposal to energy production, and producing reports, for example, on fish catches.[67] Other organisations, whose purpose is not simply facilitating exchange of information and recommendations on economic and environmental matters, but are concerned with promoting free trade, have had greater difficulties in taking on board environmental considerations.

The GATT was heavily criticised by the environmental lobby on the basis that free trade and environmental protection are incompatible, and many trade experts would agree that 'environmental regulations, perhaps setting standards for products, are *prima facie* barriers to trade and one of the fundamental purposes of the GATT is to remove trade barriers'.[68] At the 1992 UN Earth Summit in Rio, the answer to this conundrum was the panacea of 'sustainable development', Agenda 21 requiring States to 'ensure that environmental and trade policies are mutually supportive, with a view to achieving sustainable development', while urging multilateral trade organisations such as GATT to further these ends. As has been stated, the concept of 'sustainable development' by which economic growth and resource conservation are both assured so that the needs of the current generation are met without compromising the needs of future generations,[69] depends on vast advances in science and technology. Principle 12 of the Rio Declaration of 1992 explicitly states that in reality, when there is confrontation between free trade and unilateral environmental protection by States, free trade will generally prevail, unless, 'an international consensus' can be achieved for the adoption of 'environmental measures addressing transboundary or global environmental issues'.

The fear, reflected in Principle 12, that environmental regulations may be (mis)used by States as 'a means of arbitrary or unjustifiable discrimination or a disguised restriction on international trade', is directly derived from Article 20 of the GATT Agreement of 1947, illustrating how the GATT free trade system has become a fundamental aspect of international relations. Article 20 allows exceptions to free trade subject to the prohibition on arbitrary and discriminatory trade barriers based, *inter alia*, on environmental legislation. Article 20(b) permits measures 'necessary to protect human, animal or plant life or health'; and 20(g) allows for measures 'relating to the conservation of exhaustible natural resources if such measures are made effective in conjunction with restrictions on domestic production or consumption'. However, the presumption is that free trade prevails, given that the burden of proof that such measures are necessary and are not arbitrary is upon the State attempting to introduce environmental standards into free trade. The 1991 GATT dispute panel ruling in the *Mexican Tuna/Dolphin* dispute,[70] illustrates how the trade organisation's rules prevented effective environmental protection. The 1988 US ban on the import of tuna caught by purse-seine methods, which kills dolphins, was challenged by Mexico before a GATT dispute panel, which ruled that the ban was unlawful under GATT and did not come within either of the exceptions mentioned in Article 20. The 'panel openly acknowledged that the GATT was ill-equipped to strike a balance between free trade and environment protection'.[71]

Despite this apparent unconcernedness with environmental protection, the Uruguay Round of trade negotiations in December 1993 did result in, if not a reinvention of GATT (from 1 January 1995, the WTO), at least a partial greening of the new Organisation and the accompanying trade rules, although the primary aim of the latest trade accord was to 'lower trade barriers around the world, and thus boost national incomes of participating states'.[72] A brief summary of these 'greenwashing' efforts include a cursory mention of environmental protection in the Preamble to the Agreement Establishing the World Trade Organisation,[73] in which the parties:

> Recognizing that their relations in the field of trade and economic endeavour should be conducted with a view to raising standards of living, ensuring full employment and a large and steadily growing volume of real income and effective demand, and expanding the production in trade in goods and services, while allowing for the optimal use of the world's resources in accordance with the objective of sustainable development, seeking both to protect and preserve the environment and enhance the means for doing so in a manner consistent with their respective needs and concerns at different levels of economic development.

This constitutes a fairly weak commitment to environmental protection which is not effectively built into the body of the trade rules themselves, although it has been argued that the introduction of international, as opposed to national, standards into environmental and health matters 'may induce countries to raise their health and environmental standards, resulting in a trend towards harmonization'.[74] Furthermore, the members of GATT agreed to establish a Committee on Trade and the Environment under the auspices of the WTO.[75] The members did not see 'any policy contradiction between upholding and safeguarding an open, non-discriminatory and equitable multilateral trading system on the one hand, and acting for the protection of the environment, and the promotion of sustainable development on the other', although the Committee's terms of reference would be in part 'to identify the relationship between trade measures and environmental measures, in order to promote sustainable development', and to make appropriate recommendations on whether any modifications to the GATT/WTO rules are necessary, subject to the 'avoidance of protectionist trade measures'. Again although the creation of this Committee within the WTO is to be welcomed, it can only produce a partial improvement as far as environmental protection is concerned in that its mandate clearly places protectionist measures as secondary to free-trade measures. Furthermore, the Committee is asked to look at the relationship between the GATT/WTO Agreement of 1994 and the earlier environmental treaties on the ozone layer, biodiversity and climate change for instance, which may require protectionist measures to implement them, the problem being that the later trade treaty may prevail over the earlier ones, thus entrenching the dominance of free trade over environmental protection.[76]

In addition, the new 'improved' dispute settlement procedures introduced by the Uruguay Round, do not favour environmental protection in that the burden of proof still lies with the State introducing the protective measure to defend its necessity within the overall context of free trade.[77] The placing of the burden of proof on the State attempting environmental protection in these trade versus environment conflicts is contrary to the 'precautionary principle' necessary for effective environmental protection. This principle provides that 'where there are threats of serious or irreversible damage, lack of full scientific certainty should not be used as a reason for postponing measures to prevent environmental degradation'. 'At its most profound, the precautionary principle dictates the institutionalization of precaution, which would itself entail the shifting of the burden of proof from those opposing environmental degradation to those engaged in the challenged activity'.[78]

Another recent trade treaty, however, does appear to include the precautionary principle in its make-up, in that in its dispute settlement procedures and in its substantive provisions on the environment, the burden of proof falls on the party challenging the protectionist measure.[79] Although NAFTA,[80] agreed between the United States, Canada and Mexico in December 1992, is not an autonomous international organisation as such, it does include institutional mechanisms whose aim is to enhance environmental protection in a free-trade area, and in many ways it was NAFTA's innovative provisions on attempting to make a trade agreement environmentally friendly, which led to the 'last minute' introduction of environmental provisions in the GATT/WTO make-up.[81]

Although there are ambiguous statements in the Preamble to NAFTA resolving to promote free trade and sustainable development in a manner consistent with environmental conservation and protection, the objectives of the Agreement in Article 102 simply oblige the parties to eliminate trade barriers, promote fair competition, increase investment and protect intellectual property rights. Clearly the primary aim of the Agreement is the creation of a free-trade area, but it does attempt to include environmental protection perhaps more so than the GATT/WTO in view of the environmental pressure coming from Canada and the United States. The Agreement includes provisions which aim to prevent investment flight to countries (namely Mexico) which might have a laxer attitude to environmental issues, although the provisions on this are marked by a lack of enforcement machinery.[82] Furthermore, its attempts to increase the harmonisation of environmental standards is largely based on voluntary co-operation.[83] In addition, Article 104 provides that if there is any inconsistency between the provisions of NAFTA and *listed* international environmental agreements, the latter 'shall prevail to the extent of the inconsistency, provided that where a Party has a choice among equally effective and reasonably available means of complying with such obligations, the Party chooses the alternative that is the least inconsistent with' NAFTA. The list of environmental treaties can be added to by unanimous consent of the parties.[84] Although an improvement on the GATT/WTO which is silent on this point, it does mean that one of the parties can block new treaties from being added and furthermore, the 'least inconsistent' language of Article 104 may lead to actions taken by the parties to protect the environment in accordance with a main environmental treaty being challenged even if the Treaty is one of those listed.[85]

However, the most important elements of environmental protection occurred in parallel to NAFTA, in a separate agreement – the North American Agreement on Environmental Co-operation concluded between the three States in September 1993.[86] Under the Agreement, Articles 3, 4 and 5, the parties are obliged to ensure high levels of environmental protection and the enforcement of laws protecting the environment. To this end the Agreement, in Article 8, creates a trilateral Commission for Environmental Co-operation, whose powers include the effective enforcement of environmental laws. The Commission has a dispute settlement procedure based upon complaint by one of the parties. The panel can impose a 'monetary enforcement assessment' against a party found guilty of failing to implement its environmental laws. Further, if that party refuses to pay the assessment or continues to ignore breaches of its environmental laws, the complaining party may suspend the application of benefits to be obtained under NAFTA by the guilty party, such as tariff reductions.[87] This constitutes one of the few examples of enforcement of laws protecting the environment by an international institution, though it must be noted that the laws being enforced are municipal laws not necessarily international standards. The presence of enforcement powers in NAFTA reflects the dominance of that Treaty by developed States, in contrast with the much more diverse GATT/WTO.

Institutions created by environmental treaties

The impact of international organisations in the field of environmental protection is much less developed than in the areas of collective security or human rights. Nevertheless, there has been an evolution, not only in the work of the United Nations, regional organisations and even trade organisations, but also in the development of institutions established under environmental treaties. Older conventions did not contain any institutional machinery to review implementation of the Treaty, whereas beginning in the late 1950s, treaties began to include institutions, usually in the form of a review conference of all the parties. Such a review conference is an inefficient way of supervising treaties, particularly when any further measures must be taken by consensus. There is recent evidence that treaty machinery is becoming more sophisticated, with provision for majority voting, as well as the creation of commissions representing State parties, although the latter can be traced as far back as the International Whaling Commission created by treaty in 1946.[88] Nevertheless, it is true to say that the supervisory bodies created by treaty, 'whether a meeting of the parties or a Commission, is in substance no more than a diplomatic conference of States, and the existence in some of these cases of a separate legal personality does not alter the reality that the membership of these institutions is in no sense independent of the States they represent'.[89]

Nevertheless, despite their relative crudity, it can be argued[90] that such review conferences or commissions are a more effective method of promoting international environmental law than judicial or quasi-judicial methods of dispute settlement, which predominate in the human rights area for instance. Whereas individual civil and political, or indeed, economic and social rights, are suited to the judicial process, a collective 'right' such as the right to a decent environment, is perhaps less so. Besides which, environmental law has not developed to any great extent down the traditional human rights path, with individuals having virtually no environmental rights, as such, on the international plane. Furthermore, the aims of environmental law have developed beyond the simple claiming of damage done by one State polluting another, towards preventing environmental harm before damage is done. In many ways a system of judicial remedies for damage done by pollution is only a secondary method of protecting the environment. This is particularly so given the underdeveloped, consent-based, judicial system that operates at State level. Here, as we have seen in chapter 5, the International Court of Justice has a limited role to play in the promotion of international law. In the area of environmental law, there have been very few significant environmental decisions. Indeed, one of the World Court's decisions most relied upon by writers, the *Corfu Channel* case of 1949, did not directly raise environmental issues, although it did establish the basis of State responsibility developed by Principle 21 of the Stockholm Declaration of 1972.[91] The ageing body of World Court, and arbitral, decisions on environmental matters is not significantly useful in creating a legal framework to prevent a further deterioration in the environment and to deal with the emergence of fresh problems.

Though there is some limited evidence of a possible renaissance of the World Court in environmental matters,[92] it is far outweighed in terms of significance, by the proliferation of supervisory bodies created by treaty, some of which will be reviewed here.[93] One of the early examples of this development, can be found in the Antarctic Treaty of 1959,[94] which has had a major impact on the preservation of the unique Antarctic environment by obliging parties to keep the area free from nuclear and military uses, and by freezing all territorial claims there. Article 9 of the Treaty provides for the regular Consultative Meetings on the contracting parties, consisting of the twelve original States and acceding parties who conduct scientific research in Antarctica. These Meetings not only serve the purpose of information exchange and consultation but also formulate recommendations regarding 'measures in furtherance of the principles and objectives of the treaty', including measures for the 'preservation and conservation of living resources in Antarctica'. Such measures 'shall become effective when approved of by all the Contracting parties whose representatives were entitled to participate in the meetings held to consider those measures'. Despite this requirement of unanimity, at least of those State parties entitled to be at the Consultative Meetings, the system has produced significant environmental instruments, including the Madrid Proto-col on Environmental Protection of 1991, which imposed a ban on mineral activities for a period of fifty years, on environmental grounds.[95]

Although a reasonably effective system, the Antarctic Treaty System (ATS), suffers from a lack of representation, in that the decisions, although unanimous, are made by a minority of States, and perhaps do not represent the views of the majority.[96] The argument that the very reason for its success is the small and there-fore workable nature of its Consultative Meetings, is countered by the evidence from other similar systems. The Convention on Trade in Endangered Species (CITES) 1973,[97] which, as its title suggests, is a treaty aimed at preventing inter-national commercial trade in endangered species, has over one hundred and fif-teen State parties, all entitled to be represented and to vote at the Conference of the Parties in accordance with Articles 11 and 15. The most important function of the Conference is to review and amend the species listed in the appendices to the Convention, which, put simply, list, in Appendix 1 species which are threatened with extinction and in which trade is prohibited, whereas trade is controlled as regards species listed in Appendix 2.

However, the unwieldiness of the review conference is offset by the fact that the Convention does not require unanimity in the Conference for an amendment to Appendix 1 or 2, allowing such amendments to be carried by a two-thirds majority.[98] A treaty obligation not to trade for Appendix 1, or, to control trade for Appendix 2, is created upon listing, although State sovereignty is respected by Article 15(3), which allows a State to lodge a reservation to a particular listing with the result that the reserving party 'shall be treated as a State not a party to the present Convention with respect to trade in the species concerned'. This means that a State cannot be obliged to protect a species without its consent, emphasis-ing the real lack of personality of the conference. Despite this deficiency, the Con-ference, aided by a very efficient Secretariat,[99] has managed the appendices with reasonable success,[100] for example with the listing in Appendix 1 of the African elephant in 1987, with a subsequent significant reduction in trade.[101] The activity within the simple institutional structure of the Conference is reflected in the fact that at the Ninth Conference of the Parties in November 1994, there were 155 list-ing proposals covering 150 species. However, attempts at that Conference to improve enforcement measures, which under the Convention are the responsi-bility of national authorities, largely failed, again preventing CITES from devel-oping any real autonomous powers on the international plane.[102]

A move towards greater international enforcement of environmental norms in the form of empowering a treaty review body with the ability to bind States by a majority decision, has been made by the 1987 Montreal Protocol on Substances that Deplete the Ozone Layer,[103] a much more intrusive instrument than its parent treaty – the 1985 Vienna Convention for the Protection of the Ozone Layer.[104] The latter was weak in substance and machinery in that it simply obliged 'the Parties to take appropriate measures in accordance with the provisions of this Conven-tion … to protect human health and the environment against adverse effects resulting or likely to result from human activities which modify or are likely to modify the ozone layer',[105] reflecting the uneasy compromise between some developed countries wishing to see tight restrictions on CFCs, and developing countries who did not wish to see their development restricted. Structurally the Vienna Convention simply provides, in Article 7, for a Secretariat, and in Article 6 for a Conference of the Parties which reviews implementation from information received in part in reports by State parties. Furthermore, the conference can, according to Article 8, adopt new protocols to further the obligation of the parties in Article 2. Although a limited departure from consensus is permitted for amendments to the Convention or to Protocols,[106] the assumption appears to be one of unanimity, in contrast to the 1987 Montreal Protocol.

The 1987 Protocol is much more intrusive both substantively, in that it imposes firm targets for the reduction and eventual elimination of ozone-depleting substances, a reporting obligation, as well as containing innovative technology transfer provisions;[107] and institutionally, in that although the basic organ is the Meeting of the Parties to the Protocol, provision is made for majority voting as well as imbuing the decisions made with mandatory force. Article 2(9) (as amended in 1990) allows the parties to adjust the targets and the substances prohibited, subparagraph (c) providing:

> In reaching such decisions, the Parties shall make every effort to reach agreement by consensus. If all efforts at consensus have been exhausted, and no agreement reached, such decisions shall, as a last resort, be adopted by a two-thirds majority vote of the parties present and voting representing a majority of the parties operating under paragraph 1 of Article 5 present and voting and a majority of the Parties not so operating present and voting.

The reference to Article 5(1) ensures that these decisions must be supported by separate majorities of both developing and developed countries. Furthermore, Article 2(9)(d) provides that 'the decisions … shall be binding on all Parties'. Subsequent developments have also shown the Meeting of Parties moving towards enforcement of its decisions. Article 8 permits the parties to create mechanisms to determine non-compliance with the Treaty and for treatment of State parties found to be in breach. The State parties agreed in 1990 that an Implementation Committee should hear complaints on the basis of a unilateral application by a State party. That committee seeks an amicable solution and if one is not forthcoming then the Meeting of the Parties may 'decide upon and call for steps to bring about full compliance'.[108] Furthermore, in November 1992, the non-compliance procedure was expanded to include a list of measures that might be taken by the Meeting of Parties, including the issuing of cautions, the suspension of rights and privileges under the Protocol covering, for example, the transfer of technology and the availability of resources under the financial mechanisms.[109]

Unfortunately, this dynamic evolution of institutions[110] created by environmental treaties seems to have faltered with the conventions agreed upon at the Rio Conference of 1992, on Biological Diversity and Climate Change. The Convention on Biological Diversity has few innovative institutional mechanisms, its provisions creating a supervisory Conference of the Parties to which State parties report and a Secretariat (Articles 23, 24 and 26) are standard fare with no mandatory powers and limited majority decision-making powers, although Article 25 does provide for a subsidiary body on Scientific, Technical and Technological Advice. The Climate Change Convention has greater institutional development. As well as innovative provisions as regards its financial mechanism,[111] as has already been seen when discussing the World Bank and the GEF, there is provision in Article 10 for the creation of a Subsidiary Body for Implementation of the Treaty,[112] in addition to the standard supervisory Conference of the Parties and the Secretariat (Articles 7 and 8), and a Subsidiary Body for Scientific and Technological Advice (Article 9). Furthermore, Article 7(3) does permit the Conference of the Parties to adopt its own 'decision-making procedures for matters not already covered by decision-making procedures stipulated in the Convention. Such procedures may include specified majorities required for the adoption of particular decisions', thus explicitly allowing the Conference in this particular Treaty to move towards majority decision making on a wider number of issues.[113] It is questionable whether the lack of such a provision in the Convention on Biological Diversity would prevent the Conference from moving more towards majority decision making at subsequent meetings, the matter of decision making being left open in Article 23, though the presumption seems to be for consensus.

Concluding remarks

It can be seen that there has been a growth of simple institutions to deal with specific common environmental problems – Antarctica, endangered species, ozone depletion, climate change, and biodiversity, are the areas mentioned here. In many ways this is in accord with the functionalist approach, although the institutions created, principally the conferences of the parties, are an inefficient way of dealing pragmatically with such problems. The conferences suffer, as does the United Nations and its bodies, from politicisation, with the end result often being a compromise which is not sufficient to achieve the objective of preventing further environmental damage. The panacea of 'sustainable development' has been crafted as the overarching principle and is, in many ways, the ultimate Marxist political compromise in that it satisfies the developing States' desire for development *and* the developed States (weaker) desire for improved environmental protection, without really reconciling the two. Trade, financial and economic institutions, in particular, have found great difficulty in adopting effective environmental policies, reflecting the conflict between the dominant free trade and economic development ideology and the subservient green ideology, resulting in what is known as the 'greenwashing' of these institutions.

Although the UN has attempted to set universal standards in this area, as it has done in the field of human rights, the political compromises necessary for consensus have resulted in unclear and weak 'soft' laws. However, the hope that regional organisations may step in to fill this lacuna has, with the limited exception of the EU, proved false. Regional and sub-regional bodies, either tend to be based on trading blocs and hence have an inherent antipathy towards environmental protection, or are composed of developing States wishing to enhance their development. More so than human rights, environmental matters require a clear and effective lead from the global organisation. Nevertheless, despite these deficiencies in institutional competence, environmental protection is much higher on the agendas of universal, regional and even trade organisations, and has led to the creation of new organisations, developments which may eventually lead to an effective unitary environmental organisation along rationalist lines, one with mandatory and enforcement powers vested in an executive body. It is to be hoped that this development is not too late.

Notes

[1] P. W. Birnie and A. E. Boyle, *International Law and the Environment*, 1, 10 (1992).

[2] P. M. Haas, R. O. Keohane, and M. E. Levy, *Institutions for the Earth: Sources of International Environmental Protection*, 1 (1993).

[3] Birnie and Boyle, *Environment*, 86. See chapter 9 on the limited development of a human right to a decent environment.

[4] Haas, Keohane, and Levy, *Institutions*, 4–5. Author's italic.

[5] M. Pallemaerts, 'International Environmental Law from Stockholm to Rio: Back to the Future?', in P. Sands (ed.), *Greening International Law*, 17 (1993).

[6] Birnie and Boyle, *Environment*, 10, 27.

[7] *Ibid.*, 102.

[8] See generally A-C Kiss, 'La Notion de Patrimoine Commun de l'Humanité', 175 *Hague Receuil* (1982), 99.

[9] See I. Detter de Lupis, 'The Human Environment: Stockholm and its follow up', in P. Taylor and A. J. R. Groom (eds), *Global Issues in the United Nations' Framework*, 222 (1989).

[10] See A-C. Kiss and D. Shelton, *International Environmental Law*, 129 (1991).

[11] SC Res. 687, 46 UN SCOR Resolutions (1991), para.16. Author's italic.

[12] UN doc. S/23500 (1992).

[13] GA Res. 2398, 13 UN GAOR (1968).

[14] UN doc. A/CONF 48/14 (1972); 11 *I.L.M.* (1972), 1416. See further L. B. Sohn, 'The Stockholm Declaration and the Human Environment', 14 *Harvard International Law Journal* (1973), 423.

[15] GA Res. 2997, 27 UN GAOR (1972).

[16] D. W. Bowett, *The Law of International Institutions*, 57–8, 4th edn (1982).

[17] Sixteen seats for African States, 13 seats for Asian States, 6 seats for Eastern European States, 10 seats for Latin American States, 13 seats for Western European and other States.

[18] Birnie and Boyle, *Environment*, 47–52.

[19] *Ibid.*, 50. On the World Commission on Environment and Development see Pallemaerts, in Sands (ed.), *Greening*, 3–4.

[20] GA Res. 37/7, 37 UN GAOR Supp. (No. 51) 17 (1982).

[21] But see Pallemaerts, in Sands (ed.), *Greening*, 3.

[22] Birnie and Boyle, *Environment*, 50–1.

[23] Reviewed at the end of this chapter.

[24] UNEP Res. 15/3 (1989); ECOSOC Res. 1989/87 (1989). Author's italics.

[25] GA Res. 44/228, 44 UN GAOR (1989).

[26] 31 *I.L.M.* (1992), 848.

[27] At the Berlin Conference of April 1995, the parties agreed to adopt a protocol on further restricting emissions to be adopted by 1997, without setting specific targets. The conference was riven by developed and developing States demanding that the other group should be subject to greater restrictions. A proposal by an alliance of 36 island countries wanting to make a binding 20 per cent cut in carbon dioxide emissions by industrialised countries by the year 2005 was rejected. *Keesing's* (1995), 40531.

[28] 31 *I.L.M.* (1992), 818.

[29] UN doc. A/CONF.151/6/Rev. 1 (1992); 31 *I.L.M.* (1992), 882.

[30] UN doc. A/CONF.151/5/Rev. 1 (1992); 31 *I.L.M.* (1992), 876.

[31] UN doc. A/CONF.151/26 (1992), ch. 2.

[32] *Ibid.*, ch. 38.

[33] GA Res. 47/191, 47 UN GAOR (1993).

[34] UN doc. E/1994/33/Rev. 1 (1994).

[35] GA Res. 49/111, 49 UN GAOR (1994).

[36] UN doc. A/CONF.151/26 (1992), ch. 1.

[37] 327 UNTS 3.

[38] UKTS 2 (1985), Cmnd 9424.

[39] See above chapter 4.

[40] Birnie and Boyle, *Environment*, 58. But see the UN Convention on Straddling and Highly Migratory Fish Stocks, adopted in August 1995.

[41] J. D. Werksman, 'Greening Bretton Woods', in Sands (ed.), *Greening*, 65.

[42] S. C. Guyett, 'Environment and Lending: Lessons of the World Bank, Hope for the European Bank for Reconstruction and Development', 24 *New York University Journal of International Law and Politics* (1992), 889.

[43] Werksman, in Sands (ed.), *Greening*, 68.

[44] Guyett, 24 *New York University Journal of International Law and Politics* (1992), 897.

[45] Res. of IBRD Board of Executive Directors, 14 March 1991.

[46] See chapter 6.

[47] Werksman, in Sands (ed.), *Greening*, 68.

[48] See above n. 30. Author's italics.

[49] Werksman, in Sands (ed.), *Greening*, 82.

[50] R. McCluney, 'Sustainable Values', in N. J. Brown and P. Quiblier (eds), *Ethics & Agenda 21*, 16–18 (1994). See further, R. Lipschutz, 'Wasn't the Future Wonderful? Resources, Environment, and the Emerging Myth of Sustainable Development', 2 *Colombia Journal of International Law and Policy* (1991), 35.

[51] Guyett, 24 *New York University Journal of International Law and Politics* (1992), 889–90.

[52] 29 *I.L.M.* (1990), 1083.

[53] Guyett, 24 *New York University Journal of International Law and Politics* (1992), 917.

[54] M. Wheeler, 'Greening the EEC Treaty', in Sands (ed.), *Greening*, 85–7.

[55] Birnie and Boyle, *Environment*, 69. See generally P. Sands, *Principles of International Environmental Law*, ch. 14, vol. I (1995).

[56] Wheeler, in Sands (ed.), *Greening*, 89–90. See Case 120/78, *Rewe v Zentralverwaltung* [1979] ECR 649; Case 240/83, *Procureur de la République v Association de Défense des Brûleurs d'Huiles Usagées* [1985] ECR 4607; Case 302/86, *Commission v Denmark* [1988] ECR 531. For a summary of recent European Court decisions on the environment see 7 *Journal of Environmental Law* (1995), 99.

[57] 1001 UNTS 3.

[58] Birnie and Boyle, *Environment* 65.

[59] ECA is a subsidiary organ of ECOSOC established by ECOSOC Res. 671A (25) (1958). ECA is mandated to help Africa's economic development.

[60] T. Maluwa, 'Environment and Development in Africa: An Overview of Basic Problems of Environmental Law and Policy', 1 *African Journal of International and Comparative Law* (1989), 650 at 660.

[61] 161 UNTS 229.

[62] 15 *Environmental Policy and Law* (1985), 64. See further S. Sucharitkul, 'ASEAN Activities with Respect to the Environment', 3 *Asian Yearbook of International Law* (1993), 317.

[63] See R. Desgagné, 'Integrating Environmental Values into the European Convention on Human Rights', 89 *American Journal of International Law* (1995), 263 at 294. Desgagné writes that though certain rights in the Convention can be violated by environmental degradation, for example the right to a private life, 'human rights litigation under the Convention presents limited opportunities to foster the protection of the environment in general. Environmental protection has an important public facet that cannot be translated into an individual perspective and involves social choices that cannot be dealt with piecemeal. A system of protection of human rights, given its individualist bias, is not the best forum to further objectives that go beyond individual interest'.

[64] Birnie and Boyle, *Environment*, 72–3.

[65] See generally D. Wightman, *Economic Co-operation in Europe: A Study of the United Nations Economic Commission for Europe* (1956).

[66] 30 *I.L.M.* (1991), 802.

[67] Birnie and Boyle, *Environment*, 71–2.

[68] J. Cameron, 'The GATT and the Environment', in Sands (ed.), *Greening*, 100 at 101.

[69] World Commission on Environment and Development, *Our Common Future*, 8 (1987). 'In Pursuit of Sustainable Environmentally Sound Development', (Extracts from the 1994 Environmental Report of the German Council of Environmental Advisers), 25(3) *Environmental Policy and Law* (1995), 90.

[70] GATT Dispute Settlement Panel, *United States-Restrictions on Imports of Tuna* (16 August 1991), 30 *I.L.M.* (1991), 1594.

[71] Wheeler in Sands (ed.), *Greening*, 98.

[72] J. Schultz, 'The GATT/WTO Committee on Trade and the Environment – Toward Environmental Reform', 89 *A.J.I.L.* (1995), 423 at 425.

[73] 33 *I.L.M.* (1994), 15.

[74] Schultz, 89 *A.J.I.L.* (1995), 429.

[75] 33 *I.L.M.* (1994), 1267.

[76] Article 30 of the Vienna Convention on the Law of Treaties, 1969. Schultz, 33 *A.J.I.L.* (1995), 434.

[77] 33 *I.L.M.* (1994), 1226, Article 3.8.

[78] Cameron, in Sands (ed.), *Greening*, 118.

[79] NAFTA Agreement, Articles 712.3, 715.4, 723.6, 907.3, 914.4. 32 *I.L.M.* (1993), 289.

[80] See chapter 6.

[81] R. Housman, 'The North American Free Trade Agreement's Lessons for Reconciling Trade and the Environment', 30 *Stanford Journal of International Law* (1994), 379 at 380.

[82] Article 1114.2.

[83] Housman, 30 *Stanford Journal of International Law* (1994), 405. Articles 713.3, 905.3.

[84] Article 104.2.

[85] Housman, 30 *Stanford Journal of International Law*, (1994) 399.

[86] 32 *I.L.M.* (1993), 1480.

[87] Article 8, 34 and 36.

[88] International Convention for the Regulation of Whaling, 161 UNTS 72.

[89] Birnie and Boyle, *Environment*, 165.

[90] *Ibid.*, 136–9.

[91] I.C.J. *Rep.* (1949), 72.

[92] Sands, 'Enforcing Environmental Security', in Sands (ed.), *Greening*, 51, 57–9. On the creation of an ICJ Chamber for Environmental Matters see 23(6) *Environmental Policy and Law* (1993), 243.

[93] For a more comprehensive review see, Birnie and Boyle, *Environment*, 160–79.

[94] 402 UNTS 71.

[95] 30 *I.L.M.* (1991), 1455.

[96] But see GA Res. 49/80, 49 UN GAOR (1994).

[97] 993 UNTS 243.

[98] Article 15(1)(b).

[99] Article 12.

[100] S. Lyster, *International Wildlife Law*, 267–7 (1985); W. Wijnstekers, *The Evolution of CITES*, chs 12, 16, 3rd edn (1992).

[101] Birnie and Boyle, *Environment*, 478.

[102] 25(3) *Environmental Policy and Law* (1995), 88.

[103] 26 *I.L.M.* (1987), 1550.

[104] 26 *I.L.M.* (1987), 1529.

[105] Article 2(1).

[106] Article 9(3).

[107] A further tightening of the targets and an extension on the number of prohibited substances was agreed upon by the parties to the Protocol in June 1990, 30 *I.L.M.* (1991), 537.

[108] Decision 2/5 (non-compliance) of UNEP, Report of the Second Meeting of the Parties to the Montreal Protocol, UNEP doc. OzL Pro 2/3 (29 June 1990), Annex 3, paras 6–7.

[109] Report of the Fourth Meeting of the Parties to the Montreal Protocol, UNEP doc. OzL Pro 4/15 (5 November 1992), Annex 5.

[110] See also the International Sea-bed Authority created by the 1982 Law of the Sea Convention, 21 *I.L.M.* (1982), 1261. R. R. Churchill and A. V. Lowe, *Law of the Sea*, ch. 12, 2nd edn (1988). For its entry into force and provisional institutional arrangements see 25 (1,2) *Environmental Policy and Law* (1995), 18.

[111] There is no explicit link between the financial mechanism in the Biological Diversity Convention and the World Bank although this may evolve in the future, see Article 21.

[112] See also Article 13.

[113] For the first conference at Berlin see above n. 27. At the preparatory meeting for the

Berlin Conference a draft rule was proposed requiring the parties to strive for consensus on matters of substance but allowing for a two-thirds majority as a last resort (three-quarters in the case of the adoption of a protocol), 24(6) *Environmental Policy and Law* (1994), 302. No mechanism was established for majority voting – *Keesing's* (1995), 40531.

Index